MANUAL OF BUSINESS GERMAN

The **Manual of Business German** is the essential companion for all who use German for business communication.

The *Manual* is divided into five sections covering all the requirements for business communication, whether written or spoken. Fully bilingual, the *Manual* is of equal value to the relative beginner or the fluent speaker.

Features include:
- 40 spoken situations, from booking a ticket to making a sales pitch
- 80 written communications covering memos, letters, faxes and résumés
- facts and figures on the countries that use the language
- a handy summary of the main grammar points
- a 5000-word two-way glossary of the most common business terms

Written by an experienced native and non-native speaker team working in business language education, this unique *Manual of Business German* is an essential one-stop reference for all students and professionals studying or working in business and management where German is used.

Paul Hartley is Dean of the School of International Studies and Law at Coventry University. **Gertrud Robins** is Lecturer in German at Rugby College.

In the same series

*French Business Situations**
Stuart Williams and Nathalie McAndrew-Cazorla
*German Business Situations**
Paul Hartley and Gertrud Robins
*Italian Business Situations**
Vincent Edwards and Gianfranca Gessa Shepheard
*Spanish Business Situations**
Michael Gorman and María-Luisa Henson
Manual of Business French
Stuart Williams and Nathalie McAndrew-Cazorla
Manual of Business Italian
Vincent Edwards and Gianfranca Gessa Shepheard
Manual of Business Spanish
Michael Gorman and María-Luisa Henson

*Accompanying cassettes available

MANUAL OF BUSINESS GERMAN

A comprehensive language guide

Paul Hartley
and
Gertrud Robins

London and New York

In the preparation of the Business Situations and Business Correspondence sections of this handbook every effort was made to avoid the use of actual company names or trade names. If any has been used inadvertently, the publishers will change it in any future reprint if they are notified.

First published 1996
by Routledge
11 New Fetter Lane, London EC4P 4EE

Simultaneously published in the USA and Canada
by Routledge
29 West 35th Street, New York, NY 10001

© Paul Hartley and Gertrud Robins 1996

Typeset in Rockwell and Univers by Solidus (Bristol) Ltd
Printed and bound in Great Britain by Clays Ltd, St Ives plc

British Library Cataloguing in Publication Data
A catalogue record for this book is available from the British Library

Library of Congress Cataloguing in Publication Data
A catalogue record for this book has been requested

ISBN 0–415–09266–3 (hardback)
ISBN 0–415–12902–8 (pbk)

19958714

Contents

Business Situations

How to use the Business Situations

The spoken situations which follow are intended to cover a wide range of business interactions, from the brief and informal through to the more formal and prolonged exchange typical of the negotiating or interview situation. The user is encouraged not simply to read the situations together with their parallel English version, but to attempt, individually or in group work, with the help of the recording if applicable, the following exploitation exercises:

- using the original situations as models, construct dialogues on similar lines with the available vocabulary
- use the situations, or sections of them, as the basis for role-play exercises
- interpreting practice German/English, English/German
- practice in oral summary (i.e. listen to the recorded German version, and then summarize the content, in English or in German)
- oral paraphrase: listen to one version, then recount it using different expressions, but attempting to keep the same meaning
- transcription/dictation practice from the recording
- translation practice German/English, English/German

The material in the situations is intended as a basis for further expansion and exploitation, and is ideal for use in in-house training programmes, or in open learning centres, as well as for individual use.

Teil I
Section I

Am Telefon
On the telephone

1 Making an enquiry

(a) Can I visit?

Maureen Simmons	Good morning. Robinson's Motors.
Mr Lewis	Hello, my name is Lewis. I've just seen your advert for the Riva 25s available on fleet terms. We've been looking for half a dozen vehicles at the right price for a while and your offer interests us.
Maureen Simmons	Fine. Would you like me to send you more information?
Mr Lewis	No, thanks. I'd rather come down to your salesroom this afternoon with a colleague to discuss the matter with you.
Maureen Simmons	No problem, sir. My name is Maureen Simmons and I'll be available from 2.30. Can you give me your name again and your company, please?
Mr Lewis	Of course. It's Alan Lewis, from Stafford Electronics. I know where you are, so we'll be there for 2.30.
Maureen Simmons	Thanks, see you later.

(b) Sales enquiry

Telephonist	Preece and Pritchard. Good morning.
Mr Colman	Good morning. Could you put me through to Sales?
Telephonist	Certainly. Just a moment.
Assistant	Sales, good morning. Can I help you?
Mr Colman	My name is James Colman, from Goodright Inc. Can you tell me if you sell water pumps?
Assistant	Yes, we do. Industrial and domestic.
Mr Colman	Can you send me a copy of your catalog and price list?
Assistant	Certainly, just give me your address. We'll get it off to you later today.

1 Anfrage

(a) Vereinbarung eines Besuchs

Maria Simmern	Fahrzeughandel Robert. Guten Tag.[1]
Herr Lüders	Guten Tag. Mein Name ist Lüders. Ich sehe da gerade Ihre Anzeige, in der Sie den Riva 25s zum Sonderpreis als Firmenwagen anbieten. Wir halten schon längere Zeit Ausschau nach einem geeigneten Angebot für sechs Autos und Ihre Preise scheinen zu stimmen.
Maria Simmern	Gut. Möchten Sie weitere Informationen[2] erhalten?
Herr Lüders	Danke, nein. Aber ich würde gern selbst mit einem Geschäftskollegen zu Ihnen in Ihr Verkaufsbüro kommen und die Angelegenheit besprechen.
Maria Simmern	Das geht ohne weiteres. Mein Name ist Simmern und ich wäre ab halb drei frei. Darf ich Ihren Namen und den Namen Ihrer Firma nochmal haben?
Herr Lüders	Sicher. Mein Name ist Lüders von der Firma Jensen Elektronik. Also bis halb drei – wir wissen, wo Ihre Firma ist.
Maria Simmern	Gut, also bis später.

1 This is a typical 'opening': the name of the company, followed by the greeting.
2 Note the use of the plural 'Informationen'.

(b) Anfrage

Telefonist	Preece and Pritchard. Good Morning.
Herr Koller	Guten Tag. Bitte verbinden Sie mich mit der Verkaufsabteilung.
Telefonist	Einen Moment bitte.
Verkäufer	Verkaufsabteilung. Guten Tag.
Herr Koller	Mein Name ist Koller von der Firma Ruprecht GmbH in Köln. Ich möchte anfragen, ob Sie Wasserpumpen verkaufen.
Verkäufer	Ja, wir haben Wasserpumpen für Industrie und Haushalt zum Verkauf.
Herr Koller	Könnten Sie mir Ihren Katalog und Ihre Preisliste zukommen lassen?[1]
Verkäufer	Ja, gerne. Ich brauche nur Ihre Adresse und wir senden Ihnen alles heute nachmittag.

1 Alternatives: *schicken* or *senden*.

2 Ordering

(a) Placing an order

Tracy	DIY Stores, Tracy speaking. How can I help you?
Customer	I should like to order some plywood please.
Tracy	Certainly, sir, putting you through.
Wood department	Wood department.
Customer	I would like to order quite a large quantity of plywood.
Wood department	Certainly, sir. Do you know what quality or can you tell me what it is for?
Customer	The purpose is to make shelving and the quality should be good enough to hold books.
Wood department	Right, then I would suggest three-ply 1½ cm thickness. How many metres do you want to order?
Customer	I need 150 metres. Is there a discount for quantity?
Wood department	There are progressive discounts from 50 metres.
Customer	Very good. I will give you my address and you can tell me when your earliest delivery date is and what invoicing procedure you operate.

(b) Changing an order

Dave Brown	Please put me through to Steve Jones in Sales. . . . Hello, Steve. Dave here. I've had a think about what you suggested yesterday regarding the photocopier we ordered. We've decided to change our order from the CF202 to the FC302. I think that will meet our requirements better. Shall I send you a new order?
Steve Jones	That would be a good idea. Please send it with a note cancelling the initial order.
Dave Brown	Thanks Steve. Bye.

2 Bestellung

(a) Auftragserteilung

Tina	Bauhof. Guten Tag, kann ich Ihnen helfen?
Kunde	Ich möchte Sperrholz bestellen, bitte.
Tina	Augenblick. Ich verbinde.
Holzabteilung	Holzabteilung.
Kunde	Ich möchte gerne eine größere[1] Menge Sperrholz bestellen.
Holzabteilung	Gerne. Wissen Sie die Qualität oder können Sie mir sagen, wofür Sie das Sperrholz brauchen?
Kunde	Ich möchte Regale bauen und das Holz sollte fest genug für Bücher sein.
Holzabteilung	Ja, dann würde ich in diesem Fall dreischichtiges Sperrholz mit einer Dicke von 1,5 cm vorschlagen. Wieviele Meter möchten Sie bestellen?
Kunde	Ich brauche 150m. Geben Sie Mengenrabatt?[2]
Holzabteilung	Rabatt gibt es ab 50m.
Kunde	Ausgezeichnet. Ich gebe Ihnen meine Adresse und Sie sagen mir, wann Sie frühestens liefern können und wie Ihre Rechnung beglichen werden kann.

1 The comparative of the adjective is used here to express 'quite' a large amount.
2 *Mengenrabatt* means 'discount' for large orders. cf. *Menge* above.

(b) Bestellungsänderung

Herr Braun	Bitte verbinden Sie mich mit Herrn Müller im Verkauf. . . . Guten Tag, Herr Müller. Hier Braun. Es ist wegen des Photokopiergeräts, das wir bestellt haben. Ich habe über Ihren gestrigen Vorschlag nachgedacht und wir haben beschlossen, unseren Auftrag zu ändern. Wir bestellen jetzt nicht das Modell CF202 sondern das Modell FC302. Ich glaube, das entspricht unseren Anforderungen besser.[1] Soll ich Ihnen einen neuen Auftrag schicken?
Herr Müller	Ja, das wäre besser. Und könnten Sie auch beiliegend den ursprünglichen Auftrag widerrufen?
Herr Braun	Alles klar. Auf Wiederhören.

1 Note the use of the dative with *entsprechen*.

(c) Cancelling an order

Store manager	Hello, Sandhu's Wholesale.
Customer	Morning. It's Mr Wilson here, of Lomas Supermarket. I'm ever so sorry, but my brother has got our order wrong this week. Do you mind if we change it over the phone?
Store manager	No, as long as there's nothing perishable that we've had to order specially. Can you give me the order number?
Customer	Yes, it's SCC 231. We only put it in three days ago and it's all packaged catering goods. All we want to do is cancel the soft drinks and the cereals, and have instead another 15 large boxes of Mercury. Is that all right?
Store manager	I've found the order and the invoice. We can change that before you call tomorrow and I'll make you out another bill. Will you pay on the spot?
Customer	Yes, by cheque as usual. Thanks for your help. Goodbye.

(d) Confirming receipt of an order

Telephonist	Klapp and Weaver. Good morning.
Julie Little	Morning. Can I speak to Mr Preece, please?
Telephonist	Yes, putting you through now.
George Preece	Hello, Preece here.
Julie Little	Morning, Mr Preece. Julie Little here. I'm ringing to confirm receipt of our order number B/397/386.
George Preece	The radial tyres?
Julie Little	Yes, that's the one. They arrived today. You asked me to confirm receipt as soon as possible.
George Preece	Well, thanks for getting back to me.
Julie Little	We'll get your invoice processed in the next few days.
George Preece	Fine. Thanks for ringing. Goodbye.
Julie Little	Goodbye.

(c) Widerrufung einer Bestellung

Geschäftsführer	Großhandel Niederegger. Guten Tag.
Kundin	Tag. Hier Willmer, Alti Supermarkt. Es tut mir schrecklich leid, aber mein Bruder hat Ihnen diese Woche irrtümlicherweise eine falsche Bestellung geschickt. Geht es, daß ich sie telefonisch ändere?
Geschäftsführer	Ja, sicher, wenn nichts Verderbliches dabei war, das wir speziell bestellen mußten. Können Sie mir die Auftragsnummer geben?
Kundin	Ja, die ist SCC 231. Die Bestellung wurde vor drei Tagen gemacht und es handelt sich nur um verpackte Lebensmittel. Was wir absagen möchten, sind die alkoholfreien Getränke und die Cornflakes und dafür 15 Großpackungen Merkur bestellen. Ist das möglich?
Geschäftsführer	Da habe ich die Bestellung und die Rechnung. Wir ändern das alles, bevor Sie morgen die Waren abholen. Ich stelle Ihnen eine neue Rechnung aus. Ist das gegen sofortige Bezahlung?[1]
Kundin	Ja. Und wie gewöhnlich mit Scheck. Danke für Ihr Entgegenkommen. Auf Wiederhören.

1 *gegen* means 'for' in this context.

(d) Bestätigung eines Auftragsempfangs

Telefonist	Klapp und Weber. Guten Tag.
Julia Klein	Tag. Kann ich bitte mit Herrn Preiss sprechen?
Telefonist	Augenblick. Ich verbinde.
Herr Preiss	Hallo. Hier Preiss.
Julia Klein	Guten Tag, Herr Preiss. Hier Julia Klein. Ich wollte nur den Empfang unseres Auftrags Nr. B/397/386 bestätigen.
Herr Preiss	Ist das der Auftrag über[1] Gürtelreifen?
Julia Klein	Ja, genau. Die sind heute angekommen. Sie wollten, daß wir den Erhalt so bald wie möglich bestätigen.
Herr Preiss	Ja, vielen Dank für Ihren Anruf.
Julia Klein	Ihre Rechnung wird in den nächsten Tagen erledigt.
Herr Preiss	Gut. Danke nochmals für Ihren Anruf. Auf Wiederhören.
Julia Klein	Auf Wiederhören.

1 *Auftrag über/Bestellung über*, 'order for'.

(e) Clarifying details of an order

Edward	Good afternoon, DIY Stores, Edward speaking.
Customer	Hello, I am ringing about an order I made on the 24th. My name is Jones.
Edward	Just a moment ... Mr B Jones, 24 litres of paint to be delivered on the 4th?
Customer	Yes, that's it. But I would like to change one or two details if I may.
Edward	No problem. Go ahead.
Customer	I originally ordered 6 litres of eggshell blue matt, I would like to change that to sky blue vinyl silk. Is that OK?
Edward	Yes that is all right. We have it in stock. Anything else?
Customer	Just the delivery address. Could you deliver the paint to the site, 34 Western Way, on the 4th as agreed?
Edward	No problem, sir.

3 Making an appointment

Receptionist	Good morning, Chiltern International. Can I help you?
Mr Wignall	Good morning, I would like to speak to Mrs Mills's secretary.
Receptionist	One moment, please.
Secretary	Sue White.
Mr Wignall	Good morning, Ms White. My name is Wignall, from Whitnash Industries. I shall be in your area next week and would like to discuss product developments with Mrs Mills. Tuesday or Wednesday would suit me best.
Secretary	Just a moment. I'll check Mrs Mills's diary. She could see you Wednesday morning at 10.
Mr Wignall	That would be fine. Thank you very much.
Secretary	Thank you.
Mr Wignall	Goodbye.
Secretary	Goodbye.

(e) Änderung von Bestellungsdetails

Erler	Hier Baumarkt. Erler. Guten Tag.
Kunde	Hallo. Ich rufe an wegen meiner Bestellung vom vierundzwanzigsten. Mein Name ist Jäger.
Erler	Moment, bitte. . . . Herr Franz Jäger, 24 Liter Farbe für Zustellung am vierten?
Kunde	Ja, genau. Aber, wenn es geht, möchte ich ein paar Einzelheiten ändern.
Erler	Kein Problem. Worum handelt es sich?
Kunde	Ursprünglich habe ich 6 Liter in Eierschale matt bestellt. Kann ich das auf[1] himmelblau, Vinyl seidig abändern?
Erler	Ja, das geht. Wir haben die Farbe auf Lager. Sonst noch etwas?
Kunde	Ja, die Zustelladresse. Können Sie die Farbe wie vereinbart am vierten an die Werksanlage, Weststraße 34 liefern?
Erler	Geht in Ordnung.[2]

1 Note the use of *auf* to indicate change 'to'.
2 Just '*in Ordnung*' would also be possible.

3 Terminvereinbarung

Empfang	Metall International. Guten Tag. Kann ich Ihnen helfen?
Herr Winter	Guten Tag. Kann ich mit Frau Möllers Sekretärin sprechen?
Empfang	Einen Moment, bitte.
Sekretärin	Weiß.
Herr Winter	Guten Tag, Frau Weiß. Mein Name ist Winter von der Firma Steiff GmbH. Ich bin nächste Woche in Ihrem Gebiet und würde bei der Gelegenheit gern mit Frau Möller über die Produktentwicklung sprechen. Dienstag oder Mittwoch würde mir am besten passen.
Sekretärin	Moment. Ich sehe in Frau Möllers Terminkalender nach. Sie wäre Mittwoch um 10 Uhr vormittag frei.
Herr Winter	Paßt ausgezeichnet. Vielen Dank.
Sekretärin	Bitte sehr.
Herr Winter	Auf Wiederhören.
Sekretärin	Auf Wiederhören.

4 Invitation to attend a meeting

Secretary	Hello, Mr Anguita?
Director	Yes, speaking.
Secretary	Javier Clemente here. I'm secretary to Lucía Ordóñez, public relations manager at Agencia Rosell, Barcelona.
Director	Oh, yes. We met last month at the trade fair in Tarragona. She mentioned that your agency might be able to help my company.
Secretary	That's right. Well, since then she has been in touch with a number of local firms who wish to set up joint projects elsewhere in Europe. A meeting is scheduled for Tuesday, 6 October, at our offices here in Barcelona. An invitation is on its way to you. I'm ringing now to give you advance warning.
Director	That's very kind. I'll check my diary and either way I'll get my secretary to ring you before the weekend. Will you thank Ms Ordóñez for the invitation and tell her I hope I will be able to make it on the 6th?
Secretary	I will. Thank you, Mr Anguita. By the way, our number is 3516784.
Director	Sorry, I nearly forgot to ask you! Send Ms Ordóñez my regards, and thanks again. Goodbye.
Secretary	Good afternoon.

4 Einladung zu einer Besprechung

Sekretär	Hallo. Herr Dr. Reiter?[1]
Direktor	Am Apparat.[2]
Sekretär	Hier spricht[3] Klaus Pichler. Ich bin Sekretär von Frau Martin, der Leiterin für Public Relations bei der Werbeagentur Trend.
Direktor	Oh ja. Wir haben uns im letzten Monat auf der Messe in Hannover kennengelernt. Sie erwähnte damals, daß Ihre Agentur unserer Firma eventuell behilflich sein könnte.
Sekretär	Richtig. Also, Frau Martin hat neulich ein paar hiesige Firmen kontaktiert, die an einem gemeinsamen Projekt für Europa interessiert sind. Wir haben diesbezüglich eine Besprechung für Dienstag, 6. Oktober, hier in unserem Hamburger Büro angesetzt. Ihre Einladung ist schon unterwegs. Mein Anruf soll Sie nur schon vorher in Kenntnis setzen.
Direktor	Das ist sehr freundlich von Ihnen. Ich werde gleich in meinem Terminkalender nachsehen, aber auf jeden Fall wird Sie meine Sekretärin noch vor Ende der Woche anrufen. Danken Sie inzwischen Frau Martin für die Einladung und sagen Sie ihr, daß ich hoffe, am 6. in Hamburg zu sein.
Sekretär	Gern. Vielen Dank, Herr Dr. Reiter. Übrigens, unsere Telefonnummer ist 35 16 784.
Direktor	Oh danke. Das hätte ich beinahe vergessen. Also auf Wiederhören und Empfehlungen an Frau Martin.
Sekretär	Danke schön. Auf Wiederhören.

1 Note the use of the full title. Formality is required here.
2 *Am Apparat*, 'speaking' (lit: 'on the phone').
3 The *spricht* could be omitted.

5 Apologizing for non-attendance

(a) At a future meeting

Nancy Richards	Nancy Richards.
Bill Simpkins	Morning, Nancy. Bill Simpkins here.
Nancy Richards	Hello, Bill, how are you?
Bill Simpkins	Fine thanks. Look, I've just received notice of the sales meeting next Tuesday.
Nancy Richards	Yes, is there a problem?
Bill Simpkins	Afraid so. I'll have to send my apologies. I'm already committed to a trade fair trip.
Nancy Richards	OK. I'll pass on your apologies. Can you send someone else?
Bill Simpkins	I've a colleague who can probably come. Her name is Susie Green. She'll contact you later today.
Nancy Richards	Fine. Well, have a nice trip. I'll see you when you get back.

5   Entschuldigung für Abwesenheit

(a) Absage der Teilnahme an einer Besprechung

Frau Röder	Röder.
Herr Schnabel	Morgen, Frau Röder. Hier Schnabel.
Frau Röder	Grüß Gott, Herr Schnabel.[1] Wie geht's?
Herr Schnabel	Gut, danke. Also, ich habe da gerade die Mitteilung über die Verkaufsbesprechung am Dienstag bekommen.
Frau Röder	Ja, und gibt's ein Problem?
Herr Schnabel	Ja, ich muß leider meine Teilnahme absagen. Ich muß zu der Zeit auf eine Messe fahren.
Frau Röder	OK. Ich werde Sie entschuldigen. Können Sie jemanden als Vertretung schicken?
Herr Schnabel	Ja, möglicherweise meine Kollegin, Frau Grün. Sie wird Sie heute im Laufe des Tages anrufen.
Frau Röder	Schön. Also, dann gute Reise und auf Wiedersehen.

1   *Grüß Gott* is used in Southern Germany, particularly in Bavaria, and in Austria.

(b) At a meeting that has already been held

George Sands	Could you put me through to the Managing Director please.
Secretary	Certainly, sir. One moment.
Henry Curtis	Hello, George. We missed you yesterday.
George Sands	I am calling to apologize. I didn't write because I intended to come and was prevented at the last moment.
Henry Curtis	I gather there's a spot of bother in the Gulf.
George Sands	Oh, you've heard. Bad news travels fast. Yes, we have a container ship on its way and rumours of war at its destination.
Henry Curtis	What will you do? Send it somewhere else pro tem?
George Sands	Yes, but don't worry – I'll sort it out. Meanwhile how did your 'do' go?
Henry Curtis	Very well. All the important people came. Barry Clerkenwell from the BOTB was asking for you. I said you'd give him a bell.
George Sands	Will do, and sorry again that I couldn't make it.

(b) Entschuldigung im Nachhinein für Nichtanwesenheit

Herr Schranz	Bitte, verbinden Sie mich mit dem Geschäftsleiter.
Sekretärin	Einen Moment, bitte.
Herr Kurtz	Hallo, Herr Schranz. Wir haben Sie gestern vermißt.[1]
Herr Schranz	Ja, deshalb rufe ich an. Es tut mir leid. Ich habe nicht schriftlich abgesagt, denn ich wollte ja kommen, aber dann wurde ich in letzter Minute aufgehalten.
Herr Kurtz	Ja, soviel ich höre, gibt es da Schwierigkeiten mit den Golfstaaten.
Herr Schranz	Sie wissen also schon. Schlechte Neuigkeiten verbreiten sich schnell. Ja, wir haben ein Kontainerschiff unterwegs in ein Gebiet, in dem von Krieg gemunkelt wird.
Herr Kurtz	Und was ist da zu machen? Das Schiff einstweilen umleiten?
Herr Schranz	Ja, doch keine Bange. Wir schaffen das schon. Übrigens, wie ging die Sitzung?
Herr Kurtz	Ausgezeichnet. Alle wichtigen Leute waren da. Dr. Olten von der Handelskammer hat nach Ihnen gefragt. Ich sagte, Sie würden ihn gelegentlich anrufen.
Herr Schranz	Klar. Mach ich. Nochmals, bedaure, daß ich nicht bei der Sitzung war.

1   *Vermissen*, 'to miss (the presence of a person)' *Verpassen* is used for 'to miss (a bus, train, etc.)'.

6 Making a complaint

Mr Russell	Service Department, please.
Assistant	Service Department.
Mr Russell	Hello, my name's Russell, from Littleborough Plant & Equipment. Item IP/234 was ordered by us two weeks ago and has still not been delivered. I rang on Wednesday and was promised delivery by 5 p.m. yesterday. We're still waiting to receive the part.
Assistant	I'm sorry, Mr Russell, let me check . . . I'm afraid the part still hasn't come in to us. It's still on order from the manufacturer.
Mr Russell	Look, I'm not interested in all that. I just want to know when we'll get the part. I stand to lose a good customer if I don't repair his machinery. If I don't get the part today, I'll go to another supplier.
Assistant	I'll chase up the manufacturer and see what I can do. I'll get back to you by 1 o'clock and let you know what the situation is.

6 Beschwerde

Herr Ruprecht	Abteilung Kundendienst, bitte.
Verkäufer	Kundendienst. Guten Tag.
Herr Ruprecht	Hallo. Hier Ruprecht von der Firma Kleinburg. Vor zwei Wochen haben wir Artikel IP/234 bei Ihnen bestellt und haben bis jetzt noch nichts erhalten. Ich habe schon am letzten Mittwoch angerufen und man hat mir da versprochen, bis spätestens gestern 17 Uhr zu liefern. Wir warten aber noch immer auf die Lieferung der Ersatzteile.
Verkäufer	Das tut mir sehr leid, Herr Ruprecht. Lassen Sie mich mal nachsehen . . . Ich bedaure, aber die Teile sind noch nicht bei uns eingetroffen, sie sind noch immer beim Hersteller in Auftrag.
Herr Ruprecht	Schauen Sie, das interessiert mich alles überhaupt nicht. Ich will nur wissen, wann wir die Ersatzteile bekommen werden. Möglicherweise verliere ich einen guten Kunden, wenn ich seine Maschinen nicht reparieren kann. Entweder ich bekomme die Teile noch heute oder ich gehe zu einem anderen Lieferanten.
Verkäufer	Ich werde mal beim Erzeuger ein bißchen Dampf machen und sehen, was sich machen läßt. Ich rufe Sie vor ein Uhr an und gebe Ihnen dann Bescheid.

7 Reminder for payment

Tardy customer	Good day. Des Morrison speaking.
Supplier	Hello, Mr Morrison. It's Bankstown Mouldings here. Did you receive a letter from us last week reminding you about the outstanding account you have with us?
Tardy customer	No, can't say I did. Mind you, that's no surprise when you see the state of this office. We've just moved from the middle of town.
Supplier	Oh. Sorry to hear that. Well, it's an invoice for $2,356 which we sent out on 17 April; it probably arrived on 19 or 20 April.
Tardy customer	Can you refresh my memory and tell me what it was for?
Supplier	Of course. We supplied you in March with several hundred wood and plastic ceiling fittings for the houses you were working on at the time. The invoice code is QZ163P.
Tardy customer	OK. I'll ask my wife to have a good look for it. In the meantime, what about sending me a copy so that we can pay up at the end of the month even if we can't trace the original?
Supplier	That's no problem. I'll fax it to you this afternoon if you have a machine.
Tardy customer	No way. I haven't seen ours since we moved! Send it by post to this address: Unit 12, Trading Estate, Pacific Highway. Sorry for the hassle. We'll settle up as soon as we get it.
Supplier	I'll post a copy today, and rely on you to keep your word.

7 Mahnung

Kunde im Zahlungsrückstand	Guten Tag. Hier Moser.
Lieferant	Guten Tag, Herr Moser. Hier Firma Bankstetter. Haben Sie von uns letzte Woche einen Brief bezüglich Ihrer unbezahlten Rechnung erhalten?
Kunde im Zahlungsrückstand	Nicht daß ich wüßte, aber beim Zustand meines Büros ist das keine Überraschung. Wir sind nämlich gerade aus dem Stadtzentrum umgezogen.
Lieferant	Oh, Entschuldigung. Also, es handelt sich um eine Rechnung über[1] 23 560,– DM, die wir Ihnen am 17. April geschickt haben. Vermutlich haben Sie sie am 19. oder 20. bekommen.
Kunde im Zahlungsrückstand	Können Sie meinem Gedächtnis nachhelfen und mir sagen, wofür die Rechnung war?
Lieferant	Sicher. Wir haben Ihnen im März mehrere hundert[2] Deckenverkleidungen aus Holz und Kunststoff geliefert – für die Häuser, an denen Sie damals gearbeitet haben. Die Rechnungsnummer ist QZ163P.
Kunde im Zahlungsrückstand	OK. Ich sage meiner Frau, sie soll danach suchen. Wie wäre es aber, wenn Sie mir inzwischen eine Kopie der Rechnung senden könnten, sodaß wir am Monatsende zahlen können, auch wenn wir das Original nicht finden?
Lieferant	Kein Problem. Ich schicke Ihnen heute nachmittag ein Fax. Sie haben doch eine Maschine?
Kunde im Zahlungsrückstand	Bitte nicht! Ich habe unsere Faxmaschine seit dem Umzug nicht mehr gesehen. Geht es mit der Post an folgende Adresse: Industriepark, Standplatz 30, Lübecker Hauptstraße? Entschuldigen Sie das ganze Theater, aber Sie kriegen[3] Ihr Geld, sowie wir die Rechnung erhalten.
Lieferant	Ich nehme Sie beim Wort. Wir senden die Kopie noch heute.

1 *Rechnung über*, 'invoice for'. Similarly, *ein Scheck über*, 'a cheque for'.
2 Note the use of the singular *hundert* (similarly, *ein paar hundert Leute*, 'a few hundred people').
3 *Kriegen* is very colloquial.

8   Enquiry about hotel accommodation

Telephonist	Good morning, Hotel Brennan. Can I help you?
Customer	Hello. Can you put me through to Reservations?
Telephonist	Certainly. Putting you through now.
Reservations desk	Reservations. Good morning.
Customer	Morning. Could you tell me if you have a double room free from 14 to 16 May, or from 18 to 20 May?
Reservations desk	Just a moment. I'll check for you. Yes, we do. On both dates.
Customer	What's the price?
Reservations desk	The price per night, with bath and including breakfast, is £160. That includes service and VAT. Do you want to make a reservation?
Customer	Not yet. I'll get back to you. Goodbye.
Reservations desk	Goodbye.

8 Hotelanfrage

Telefonist	Hotel Brenner. Guten Morgen. Bitte schön?
Kunde	Hallo. Bitte verbinden Sie mich mit Reservierungen!
Telefonist	Gerne. Ich verbinde.
Reservierungen	Reservierungen. Guten Morgen.
Kunde	Guten Tag. Können Sie mir sagen, ob Sie ein Doppelzimmer vom 14. bis 16. Mai oder vom 18. bis 20. Mai frei haben?
Reservierungen	Augenblick. Ich sehe nach. Ja, beide Daten gehen.
Kunde	Und was kostet das?
Reservierungen	Der Preis, mit Bad und Frühstück beträgt pro Nacht DM 368,–, inklusive Bedienung und Mehrwertsteuer. Möchten Sie ein Zimmer reservieren?
Kunde	Nicht im Moment. Ich werde zurückrufen. Auf Wiederhören.
Reservierungen	Auf Wiederhören.

9 Changing an appointment

Susan Lipman	Hello. May I speak to Helen Adler?
Helen Adler	Speaking.
Susan Lipman	Hello, this is Susan Lipman. I rang yesterday to see if I could visit the Ministry on Friday to discuss with your staff the new plans for tax reforms in the recent Budget. Unfortunately, my boss has just told me that the time we fixed is no good as I have to attend an urgent meeting with him. Could we possibly change our appointment?
Helen Adler	I'm sorry that's happened, but don't worry. When do you think you can come?
Susan Lipman	Any chance of the following week, maybe Tuesday afternoon?
Helen Adler	It looks unlikely, I'm afraid. How about Thursday at about 10.30? All the key staff should be here then.
Susan Lipman	If you can give me a moment, I'll check . . . Yes, that's fine as long as you don't object to our having to leave by 1 p.m. – my boss has to fly to the States in the afternoon.
Helen Adler	That will suit us. When you arrive, please inform the security staff and they will direct you to the relevant department, which is on the fourth floor. OK?
Susan Lipman	Many thanks for being so helpful. Looking forward to seeing you on the 8th.
Helen Adler	Me too. Goodbye.

9 Terminänderung

Susanne Liebermann	Hallo. Kann ich mit Frau Adler sprechen, bitte?
Frau Adler	Am Apparat.
Susanne Liebermann	Guten Tag. Hier spricht Susanne Liebermann. Ich rief bereits gestern an bezüglich meines Besuchs bei Ihren Mitarbeitern im Ministerium am Freitag zur Besprechung der neuen Steuerreformpläne im letzten Budget. Leider findet mein Chef die von uns vereinbarte Zeit ungünstig, denn er braucht mich bei einer dringenden Sitzung. Wäre es möglich, unseren Termin zu ändern?
Frau Adler	Ach bestimmt. Machen Sie sich keine Sorgen. Wann würde es Ihnen dann passen?
Susanne Liebermann	Wie wäre es mit nächster Woche, sagen wir Dienstag nachmittag?
Frau Adler	Tut mir leid, aber da geht es nicht. Könnten Sie am Donnerstag um 10.30 Uhr kommen? Alle wichtigen Mitarbeiter dürften dann anwesend sein.
Susanne Liebermann	Moment, ich seh' mal nach. . . . Ja, das geht wunderbar, nur wenn es Ihnen nichts ausmacht, daß wir schon um ein Uhr wieder weg müssen. Mein Chef muß nämlich am Nachmittag in die Staaten fliegen.
Frau Adler	Nein, das macht überhaupt nichts. Könnten Sie bei Ihrer Ankunft dem Sicherheitspersonal Bescheid geben und man wird Sie dann in die betreffende Abteilung im 4. Stock führen. Geht das?
Susanne Liebermann	Ja. Vielen Dank für Ihr Entgegenkommen. Also auf Wiedersehen am achten.
Frau Adler	Bis dann. Auf Wiedersehen.

10 Informing of a late arrival

Brian Kennon	Brian Kennon.
Paul Kelvin	Morning Brian, Paul here.
Brian Kennon	Hi, Paul. Where are you?
Paul Kelvin	I'm still at Heathrow – the flight has been delayed.
Brian Kennon	So you'll be late for the meeting.
Paul Kelvin	Yes, afraid so! I'm now due to arrive at Düsseldorf at 11.15. I should be with you about 12.
Brian Kennon	Don't worry. We'll push the start of the meeting back to 11.30 and take the less important agenda items first.
Paul Kelvin	Fine. Thanks for that. Look, I'd better dash – they've just called the flight.
Brian Kennon	OK. See you later. Bye for now.
Paul Kelvin	Bye.

11 Ordering a taxi

Taxi firm	Hello.
Customer	Hello, is that A & B Taxis?
Taxi firm	Yes. What can we do for you?
Customer	We would like a cab straightaway to take our Sales Manager to the airport.
Taxi firm	Birmingham Airport?
Customer	Yes. It's quite urgent. He has to check in in 35 minutes.
Taxi firm	Don't worry we'll get him there. Give me your address and a cab will be with you in 5 minutes.

10   Verspätete Ankunft

Benno König	Hier König.
Paul Klein	Hallo Benno. Hier ist Paul.[1]
Benno König	Hallo Paul. Wie geht's?
Paul Klein	Ich bin noch immer in Heathrow – der Flug hat Verspätung.
Benno König	Das heißt, daß du zu spät zur Besprechung kommst.
Paul Klein	Ja, tut mir leid. Wir sollen jetzt um 11.15 Uhr in Düsseldorf ankommen. Da müßte ich es bis 12 Uhr schaffen, bei dir zu sein.
Benno König	Kein Problem. Wir verlegen den Anfang der Sitzung einfach auf 11.30 Uhr und nehmen die weniger wichtigen Punkte der Tagesordnung zuerst dran.
Paul Klein	Super. Vielen Dank. Aber ich gehe jetzt besser. Mein Flug wurde gerade aufgerufen.[2]
Benno König	OK. Bis später. Tschüß[3] denn!
Paul Klein	Tschüß!

1   The *ist* could be omitted.
2   *Einen Flug aufrufen*, 'to call a flight'.
3   This is a very colloquial expression which is frequently used.

11   Ein Taxi bestellen

Taxiunternehmen	Hallo.
Kunde	Ist dort A & B Taxis?
Taxiunternehmen	Ja. Sie wünschen?
Kunde	Bitte können Sie uns direkt einen Wagen schicken? Unser Verkaufsdirektor muß zum Flughafen.[1]
Taxiunternehmen	Flughafen Düsseldorf?
Kunde	Ja. Es ist dringend. Er muß in 35 Minuten einchecken.
Taxiunternehmen	Keine Sorge. Wir schaffen das schon rechtzeitig. Geben Sie mir Ihre Adresse. Ein Wagen wird in 5 Minuten da sein.

1   The verb of motion is omitted, since the sense of this is contained in the words here.

12 Checking flight information

Travel agent	Russell's Travel, good morning.
Customer	Could you confirm my travel details for me, please?
Travel agent	Certainly, sir. Do you have your ticket to hand?
Customer	I am travelling on flight EA739 to Prague next Wednesday and then on to Bratislava the next day.
Travel agent	Flight EA739 leaves Heathrow at 11.35 a.m. and arrives in Prague at 15.05. Flight CZ417 leaves Prague at 16.30 and gets to Bratislava at 17.20. Is it an open ticket?
Customer	No, it's an Apex ticket.
Travel agent	That's fine, then. You must check in one hour before departure.
Customer	Thank you very much for your help.
Travel agent	Don't mention it.

13 Booking a flight

Customer	Hello. Sunline Air Services?
Airline clerk	Yes, madam. This is Paul Wagner. Can I help you?
Customer	Thank you. My name is Robertson. I'd like to book a direct flight to Antigua. How many times a week do you offer Luxury Class travel on your flights?
Airline clerk	There are departures from London each Monday afternoon and Thursday morning. Obviously, there are flights on other days with different airlines, but our tariffs are very competitive.
Customer	Yes, that's what they told me at the travel agency, but I wanted to check for myself. Could you quote me for two return tickets leaving on Thursday, 7 May?
Airline clerk	Can we first check flight details and then look again at prices?
Customer	Yes, fine. So how does the 7th look?
Airline clerk	On the 9.30 departure there are several pairs of seats available still; for your return journey you can make arrangements in Antigua. Shall I pass you over to my colleague, Janet, who can give you more information on costs? Everything else will be dealt with by her, including your personal details, form of payment and delivery of tickets to you.
Customer	Thank you for your help.
Airline clerk	My pleasure.

12   Fluginformation einholen

Reisebüro	Reisebüro Globus. Guten Tag.
Kunde	Könnten Sie bitte meine Reiseeinzelheiten bestätigen?
Reisebüro	Gerne. Haben Sie Ihre Flugkarte bei der Hand?
Kunde	Ja. Also ich fliege mit Flug EA739 nächste Woche nach Prag und am nächsten Tag weiter nach Bratislava.
Reisebüro	EA739 fliegt um 11.35 Uhr von Heathrow ab und kommt um 15.05 Uhr in Prag an. Flug CZ417 von Prag, Abflug 16.30 Uhr, Ankunft in Bratislava 17.20 Uhr. Haben Sie ein offenes Flugticket?
Kunde	Nein, es ist APEX.
Reisebüro	Gut. Sie müssen spätestens eine Stunde vor Abflug einchecken.
Kunde	Vielen Dank für Ihre Hilfe.
Reisebüro	Bitte schön.

13   Buchung eines Fluges

Kunde	Hallo. Fluglinie Sonnenstrand?
Angestellter	Ja. Hier Paul Wagner. Kann ich Ihnen behilflich sein?
Kunde	Mein Name ist Reinert. Ich möchte einen Direktflug nach Antigua buchen. Wie oft pro Woche kann man auf Ihren Flügen Luxusklasse fliegen?
Angestellter	Es gibt einen Flug jeden Montag nachmittag und jeden Donnerstag vormittag. Natürlich gibt es auch Flüge verschiedener Fluggesellschaften an den anderen Tagen, aber unsere Flugtarife sind äußerst konkurrenzfähig.
Kunde	Ja. Das hat man mir auch im Reisebüro gesagt, aber ich wollte das selbst überprüfen. Können Sie mir sagen, wieviel zwei Flugkarten hin und zurück, Abflug 7. Mai kosten würden?
Angestellter	Sehen wir uns zuerst die Flugeinzelheiten an bevor wir zu den Preisen kommen.
Kunde	Gut. Also wie sieht es für den 7. aus?
Angestellter	Es gibt noch etliche freie Plätze nebeneinander im Flug um 9.30 Uhr. Für Ihren Rückflug können Sie von Antigua aus Anordnungen treffen. Ich kann Sie jetzt an meine Kollegin, Frau Wolf, weitergeben. Sie gibt Ihnen weitere Auskunft über die Kosten. Das Restliche, das heißt Personaldaten, Zahlungsweise und Zustellung der Flugkarten, erledigt meine Kollegin.
Kunde	Vielen Dank.
Angestellter	Bitte, gern. Auf Wiederhören.

14 Thanking for hospitality

Jennie Denning	Jennie Denning.
Rachel Green	Hello, Ms Denning. Rachel Green here, from Galway plc.
Jennie Denning	Hello, Mrs Green. Did you have a good flight back?
Rachel Green	Yes, very good thanks. I'm ringing to thank you for your hospitality last night. It was a very enjoyable evening, and it was very kind of you to ask us all round – particularly at such short notice!
Jennie Denning	I'm pleased you found it enjoyable. It was very interesting for me to meet you all.
Rachel Green	It really was kind of you. So thanks once again. If you ever come over here, you must visit us.
Jennie Denning	Yes, I'll do that. Thanks for ringing.
Rachel Green	And thank you. Goodbye.
Jennie Denning	Bye.

14 Dank für Gastlichkeit

Frau Denniger	Hier Denninger.
Ruth Grüner	Hallo, Frau Denninger, hier spricht Ruth Grüner von Urbann GmbH.
Frau Denniger	Guten Tag, Frau Grüner. Hatten Sie einen guten Rückflug?
Ruth Grüner	Ja, danke. Ich möchte mich noch sehr herzlich für Ihre Gastfreundschaft gestern abend bedanken. Es war ein wirklich reizender Abend, und es war so nett von Ihnen, uns alle zu Ihnen nach Hause einzuladen – und mit so wenig Zeit zur Vorbereitung!
Frau Denniger	Schön, daß Sie sich gut unterhalten haben. Es hat mich sehr gefreut, Sie alle kennenzulernen.
Ruth Grüner	Es war wirklich sehr freundlich von Ihnen. Nochmals vielen Dank. Sollten Sie einmal in unsere Gegend kommen, müssen Sie uns unbedingt besuchen.
Frau Denniger	Oh, sehr gerne. Vielen Dank für Ihren Anruf.
Ruth Grüner	Ich danke Ihnen. Auf Wiederhören.
Frau Denniger	Wiederhören.

15 Invitations

(a) Accepting

John Brown	Hello, this is John Brown of International Tool & Die. I am calling to accept your invitation to the lunch in honour of Mr Aspley.
Chamber of Commerce employee	You are only just in time Mr Brown. I am fixing the final number of guests at 12 noon today.
John Brown	I'm sorry I did not reply sooner and in writing, but I've just come back from a business trip. I'm so glad not to miss this occasion.
Chamber of Commerce employee	A lot of people think highly of our Euro MP. There's going to be a good turnout.
John Brown	I am pleased to hear it. Mr Aspley has certainly helped my business to get into the EU market. Are any other VIPs coming?
Chamber of Commerce employee	The Lord Mayor is coming and so is the president of the European Parliament. I don't know about our local MPs.
John Brown	Anyway, you've got me on your list?
Chamber of Commerce employee	Yes, Mr Brown. You are on the list.

15 Einladung

(a) Annehmen

Herr Braun	Hallo, hier Braun von MABO Werkzeugmaschinen. Ich nehme gerne Ihre Einladung zum Mittagessen zu Ehren von Herrn Dr. Alpert an.
Handelskammerangestellte	Oh, gut. Sie rufen gerade rechtzeitig an, Herr Braun. Heute mittag wird die endgültige Gästeliste festgesetzt.
Herr Braun	Es tut mir leid, daß ich nicht schon früher und schriftlich geantwortet habe, aber ich bin gerade eben von einer Geschäftsreise zurückgekehrt. Ich bin so froh, daß ich diesen Anlaß nicht verpasse.[1]
Handelskammerangestellte	Ja, unser Abgeordneter im Europäischen Parlament wird sehr geschätzt und viele Leute werden da sein.
Herr Braun	Das freut mich zu hören. Herr Dr. Alpert hat jedenfalls meinem Unternehmen sehr geholfen, auf dem EU Markt Fuß zu fassen. Kommen irgendwelche hohen Tiere?
Handelskammerangestellte	Ja, der Oberbürgermeister und der Präsident des Europäischen Parlaments. Ich bin nicht sicher, ob unser Bundestagsabgeordneter kommt.
Herr Braun	Aber Sie haben mich jetzt auf der Liste, nicht wahr?
Handelskammerangestellte	Ja, Herr Braun. Haben wir.

1 *Verpassen*, 'to miss' i.e. an opportunity, train, etc. *Vermissen* is used in the sense: 'to miss' a person, place (i.e. emotionally).

(b) Declining

John Gregory	Hello, Michael. This is John Gregory from Car Products International. We've organized a trip to the Indycar road race at Long Beach for our most valued clients. It's the last weekend of April. Would you be able to come?
Michael Mills	Let me check my diary. I'm sorry, John, but I'm down to go to a company sales convention in Malta that weekend. I'm afraid there's no way I can get out of that.
John Gregory	That's a real pity. It would have been great to get together again. If you would like to send one of your staff, just let me know.
Michael Mills	Will do. Goodbye.
John Gregory	So long.

16   Travel enquiries

(a) Rail

Passenger	Good afternoon. Could you tell me if there is a train out of Seville in the early afternoon going to Madrid?
Booking clerk	Do you mind how long the journey takes?
Passenger	Well, I have to be at a conference in the capital by 6 o'clock in the evening.
Booking clerk	There's a high-speed train which leaves Seville every day at 12 midday. You'll be in Madrid by mid-afternoon.
Passenger	That sounds fine. Can I purchase my tickets by phone?
Booking clerk	No, I'm afraid you have to come and pay in person.
Passenger	Surely it's possible for a colleague or my personal assistant to make the purchase for me?
Booking clerk	Yes, sir, of course.
Passenger	Very well. I shall be travelling on Friday of this week and will require two singles. How much is that?
Booking clerk	34,000 pesetas in first class or 21,000 in second.
Passenger	Fine. Thanks for your assistance.

(b) Ablehnen

Herr Gärtner Hallo, Herr Miltner? Hier spricht Gärtner von Möller Autozubehör. Wir haben einen Ausflug nach Hockenheim zum Autorennen für unsere ganz speziellen Kunden organisiert. Das wäre am letzten Wochenende im April. Könnten Sie mitkommen?

Herr Miltner Ich sehe mal schnell im Terminkalender nach. Oh wie schade! Ich muß zu einer Verkaufskonferenz[1] unserer Firma nach Malta an diesem Wochenende und da kann ich leider nicht absagen.

Herr Gärtner Ja, das ist wirklich sehr schade.Ich hätte mich sehr gefreut, Sie wieder einmal zu sehen. Aber wenn Sie einen Ihrer Mitarbeiter schicken wollen, lassen Sie es mich doch wissen.

Herr Miltner Sehr gerne. Auf Wiederhören.

Herr Gärtner Wiederhören.

1 The omission of the verb of motion in this type of construction is quite common, for example: *ich muß in die Stadt*; *wir müssen heute nach Wien*.

16 Auskünfte

(a) Zugauskunft

Reisender Guten Tag. Können Sie mir sagen, ob es einen Zug von Hamburg nach Frankfurt am frühen Nachmittag gibt?

Bahnbeamter Wie lang darf die Reise dauern? Oder spielt das keine Rolle?

Reisender Also, ich muß um 6 Uhr abends in Frankfurt bei einer Tagung sein.

Bahnbeamter Es geht täglich ein Schnellzug von Hamburg um 12 Uhr; Sie wären dann am späten Nachmittag in Frankfurt.

Reisender Ja, das paßt gut. Kann ich meine Fahrkarten telefonisch lösen?

Bahnbeamter Leider nein. Sie müßten das hier selbst erledigen.

Reisender Aber es muß doch möglich sein, daß ein Mitarbeiter oder meine Sekretärin das für mich machen kann.

Bahnbeamter Ja, selbstverständlich.

Reisender Gut. Also, ich fahre am Freitag dieser Woche und brauche zwei einfache Fahrkarten. Was macht das, bitte?

Bahnbeamter 374,– DM erster Klasse und 230,– DM zweiter Klasse.[1]

Reisender Schön. Vielen Dank für Ihre Hilfe.

1 Note the use of the genitive here: *erster* and *zweiter Klasse*.

(b) Ferry

Booking clerk   Speedline Ferries. Can I help you?

Passenger   Yes, I'm taking my car over to France next week, from Dover to Calais. Can you give me the times of the crossings?

Booking clerk   Well, they're very frequent. About what time do you want to leave?

Passenger   About 8 a.m.

Booking clerk   Well, there's one at 8.45. The next one is at 10.45.

Passenger   Is there an earlier one?

Booking clerk   Yes, but that one goes at 6 a.m.

Passenger   And what's the return fare?

Booking clerk   Your vehicle and how many passengers?

Passenger   Just me.

Booking clerk   The fare is £185.

Passenger   That's fine. Can I book by phone using my credit card?

Booking clerk   Certainly sir.

Passenger   Thanks for your help. I'll call back later. Goodbye.

Booking clerk   Bye, and thanks for calling.

(b) Fährenauskunft

Beamter	Speedline Ferries.
Reisender	Ich möchte nächste Woche die Autofähre von Ostende nach Dover nehmen. Könnten Sie mir die Zeiten der Überfahrt geben, bitte?
Beamter	Also, die Fähren gehen sehr oft. Wann ungefähr möchten Sie fahren?
Reisender	So um 8 Uhr früh.
Beamter	Nun, es gibt eine Fähre um 8.45 Uhr. Die nächste wäre dann um 10.45 Uhr.
Reisender	Gibt es denn keine frühere?
Beamter	Ja, aber die geht schon um 6 Uhr.
Reisender	Und was kostet eine Rückfahrkarte?
Beamter	Für Ihren Wagen und für wieviele Mitreisende?
Reisender	Ich fahre allein.
Beamter	Das kostet dann 425,– DM.
Reisender	Gut. Kann ich dann die Fahrt telefonisch mit Kreditkarte buchen?
Beamter	Ja, natürlich.
Reisender	Danke für Ihre Hilfe. Wiederhören.
Beamter	Auf Wiederhören. Danke für Ihren Anruf.

17 Arranging delivery of goods

Customer	Hello, Mr King? You wanted me to ring you back.
Supplier	Thanks for calling. I wanted directions for the delivery of parts that we are making to your factory on Monday.
Customer	Ah right, this will be your first delivery. Well, take the motorway north. Come off at exit 27 and head towards Northam.
Supplier	How do you spell that? N-O-R-T-H-A-M?
Customer	That's it. After five miles you'll come to the Eastfield road.
Supplier	E-A-S-T-F-I-E-L-D?
Customer	Yes. After two miles you meet the Eastfield ringroad, clearly indicated, at a set of traffic lights. Go straight ahead and go through the next two traffic lights.
Supplier	So, that's two miles and three traffic lights . . .
Customer	At the fourth traffic light you turn left and then second right. This is Alverton Road and our premises are 150 yards down on the left.
Supplier	Thanks very much; our lorry will be there on Monday.

17 Anweisungen zur Lieferung

Kunde	Hallo, Herr Kienzl. Sie wollten, daß wir Sie zurückrufen.
Lieferant	Danke für Ihren Anruf. Können Sie mir sagen, wie ich zu Ihrem Betrieb komme? Wir liefern die Ersatzteile am Montag.
Kunde	Ach richtig. Das ist Ihre erste Lieferung an uns. Also, nehmen Sie die Autobahn in Richtung Norden. Fahren Sie ab bei Ausfahrt 27 in Richtung Neustadt.
Lieferant	Wie schreibt man das? N-E-U-S-T-A-D-T?
Kunde	Genau. Nach etwa 8 km kommen Sie zu einem Kreisverkehr und nehmen von dort die Straße nach Erfurt.
Lieferant	E-R-F-U-R-T?
Kunde	Stimmt. Nach ungefähr 3 km kommen Sie zur klar gekennzeichneten Umfahrung von Erfurt bei einer Verkehrsampel. Sie fahren dann immer geradeaus durch zwei geregelte Kreuzungen.
Lieferant	Also, ein Kreisverkehr und drei Verkehrsampeln . . .
Kunde	Bei der vierten Ampel biegen Sie links ein und nehmen dann die zweite Straße rechts. Das ist Adenauerstraße und unsere Firma ist etwa 100 m weiter auf der linken Seite.
Lieferant	Vielen Dank. Unser Lieferwagen wird am Montag bei Ihnen sein.

Teil II
Section II

Persönliches Gespräch
Face to face

18 Arriving for an appointment

Receptionist	Good morning, can I help you?
Frances Jones	Good morning, my name is Frances Jones. I have an appointment with Mrs Fisher at 10.
Receptionist	One moment, please. Mrs Fisher's secretary will come down to meet you. Please take a seat.
Frances Jones	Thank you.
Receptionist	Would you like a coffee while you are waiting?
Frances Jones	Yes, thank you.
Receptionist	Please help yourself, the coffee machine and the cups are on your left.

18 Ankunft zu einem Termin

Empfang	Guten Tag. Bitte schön?
Frau Jörger	Guten Tag. Mein Name ist Jörger. Ich habe einen Termin mit Frau Fischer um 10 Uhr.
Empfang	Einen Moment, bitte. Frau Fischers Sekretärin wird gleich zu Ihnen herunterkommen. Bitte nehmen Sie einstweilen Platz!
Frau Jörger	Danke.
Empfang	Möchten Sie vielleicht einen Kaffee, während Sie warten?
Frau Jörger	Oh ja, bitte.
Empfang	Bitte, bedienen Sie sich! Die Kaffeemaschine und die Tassen sind hier links.

19 Arranging further contacts with a company

Mr Calder	Thank you very much for your help this morning, Mr Winter. I think we've made a lot of progress on the matter of financing the deal.
Mr Winter	Yes, I agree. It's been useful to clear the air after the initial difficulties we experienced. Presumably, this will not be our last meeting as we must await the final decision and then act quickly.
Mr Calder	Indeed. Do you have any idea of when that will be?
Mr Winter	I've been promised an answer by the end of June, so if we say early July there will still be a couple of weeks before we close for the summer vacation.
Mr Calder	Fine. How about Monday the 3rd?
Mr Winter	I can't make the morning, but I shall be free all afternoon. More importantly, the main people involved will be able to work on the final proposals that week. If we need to develop our plans further, bringing in other companies or arranging further contacts, there should be time enough to do that.
Mr Calder	Shall we say 2 p.m. here? In the meantime we can still explore the possibilities or value of involving other parties both within and outside our companies.
Mr Winter	Very well. I'll get that organized. I'll give you a ring by the 14th to confirm everything we might know in the meantime.
Mr Calder	Right. Thanks again. . . . Can I get to the carpark by going straight down in the elevator?
Mr Winter	Yes. First floor, first door on the left. See you in July if not before.

19 Weitere Terminvereinbarungen

Herr Kuhn	Sie haben uns heute vormittag sehr geholfen, Herr Winter. Vielen Dank. Ich denke, daß wir in der Sache Projektfinanzierung sehr viel weitergekommen sind.
Herr Winter	Ja, bestimmt. Nach den Anfangsschwierigkeiten war es nützlich, alle Unklarheiten aus dem Weg zu räumen. Es wird sicherlich noch weitere Besprechungen geben vor dem Endbeschluß, und dann heißt es schnell handeln.
Herr Kuhn	Genau. Haben Sie eine Ahnung, wann das ist?
Herr Winter	Mir wurde eine Antwort bis Ende Juni versprochen. Also nehmen wir Anfang Juli an, dann bleiben uns immer noch zwei Wochen, bevor der Betrieb Sommerurlaubssperre hat.
Herr Kuhn	Schön. Wie wäre es also mit Montag dem dritten?
Herr Winter	Vormittag geht es bei mir nicht, aber ich wäre den ganzen Nachmittag frei. Was aber noch wichtiger ist – die Hauptbeteiligten können in dieser Woche noch die letzten Vorschläge ausarbeiten. Und falls es nötig ist, unsere Pläne zu erweitern, etwa andere Firmen einzubeziehen oder weitere Termine zu vereinbaren,[1] so bleibt uns noch genug Zeit dafür.
Herr Kuhn	Sagen wir also um 14 Uhr hier? In der Zwischenzeit können wir noch untersuchen, welche Möglichkeiten oder welchen Sinn es haben würde, andere Gruppen innerhalb oder außerhalb unserer Firmen heranzuziehen.
Herr Winter	Also gut. Ich sehe dazu und rufe Sie dann noch vor dem 14. an und halte Sie auf dem laufenden.
Herr Kuhn	In Ordnung. Nochmals besten Dank. . . . Komme ich mit dem Lift direkt hinunter zum Parkplatz?
Herr Winter	Ja. Fahren Sie ins Erdgeschoß und dann ist es die erste Tür links. Auf Wiedersehen im Juli wenn nicht schon früher.

1 *Einen Termin vereinbaren*, 'to fix', 'make an appointment'. *Einen Termin einhalten* means 'to keep an appointment'.

20 Presenting a proposal

Helen Green	Morning, John. Do come in and take a seat.
John Stevens	Morning, Helen. Thanks.
Helen Green	You wanted to see me about our new product launch?
John Stevens	Yes, I think we should try to bring it forward to December.
Helen Green	That might be a bit tight. Any particular reason why?
John Stevens	Well, we'd catch the important Christmas business, and we'd be ahead of the opposition.
Helen Green	I'm not sure our production people could handle it.
John Stevens	Not a major problem. Our plant in Wellington can take on more of the production. We have spare capacity there.
Helen Green	Have you discussed this with your people over there?
John Stevens	Yes, and they're convinced they can deal with it.
Helen Green	We can't risk any slip-up on this – the launch is very important. And what about the advertising schedule?
John Stevens	That's OK. The advertising copy is virtually ready. The ads could be pulled forward to December.
Helen Green	Look, there's some advantage in doing this, but I'd like to talk about it with the board first. There's a meeting tomorrow at 2. Can you make it?
John Stevens	I've got one or two things on, but I can reshuffle them.
Helen Green	Fine. Look, I've another meeting now, but I'll catch up with you later.
John Stevens	OK. See you later.

20 Einen Geschäftsvorschlag machen

Frau Groß	Guten Tag, Herr Steiner. Kommen Sie doch herein und nehmen Sie Platz!
Herr Steiner	Danke, Frau Groß.
Frau Groß	Sie wollten mich wegen der Lancierung unseres neuen Produktes sehen?
Herr Steiner	Ja, ich glaube, wir sollten das auf Dezember vorverlegen.
Frau Groß	Das könnte ein bißchen knapp werden. Haben Sie bestimmte Gründe dafür?
Herr Steiner	Also, wir würden damit noch ins Weihnachtsgeschäft kommen, was wichtig wäre. Und außerdem hätten wir einen Vorsprung vor der Konkurrenz.[1]
Frau Groß	Ich bin mir nicht sicher,[2] ob das die Leute in der Herstellung schaffen können.
Herr Steiner	Das ist eigentlich kein größeres Problem. Unsere Fabrik in Hamburg kann einen weiteren Teil der Produktion übernehmen. Wir haben freie Kapazitäten da.
Frau Groß	Haben Sie das schon mit Ihren Leuten vor Ort besprochen?
Herr Steiner	Ja und die sind sicher, daß sie damit zurechtkommen.
Frau Groß	Die Lancierung ist äußerst wichtig für uns. Wir dürfen uns dabei keine Fehler erlauben. Und wie steht es mit dem Werbeplan?
Herr Steiner	Das ist klar. Der Werbetext ist schon so gut wie fertig. Die Reklame könnte also leicht schon im Dezember herauskommen.
Frau Groß	Ja, das hätte sicher einige Vorteile, aber ich muß das alles erst mit dem Vorstand besprechen. Er hat morgen eine Sitzung um zwei. Geht das bei Ihnen?
Herr Steiner	Ich hab zwar ein paar Sachen zu tun, aber die lassen sich verschieben.
Frau Groß	Gut. Und jetzt habe ich gleich noch eine andere Besprechung, aber ich sehe Sie dann später.
Herr Steiner	OK. Also Tschüß!

1 *Konkurrenz* can be used in the sense of 'competition' (abstract), and 'competitors'. 'Competitors' can also be rendered as *Konkurrenten*.
2 *Mir* is not essential here.

21 Exploring business collaboration

Mr Berryman	Pleased to meet you, Monsieur Maurois, and thank you for arranging my hotel.
M. Maurois	The pleasure is mine, Mr Berryman. You wanted to discuss possible joint ventures with us.
Mr Berryman	Yes, we are both in building and civil engineering. We want to expand into Europe. You might find us useful partners.
M. Maurois	It's a pity we didn't begin these discussions three months ago; we recently wanted to bid for a stretch of motorway in this region but we did not quite have the resources.
Mr Berryman	Was there no local company you could combine with?
M. Maurois	Unfortunately we are the only firm in the region with the necessary expertise. You would have been a good partner – we have made a study of your past projects.
Mr Berryman	And we have studied yours, of course. We were thinking of the proposed port development just down the road.
M. Maurois	You are really on the ball Mr Berryman. We have just received the detailed specifications and were contemplating a tender.
Mr Berryman	And I have the spec in English in my briefcase! Shall we roll our sleeves up and work out a joint tender?

21 Besprechung der Möglichkeit eines Joint Venture Projekts

Mr Berryman	Freut mich, Sie kennenzulernen, Herr Manstein, und vielen Dank, daß Sie ein Hotel für mich organisiert haben.
Herr Manstein	Ganz meinerseits, Mr Berryman. Sie möchten die Möglichkeit eines Joint Venture Projekts für unsere Firmen besprechen, nicht wahr?
Mr Berryman	Ja. Unsere Firmen sind beide in der Baubranche und wollen ihre Geschäftstätigkeit auf ganz Europa ausdehnen. Das könnte eine äußerst fruchtbare Partnerschaft ergeben.
Herr Manstein	Wie schade, daß wir uns nicht schon vor drei Monaten darüber unterhalten konnten. Wir wollten damals ein Angebot für die Autobahnteilstrecke in dieser Gegend machen, aber es fehlte uns an den nötigen Mitteln.
Mr Berryman	Und in Kombination mit einer hiesigen Firma? War das nicht möglich?
Herr Manstein	Leider sind wir der einzige Betrieb in der Gegend mit der geeigneten Erfahrung und Sachkenntnis. Sie wären der richtige Partner für uns gewesen – wir haben Ihre bisherigen Projekte eingehend studiert.
Mr Berryman	Und wir selbstverständlich auch Ihre Projekte. Es gibt da diesen geplanten Hafenausbau gleich in der Nähe von Ihnen und da hätten wir gedacht. . . .
Herr Manstein	Mr Berryman, Sie sind wirklich auf Draht! Wir haben gerade die genaue Baubeschreibung erhalten und erwägen, ein Angebot zu machen.
Mr Berryman	Und ich habe die Baubeschreibung auf englisch in meiner Aktentasche. Na, wollen wir uns die Ärmel aufkrempeln und ein gemeinsames Angebot ausarbeiten?

22 At the travel agent's

(a) Enquiry/booking

Passenger	Could you give me details of flights to Wellington, New Zealand, please?
Booking clerk	When do you wish to fly?
Passenger	The first week of June.
Booking clerk	Let me see. Which day do you want to depart?
Passenger	Tuesday, if possible.
Booking clerk	There's a flight leaving Sydney at 8 a.m. which gets into Wellington at 1 p.m. Do you want to make a booking?
Passenger	How much is the flight?
Booking clerk	It's 725 Australian dollars return.
Passenger	Fine, OK. I'll take it.

(b) Changing a booking

Customer	I'd like to change a flight reservation for Mr David Street.
Booking clerk	Could you give me the flight details?
Customer	BY567 to Rome on 21 March. Would it be possible to change it to 23 March?
Booking clerk	I'll just check. That's OK. The flight leaves at the same time. I'll issue a new ticket and send it to you later today.
Customer	Thank you.

22 Im Reisebüro

(a) Auskunft/Buchung

Reisender	Bitte können Sie mir Einzelheiten über Flüge nach London geben?
Angestellter	Wann möchten Sie fliegen?
Reisender	In der ersten Juniwoche.
Angestellter	Augenblick. An welchem Wochentag möchten Sie fliegen?
Reisender	Wenn möglich am Dienstag.
Angestellter	Es gibt einen Flug von München um 8 Uhr morgen. Ankunft in London um 10.30 Uhr Ortszeit. Möchten Sie den Flug buchen?
Reisender	Was kostet der Flug?
Angestellter	Dreihundert DM hin und zurück.[1]
Reisender	Ja, OK. Ich nehme den Flug.

1 Outward flight is *Hinflug*; 'return flight' is *Rückflug*.

(b) Änderung einer Buchung

Kunde	Ich möchte die Flugreservierung für Herrn David Strasser ändern, bitte.
Angestellter	Können Sie mir die Einzelheiten seines Fluges geben?
Kunde	Flug BY567 nach Rom am 21. März. Können Sie das auf den 23. März ändern?
Angestellter	Augenblick, ich sehe nach. Ja, das ist OK. Der Flug geht zur selben Zeit. Ich stelle ein neues Ticket aus und schicke es noch heute an Sie ab.
Kunde	Danke schön.

(c) Flight cancellation

Customer I'm ringing on behalf of Mrs Mary Thomas. She's booked on a flight to Capetown next Thursday, but she has unfortunately fallen ill. Can she get a refund on her ticket?

Booking clerk How did she pay?

Customer By cheque, I think.

Booking clerk If she took out travel insurance she will be able to get her money back, if her doctor signs a certificate.

Customer I'd better ask her if she took out any insurance and then I'll get back to you.

23   Checking in at the airport

Assistant Good evening, sir. Can I have your ticket and passport?

Passenger Certainly.

Assistant Are you travelling alone?

Passenger Yes, that's right.

Assistant How many items of luggage are you checking in?

Passenger Just this case.

Assistant Can you put it on the belt, please? Did you pack it yourself?

Passenger Yes.

Assistant Are there any electrical items in it?

Passenger No, they're in my hand baggage.

Assistant What are they?

Passenger An electric shaver and a lap-top computer.

Assistant That's fine. Do you want smoking or non-smoking?

Passenger Non-smoking please.

(c) Flugstornierung

Kunde	Ich rufe an im Auftrag von Frau Thomas. Sie ist auf einen Flug[1] nach Kapstadt nächsten Donnerstag gebucht, aber sie ist jetzt leider krank. Kann sie das Geld für den Flugschein zurückbekommen?
Angestellter	Wie hat sie dafür gezahlt?
Kunde	Mit Scheck, glaube ich.
Angestellter	Wenn sie eine Reiseversicherung eingegangen ist und ein ärztliches Attest vorlegt, kann sie ihr Geld zurückerhalten.
Kunde	Ich frage sie da besser wegen der Versicherung und rufe Sie dann später zurück.

1 *Auf einen Flug gebucht*: accusative rather than dative.

23 Bei der Flugabfertigung (einchecken)

Bodenpersonal	Guten Abend. Bitte Ihren Flugschein und Paß!
Reisender	Bitte sehr.
Bodenpersonal	Reisen Sie allein?
Reisender	Ja.
Bodenpersonal	Wieviele Gepäckstücke checken Sie ein?
Reisender	Nur diesen Koffer.
Bodenpersonal	Bitte stellen Sie ihn auf das Förderband! Haben Sie ihn selbst gepackt?
Reisender	Ja.
Bodenpersonal	Haben Sie elektrische Geräte im Koffer?
Reisender	Nein, nur im Handgepäck.
Bodenpersonal	Welche?
Reisender	Einen Elektrorasierer und einen Laptop-Computer.[1]
Bodenpersonal	In Ordnung. Möchten Sie Raucher oder Nichtraucher?
Reisender	Nichtraucher, bitte!

1 The accusatives are required because the nouns are in apposition with *elektrische Geräte* above. (*Haben Sie . . .*).

24   Checking in at a hotel

Receptionist	Good afternoon, madam.
Guest	Good afternoon. I have a reservation in the name of Battersby.
Receptionist	A single room for two nights?
Guest	Surely that was changed to a double room? My husband is due to join me later this evening.
Receptionist	One moment please; I'll just check. Oh, yes, there is a note to that effect. Will you be having dinner at the hotel?
Guest	Yes, dinner for one. Can I also order an early call tomorrow morning and can we have a newspaper?
Receptionist	At 6 o'clock, 6.30?
Guest	That's too early. Say 7 o'clock. And could we have a copy of *The Times*?
Receptionist	I am sorry but we will not have the London *Times* until tomorrow afternoon. Would you like the *Herald Tribune* or perhaps a German newspaper?
Guest	No, thank you. I'll leave it. I'll need a taxi in half an hour. Can you call one for me? And what time is dinner by the way?

25   Checking out of a hotel

Guest	I would like to check out now.
Receptionist	Certainly, sir. What is your room number?
Guest	324.
Receptionist	Mr Lawrence? Did you make any phone calls this morning? Have you used the mini-bar?
Guest	No, I haven't made any calls since yesterday evening. Here is my mini-bar slip.
Receptionist	Thank you. Would you be so kind as to fill in the hotel questionnaire while I total your bill? How do you wish to pay?
Guest	By credit card.
Receptionist	Fine. I'll just be a minute. There you are, Mr Lawrence. Thank you very much.

24 Hotelanmeldung

Empfang	Guten Tag.
Gast	Guten Tag. Ich habe eine Reservierung unter dem Namen Battersby.[1]
Empfang	Ist das ein Einzelzimmer für zwei Nächte?
Gast	Aber das wurde doch geändert auf ein Doppelzimmer! Ich erwarte meinen Mann hier am späten Abend.
Empfang	Einen Moment, bitte. Ich sehe nach. Ach ja, hier ist eine Anmerkung mit der Änderung. Möchten Sie das Abendessen im Hotel?
Gast	Ja. Für eine Person. Und können Sie uns auch morgen früh wecken lassen, ja? Wir hätten auch gern eine Zeitung.
Empfang	Ja. Um sechs Uhr oder halb sieben?
Gast	Nein. Das ist zu früh. Sagen wir sieben Uhr. Und wir nehmen die *Times*.
Empfang	Leider bekommen wir die Londoner *Times* erst morgen nachmittag. Möchten Sie statt dessen den *Herald Tribune* oder vielleicht eine deutsche Zeitung?
Gast	Nein, danke. Dann keine Zeitung. Ich brauche in einer halben Stunde ein Taxi. Können Sie mir bitte eines bestellen? Oh, und um wieviel Uhr ist Abendessen?

1   *Unter dem Namen*, 'in the name of'. Note the preposition here.

25 Abreise

Gast	Ich reise ab. Können Sie mir die Rechnung ausstellen?
Empfang	Gerne. Was ist Ihre Zimmernummer, bitte?
Gast	Dreihundertvierundzwanzig.
Empfang	Herr Lawrence? Haben Sie heute morgen noch telefoniert? Haben Sie die Minibar benützt?
Gast	Nein. Mein letzter Anruf war gestern abend. Und hier ist mein Minibarzettel.
Empfang	Würden Sie bitte so freundlich sein und den Hotelfragebogen ausfüllen? Ich mache einstweilen Ihre Rechnung fertig. Wie möchten Sie bezahlen?
Gast	Mit Kreditkarte.
Empfang	Schön. Einen Moment, bitte. So, Herr Lawrence. Und besten Dank!

26 Ordering a meal in a restaurant

Waitress	Good afternoon, madam. Would you like the menu?
Customer 1	Yes, thank you. And may we have a dry white wine and a pint of lager whilst we are choosing our meal?
Waitress	Certainly. Here is the menu; we also have a chef's special set meal at 15 dollars.

* * *

Customer 1	Would you like to have a look first?
Customer 2	No. I'll have what you recommend as you know the local cuisine far better than I do. But I'm looking forward to my lager.
Customer 1	Fine. Here come the drinks, anyway. May we have two hors d'œuvres? And for the main course two pepper steaks with mixed vegetables and jacket potatoes. I think we'll also have a bottle of house red with the steak.
Waitress	So, a bottle of red, two hors d'œuvres and two pepper steaks. How would you like the steaks cooked?
Customer 2	Well done for me, please.
Customer 1	Medium for me.

* * *

Waitress	Have you enjoyed your meal?
Customer 1	Yes, it was fine, thank you. I think we'll skip the sweet as we are running a bit late. Just two black coffees and the bill, please.

* * *

Waitress	Your coffee and the bill, madam. Could you pay the head waiter at the till when you leave?
Customer 1	Of course. And this is for you. Many thanks.
Waitress	Thank you, madam. I'm glad you enjoyed your meal.

26 Bestellen im Restaurant

Kellnerin	Guten Tag. Möchten Sie die Speisekarte, bitte?
1. Gast	Ja, bitte. Und wir möchten einstweilen ein Glas trockenen Weißwein und ein großes Bier.
Kellnerin	Gerne. Hier ist die Karte. Wir haben auch ein Spezialmenü zu 25,– DM.

* * *

1. Gast	Wählen Sie zuerst, bitte!
2. Gast	Nein, ich nehme, was Sie mir empfehlen, denn Sie kennen die hiesige Küche besser als ich. Aber ich freue mich auf mein Bier.
1. Gast	Wunderbar. Hier kommen schon die Getränke. Können wir zweimal die Backerbsensuppe haben und als Hauptspeise zweimal Pfeffersteak mit Gemüseallerlei und Kartoffeln in der Schale? Und zum Steak nehmen wir eine Flasche roten Hauswein.
Kellnerin	Also, eine Flasche Rotwein, zwei Suppen und zwei Pfeffersteaks. Wie möchten Sie die Steaks, bitte?
2. Gast	Gut durch für mich, bitte!
1. Gast	Halb durch für mich.

* * *

Kellnerin	Hat es Ihnen geschmeckt?[1]
1. Gast	Ja, sehr gut, danke. Aber leider bleibt uns keine Zeit mehr für die Nachspeise. Bringen Sie uns noch zwei kleine Mokka und die Rechnung, bitte!

* * *

Kellnerin	Hier ist Ihr Kaffee und die Rechnung. Können Sie bitte beim Ober an der Kasse bezahlen, wenn Sie gehen?
1. Gast	Natürlich. Und das ist für Sie – vielen Dank!
Kellnerin	Ich danke Ihnen. Freut mich, daß es Ihnen geschmeckt hat.

1 A standard expression. It is possible to abbreviate it to *hat's geschmeckt?*

27 Verifying a bill

Waiter	Yes sir? Did you enjoy your meal?
Customer	Yes, but can I check the bill with you?
Waiter	Certainly – is there a problem?
Customer	I think there might be a mistake – we had four set menus at £15 and also the aperitifs and the wine.
Waiter	Yes?
Customer	But what's this item here?
Waiter	Four whiskies, sir. £10.
Customer	But we didn't have any!
Waiter	Just a moment sir, I'll check it for you. . . . Sorry, my mistake. I'll get you an amended bill at once.
Customer	Thank you.

27 Überprüfung einer Rechnung

Kellnerin	Bitte schön! Hat's geschmeckt?
Gast	Ja, aber kann ich bitte die Rechnung noch überprüfen?
Kellnerin	Gerne. Gibt es ein Problem?
Gast	Ich glaube, da ist hier ein Fehler – wir hatten vier Menüs zu 35,– DM und auch die Aperitife und den Wein.
Kellnerin	Ja?
Gast	Aber was bedeutet dieser Rechnungsposten hier?
Kellnerin	Das ist für vier Whisky. Dreiundzwanzig DM.
Gast	Aber wir hatten doch keinen!
Kellnerin	Einen Augenblick, bitte. Ich sehe das für Sie nach ... Es tut mir leid, das war mein Fehler.[1] Ich bringe Ihnen sofort eine neue Rechnung.
Gast	Danke.

1 'To make a mistake' in adding up bill, etc, *sich verrechnen* (e.g. *ich habe mich verrechnet*).

28 Drawing up a schedule of visits for reps

Senior representative	Thanks for coming to this meeting. I thought it would be useful to discuss areas for the autumn quarter.
Representative 2	Conveniently enough the schedule of leads and follow-up visits shows a roughly equal split between the northwest, northeast and southwest regions.
Representative 3	We need to consider what to do about the lack of interest in our products in the southeast.
Senior representative	There is also a scattering of trade fairs that one or other of us should attend, including one in Marseilles in mid-September.
Representative 2	Perhaps we should all be there to work out a strategy for the southeast. And we could all be at the Paris Salon des Arts Ménagers in early November.
Representative 3	Good idea. I have some contacts that might help. We'll proceed by regions as originally suggested. Me in Bordeaux, Edwin in Lille and Fred in Strasbourg?
Senior representative	Seems OK to me. Are you happy, Fred? Apart from the Marseilles and Paris fairs we can each do our regional fairs individually.
Representative 2	I am happy with that. Same budget as last year?
Senior representative	I am glad you asked. The operating budget has been increased by a meagre 5 per cent. Any requests for increased staffing need to be justified by an increase in business.
Representative 3	So what else is new? Let's get those dates in our diaries.

28 Erstellung eines Plans für Vertreterbesuche

Hauptvertreterin	Danke, daß ihr zur Besprechung gekommen seid. Ich dachte, es wäre nützlich, über unsere Gebiete im Hinblick auf das Herbstquartal zu sprechen.
2. Vertreter	Da trifft es sich ja günstig, daß sich Kontaktnahme und nachfassende Besuche auf unserer Liste im wesentlichen gleichmäßig auf die Regionen Nordwest, Nordost und Südwest verteilen.
3. Vertreter	Wir müssen uns also überlegen, was gegen den Mangel an Interesse für unsere Produkte im Gebiet Südost unternommen werden kann.
Hauptvertreterin	Es gibt da ein paar Messen, die der eine oder andere von uns besuchen könnte, einschließlich der Gewerbeausstellung in Marseille Mitte September.
2. Vertreter	Vielleicht sollten wir alle drei hinfahren und eine Taktik für den Südosten ausarbeiten. Anfang November[1] könnten wir dann alle auf der Haushaltsmesse in Paris sein.
3. Vertreter	Gute Idee. Ich habe da ein paar nützliche Kontakte. Wie ist es, bleiben wir bei unseren ursprünglichen Regionen? Ich in Bordeaux, der Egon in Lille und der Fredi in Straßburg?
Hauptvertreterin	Scheint mir OK. Was meinst du, Fredi? Abgesehen von den Messen in Marseille und Paris kann jeder auf die Ausstellungen in seinem Gebiet allein fahren.
2. Vertreter	Einverstanden. Haben wir dasselbe Budget wie im Vorjahr?
Hauptvertreterin	Gut, daß du fragst. Das Betriebsbudget wurde um[2] mickrige 5% erhöht. Jede Neuanforderung von Personal muß durch eine Geschäftszunahme gerechtfertigt werden.
3. Vertreter	Also alles wie gehabt! Füllen wir unsere Terminkalender aus!

1 When *Anfang Mitte* or *Ende* are used in the temporal sense, they do not require a preposition: *Ende November*, 'at the end of November'; *am Ende der Straße*, 'at the end of the street'.
2 *Erhöhen um*, 'to increase by'; *erhöhen auf*, 'to increase to'.

29 Conducted visit of a department

Guide	Before I show you round the department, come and meet my deputy, Frederick Fallon.
Miss Smith	Pleased to meet you, Mr Fallon.
Frederick Fallon	Welcome to the department, Miss Smith.
Guide	Frederick is responsible for the day-to-day running of the department. I'll take you round now. This is the general office, with Mrs Jones looking after reception and typists and PC operators.
Miss Smith	How many secretaries work for Mrs Jones?
Guide	Normally five. One is currently on sick leave and one on holiday. . . . This is the overseas sales office. They have their own fax machines and deal directly with our agents in Europe. . . . And this is the design section. Most of their work is now done by CAD/CAM. They've got some of the most sophisticated computer equipment in the company. Let me introduce you to David Hall. David, this is Miss Smith.
David Hall	Pleased to meet you, Miss Smith.
Guide	David has four designers working for him. And finally, this is Ted Stolzfuss, who is over here from our American parent company. Ted is with us to look at the way we operate in Europe. Ted, meet Miss Smith.

29 Besichtigung einer Betriebsabteilung

Leiter	Bevor ich Ihnen die Abteilung zeige, möchte ich Sie mit meinem Stellvertreter, Herrn Fellner, bekanntmachen.
Frau Schmid	Freut mich, Sie kennenzulernen, Herr Fellner!
Herr Fellner	Willkommen in unserer Abteilung, Frau Schmid!
Leiter	Herr Fellner ist verantwortlich für den geregelten Ablauf des Abteilungsbetriebs. Ich führe Sie jetzt weiter. Hier ist das Hauptsekretariat einschließlich Schreibdienst, Empfang, und EDV. Frau Jonas hat die Leitung hier.
Frau Schmid	Wieviele Sekretärinnen werden hier beschäftigt?
Leiter	Normalerweise fünf. Eine ist zur Zeit im Krankenstand und eine andere ist auf Urlaub. . . . Hier ist die Auslandsabteilung. Sie haben da ihre eigenen Faxgeräte und stehen in direkter Verbindung mit unseren Vertretungen. . . . Und das ist unser Konstruktionsbüro. Es wird hier fast ausschließlich nur mit CAD/CAM gearbeitet. Die Computer gehören zu[1] den technisch raffiniertesten Geräten in unserer Firma. Darf ich Ihnen Herrn Holter vorstellen? Herr Holter, das ist Frau Schmid.
Herr Holter	Angenehm.[2]
Leiter	Herr Holter hat einen Mitarbeiterstab von vier Konstrukteuren. Und hier ist Herr Stolzfuss von unserer amerikanischen Mutterfirma. Er informiert sich bei uns über die Geschäftspraxis in Europa. Herr Stolzfuss, Frau Schmid.

1 *Gehören zu*, 'belong to' (in the sense of 'are part of the group'). 'To belong to' in the sense of 'possession' is *gehören* + dative (*das Buch gehört mir*).
2 A variation on *freut mich*.

30 Informal job interview

Personnel manager	Good morning, Ms Jiménez, and welcome. I hope you had no trouble getting here.
Gloria Jiménez	Good morning. Thank you, it was nice of you to invite me in for a chat.
Personnel manager	First, let me introduce you to Brian Arthur, who is in charge of advertising. As you can see, he's always snowed under with work, eh Brian? Gloria Jiménez, Brian Arthur.
Brian Arthur	Pleased to meet you. Don't take her too seriously, Gloria, you'll see for yourself when you start next week.
Gloria Jiménez	How many staff do you have in this department?
Brian Arthur	Seven fulltimers and a couple of freelancers who help out when we have special projects on.
Gloria Jiménez	It looks a friendly set-up, anyway.
Personnel manager	Yes, you're right, they are one of our most efficient and successful departments. Would you like to meet James, with whom you will be working most closely? He is our art director.
Gloria Jiménez	Fine. Has he been with the company for a long time?
Personnel manager	No, he was brought in recently when the company merged. Oh, it looks as if he's in a meeting, so we'll wait here and talk a bit more about you. How did you get into commercial design?
Gloria Jiménez	After university I realized that there were good prospects for young people with ideas in the field of design and advertising, so I took a course in advertising in Seville not long before the World Fair was awarded to the city.
Personnel manager	Did you actually work on the World Fair project?
Gloria Jiménez	Yes, my first job was with a Japanese agency that was promoting its high-tech industries, and I carried on until the Fair closed last year.
Personnel manager	That sounds just the sort of experience we are looking for. Ah, here comes James . . .

30 Vorstellungsgespräch (nicht formell)

Personalleiterin   Guten Tag, Frau Jiménez. Herzlich willkommen! Ich hoffe, Sie
hatten eine gute Reise.

Gloria Jiménez   Guten Tag. Ja, danke. Es ist sehr freundlich von Ihnen, mich zu
einem Gespräch einzuladen.

Personalleiterin   Darf ich Ihnen gleich einmal den Werbeleiter, Herrn Benno
Artberg, vorstellen? Wie Sie sehen, ist er wie immer mit
Arbeit reichlich eingedeckt, – was, Benno? Benno Artberg,
Gloria Jiménez.

Benno Artberg   Freut mich sehr. Nehmen Sie sie nicht zu ernst, Frau Jiménez!
Sie werden ja sehen, wenn Sie nächste Woche hier anfangen.

Gloria Jiménez   Wieviele Mitarbeiter beschäftigen Sie eigentlich in dieser
Abteilung?

Benno Artberg   Sieben sind vollbeschäftigt und bei speziellen Projekten
stellen wir Freiberufler zur Aushilfe ein.

Gloria Jiménez   Es scheint hier ja sehr freundlich zuzugehen.

Personalleiterin   Stimmt. Doch die Abteilung ist auch eine unserer tüchtigsten
und erfolgreichsten. Und jetzt führe ich Sie zu unserem
Chefgraphiker, Uwe Jansen, mit dem Sie am meisten
zusammenarbeiten werden.

Gloria Jiménez   Schön. Ist er schon lange bei der Firma?

Personalleiterin   Nein. Er ist erst kürzlich durch den Firmenzusammenschluß
zu uns gekommen. Oh, es scheint, daß er gerade bei einer
Besprechung ist. Wollen wir hier warten und uns noch ein
wenig über Sie unterhalten? Wie sind Sie eigentlich zur
Werbegraphik gekommen?

Gloria Jiménez   Nach meinem Studium habe ich bemerkt, daß es gute
Aussichten für junge Leute in der Werbebranche gibt und da
habe ich einen Ausbildungskurs in Sevilla gemacht. Das war
kurz bevor die Veranstaltung der Weltausstellung an Sevilla
ging.

Personalleiterin   Und waren Sie eigentlich auch in der Weltausstellung tätig?

Gloria Jiménez   Ja. Meine erste Stelle war bei einer japanischen Agentur, die
für die High-Tech-Industrie Werbung machte. Ich war bis zum
Ende der Weltausstellung bei dieser Firma.

Personalleiterin   Das ist genau die Art von Berufserfahrung, die wir suchen. Ah,
hier kommt Herr Jansen.

31 Formal job interview

Part 1

Interviewer	Do come in, Ms Hellington, and take a seat.
Ms Hellington	Thank you.
Interviewer	Well, if I can make a start, can you tell us why you want this particular post?
Ms Hellington	As I said in my application, I'm working with quite a small company at the moment. My promotion prospects are limited because of that.
Interviewer	So that is your main reason?
Ms Hellington	Not just that. I've been with the company for five years now, and although I found the work interesting at first, I now feel that I want a more varied post which is more challenging.
Interviewer	You feel that you'll find that here?
Ms Hellington	Yes, I do. You're a big company in the process of expansion, and the department I'd be working in would give me much more variety.
Interviewer	Do you think that moving from a small department to a much larger one would be a problem?
Ms Hellington	It would be rather new at first, but I was working with a big company before my present job, and I do integrate well. So I'm confident that I can make the change.

31 Vorstellungsgespräch (formell)

Erster Teil

Leiter des Vorstellungsgesprächs	Bitte, kommen Sie herein und nehmen Sie Platz, Frau Hellinger!
Frau Hellinger	Danke.
Leiter des Vorstellungsgesprächs	Also, ich darf Sie zu Beginn gleich fragen, warum Sie sich für diese Stelle interessieren.
Frau Hellinger	Wie ich schon in meinem Bewerbungsschreiben erwähnte, bin ich zur Zeit bei einer kleinen Firma beschäftigt und da sind die Aufstiegsmöglichkeiten ziemlich begrenzt.
Leiter des Vorstellungsgesprächs	Und ist das der Hauptgrund?
Frau Hellinger	Nein, eigentlich nicht. Ich bin bei dieser Firma jetzt schon fünf Jahre, und obwohl ich die Arbeit anfangs interessant gefunden habe, möchte ich nun eine Stelle, in der ich stärker gefordert werde und die mehr Abwechslung[1] bietet.
Leiter des Vorstellungsgesprächs	Und Sie glauben das hier zu finden?
Frau Hellinger	Ja, bestimmt. Ihr Unternehmen ist groß und in Ausdehnung begriffen. Die Abteilung, in der ich arbeiten würde, gäbe mir viel mehr Spielraum.
Leiter des Vorstellungsgesprächs	Meinen Sie nicht, daß ein Wechsel von einer kleinen zu einer viel größeren Abteilung Probleme mit sich bringen könnte?
Frau Hellinger	Sicher wäre am Anfang alles neu für mich, aber vor meiner jetzigen Stellung war ich schon in einem Großbetrieb tätig. Ich bin überzeugt, daß ich bei meiner Anpassungsfähigkeit die Umstellung gut schaffen würde.

1 *Abwechslung* 'change', 'variety'. 'For a change', *zur Abwechslung*.

Part 2

Interviewer	As you know, we're a multinational organization, and that means that one of the things we're looking for in this post is a competence in languages.
Ms Hellington	Yes, well, as you'll see from my CV I studied German and Spanish at school, and I've lived and worked in France for several years.
Interviewer	How would you describe your language competence?
Ms Hellington	My French is fluent, and I can still remember the basics in German and Spanish.
Interviewer	What if we asked you to take further language training?
Ms Hellington	I'd welcome that. I feel that it's important to get them to as high a level as possible.
Interviewer	Fine. On another issue: if we were to offer you the post, when could you take it up?
Ms Hellington	In two months. I'm working on a project in my current post, and I'd like to see that through first. Would that be a problem?
Interviewer	I don't think so, but I'd have to check with the department before confirming, of course. Well now, are there any questions you want to ask us?
Ms Hellington	Just two: you mention your management training programme in your company brochure. Can you tell me more about it?
Interviewer	Yes, we expect all our middle managers to try to reach their full potential through self-development. We help them in that by running a series of in-house residential training courses.
Ms Hellington	How often?
Interviewer	Three or four times a year, and we expect everyone to attend them, as far as possible.
Ms Hellington	That's fine. One other question, if I may?
Interviewer	Certainly.

Zweiter Teil

Leiter des Vorstellungsgesprächs	Da wir bekanntlich eine multinationale Organisation sind, bedeuten Fremdsprachenkenntnisse einen wichtigen Aspekt dieser Stellung.
Frau Hellinger	Ja, also wie Sie meinem Lebenslauf entnehmen[1] können, habe ich in der Schule Englisch und Spanisch gelernt und dann habe ich mehrere Jahre in Frankreich gelebt und gearbeitet.
Leiter des Vorstellungsgesprächs	Wie würden Sie denn selbst Ihre Sprachfähigkeiten beschreiben?
Frau Hellinger	Mein Französisch ist perfekt und ich habe Grundkenntnisse im Englischen und Spanischen.
Leiter des Vorstellungsgesprächs	Was würden Sie davon halten, wenn Sie einen Perfektionskurs zu besuchen hätten?
Frau Hellinger	Ich würde das sehr begrüßen. Ich meine, es ist wichtig, Sprachkenntnisse auf ein höchstmögliches Niveau zu bringen.
Leiter des Vorstellungsgesprächs	Schön. Und nun etwas anderes: falls wir Ihnen die Stelle anbieten, wann könnten Sie frühestens bei uns anfangen?
Frau Hellinger	In zwei Monaten. In meiner jetzigen Stelle bin ich an einem Projekt beschäftigt, das ich gerne abschließen würde. Wäre das ein Problem?
Leiter des Vorstellungsgesprächs	Ich glaube nicht. Aber ich muß das zur Sicherheit natürlich erst in der Abteilung besprechen. Und nun, gibt es irgendwelche Fragen, die Sie uns stellen möchten?
Frau Hellinger	Eigentlich nur zwei. Sie erwähnten das Ausbildungsprogramm für Führungskräfte in den Informationen über Ihre Organisation. Können Sie mir etwas mehr darüber sagen?
Leiter des Vorstellungsgesprächs	Ja, es liegt uns daran, daß unsere Mitarbeiter im mittleren Management ihr volles Potential entfalten können. Wir helfen ihnen dabei durch die Abhaltung von Schulungskursen vor Ort.[2]
Frau Hellinger	Wie oft?
Leiter des Vorstellungsgesprächs	Dreimal im Jahr. Und wir erwarten, daß alle soweit möglich daran teilnehmen.
Frau Hellinger	Gut. Und dann hätte ich noch eine Frage, bitte.
Leiter des Vorstellungsgesprächs	Gern.

Ms Hellington   When will I hear if I've got the job?

Interviewer   We'll be contacting the successful candidate by phone this evening, and we'll be writing to the others.

Ms Hellington   Thanks very much.

Interviewer   Well, thank you for coming to the interview, Ms Hellington. Goodbye.

Ms Hellington   Goodbye.

Frau Hellinger	Wann werde ich hören, ob ich die Stelle bekommen habe?
Leiter des Vorstellungsgesprächs	Der erfolgreiche Bewerber wird noch heute abend telefonisch benachrichtigt. Alle anderen hören schriftlich von uns.
Frau Hellinger	Vielen Dank.
Leiter des Vorstellungsgesprächs	Frau Hellinger, wir danken Ihnen für das Gespräch. Guten Tag.
Frau Hellinger	Guten Tag.

1 Alternative: *Wie Sie aus meinem Lebenslauf ersehen*.
2 *Vor Ort*, 'on site'.

Part 3

Ms Hellington	Hello. Jane Hellington.
Brendan Carter	Good evening, Ms Hellington. Brendan Carter here, from Keystone Engineering. I'm ringing to offer you the post here.
Ms Hellington	Really? Well, thank you very much!
Brendan Carter	The first question I must ask is whether or not you wish to accept the post.
Ms Hellington	Yes, I do. Thank you.
Brendan Carter	The starting salary, as we agreed, would be £. . ., with a salary review after your first six months.
Ms Hellington	Yes, that's fine.
Brendan Carter	When could you start?
Ms Hellington	As I explained at the interview, there is a project I'm working on at the moment that I'd like to see through. So if possible I'd like to start in two months.
Brendan Carter	Shall we say the 1st of June, then?
Ms Hellington	Probably. I'll just need to discuss things with my present employer first. I'll do that after I get your offer in writing, and then ring you.
Brendan Carter	You'll need to get down here a few times before, of course, to meet one or two people and get the feel of the place.
Ms Hellington	Yes, certainly. I'd like to do that.
Brendan Carter	Well then, I'll get our personnel people to send the formal written offer to you. That should be with you in a couple of days.
Ms Hellington	Thank you for offering me the post.
Brendan Carter	Look forward to working with you. Bye.
Ms Hellington	Goodbye.

Dritter Teil

Frau Hellinger	Hallo. Hellinger.
Herr Kortner	Guten Abend, Frau Hellinger. Hier spricht Bernhard Kortner von der Firma Schüßler Maschinenbau. Ich kann Ihnen die Stelle hier bei uns anbieten.
Frau Hellinger	Wirklich? Also vielen herzlichen Dank!
Herr Kortner	Zuerst muß ich Sie aber fragen, ob Sie die Stelle annehmen wollen.
Frau Hellinger	Ja, gerne.
Herr Kortner	Ihr Anfangsgehalt beträgt wie vereinbart DM 8000, mit einer Aufbesserung nach den ersten sechs Monaten.
Frau Hellinger	Sehr gut.
Herr Kortner	Wann können Sie anfangen?
Frau Hellinger	Wie ich schon beim Interview erklärte, möchte ich das Projekt, an dem ich zur Zeit arbeite, noch abschließen. Also, wenn das geht, würde ich gerne in zwei Monaten anfangen.
Herr Kortner	Sagen wir dann am 1. Juni?
Frau Hellinger	Wahrscheinlich. Ich muß das aber erst mit meinem jetzigen Arbeitgeber besprechen, nachdem ich Ihr Angebot schriftlich erhalten habe. Daraufhin werde ich Sie anrufen.
Herr Kortner	Es wäre natürlich günstig, wenn Sie vor Ihrem Arbeitsantritt ein paar Mal hierherkommen könnten, damit Sie Ihre Mitarbeiter kennenlernen und sich auf Ihre neuen Aufgaben einstellen können.
Frau Hellinger	Ja, sicher. Das würde ich sehr gerne.
Herr Kortner	Also, dann sage ich der Personalabteilung Bescheid, daß Ihnen das offizielle Angebot schriftlich gemacht wird. Es dürfte in zwei Tagen dann bei Ihnen sein.
Frau Hellinger	Nochmals vielen Dank für Ihr Angebot.
Herr Kortner	Ich freue mich auf die Zusammenarbeit mit Ihnen. Auf Wiederhören.
Frau Hellinger	Auf Wiederhören.

32 **Planning a budget**

Managing director	All right, if I can open the meeting. This need not be too formal but I hardly need to say how important it is. We've all received a copy of our balance sheet.
Director 2	It makes very pleasant reading, 11 per cent growth on the preceding year...
Managing director	Don't get carried away, Derek. I've looked at our orders and would suggest that we should not budget for more than 5 per cent growth in the coming year.
Director 2	Does that mean an average 5 per cent increase in expenditure all round?
Director 3	Most of the increase will be forced on us. We have got to give the staff a cost of living increase, fuel for the vans is bound to increase by at least 5 per cent.
Managing director	We certainly cannot recruit extra staff at this point so I agree with that. Is there any equipment we need to replace?
Director 2	The production stuff is in good nick and we have at least 20 per cent spare capacity. The vans are OK, not too much mileage.
Director 3	Natasha needs a new printer and we could all do with a higher spec photocopier. We probably need to up our marketing effort.
Managing director	I am relying on you to watch the monthly cash flow like a hawk, Bill. Most of my time is taken looking for new business. What about production costs?
Director 2	I reckon we can increase production by 10 per cent with hardly any extra cost and no danger. How about that!
Managing director	And the bank is happy with the state of our overdraft. That all looks fairly satisfactory. As long as we continue to slave away.

32 Budgetplanung

Geschäftsführer	Also, wir eröffnen nun die Sitzung. Das braucht nicht so formell zu sein, aber ich muß nicht besonders betonen, wie wichtig die Sache ist. Wir haben alle unsere Kopie der Bilanz erhalten.
2. Direktor	Das sieht sehr positiv aus. Elf Prozent Wachstum im Vergleich mit dem Vorjahr.
Geschäftsführer	Ja, aber bleiben wir auf dem Boden. Ich habe mir unsere Auftragslage angesehen, und ich schlage vor, daß wir für nicht mehr als 5% Wachstum im kommenden Jahr veranschlagen.
2. Direktor	Bedeutet das eine durchschnittliche Erhöhung von 5% für allgemeine Aufwendungen?
3. Direktorin	Die meisten Erhöhungen sind unvermeidbar. Wir müssen unserer Belegschaft eine Lebenshaltungskostenzulage geben, der Treibstoff für unsere Transportfahrzeuge wird bestimmt um mindestens 5% teurer werden.
Geschäftsführer	Und auf jeden Fall können wir uns zur Zeit keine Neueinstellungen leisten. Aber müssen irgendwelche Geräte erneuert werden?
2. Direktor	Die Produktionsmaschinen sind in gutem Zustand und wir haben mindestens 20% freie Kapazität. Die Lastwagen sind OK, nicht zu stark abgefahren.
3. Direktorin	Frau Neuber benötigt einen neuen Drucker und wir könnten ein neues Hochleistungskopiergerät[1] gut gebrauchen, besonders wenn wir uns in Zukunft um ein verstärktes Marketing bemühen müssen.
Geschäftsführer	Ich verlasse mich darauf, daß Sie unseren monatlichen Cash Flow mit Argusaugen verfolgen. Ich werde mich hauptsächlich darauf verlegen, neue Geschäftsmöglichkeiten zu finden. Und wie steht es mit den Herstellungskosten?
2. Direktor	Ich schätze, wir können die Produktion ohne nennenswerte Kostensteigerung ruhig um 10% erhöhen. Was sagen Sie dazu!
Geschäftsführer	Und die Bank hat gegen den Stand unserer Kontoüberziehung[2] nichts einzuwenden. Also alles bestens und sonst weiterschuften[3] wie bisher.

1 *Hochleistungs . . .* in any compound implies 'high speed'/'high efficiency'. 'Efficiency' is *Leistungsfähigkeit*.
2 'Overdrawn' would be *überzogen*.
3 *Schuften*, 'slave away', 'slog' (very colloquial).

33 Organizing a product launch

Albert Archer	My suggestion is that we hire a river cruiser and take our key accounts for an evening cruise and dinner. After dinner we can unveil our new range of services.
Brian Ball	Do you think that'll be enough?
Albert Archer	Well, when we've informed the key accounts, we can do some promotion in the trade press – some ads and, if possible, a press release. The key accounts managers will just have to keep in touch with their clients. We'll have to wait and see what response we get from the trade journals.
Brian Ball	OK. Let's go ahead with this. Do you want me to get Kevin started on the arrangements?
Albert Archer	Yes, you might as well. By the way, what about hospitality for the press? Couldn't we invite them to the Clubroom for a special presentation?
Brian Ball	Good idea! I'll get Kevin to see to it.

33 Einführung eines Produktes

Herr Altdorfer	Mein Vorschlag wäre, daß wir einen Flußdampfer mieten und unsere wichtigsten Kunden zu einem Schiffsausflug mit Abendessen an Bord einladen. Nach dem Essen können wir dann unsere neuen Dienstleistungen präsentieren.
Herr Barth	Glauben Sie, daß das genug ist?
Herr Altdorfer	Also, nachdem wir unsere Hauptkunden informiert haben, könnten wir Werbung in der Branchenpresse machen – ein paar Anzeigen und eine Pressemitteilung vielleicht. Unsere Hauptabnehmer[1] werden wohl ihre eigenen Kunden informieren. Und dann wollen wir sehen, wie die Fachzeitschriften[2] reagieren.
Herr Barth	OK. Also gut, machen wir das! Soll ich Herrn Kurz ersuchen, die Sache in die Wege zu leiten?
Herr Altdorfer	Ja, warum nicht. Übrigens, wie ist das mit der Bewirtung der Presseleute? Könnten wir sie vielleicht in den Klubraum zu einer eigenen Präsentation einladen?
Herr Barth	Gute Idee! Ich sage Herrn Kurz Bescheid.

1 Alternative: *Hauptkunden*.
2 *Fachpresse* = 'specialist'/'trade press'.

34 Contacting official agencies

(a) Chamber of Commerce

Roberto Comas	How do you do? I'm Roberto Comas, from Textiles Paloma.
Arturo Castro	Pleased to meet you. Arturo Castro. My staff told me you were going to come by this morning. How can we help?
Roberto Comas	We are thinking of expanding the business, especially to focus on the '30 to 50' market, and we were advised to seek your views on how and where best to establish retail outlets for our fashion products.
Arturo Castro	Well, Sr Comas. I hope you will join the Chamber as and when you set up in the city, but for the time being you are welcome to our assistance.
Roberto Comas	Yes, I understand, but right now we are keen to obtain some information on local retail figures, the competition, some data on the local population, available premises and so on.
Arturo Castro	That's no problem. We can provide you with what you request and much more. Are you likely to be creating any jobs through your new initiative?
Roberto Comas	I think it's inevitable that we will take on new staff, both in the factory and in the local shops. Do you happen to have a good contact at the Jobcentre?
Arturo Castro	Yes, of course. If you'd like to come through to my office, we'll have a coffee and get down to business on this one.

34 Kontakt mit Ämtern

(a) Termin bei der Handelskammer

Herr Körner	Guten Tag! Gestatten Sie, Körner, von der Firma Greiff Textilien.
Frau Deinhard	Angenehm, Deinhard. Meine Mitarbeiter sagten mir schon, Sie würden heute vormittag vorbeikommen. Was können wir für Sie tun?
Herr Körner	Also, wir denken daran, unseren Geschäftsbereich zu erweitern und wollen uns dabei besonders auf den Markt für die Altersgruppe 30 bis 50 Jahre konzentrieren. Es wurde uns nahegelegt, mit Ihnen darüber zu sprechen, wo und wie sich Absatzmöglichkeiten für unsere Modewaren am besten einrichten ließen.
Frau Deinhard	Nun, Herr Körner, ich hoffe, Sie werden Mitglied der Handelskammer, nachdem Sie sich hier bei uns in der Stadt etabliert haben, aber einstweilen geben wir Ihnen natürlich gerne unsere Unterstützung.
Herr Körner	Ja, danke schön. Was für uns momentan besonders wichtig ist, sind Informationen über die hiesigen Verkaufsziffern, die Konkurrenz, Angaben über die Bevölkerung, verfügbare Geschäftslokale und so weiter.
Frau Deinhard	Kein Problem. Können Sie alles gerne haben. Werden aufgrund Ihrer Initiative möglicherweise auch neue Arbeitsplätze geschaffen?
Herr Körner	Ja, ich denke, daß wir sicher neue Mitarbeiter in der Fabrik und in den Geschäften hier einstellen werden. Haben Sie übrigens gute Kontakte zum Arbeitsamt?
Frau Deinhard	Natürlich. Würden Sie jetzt bitte in mein Büro weiterkommen. Wir trinken eine Tasse Kaffee und machen uns dann an die Arbeit.

(b) Customs and Excise

Customs and Excise official	HM Customs.
Retailer	Hello, I have a query regarding the import of meat products. I wonder if you can help me.
Customs and Excise official	Certainly. Can you explain?
Retailer	We're a meat retailer based here in Dover, and we're intending to import a range of cooked meats and sausages from a German supplier. So far we've only been supplied by British companies. I need to know what the regulations are.
Customs and Excise official	It's rather difficult and complex to explain over the phone. There is a range of regulations and restrictions. They're contained in our information brochures. When are you intending to import?
Retailer	The first shipment is coming in a couple of weeks.
Customs and Excise official	Then you'd better move fast. I'll get the information off to you. The best thing is for you to read it and then come back to us with any queries.
Retailer	Fine. Let me give you my address.

(b) Anruf beim Zollamt

Beamter	Zollamt. Guten Tag.
Einzelhändler	Guten Tag. Ich habe eine Frage bezüglich der Einfuhr von Fleischwaren. Könnten Sie mir helfen?
Beamter	Gerne. Worum handelt es sich?
Einzelhändler	Wir sind ein Fleischgeschäft hier in Bremerhaven und beabsichtigen, Fleisch- und Wurstprodukte von einem englischen Lieferanten zu importieren. Da wir bis jetzt nur deutsche Lieferanten benützt haben, kenne ich die Einfuhrvorschriften nicht.
Beamter	Also, telefonisch ist das etwas schwierig zu erklären. Es gibt da eine ganze Reihe von Vorschriften und Beschränkungen, die Sie alle in unseren Informationsbroschüren finden. Für wann haben Sie die Einfuhr geplant?
Einzelhändler	Die erste Lieferung kommt in zwei Wochen.
Beamter	Dann bleibt Ihnen nicht mehr viel Zeit. Ich schicke Ihnen die Informationen sofort. Am besten, Sie lesen die zuerst und wenden sich dann an uns, wenn Sie noch Fragen haben.
Einzelhändler	Schön. Also hier ist meine Adresse.

35 Presenting company policy

(a) Location

Managing director	As you know, it's the company's policy to set up new plants in areas which offer the most advantages. For this reason the liquid detergent plant here will close as soon as the new plant is operational in the south-east. There are both economic and social benefits in doing things this way.
Journalist	What about the people currently working at the plant? What will happen to them? Will they be made redundant?
Managing director	That's not the way we do things here. We'll look to natural wastage and early retirements throughout the company – nobody will be made redundant because of this. Clearly, some people will have to be redeployed and there may be possibilities at the new plant for some of the specialist technicians if they are willing to relocate.
Journalist	How will you reorganize the remaining staff? Would they qualify for removal assistance if they agreed to move?
Managing director	Clearly we would offer them a relocation package if they agreed to move; that's standard practice here.

35 Präsentation der Firmenpolitik

(a) Standort

Generaldirektor	Wie Sie wissen, ist es Firmenpolitik, neue Anlagen dort zu errichten, wo sich die größtmöglichen Vorteile bieten. Deshalb wird die Waschmittelfabrik hier geschlossen, sobald die neue Anlage im Südosten betriebsfähig ist. Wir profitieren dadurch sowohl wirtschaftlich als auch sozial.
Journalist	Aber die derzeitige Belegschaft! Was geschieht mit der? Werden die Arbeiter denn einfach entlassen?
Generaldirektor	Aber nein, das ist nicht unsere Art. Wir rechnen mit natürlicher Personalreduzierung und Frührenten im ganzen Unternehmen – niemand muß entlassen werden. Doch wir werden nicht umhin können, einige Mitarbeiter zu versetzen. Die neue Fabrik könnte Chancen für unsere technischen Fachleute bieten, aber nur wenn sie zu einem Umzug bereit sind.
Journalist	Und wie werden Sie die Restbelegschaft umstrukturieren? Gibt es auch für diese Mitarbeiter eine Unterstützung, wenn sie zu einer Versetzung einwilligen?
Generaldirektor	Natürlich würden wir ihnen in diesem Fall eine Umzugspauschale gewähren, wie das in unserer Firma üblich ist.

(b) Development

Personnel manager	So, as we have seen during the last half-hour, the prospects for the next few years are quite encouraging. We now need to consider precisely how we are going to develop policies to benefit the firm and its employees.
Managing director	Can I just add before you continue, Alan, that the Board will be taking very seriously whatever conclusions are drawn by this group today. So it is essential that people speak their mind.
Personnel manager	Thanks for confirming that, Victor. Frankly, recent EU legislation means that our profit margins can be increased as long as we take into account from the start matters like Health and Safety, employee compensation, maternity benefits, etc. These items, that normally and quite properly cost us a percentage of raw profits, can be reclaimed if fully documented.
Financial director	Well, that's good news as in the past we've never been able to prepare very well for this sort of cost to the company.
Personnel manager	I am proposing, therefore, that we create a small unit within the company to cover the full range of benefits that can accrue to us under the new provisions. In addition to this, we should be able to demonstrate to the workforce that by our observing these criteria they too will have an enhanced status. Before I continue with my next subject, are there any questions?
Sales manager	Alan, can anyone guarantee that our current level of sales is sustainable? What you are saying about the interests of the workforce and those of the company as a whole being convergent seems to me a rather optimistic interpretation.
Personnel manager	We've commissioned a report on this very question, so as long as everybody is prepared to wait for a week or two longer I should be able to give you an honest answer. Frankly, whatever the precise outcome of that report, we have to make plans for a future in which we balance the financial well-being of the firm with that of all the individuals who work in and for it.

(b) Gestaltung

Personalleiter	Also, wie wir in der letzten halben Stunde gesehen haben, sind die Aussichten für die nächsten Jahre recht günstig. Nun müssen wir uns genau überlegen, wie wir unsere Geschäftspolitik zum Vorteil des Unternehmens und der Arbeitnehmer gestalten werden.
Geschäftsleiter	Darf ich hier kurz einwerfen, daß der Vorstand dem Fazit unserer heutigen Besprechung große Bedeutung zumißt. Es ist daher wichtig, daß wir offen miteinander reden.
Personalleiter	Danke für Ihren Hinweis. Nun, aufgrund neuer EU Gesetzgebung können wir unsere Gewinnspannen dann vergrößern, wenn wir Belange wie Arbeitsschutz, Ausgleichszahlungen, Mutterschaftsgeld, usw. von allem Anfang an in Betracht ziehen. Diese Ausgaben, die uns eigentlich immer einen Teil unseres Bruttogewinns kosten, sind bei Vorlage von Belegen rückzahlbar.
Finanzleiterin	Ja, das sind wirklich gute Nachrichten, denn früher hatten wir immer Planungsschwierigkeiten bei derartigen Kosten.
Personalleiter	Ich schlage daher vor, wir schaffen eine kleine Firmenabteilung, die sich mit allen Vergünstigungen befaßt, welche sich für uns durch die neuen Bestimmungen ergeben könnten. Dies dürfte außerdem den Arbeitnehmern vor Augen führen, daß sich durch unsere Maßnahmen auch ihre Stellung im Unternehmen verbessern würde. Aber bevor ich zu meinem nächsten Thema übergehe, gibt es irgendwelche Fragen?
Verkaufsleiterin	Aber wer garantiert mir, daß unser derzeitiges Absatzniveau aufrechterhalten werden kann? Wenn Sie da die Interessen von Belegschaft und Unternehmen als im wesentlichen übereinstimmend sehen, so kommt mir das doch ziemlich optimistisch vor.
Personalleiter	Wir haben diesbezüglich ein Gutachten in Auftrag gegeben und wenn Sie sich noch eine oder zwei Wochen gedulden, kann ich Ihnen eine klare Antwort geben. Aber ehrlich gesagt, egal wie das Gutachten ausfällt, es liegt an uns, für eine Zukunft zu planen, in der solide Betriebsfinanzen durchaus vereinbar sind mit der Zufriedenheit jedes einzelnen Mitarbeiters.

(c) Staffing

Meeting between the personnel manager and a trade union representative

Personnel manager	I've called you in to tell you about our proposed staff changes.
TU representative	Yes, I know. I've heard that you're planning compulsory redundancies.
Personnel manager	No, that's not the case, but we do need to rationalize.
TU representative	Can you tell me why?
Personnel manager	Everyone knows why: production costs have been increasing because of outmoded plant. We've taken the decision to close one of our older plants.
TU representative	Has it been decided which one?
Personnel manager	We have a choice of either Sheffield or Gloucester. The precise figures are being worked out.
TU representative	And what happens to the workforce?
Personnel manager	We'll propose voluntary redundancies and early retirements. That should reduce the problem considerably.
TU representative	But not fully. You'll have to lay people off.
Personnel manager	We don't think so. The remaining staff can be relocated. We have other plants within 20 miles of both Sheffield and Gloucester. We're talking about streamlining production, not cutting it back.
TU representative	So what will be the total reduction in the workforce?
Personnel manager	In the region of 200 to 250.
TU representative	And when are the changes being made?
Personnel manager	We're hoping to have them complete by the end of January.
TU representative	Has it been discussed at board level yet?
Personnel manager	Of course – the board gave its approval last week. That's why we're moving on it now.

(c) Personal

Gespräch zwischen Personalleiter und Gewerkschaftsvertreter

Personalleiter	Ich habe Sie zu mir gebeten, um Sie über die beabsichtigten Änderungen in der Belegschaft in Kenntnis zu setzen.
Gewerkschaftsvertreter	Ja, ich weiß. Ich habe gehört, Sie planen zwangsweise Entlassungen.
Personalleiter	Nein, das ist nicht der Fall. Doch wir müssen rationalisieren.
Gewerkschaftsvertreter	Können Sie mir sagen, warum?
Personalleiter	Jeder weiß, warum. Wegen unserer veralteten Fabriksanlagen sind die Herstellungskosten ständig gestiegen. Wir haben daher beschlossen, eine unserer älteren Fabriken stillzulegen.
Gewerkschaftsvertreter	Hat man schon beschlossen, welche?
Personalleiter	Wir haben die Wahl zwischen Halle und Dresden. Wir arbeiten noch an den genauen Zahlen.
Gewerkschaftsvertreter	Und was geschieht mit der Belegschaft?
Personalleiter	Durch Vorruhestand und freiwilliges Ausscheiden aus dem Betrieb dürfte das eigentlich kein Problem sein.
Gewerkschaftsvertreter	Das meinen Sie. Sie werden aber doch Personal entlassen müssen.
Personalleiter	Das glauben wir nicht. Die restliche Belegschaft kann versetzt werden. Wir haben noch andere Werksanlagen in etwa 30 km Entfernung sowohl von Halle als auch von Dresden. Wir sprechen hier nicht von einer Verminderung der Produktion sondern von einer Rationalisierung.
Gewerkschaftsvertreter	Also, was ist dann die gesamte Kürzung im Belegschaftsbereich?
Personalleiter	So etwa 200 bis 250 Mitarbeiter.
Gewerkschaftsvertreter	Und wann sollen diese Änderungen vorgenommen werden?
Personalleiter	Wir hoffen, daß sie bis Ende Januar abgeschlossen sind.
Gewerkschaftsvertreter	Und wurde die Angelegenheit schon auf Vorstandsebene erörtert?
Personalleiter	Natürlich. Der Vorstand hat letzte Woche seine Zustimmung gegeben. Deshalb bringen wir die Sache in Gang.

(d) Sales

Chairman	I am pleased to open this first Board Meeting following our change of parent company. The first item on the agenda is sales policy. Over to you, Charles.
Charles	Thank you, Mr Chairman. I am instructed by the main board of our parent company to plan, with you, the introduction of a new sales policy.
Director 2	What view is taken of our existing policy? Too expensive?
Charles	In a nutshell, yes. The company's product lines are mostly good but the sales operation could be improved.
Director 2	I am not surprised. I have thought for some time that we have too large a sales force in too many regions.
Charles	That brings me to one of the proposals I have. To redraw the regions and slim down the workforce.
Director 2	By redundancy or natural wastage?
Charles	Probably a bit of both would be necessary. Also, some concern has been expressed about the size of the advertising budget.
Director 3	Hear, hear. For a company with good products we do a hell of a lot of advertising.
Charles	I gather it is proposed, subject to this board's approval, to appoint a top class Marketing Manager with the remit to review the whole operation.
Director 2	Is a system of dealerships on the cards?
Charles	Nothing is excluded based on the premise of a need to rationalize the sales operation.

(d) Verkaufsstrategie

Vorsitzender	Ich freue mich, die erste Vorstandssitzung seit der Übernahme durch unsere neue Muttergesellschaft zu eröffnen. Punkt eins der Tagesordnung betrifft Verkaufspolitik. Herr Dr. Müllner, bitte!
Herr Dr. Müllner	Danke. Der Hauptvorstand hat mich beauftragt, mit Ihnen gemeinsam die Einführung einer neuen Verkaufsstrategie zu planen.
2. Direktorin	Und wie steht man zu unserer jetzigen Strategie? Hält man die für zu kostspielig?
Herr Dr. Müllner	Schlicht gesagt, ja. Die Produktpalette der Firma ist im allgemeinen gut, aber der Verkauf könnte besser funktionieren.
2. Direktorin	Das wundert mich nicht. Ich habe schon längere Zeit den Eindruck, daß wir zu viel Verkaufspersonal und zu viele Verkaufsgebiete haben.
Herr Dr. Müllner	Und damit komme ich direkt zu einem meiner Vorschläge, nämlich Neuaufteilung der Verkaufsgebiete und Abspeckung in der Belegschaft.
2. Direktorin	Durch Entlassung oder natürliche Personalreduzierung?
Herr Dr. Müllner	Wahrscheinlich wird etwas von beidem nötig sein. Und die Höhe unseres Werbeetats hat auch Grund zur Besorgnis gegeben.
3. Direktorin	Sehr richtig! Für ein Unternehmen mit soliden Erzeugnissen machen wir verdammt viel Reklame.
Herr Dr. Müllner	Soviel ich weiß, ist beabsichtigt, im Einvernehmen mit uns einen Spitzenfachmann als Marketingmanager zur Überprüfung des ganzen Systems einzustellen.
2. Direktorin	Wird auch ein Verteilernetz ausgearbeitet?
Herr Dr. Müllner	Alles was zur Rationalisierung des Verkaufsbetriebs führen kann, wird in Betracht gezogen.

36 Visiting the bank manager

Bank manager	Good morning, Mr Ansell. I'm pleased to see you again.
Mr Ansell	Good morning, Mr Green. I have come to discuss our business plan with you. Our turnover has risen by 40 per cent for the last three years and our products have been selling really well. And so we'd like to open another shop in Loughborough.
Bank manager	Well, Mr Ansell, I have followed the success of your company. Our bank has been very happy to support its development. Your firm has always stayed within its overdraft limits. How might we help you now?
Mr Ansell	We're having to plough back most of our profits into the business in order to finance our growth. We've done market research in Loughborough and are convinced that it will be a success, what with Loughborough being a university town. What I've come to discuss with you is a loan to finance the lease of a shop and to buy start-up stock.
Bank manager	I'm sure the bank will be willing in principle to finance your business's future growth. If you send me your proposal for the shop in Loughborough, with details of the amount you wish to borrow, cash flow projections – you know, all the usual information – I will consider it as quickly as possible.
Mr Ansell	Thank you very much. I'll send you our proposal in the next few days.

36 Beim Bankfachmann

Banker	Guten Tag, Herr Anders. Freut mich, Sie wieder einmal zu sehen.
Herr Anders	Guten Tag, Herr Grüner. Ich möchte heute einen Plan unseres Unternehmens mit Ihnen besprechen. Der Umsatz ist bei uns seit den letzten drei Jahren um 40% gestiegen und unsere Waren verkaufen sich wirklich gut. Daher denken wir daran, einen anderen Laden in Bamberg zu eröffnen.[1]
Banker	Ja, Herr Anders. Ich habe den Aufstieg Ihres Unternehmens mit Interesse verfolgt und unsere Bank hat Sie gerne dabei unterstützt. Ihre Kontoüberziehung ist immer in Grenzen geblieben. Was können wir jetzt für Sie tun?
Herr Anders	Zur Finanzierung unserer Geschäftserweiterung sind wir gezwungen, einen Großteil unseres Gewinns zu reinvestieren. Marktforschung in Bamberg hat uns darin bestärkt, daß wir mit unserem Laden Erfolg haben würden, nicht zuletzt weil es sich um eine Universitätsstadt handelt. Was ich mit Ihnen besprechen möchte, ist ein Darlehen für die Miete von Geschäftsräumen und die anfängliche Erwerbung von Warenbestand.
Banker	Die Bank ist im Prinzip sicher bereit, die weitere Vergrößerung Ihres Unternehmens zu finanzieren. Schicken Sie mir doch Ihre Vorschläge bezüglich des Ladens in Bamberg sowie Einzelheiten des Darlehens, Cash-flow-Prognose – Sie wissen schon, die üblichen Informationen – ich werde mich gleich damit befassen.
Herr Anders	Vielen Dank. Ich schicke Ihnen alle Unterlagen in den nächsten Tagen.

1 *Eröffnen* means 'to open for the first time'. *Öffnen* is 'to open' daily/regularly.

37 Selling a service to a client

Teresa Allison	Good morning, Mr Tolson. I'm Teresa Allison from P and G Computer Maintenance Services. You answered one of our ads in the *Evening Mail*, so I have come to fill you in on what we have to offer small businesses.
Mr Tolson	Ah yes, thank you for coming so soon. As you can see, we recently purchased a computer system to maximize our efficiency in dealing with orders.
Teresa Allison	I assume that you have an initial service contract on the machines, but once that runs out you would be best advised to take out a plan like ours. We can provide a 24-hour breakdown cover, three-monthly servicing, immediate replacement of faulty equipment, regular updating of your software and a free consultancy service for the duration of the contract.
Mr Tolson	It sounds a good deal, but what are the conditions of payment? Is it possible to pay monthly via a standing order or does it have to be a lump sum?
Teresa Allison	You can pay either way, as long as your bank can guarantee that your account will bear it. Let me leave you some brochures to read at your leisure; you'll be able to compare our prices and conditions with others, though I can assure you that it's the most favourable deal available at present.
Mr Tolson	OK, fair enough. Can you give me a ring in about a week and I'll let you know what I think?
Teresa Allison	I certainly will. Give me your number and I'll be in touch early next week.

37 Dienstleistungsangebot

Frau Amberg	Grüß Gott, Herr Tölz. Mein Name ist Gerda Amberg von der Firma P & G Computer Service. Nachdem Sie uns aufgrund unserer Anzeige in der Tagespost kontaktiert haben, möchte ich Ihnen noch mehr über unser Serviceangebot für Kleinbetriebe erzählen.
Herr Tölz	Ach ja. Danke, daß Sie so bald gekommen sind. Wie Sie sehen, haben wir uns vor nicht sehr langer Zeit ein Computersystem angeschafft, um unsere Auftragserledigung so weit wie möglich zu rationalisieren.
Frau Amberg	Ich nehme an, Sie haben für die erste Zeit einen Sevicevertrag für die Geräte, aber wenn der ausläuft, wäre es am besten, einen Plan wie unseren zu verwenden. Wir bieten Ihnen 24 Stunden Service bei Computerversagen, Wartung alle drei Monate, sofortigen Ersatz fehlerhafter Geräte. Wir bringen Ihre Software auf den neuesten Stand der Dinge und beraten Sie[1] kostenlos für die Dauer des Vertrags.
Herr Tölz	Scheint mir ein gutes Angebot. Wie sind Ihre Zahlungsbedingungen? Ist es möglich, per Dauerauftrag monatlich zu bezahlen oder muß es pauschal sein?
Frau Amberg	Wie Sie wollen. Solange Ihre Bank Ihre Zahlungsfähigkeit garantiert. Ich lasse Ihnen ein paar Broschüren hier. Lesen Sie sie in Ruhe durch! Sie können dann unsere Preise und Bedingungen vergleichen, aber ich kann Ihnen versichern, daß unser Angebot das zur Zeit günstigste ist.
Herr Tölz	Na, schön! Können Sie mich vielleicht in einer Woche anrufen? Dann sage ich Ihnen Bescheid.
Frau Amberg	Gerne. Geben Sie mir bitte Ihre Nummer und ich melde mich Anfang nächster Woche.

1 *Beraten* takes the accusative. *Raten* would take the dative (*ich rate Ihnen . . .*).

38   Selling a product to a client

Salesman   This motor is very good value, sir, if you prefer not to buy new.

Customer   It certainly looks to be in immaculate condition. About two years old is it?

Salesman   Eighteen months. It only has 6,000 miles on the clock.

Customer   That's unusual, isn't it? Who was the previous owner?

Salesman   It's been a demonstration model. That explains the complete lack of any dents and no rust of course.

Customer   What sort of discount could I have or can you offer a hire purchase deal?

Salesman   We are offering a 5 per cent discount off the list price and you could repay over one or two years.

Customer   That sounds quite interesting. And you would offer me the trade-in price for my present car that we discussed earlier?

Salesman   Yes indeed, sir. Would you like to go for a test drive?

39   Giving an informal vote of thanks

Speaker   Ladies and gentlemen, I'd like to take this opportunity of thanking Leonard White and his colleagues for arranging the seminar over the last few days. I'm sure we've all found it most interesting and stimulating, and we all have good ideas to take back with us.

I'd like to thank them for their hospitality over the last two evenings, and I'm sure I speak for all of us when I say that the seminar has been a great success.

As you all know, we intend to hold a similar seminar next year at our headquarters, and that will give us the opportunity to return the hospitality. Thanks again, Leonard and colleagues, for a most successful event.

38 Verkaufsgespräch

Verkäufer	Dieser Wagen ist sehr preiswert, wenn Sie keinen neuen kaufen wollen.
Kunde	Ja, der scheint wirklich in tadellosem Zustand zu sein. Wie alt ist er eigentlich?
Verkäufer	Achtzehn Monate. Und er hat nur neuntausend Kilometer auf dem Tacho.
Kunde	Das ist aber ungewöhnlich, nicht? Wem hat das Auto vorher gehört?
Verkäufer	Es war ein Vorführwagen. Deshalb ist es überhaupt nicht verbeult oder verrostet.
Kunde	Kriege[1] ich einen Rabatt oder kann ich den Wagen auf Raten kaufen?
Verkäufer	Wir bieten Ihnen 5% vom Listenpreis und Sie können in ein bis zwei Jahren abzahlen.
Kunde	Das klingt ja sehr interessant. Und – wie besprochen – bleibt es bei Ihrem Angebot, mir meinen Wagen zu einem guten Preis abzunehmen?
Verkäufer	Selbstverständlich. Möchten Sie eine Probefahrt machen?

1   Very colloquial. Less colloquial would be *bekomme ich*.

39 Inoffizielle Dankadresse

Rednerin   Meine Damen und Herren! Ich möchte hier die Gelegenheit ergreifen, Herrn Weiß und seinen Kollegen für die Veranstaltung des Seminars zu danken. Die vergangenen Tage waren für uns sehr interessant und anregend und ich bin sicher, daß wir alle gute Ideen mit nach Hause nehmen.

Ich möchte unseren Veranstaltern auch herzlich für ihre Gastlichkeit an den beiden Abenden danken, und ich spreche bestimmt im Namen aller, wenn ich sage: Das Seminar war ein großer Erfolg.

Wie Sie wissen, wollen wir eine ähnliche Veranstaltung im nächsten Jahr bei uns abhalten und dabei Gelegenheit haben, Ihre Gastfreundschaft zu erwidern. Nochmals vielen Dank für das erfolgreiche Seminar.

40 Discussing contracts

(a) Sales conditions

Client   I'm pleased to inform you that we are prepared to include your company as one of our suppliers. Before we sign an agreement, we need to agree on terms and conditions.

Supplier   We're delighted. What in particular do we need to agree?

Client   Firstly, our terms of payment are 20 per cent on receipt of the goods and the remainder within 90 days.

Supplier   We normally expect to be paid in full within 60 days, but if we can have a two-year agreement, we could accept 90 days.

Client   Fine. We also want a 10 per cent discount for orders of over 5,000 parts. Deliveries must also be made by the specified date, with penalties for late delivery. I think you've been given some details.

Supplier   Yes, and I can assure you that we are accustomed to just-in-time delivery. I'm sure that you know already that we offer good service at a good price. We're ready to sign.

Client   That's good. I have the agreement here.

40 Verträge besprechen

(a) Verkaufsbedingungen

Kunde	Ich freue mich, Ihnen sagen zu können, daß wir bereit sind, Ihre Firma zu unseren Lieferanten zu zählen. Aber bevor wir den Vertrag unterschreiben, müssen wir uns noch über die Konditionen[1] einig werden.
Lieferant	Ausgezeichnet. Worum handelt es sich?
Kunde	Also zuerst einmal unsere Zahlungsbedingungen. Wir zahlen 20% bei Erhalt der Waren und den Rest innnerhalb von 90 Tagen.
Lieferant	Nun, normalerweise geben wir eine Zahlungsfrist von 60 Tagen, aber bei einem Zweijahresvertrag mit Ihnen akzeptieren wir 90 Tage.
Kunde	Gut. Und dann möchten wir auch 10% Rabatt bei Aufträgen von über 5 000 Bestandteilen. Die Lieferungen müßten zum gegebenen Termin stattfinden und Lieferverzögerungen gehen zu Ihren Lasten. Ich glaube, Sie haben schon diesbezügliche Einzelheiten erhalten.
Lieferant	Ja, ich kann Sie beruhigen. Wir sind gewöhnt, pünktlich zu liefern. Wie Sie sicher bereits wissen, ist unser Leistungsangebot äußerst günstig. Wir sind bereit zu unterschreiben.
Kunde	Prima. Hier ist der Vertrag.

1 Alternative: *Bedingungen*.

(b) Payment conditions

Client   When is the last payment of the instalments on the new equipment due?

Supplier   There are several plans under which you have maximum flexibility of conditions. Obviously, you can pay the full amount in a óne-off sum, which would mean a substantial saving overall as interest costs are always high in the transport sector.

Client   Suppose I could pay you 50 per cent of the total cost now, what sort of arrangements would best suit us both for the other half over a couple of years?

Supplier   That would depend on how we structure our own borrowing requirement, but in principle there is no reason why payments cannot be adjusted exactly to suit your circumstances.

Client   Fine. Give me a few days to discuss this with my accountant. If the bank is willing to lend me more than I had first thought, it may be possible for me to buy outright.

Supplier   Why not? With general interest rates as they are it could be worth risking a big outlay. Remember: either way we can help, as our own finances are secured by the parent company.

Client   That's reassuring to know. I'll come back to you ASAP.

(b) Bedingungen für einen Kauf auf Abzahlung

Kunde	Wann ist die letzte Rate für das neue Gerät fällig?
Lieferant	Es stehen Ihnen verschiedene Zahlungsmöglichkeiten offen und alle zu höchst flexiblen Bedingungen. Natürlich können Sie auch den Gesamtbetrag mit einer einmaligen Zahlung begleichen. Ihre Ersparnisse wären dabei beträchtlich, denn die Zinskosten sind im Transportsektor immer hoch.
Kunde	Angenommen, ich zahle jetzt die Hälfte der Gesamtkosten, welche beiderseits akzeptable Vereinbarung könnten wir für die Abzahlung der zweiten Hälfte innerhalb von zwei Jahren treffen?
Lieferant	Das würde von unserem eigenen Kreditbedarf abhängen, aber prinzipiell sehe ich keinen Grund, warum die Ratenzahlung nicht Ihren Verhältnissen angepaßt werden könnte.
Kunde	Schön. Geben Sie mir ein paar Tage, damit ich die Sache mit meinem Steuerberater besprechen kann. Wenn die Bank zu einem höheren Darlehen als ursprünglich angenommen bereit ist, dann kann ich eventuell den ganzen Preis sofort bezahlen.
Lieferant	Warum nicht? Beim derzeitigen Zinssatz lohnen sich große Ausgaben. Aber denken Sie daran, wir können Ihnen auf alle Fälle behilflich sein, denn unsere eigenen Finanzen sind durch unsere Muttergesellschaft gesichert.
Kunde	Das ist beruhigend zu wissen. Ich gebe Ihnen also so bald wie möglich Bescheid.

(c) Breach of contract

Client	Well, here we have the order contract that you wanted to discuss.
Supplier	Yes, thanks. The paragraph I wanted to look at was this one, 9b.
Client	Is there a problem?
Supplier	It says here that unless we deliver within three days of the date indicated, we are in breach of contract and the order can be cancelled.
Client	That's part of our normal contract. Would you have a problem with that?
Supplier	I find it a bit unusual.
Client	We've had to introduce it, because in the past we had lots of problems with suppliers missing the delivery dates by weeks. We lost a lot of customers because of that. Since we introduced the modified contract we've had far fewer problems with delay.
Supplier	But is it possible to vary it a little?
Client	In what way?
Supplier	Well, I find three days very restrictive. We'd be much happier with one week.
Client	I'm sure you would! Any particular reason? Have you had difficulties meeting dates in the past?
Supplier	Only rarely, but it does happen. And it's usually because a supplier has let us down. I'd like to modify that paragraph a bit, to give us a little more time.
Client	Let me check it out with our manager. I'll get back to you in the next 24 hours.
Supplier	Thanks.

(c) Nichteinhaltung eines Vertrags

Kunde   Also, hier ist der Liefervertrag, den Sie besprechen wollen.

Lieferant Ja, danke. Ich möchte besonders Klausel 9b ins Auge fassen.

Kunde   Gibt es ein Problem damit?

Lieferant Ja, hier wird angedeutet, daß wir uns eines Vertragsbruches schuldig[1] machen, wenn wir den Liefertermin um mehr als drei Tage überschreiten, und daß dann der Auftrag storniert werden kann.

Kunde   So steht es normalerweise in unseren Verträgen. Hätten Sie damit Schwierigkeiten?

Lieferant Ich finde das etwas ungewöhnlich.

Kunde   Wir waren zur Einführung der Klausel gezwungen, da wir früher ziemliche Sorgen mit Lieferanten hatten, die ihre Termine um Wochen überschritten. Wir haben dadurch manche Kunden verloren. Seit der Vertragsänderung haben wir kaum Probleme mit Lieferverzögerungen.

Lieferant Aber können Sie nicht vielleicht doch eine kleine Änderung machen?

Kunde   Inwiefern?

Lieferant Also, ich finde drei Tage etwas knapp. Eine Woche würde uns besser zusagen.

Kunde   Sicher. Aber warum? Fanden Sie es früher schwierig, Termine einzuhalten?

Lieferant Nur selten, aber es kann passieren. Und meistens, weil uns ein Lieferant im Stich gelassen hat. Ich wäre sehr für eine Änderung der Klausel. Das würde uns etwas mehr Zeit geben.

Kunde   Kann ich das mit unserem Geschäftsleiter besprechen? Sie erhalten dann in den nächsten 24 Stunden von mir Bescheid.

Lieferant Danke schön.

1 Note the cases here. *sich einer Sache* (genitive) *schuldig machen*.

41 Meeting a visitor at the airport

John Andrew	Messrs Martin and Bertot from Toulouse?
M. Martin	Are you Mr Andrew from Perkins Industrial?
John Andrew	Yes, that's me. I am glad to hear that you speak English, I was trying to remember my schoolboy French on the way to the airport.
M. Martin	My colleague Bertot cannot speak English I am afraid, so you may need some of your schoolboy French, or perhaps an interpreter, when we come to discuss the contract.
John Andrew	Right, I'll see to it. Are these your bags? My car is just outside. Did you have a good journey?
M. Martin	Fairly good. For some reason our plane from Toulouse to Paris was delayed so we nearly missed the Paris–Birmingham flight.
John Andrew	I am sure our Chairman will be pleased that you made it. We have high hopes for our proposed deal. Would you like to have a coffee before we set off?
M. Martin	No, don't worry, we had an excellent breakfast during the flight.
John Andrew	Before we get back to talking shop can I just ask you what time you need to check in for this evening's return flight?

41   Einen Besucher vom Flughafen abholen

Herr Anderbach	Herr Martin und Herr Bertot aus Toulouse?
Herr Martin	Sind Sie Herr Anderbach von der Firma DAMO?
Herr Anderbach	Ja, bin ich. Ich bin froh, daß Sie deutsch sprechen. Auf dem Weg zum Flughafen habe ich mich bemüht, mich an mein Schulfranzösisch zu erinnern.
Herr Martin	Mein Kollege Bertot spricht leider kein Deutsch, also werden wir Ihr Schulfranzösisch manchmal brauchen. Oder vielleicht einen Dolmetscher, wenn wir über den Vertrag verhandeln.
Herr Anderbach	Gut. Wird gemacht. Ist das Ihr Gepäck? Mein Wagen steht gleich da draußen. Hatten Sie einen guten Flug?
Herr Martin	Ja, es geht. Aus irgendwelchen Gründen hatten wir mit dem Flug von Toulouse nach Paris Verspätung und hätten fast den Flug von Paris nach München verpaßt.
Herr Anderbach	Unser Generaldirektor wird sich freuen, daß Sie es geschafft haben. Wir erwarten uns sehr viel von unserem Geschäftsvorschlag. Möchten Sie einen Kaffee bevor wir fahren?
Herr Martin	Nein, danke. Das ist nicht nötig. Das Frühstück während des Fluges war ausgezeichnet.
Herr Anderbach	Und dann frage ich Sie besser gleich jetzt, bevor wir über die Arbeit sprechen, wann Sie heute abend zur Abfertigung für Ihren Rückflug müssen.

Business Correspondence

German commercial correspondence – some general notes

1 Note on translations

The documents presented here in parallel text are not a word-for-word translation of each other. Owing to obvious differences in letter-writing style in Germany, and the business terms used, it is possible to offer only an equivalent version of the German letter in the English text.

2 Letterheads

Various terms crop up consistently on German letterheads:

Betreff (sometimes *betrifft*): 're', 'subject'
Ihr Zeichen: your reference
Unser Zeichen: our reference
Ihre Nachricht vom: your letter of . . .

3 Opening sentences

The most usual opening sentences are now:

Sehr geehrte Herren (despite political correctness, still very widely used); *Sehr geehrte Damen und Herren*.

The singular form *Sehr geehrter Herr/Sehr geehrte Frau* is never used. *Frau* or *Herr* must be followed by the name or the designation of the addressee, for example:

Sehr geehrter Herr Oberstudiendirektor
Sehr geehrte Frau Oberstudienrätin
Sehr geehrter Herr Bulowski
Sehr geehrte Frau Schiller.

It was once very common to insert an exclamation mark after the opening: *Sehr geehrte Herren!*; *Sehr geehrte Frau Liesing!* This is now fast disappearing in favour of a comma:

Sehr geehrte Herren,

wir bestätigen den Empfang . . .

(note the use of the lower case letter after the comma.) OR in favour of open punctuation:

Sehr geehrte Frau Derrig

Wir haben soeben . . .

(in this case the first word of the letter begins with a capital letter).

4 Close of the letter

The most common formulation is *Mit freundlichen Grüßen*.

A very formal close, which is still used quite frequently but is losing popularity, is *Hochachtungsvoll*. Other possibilities are *Mit besten Grüßen* or *Mit bestem Gruß*.

5 Style

It is also important to note that, as in the case of English, the tendency now is to a more informal approach in letter writing, and toward the avoidance of excessive verbiage.

1 Enquiry about a product

Augustin SA
Z.I. de l'Empereur
F-19200 Ussel
France

Dear Sir/Madam

RE: TOOTHPICK MAKING & PACKAGING MACHINE

We represent a major distributor of foodstuffs and related materials.

We have found your name in *Kompass* under the category of suppliers of toothpick-making machinery. Our present requirement is for a special toothpick-making and packaging machine. If you do produce such equipment or can supply it we would be pleased to receive your earliest quotation CIF Mombasa, prices for this machine and its equipment, together with a stated delivery time.

Please would you also quote for the installation of this machine in the Ususu factory in Mombasa.

We look forward to your earliest reply and remain

Yours faithfully

John Mason
Technical Director

1 Produktanfrage

Storsberg Maschinen GmbH
Franzensstr. 34

D–38441 Einbeck

Gerät zur Herstellung und Verpackung von Zahnstochern

Sehr geehrte Damen und Herren,[1]

wir vertreten ein Großhandelsunternehmen von Lebensmitteln und branchenverwandten Waren.

Wir fanden Ihren Namen in 'Kompass' klassifiziert als Lieferant von Geräten zur Zahnstocherherstellung. Zur Zeit benötigen wir eine Spezialmaschine für die Erzeugung und Verpackung von Zahnstochern. Wenn Sie derartige Geräte herstellen oder liefern, wären wir Ihnen dankbar für Ihr baldmöglichstes Angebot CIF Mombasa, Preise für diese Maschine samt Zubehör sowie Angabe der Lieferzeit.

Könnten Sie uns auch eine Preisangabe für die Installierung dieser Maschine in der Ususu Fabrik in Mombasa zukommen lassen.[2]

Wir freuen uns, so bald wie möglich von Ihnen zu hören und verbleiben[3]

mit besten Grüßen

Gianni Mussini
Technischer Leiter

1 *Sehr geehrte Damen und Herren*: this opening is gaining in popularity, but *Sehr geehrte Herren* is still quite common.
2 *Zukommen lassen*: this is very formal, but in common use. *Schicken* or *senden* would also be possible.
3 *Und verbleiben*: the use of this phrase is not strictly necessary.

2   Enquiry about prices

Bandani Detergenti SpA
Via A. Lamarmora 75
20093 COLOGNO MONZESE (MI)
Italy

Dear Sir/Madam

RE: QUOTATION RMS34/16 JAN 199-/TOILET CLEANSER

On 16 January we received a quotation from your company for the supply of
4,000 litres of industrial toilet cleanser and disinfectant. We were unable to justify
ordering this at the time, because we had sufficient stocks from our previous
order at the end of last year.

We would like to enquire now if the prices quoted at the time are still valid for this
commodity.

If you are unequivocally able to confirm that this is the case, please take this
letter as an order for a further 10,000 litres. If there has been any price increase,
please fax this to us or phone the undersigned to enable us to proceed and agree
a price in due course.

Yours faithfully

Dick DeZwart
Buyer

2 Preisanfrage

Fa Volker & Roth[1]
Grabenzeile 14

D–04251 Leipzig

Betreff: Preisangabe RMS34/16.01.9-/Toilettenreiniger

Sehr geehrte Damen und Herren,

am 16.01. erhielten wir eine Preisangabe von Ihrer Firma bezüglich der Lieferung von 4000l Toilettenreinigungs- und Desinfektionsmittel[2] für Industriezwecke. Da wir noch genügend Vorrat von unserer vorherigen Bestellung am Ende letzten Jahres hatten, fanden wir einen Auftrag zu dieser Zeit nicht gerechtfertigt.

Nun möchten wir gerne anfragen, ob die damals angegebenen Preise für diese Ware noch gültig sind.

Wenn Sie eindeutig bestätigen können, daß dies der Fall ist, dann betrachten Sie bitte dieses Schreiben als Auftrag für weitere 10 000l. Im Falle[3] einer Preissteigerung faxen Sie uns bitte oder rufen Sie mich an, sodaß wir zu gegebener Zeit zu einer Preisabsprache kommen können.

Mit besten Grüßen

F. DeZwart
Einkäufer

1 *Fa*: abbreviation of 'Firma'.
2 *Toilettenreinigungs-*: note that the second part of the compound noun is contained in the following noun (*Desinfektionsmittel*).
3 *Im Falle einer Preissteigerung*: avoids a verbal construction (*wenn wir*...). Note that *Preiserhöhung* would be a suitable alternative.

3 Enquiry about a company

Giardin Prati SpA
Via Cassia Km 89
Val di Paglia
53040 RADICOFANI
Siena
Italy

Dear Sir/Madam

RE: ORDER LAWN-IND/CZ28

We refer to your quotation for 30 industrial mowing machines, model CZ28.

Our client is now eager to proceed with finalizing the order for this equipment as we are slowly approaching spring time. As we have never placed an order with your company, we would like to receive your full audited accounts for the last four trading years.

Please ensure that the above accounts reach us within the next five working days, as we are eager not to miss the six-week delivery time which will enable us to have the equipment in our hands as soon as possible.

Yours faithfully

Sales Department

3 Firmenanfrage

Gartenwies GmbH[1]
Lilienstr. 15

A 6020 Innsbruck

Betr.: Auftrag MÄH-IND/CZ28

Sehr geehrte Damen und Herren,

wir beziehen uns auf Ihre Preisangabe für Großmähmaschinen, Typ CZ28.

Wegen des bevorstehenden Frühjahrsbeginns möchte unser Kunde unbedingt
den Auftrag für diese Geräte abschließen. Da wir aber Ihrer Firma noch nie einen
Auftrag erteilt haben,[2] wären wir dankbar, Ihre Bücher der letzten vier
Geschäftsjahre geprüft zu erhalten.

Bitte veranlassen Sie, daß uns die obigen Bücher bestimmt innerhalb der
nächsten fünf Arbeitstage erreichen, da wir die sechswöchige Lieferfrist
keineswegs versäumen möchten, um die Geräte baldmöglichst[3] zur Hand zu
haben.

Hochachtungsvoll

Luigi Ravanelli
Verkaufsabteilung

1 GmbH: *Gesellschaft mit beschränkter Haftung* (company with limited liability).
2 *Einen Auftrag erteilen*: 'place an order'. *Einen Auftrag geben* would also be possible.
3 *Baldmöglichst*: very common in commercial correspondence. *So bald wie möglich* also
   possible.

4   Enquiry about a person

ROPER Industriale
Viale San Benedetto 39–43
20084 Lacchiarella
Milano

Dear Sirs

RE: Mr Samuel Smith

We write to you as a fellow producer of machine tools. We have recently received an application from Mr Samuel Smith of Reading (England). He is applying for a post as technical support engineer with our company and has given your company's name both as a previous employer and as a character referee.

From our reading of Mr Smith's CV he would appear most suitable for the post. However, we are also keen that people should fit into our factory and we are most concerned that in his early twenties Mr Smith was a very active member of the European Pro-Whale Organization. We would appreciate your comments on this as we are keen to be better informed about this candidate.

Yours faithfully

Carlo Ruggeri
Personnel Manager

4   Einholung einer Personalreferenz

EFI Maschinenbau
Postfach 2340

D–70414 Stuttgart

Betrifft: Referenz für Herrn Günther Schmidt[1]

Sehr geehrte Damen und Herren,

Wir möchten uns an Sie als Kollegen in der Werkzeugmaschinenbranche in folgender Angelegenheit wenden:

Vor kurzem erhielten wir eine Bewerbung von Herrn Günther Schmidt aus Passau. Er sucht bei uns um die Stelle als Hilfstechniker an und gab Ihre Firma als früheren Arbeitgeber und als Charakterreferenz an.

Seinem Lebenslauf nach zu beurteilen erscheint uns Herr Schmidt als äußerst fähig.

Da wir jedoch großen Wert auf Anpassungsfähigkeit in unserem Betrieb legen und uns Herrn Schmidts aktive Mitgliedschaft bei der Europa-Organisation 'Rettet den Wal' in seinen Zwanzigern[2] etwas zu denken gibt, wären wir über Ihren Kommentar zu unserer besseren Information über den Bewerber äußerst dankbar.

Mit besten Grüßen

Carlo Ruggeri
Firmeninhaber

1   *Betrifft*: note the use of the verb as an alternative to *Betreff*.
2   *In seinen Zwanzigern*: 'in his twenties'. Note however: 'in the twenties' (period) is *in den zwanziger Jahren*.

5 Enquiry asking for a specific quote

Sales Manager
OFFICE 2000
89–91 Scott Road
Olton
Solihull
West Midlands
B92 7RZ

Dear Sir/Madam

RE: LASER PHOTOCOPIER PR3000

We have been in correspondence with your company over the last six months and have in that time received a number of different quotations for different models of the industrial laser photocopying machines produced by your company. We have decided that the most suitable machine for our requirement is the PR3000.

We note however that your price of £4,000 was for one machine only. We are keen to purchase 20 printers of this particular model and we would like to know what your discount is on an order of this magnitude.

We are also keen to have the delivery time for this equipment. If it were possible to deliver the printers in two separate batches of 10 each, we would require the first delivery in three months' time and the second some two months after that, when our new British office is set up in Cromer.

Yours faithfully

Luca Evangelista
Sales Manager

5 Anfrage – Ersuchen um Spezialpreisangabe

Büro 2000
z. H. Verkaufsabteilung
Schottenstr. 89–91

D–27124 Bremen

Betr.: Laserphotokopiergerät PR 3000

Sehr geehrte Damen und Herren,

während unserer sechsmonatigen Geschäftsbeziehungen erhielten wir von Ihnen eine Reihe von Preisangaben für verschiedene Typen der von Ihnen hergestellten[1] Lasergroßkopiermaschinen.

Wir haben nun beschlossen, daß das für unsere Anforderungen am besten geeignete Gerät der Typ PR3000 ist.

Wir sehen aber, daß Ihr Preis von 9200 DM nur auf ein Gerät bezogen ist. Da wir jedoch 20 Kopierer dieses bestimmten Typs anschaffen[2] möchten, würden wir gerne Ihren Rabatt für einen Auftrag dieser Größenordnung erhalten.

Die Lieferfrist für die Geräte ist auch sehr wichtig für uns. Sollte es möglich sein, die Kopierer in zwei Teillieferungen von je 10 Stück zu senden, würden wir die erste Lieferung in drei Monaten und die zweite Lieferung in etwa zwei Monaten darauf benötigen, wenn unser neues Büro in München fertiggestellt ist.

Mit freundlichen Grüßen

G. Platini

1 This construction avoids a further clause (*der . . . Maschinen, die Sie hergestellt haben*).
2 *Anschaffen. Kaufen* would obviously also be possible.

6 Soliciting an agency

Erwin Page plc
Electrical appliances & supplies
29 Landon Place
London
SE45 9AS

Dear Sirs

We have heard from business associates that you are looking for an agency for the promotion of your products in the US and we feel that we may be of assistance to you.

We are a long established agency with offices in the midwest and on the west coast, and are experienced in the sale and promotion of domestic electrical equipment. We have helped several British firms to boost their US sales, and are convinced that you too could benefit from our experience. Our UK representative, Charles J Parker, would be pleased to call on you to discuss your needs further: you can contact him on 0171 745 4756. He will in any event be in your locality in the coming week, and will take the opportunity of calling on you.

Yours faithfully

Peter Bowles

6 Vertretungen – erste Kontaktnahme

Erwin Plattner GmbH
Industrieweg 27–29

D 61253 Frankfurt a. Main

Sehr geehrte Herren![1]

Von Geschäftsfreunden erfahren wir, daß Sie auf Suche nach einer Vertretung zur Einführung Ihrer Produkte in den Vereinigten Staaten sind, und wir glauben, daß wir Ihnen dabei behilflich sein könnten.

Wir sind eine gut eingeführte Agentur mit Büros im Mittelwesten und an der Westküste und haben Erfahrung im Verkauf und in der Verkaufsförderung von Elektrogeräten für den Haushalt.

Wir haben verschiedenen deutschen Firmen zu einer Absatzsteigerung in den USA verholfen und sind überzeugt, daß auch Sie von unserer Erfahrung profitieren würden.

Herr Friedrich Gärtner, unser Vertreter in Deutschland, wäre gerne bereit, Sie zu einer Besprechung Ihrer Bedürfnisse aufzusuchen.

Sie erreichen ihn unter[2] der Telefonnummer 071-23572. Er würde kommende Woche in Ihrer Gegend sein und könnte bei dieser Gelegenheit bei Ihnen vorsprechen.

Mit freundlichen Grüßen

Peter Bowles

1 *Sehr geehrte Herren!* The use of the exclamation mark in the opening is declining, but it is still occasionally found.
2 Note use of *unter*: on/at the following number.

7 Requesting information about agents

Duperrier SA
24 avenue des Sylphides
Brignoles
83170 Var
France

Dear Sirs

RE: LÜTTICH GmbH

We have heard from colleagues that you have recently used the services of Lüttich GmbH as agents for your products in Germany. We are in a different line of business from yourselves, but I believe that Lüttich represents companies of various kinds. We are looking for agents in Germany and Switzerland for our stationery products. I should be grateful if you could let us have further information on the above-named firm. Any information you send us will be treated with the strictest confidence.

Yours faithfully

P Brandauer

7 Erkundigung über Vertretung

Lettich GmbH
Postfach 4816

D–61422 Rüsselsheim

Sehr geehrte Damen und Herren,

wir hören von Geschäftskollegen,[1] daß Sie seit einiger Zeit die Dienste der Firma
Duperrier SA als Vertretung Ihrer Waren in Frankreich in Anspruch nehmen.

Unsere Firmen sind zwar nicht branchenverwandt, aber wir glauben, daß
Duperrier Unternehmen verschiedener Art vertritt.

Da wir Vetretungen für unsere Schreibwaren in Frankreich und in der Schweiz[2]
suchen, wären wir Ihnen dankbar, wenn Sie uns weitere Informationen über die
obige Firma könnten zukommen lassen.[3]

Wir werden Ihre Äußerungen selbstverständlich streng vertraulich behandeln.

Hochachtungsvoll

E. H. Porter

1 *Geschäftskollegen. Geschäftsfreunden* would also be possible.
2 Note *in der Schweiz*, as *Schweiz* is feminine. Also *in der Türkei*, etc.
3 Note the word order here. The finite verb precedes the two infinitives.

8 Giving information about agents

Herrn H Pike
Heinrich Pittmann GmbH
Ofterdingenstraße 69
D 68212 Mannheim
Germany

Dear Mr Pike

RE: DIETER & HELLER

Thank you for your enquiry about the company Dieter and Heller, who have been agents for our products for several years. This company has represented our interests in Eastern and Central Europe very effectively and our sales in those regions have been buoyant as a result. You will find their Bonn-based manager, Max Lettmann, particularly helpful, and I am sure he will be interested in co-operating with you.

If you do contact him, don't hesitate to mention my name.

Yours sincerely

Maria Fischer

8 Agenturauskunft

Herrn H. Pike
Heinrich Pittmann GmbH
Ofterdingenstr. 69

D–68212 Mannheim

Sehr geehrter Herr Pike,

wir danken Ihnen für Ihre Anfrage bezüglich der Firma Dieter und Heller, die seit Jahren die Vertretung unserer Waren innehat.

Ihre wirksame Vertretung unserer Interessen in Ost- und Mitteleuropa zog einen regen Absatz[1] unserer Produkte in diesen Gebieten nach sich.

Sie werden Herrn Max Lettmann, den Geschäftsleiter in Bonn, besonders entgegenkommend finden, und ich bin sicher, daß er an einer Zusammenarbeit mit Ihnen interessiert sein wird.

Wenn Sie sich mit ihm in Verbindung setzen, können Sie gerne meinen Namen erwähnen.

Mit freundlichen Grüßen

Maria Fischer

1 *Absatz* is invariably used in the singular, and usually preferred in correspondence to *Verkäufe*.

9   Request for a business reference

CONFIDENTIAL

Mr G Le Blanc
Sales Director
CURTAINS & BLINDS Ltd
PO Box 181
Croydon
CR0 5SN

Dear Mr Le Blanc

RE: CASELLACCI SpA

We would like to introduce our company as a major supplier of castors for office furniture. We have been approached by Casellacci SPA of Pisa as potential distributors of our products in the Italian market. Mr Casellacci has explained that he has been supplying your range of curtain fittings in the Italian market for some fifteen years and has a proven track record of both successful sales and prompt payment with your company.

We are eager to proceed in the Italian market, but we wish to have some reassurance about this company, as we do not know either the company or the individuals concerned. It would appear that they are selling only high quality products and that our range of castors would fit very well into their sales range.

We would appreciate your earliest comments and thank you in advance for providing this information, which we would treat in the utmost confidence.

Yours sincerely

Steve Watwood
Export Manager

9 Ersuchen um Geschäftsreferenz

Fensterschön Gmbh
z.H. Herrn Georg Weiß, Verkaufsdirektor
Postfach 189
D 55314 Linz a. Rhein

Betr.: Casellacci SpA – Vertraulich[1]

Sehr geehrter Herr Weiß,

dürfen wir uns als Großlieferant von Möbelrollen für Büroeinrichtungen
vorstellen und in folgender Angelegenheit an Sie wenden:
Die Firma Casellacci SpA aus Pisa ist als möglicher Verteiler unserer Erzeugnisse
auf dem italienischen Markt an uns herangetreten.

Herr Casellacci erwähnte, daß er seit etwa 15 Jahren den italienischen Markt mit
Ihrem Vorhangzubehör beliefert. Er stellte auch seine Leistungen in bezug auf
Verkaufserfolg und Pünktlichkeit der Abrechnung mit Ihrer Firma unter Beweis.

Das Geschäft mit Italien liegt uns zwar sehr am Herzen, aber wir benötigen eine
gewisse Sicherheit, da uns weder die Firma noch Einzelpersonen der Firma
bekannt sind.

Es scheint, daß das Unternehmen nur erstklassige Waren verkauft und unser
Möbelrollensortiment ausgezeichnet in ihr Angebot[2] passen würde.

Wir würden uns freuen, so bald wie möglich von Ihnen zu hören und danken
Ihnen im voraus für Ihre Information, die wir streng vertraulich behandeln
werden.

Mit besten Grüßen

S. Watwood
Exportleiter

1 *Vertraulich*: 'confidential'. 'Strictly confidential' is *streng vertraulich*.
2 *Angebot*: 'offer' or (here) 'range'.

10 Favourable reply to request for a business reference

Mr S Watwood
CASTASSIST
158–161 Cressex Estate
New Malden
Surrey
KT13 4EY

Dear Mr Watwood

RE: CASELLACCI SpA of Pisa

We thank you for your letter of 11 March, regarding the company Casellacci of Italy as potential distributors of your range of castors.

We have indeed been working with Casellacci now for 23 years and know both Andrea Casellacci and his son Antonio, who has become more active in the company over the last few years. Casellacci have a number of most competent sales personnel covering the whole of Italy and the islands and have performed most effectively for our company against our large German competitors within the market. Casellacci have over this period of time proven to be most prompt in their payment. At the time of writing I cannot recall any undue delay in the settlement of their bills.

I have some awareness of your company and its products and I am sure they are suited to the Italian market. I hope the Casellacci company will prove a dependable and successful distributor for your product.

We hope you find this information sufficient to your requirements. Should you need any further comments please do not hesitate to contact us.

Yours sincerely

George Le Blanc
Sales Director

10 Günstige Geschäftsreferenz

Castassist
z.H. Herrn S. Watwood
158–161 Cressex Estate
New Malden
Surrey
KT13 4EY

Betrifft: Casellacci SpA, Pisa

Sehr geehrter Herr Watwood,

wir danken Ihnen für Ihren Brief vom 11.03. bezüglich der Firma Casellacci als potentieller Verteiler Ihrer Möbelrollen.

Es stimmt, daß wir seit 23 Jahren mit Casellacci zusammenarbeiten, und wir kennen sowohl Andrea Casellacci als auch seinen Sohn Antonio, der seit einigen Jahren in der Firma tätig ist.[1]

Casellacci beschäftigt tüchtige Verkaufskräfte, die für ganz Italien samt Inseln zuständig sind und für unsere Firma mit Erfolg gegenüber der französischen Konkurrenz[2] tätig waren.

Firma Casellacci zeigte sich immer pünktlich in ihren Zahlungen; ich weiß von keiner ungebührlichen Verzögerung in ihrer Abrechnung.

Mir ist Ihr Unternehmen teilweise bekannt, und ich bin sicher, daß Ihre Waren für den italienischen Markt geeignet sind. Ich hoffe, daß sich die Firma Casellacci als verläßlicher und erfolgreicher Verteiler Ihrer Produkte erweisen wird.

Wir hoffen, Ihnen mit dieser Auskunft gedient zu haben. Sollten Sie weitere Einzelheiten benötigen, bitte zögern Sie nicht, sich mit uns in Verbindung zu setzen.

Mit freundlichen Grüßen

Georg Weiß
Verkaufsleiter

1 Alternatives to *tätig ist*: *arbeitet*, or *beschäftigt ist*.
2 *Konkurrenz* can mean 'competition' or 'competitors'. 'Competitors' (lit.): *Konkurrenten*.

11 Unfavourable reply to request for a business reference

Mr S Watwood
CASTASSIST
158–161 Cressex Estate
New Malden
Surrey
KT13 4EY

Dear Mr Watwood

RE: CASELLACCI SpA OF PISA

We are in receipt of your letter regarding the company of Andrea Casellacci with whom you have been discussing the potential distribution of your products in the Italian market.

We must first ask you to accept our comments on this company in the most confidential terms. We have indeed been working with Casellacci for many years, but unfortunately six months ago Mr Andrea Casellacci was detained by the Italian police and certain irregularities within the company have come to light. A direct result of this situation, in our particular case, is that we have not received payment for the last three major shipments of goods to Casellacci, which were due to us at different times. We are at the moment in discussions with our solicitors who will be undertaking the appropriate action on our behalf.

It is our view, therefore, that although this company has performed successfully in the past, it is obviously not in a position to continue this work on our behalf and therefore it is fair to put to you that it would not be a suitable partner for you at this time.

Yours sincerely

George Le Blanc
Sales Director

11 Ungünstige Geschäftsreferenz

Castassist
z.H. Herrn S. Watwood
158–161 Cressex Estate New Malden
Surrey
KT13 4EY

Betr: Casellacci SpA, Pisa

Sehr geehrter Herr Watwood,

wir haben Ihren Brief bezüglich der Firma Casellacci erhalten, mit der Sie über den möglichen Vertrieb Ihrer Waren auf dem italienischen Markt im Gespräch sind.

Zunächst müssen wir Sie ersuchen, unsere Äußerungen über diese Firma mit strengster Vertraulichkeit zu behandeln. Wir haben zwar mit Casellacci längere Zeit zusammengearbeitet, aber Herr Andrea Casellacci war leider vor sechs Monaten in Polizeigewahrsam, und gewisse betriebliche Unregelmäßigkeiten stellten sich heraus.

Dieses Problem hatte zur Folge, daß wir unsererseits drei zu verschiedenen Terminen[1] fällige Zahlungen für Warenlieferungen an Casellacci noch nicht erhalten haben.

Zur Zeit besprechen wir die Angelegenheit mit unserem Anwalt, der in unserem Auftrag entsprechende Schritte unternehmen wird.

Aus unserer Sicht ist die Firma trotz guter Leistung in der Vergangenheit keineswegs mehr in der Lage, für uns weiter tätig zu sein, und daher ist es nur recht und billig, Ihnen offen zu sagen, daß die Firma Casellacci zur Zeit für eine Zusammenarbeit ungeeignet ist.

Mit besten Grüßen

Georg Weiß
Verkaufsleiter

---

1 *Termin* is a very common term in commercial correspondence, e.g. *ich habe einen Termin bei* . . .: 'I have an appointment with . . .'

12 Evasive reply to request for a business reference

Mr S Watwood
CASTASSIST
158–161 Cressex Estate
New Malden
Surrey
KT13 4EY

Dear Mr Watwood

RE: CASELLACCI SpA OF PISA/ITALY

We are in receipt of your letter regarding the company Casellacci SpA with whom you have been discussing the distribution of your products in the Italian market.

Casellacci are a very good company, but we are concerned that they might have already stretched themselves with the selling of our products in Italy. We feel that, if they did take on your range of products, they would probably have to employ a further product manager and perhaps another half a dozen regional sales people to cover the Italian market adequately.

We trust this information is sufficient, but should you require any further comments please do not hesitate to contact us.

Yours sincerely

George Le Blanc
Sales Director

12   Ausweichende Antwort auf Ersuchen um Geschäftsreferenz

Castassist
z.H. Herrn S. Watwood
158–161 Cressex Estate
New Malden
Surrey
KT13 4EY

Betr: Casellacci SpA, Pisa

Sehr geehrter Herr Watwood,

wir haben Ihr Schreiben bezüglich der Firma Casellacci erhalten, mit der Sie über den Verkauf Ihrer Waren auf dem italienischen Markt in Verhandlung stehen.[1]

Casellacci ist ein sehr guter Betrieb, aber wir fürchten, daß er mit dem Vertrieb unserer Waren in Italien bereits voll ausgelastet ist.

Bei Übernahme Ihres Sortiments, glauben wir, würde wahrscheinlich der Einsatz eines weiteren Produktleiters und weiterer sechs Gebietsvertreter zur ausreichenden Erfassung[2] des italienischen Marktes notwendig sein.

Wir hoffen, daß diese Information ausreichend ist. Sollten Sie jedoch weitere Einzelheiten benötigen, bitte zögern Sie nicht, sich mit uns in Verbindung zu setzen.

Mit freundlichen Grüßen

Georg Weiß
Verkaufsleiter

1   *In Verhandlung stehen*: 'be in negotiations with'.
2   *Zur* plus the noun avoids a long verbal construction (*um . . . zu*, or *damit wir . . . können*).

13 Placing an order

Jenkins Freeman plc
Unit 36
Heddington Industrial Estate
Birmingham
B34 9HF

Dear Sirs

We thank you for your catalogue and price list, which we read with interest. On the basis of your current prices, we wish to order the following:

50 electric drills, model 1456/CB
50 chain saws, model 1865/CH

Delivery is required by 3.5.199-, and the goods should be delivered to our warehouse in Riddington Way, Battersea. As agreed, payment will be by banker's draft.

Yours faithfully

Gillian Brookes
Purchasing Department

13 Auftragserteilung

Jeschke und Freimann GmbH
Industriepark Süd
Standplatz 12

D–40697 Düsseldorf

Sehr geehrte Herren,

wir danken Ihnen für Ihren Katalog samt[1] Preisliste, die wir mit Interesse zur Kenntnis genommen haben.

Auf der Basis Ihrer derzeitigen Preise möchten wir Ihnen folgenden Auftrag erteilen:

    50 Elektrobohrer, Typ 1456/CB
    50 Kettensägen, Typ 1865/CH

Die Lieferung wird bis 03.05. benötigt,[2] mit Zustellung der Waren an unser Lagerhaus in Riddington Way, Battersea. Zahlung durch Wechsel, wie vereinbart.[3]

Mit besten Grüßen

Gillian Brookes
Einkauf

1 *Samt* is very formal, and would rarely, if ever, be used in spoken German.
2 *Bis*: 'up to and including'. Strictly speaking, 'before' would be *vor*.
3 Note the contracted form of this sentence. There is a tendency towards this style in commercial correspondence.

14 Cancellation of order

Porzellanfabrik Hering
Langauer Allee 18
D–70102 Stuttgart
Germany

Dear Sirs

RE: ORDER NO. HGF/756

We recently placed an order for 60 bone china coffee sets (model 'Arcadia'). The order reference: HGF/756.

We regret that due to circumstances beyond our control, we now have to cancel the order. We apologize for any inconvenience this may cause you.

Yours faithfully

D Grey

14 Widerrufung einer Bestellung

Porzellanfabrik Hering
Langauer Allee 18

D 70102 Stuttgart

Sehr geehrte Damen und Herren,

wir stellten Ihnen neulich einen Auftrag über[1] 60 Porzellan Kaffeeservices (Typ 'Arcadia') unter Bestellnummer HGF/756.

Umständehalber müssen wir diesen Auftrag leider widerrufen, und wir bitten für alle dadurch entstandenen Unannehmlichkeiten vielmals um Entschuldigung.

Mit freundlichen Grüßen

D. Grey

1 *Auftrag über*: 'order for'. *Erteilen* could also be used instead of *stellen*.

15 Confirming a telephone order

Henning & Söhne GmbH
Schillerstraße 45
D–43002 Essen
Germany

Dear Mr Hartmann

Following the visit of your representative Dieter Höne last week, we are confirming our telephone order for

    250 car seat covers, model AS/385/C

The total price of the order, inclusive of your discount, is £4,600. Payment will follow immediately upon delivery. The covers should be delivered by Tuesday 3 February, to our warehouse on the Pennington Industrial Estate, Rochdale.

Yours sincerely

Derek Batty

15 Bestätigung eines telephonischen Auftrags

Henning & Söhne GmbH
Schillerstraße 45

D 43002 Essen

Sehr geehrter Herr Hartmann,

im Anschluß an den Besuch Ihres Vertreters Herrn Dieter Höne in der letzten Woche bestätigen wir unseren telephonischen Auftrag über

250 Autositzüberzüge, Typ AS/385/C

Der Gesamtpreis für die Bestellung beträgt 4600 Pfund,[1] inklusive[2] Rabatt. Zahlung unmittelbar nach Erhalt[3] der Lieferung.

Die Überzüge sollten bis Dienstag, 3. Februar an unser Lagerhaus, Industriegelände Pennington, Rochdale, geliefert werden.

Mit besten Grüßen

Derek Batty

1 *Pfund*: note the use of the singular. (50 *Mark*: 50 Marks).
2 Alternative to *inklusive*: *einschließlich*.
3 *Unmittelbar nach Erhalt*: it is common to omit the definite article in such expressions in commercial correspondence.

16   Making an order for specific items of office equipment

Your ref.
Our ref. HB/LP

Garzón y Hijos
Plaza de la Catedral 8
Bogotá

Dear Sir/Madam

Please supply the following items, using the Order Number E183, to the above address at your earliest convenience; payment will be made within 14 days of receipt of your invoice and of the goods as ordered.

   6 artists' stools (aluminium)

   20 sets of 5 painting brushes

   10 reams of A5 drawing paper

   2 drawing tables: 2m × 1m

   1 Sanchix camera: FB4X model

   1 QRM computer: portable TGs model

Before you prepare and invoice us for these goods, please inform us by telex or phone of the cost per item, in order to avoid any unexpectedly high sums in the final bill, as this is something which has occasionally happened in the past.

We thank you in anticipation of your prompt reply.

Yours faithfully

Herberto Baza
Studio Supervisor

16   Auftrag für spezielle Büroartikel

Firma Böcklin & Schiele
Ritterplatz 42b

50992 Leverkusen

Sehr geehrte Damen und Herren,

bitte senden Sie so bald wie möglich folgende Artikel an die obige Adresse unter Benutzung der Bestellnummer E183. Zahlung erfolgt innerhalb von zwei Wochen nach Erhalt der Rechnung und der bestellten Waren.

> 6 Malerschemel (Aluminium)
> 20 Garnituren zu je 5 Malerpinseln[1]
> 10 Ries A5 Zeichenpapier
> 2 Zeichentische 2m × 1m
> 1 Sanchix Photoapparat, Modell FB4X
> 1QRM Computer, Modell TGs, tragbar

Bevor Sie uns diese Waren in Rechnung stellen, wären wir Ihnen dankbar, wenn Sie uns telefonisch oder per Fernschreiben[2] den Einzelpreis der Waren angeben könnten, da wir in der Vergangenheit manchmal unerwartet hohe Rechnungen erhalten haben.

Wir danken Ihnen im voraus für eine umgehende Antwort und verbleiben

mit besten Grüßen

Herbert Bart
Verwaltung

1   *Je*: 'each'. cf: *drei Bücher zu je 17 Mark*: 'three books at 17 Marks each'.
2   *Per Fernschreiben*: 'by telex'; by fax: *per Fax*.

17 Acknowledgement of an order

Mr Henry Putton
33 Flintway
West Ewell
Surrey
KT19 9ST

Dear Mr Putton

Thank you for your signed order given to our Adviser for a bed to be constructed to your specific requirements.

We shall now pass your order to our Design Department complete with your personal specification.

Delivery time will be in approximately seven weeks and you will be advised of the exact date in due course.

Once again many thanks for your order.

Yours sincerely

Janet Craig
Customer Relations Manager

17 Auftragsbestätigung

Herrn
Heinrich Pitter
Flintweg 33

D 04 Leipzig

Sehr geehrter Herr Pitter,

wir danken Ihnen für Ihre unserem Berater unterzeichnet übergebene Bestellung über ein für Ihre Bedürfnisse speziell angefertigtes Bett.[1]

Wir werden Ihren Auftrag samt Ihren Anweisungen an unsere Konstruktionsabteilung weiterleiten.

Die Lieferfrist beträgt etwa sieben Wochen und wir werden Ihnen das genaue Datum rechtzeitig bekanntgeben.

Nochmals besten Dank für Ihren Auftrag.[2]

Mit freundlichen Grüßen

Janet Craig
Kundendienst

1 The first paragraph has a very complex but compact structure. It avoids the use of several clauses, but care must be taken with the adjective endings.
2 Note the accusative. *Dank* is the object of the understood verb.

18   Payment of invoices –
Letter accompanying payment

Dr V Meyer
Neue Marktforschung GmbH
Kastanienallee 14
D–45023 Osnabrück
Germany

Dear Dr Meyer

I enclose an international money order to the value of 450DM as payment for the three market research reports published by your organization this year.

As agreed during our telephone conversation on 15.1.199-, the sum enclosed includes postage.

I look forward to receiving the reports as soon as possible.

Yours sincerely

Maria Meller

Enc.

18   Begleitbrief zur Begleichung einer Rechnung

Frau
Dr. V. Meyer
Neue Marktforschung GmbH
Kastanienallee 14

D 45023 Osnabrück

Sehr geehrte Frau Dr. Meyer,

in der Anlage[1] finden Sie eine internationale Postanweisung im Werte von DM 4500 als Zahlung für drei von Ihrer Organisation in diesem Jahr veröffentlichte Marktberichte.

Wie am 15.01.199- telefonisch vereinbart, enthält dieser Betrag auch die Postgebühr.

Wir freuen uns darauf, die Berichte so bald wie möglich zu erhalten.

Mit besten Grüßen

Maria Weller

Anlage
Internationale Postanweisung

1   Alternatives to *in der Anlage*: *als Anlage, beiliegend, beigelegt,* or *wir legen ... bei.*

19 Payment of invoices – request for deferral

South East Finance Ltd
Dovehouse Lane
Sutton
Surrey
SM2 6LY

Dear Sirs

RE: MAXITRUCK 2000

I refer to our recent agreement of 30 November 199- regarding payment for one 40-ton Maxitruck 2000.

As you will recall, we paid an initial instalment of £10,000 and agreed to 10 further monthly instalments of £3,000. The December and January instalments, as you will know, have been paid promptly.

However, owing to the serious economic situation we find ourselves in, we are at the moment unable to make payments as agreed. Because of our reduced cash flow we are unable to pay more than £2,000 a month. We would, therefore, appreciate the opportunity to discuss this matter with you and reach a mutually satisfactory arrangement.

Yours faithfully

Tom Page
Finance Manager

19 Rechnungsbegleichung –
Bitte um Stundung

Süd-Ost Finanzen GmbH
Taubenschlagweg 12

D 44003 Dortmund

Sehr geehrte Damen und Herren,

wir beziehen uns auf unsere jüngste Absprache am 30.11.199- bezüglich der
Zahlung für den 40t Großlaster Maxi 2000.

Wie Sie sich erinnern werden, bezahlten wir eine anfängliche Rate von 23 000 DM
und vereinbarten weitere zehn Monatsraten zu je 6900 DM.[1] Die Raten für
Dezember und Januar wurden, wie Sie wissen, pünktlich überwiesen.[2]

Da wir uns zur Zeit jedoch in wirtschaftlichen Schwierigkeiten befinden, sind wir
leider nicht in der Lage, den Zahlungen, wie vereinbart, nachzukommen.

Aufgrund von begrenzter Liquidität können wir nicht mehr als 4600 DM pro
Monat aufbringen. Wir wären Ihnen daher dankbar für eine Gelegenheit, diesen
Punkt zur beiderseitigen Zufriedenstellung mit Ihnen erörtern zu können.

Mir freundlichen Grüßen

Tom Page
Finanzleiter

1   *Zu je 6900 Mark*: 'at 6900 Marks each'.
2   *Überweisen*: 'to transfer'. 'To transfer to an account': *auf ein Konto überweisen*.

20 Payment of invoices – refusal to pay

Johnson (Builders) Ltd
Nugget Grove
Christchurch

Dear Sirs

RE: INVOICE NO. L28/4659

We refer to your invoice No. L28/4659 regarding repairs to the roof of workshop 17 at Heath End.

In spite of the repair work carried out by your employees the roof still leaked in a number of places during the recent rains, causing a shut-down of the workshop for safety reasons.

We look forward to a speedy response by you to resolve this problem and assure you that your invoice will be paid as soon as this matter has been resolved to our satisfaction.

Yours faithfully

20 Zahlungsverweigerung

Baubetrieb Sieger
Nußbaumstr. 2

27458 Bremen

Sehr geehrte Herren!

Wir beziehen uns auf Ihre Rechnung Nr. L28/4659 betreffend die Dachreparatur unserer Werkstatt 17 in der Heidenstraße.

Trotz der von Ihren Arbeitern durchgeführten Reparatur erwies sich das Dach während des neulichen Regens an mehreren Stellen als undicht, was eine Schließung der Werkstatt aus Sicherheitsgründen zur Folge hatte.

Wir erwarten nun, daß Sie unverzüglich Schritte zur Lösung dieses Problems unternehmen, und versichern Ihnen, daß Ihre Rechnung beglichen wird, sobald diese Angelegenheit zu unserer Zufriedenheit beigelegt ist.

Hochachtungsvoll[1]

M. Meier

1 Although *Hochachtungsvoll* is declining in popularity, it is still appropriate in letters of this type which are making a complaint/demanding payment, etc.

21 **Apologies for non-payment**

Mr I Sahani
Michigan Lake Trading Co.
974 South La Salle Street
Chicago
Illinois 60603
USA

Dear Mr Sahani

I refer to our telephone conversation yesterday.

I must once again apologize for the fact that you have not yet received payment for order No. 072230/5310.

Payment was duly authorized by me on the 10 July, but due to staff holidays the paperwork appears to have gone astray between our sales and finance departments.

We have now traced the relevant documentation and I can assure you that the matter is being attended to with the utmost urgency.

If you do not receive payment by Monday, 22 August, I would be grateful if you would contact me immediately.

I apologize once again for the inconvenience this has caused you and assure you of our best intentions.

Yours sincerely

21 Entschuldigung für Nichtbegleichung einer Rechnung

Firma Bergmann & Co
z.H. Herrn F. Sacher
Blücherweg 27

D–14800 Berlin

Sehr geehrter Herr Sacher,

darf ich mich noch einmal dafür entschuldigen, daß Sie noch keine Bezahlung für Auftrag Nr. 072230/5310 erhalten haben.

Zwar habe ich ordnungsgemäß die Zahlung am 10. Juli veranlaßt, doch die Unterlagen schienen wegen Personalurlaub in der Verkaufs- und der Rechnungsabteilung in Verlust geraten zu sein.

Wir haben aber nun die diesbezüglichen Papiere gefunden, und ich kann Ihnen versichern,[1] daß die Angelegenheit als äußerst dringlich behandelt wird.

Sollten Sie die Zahlung bis Montag, 22. August nicht erhalten haben, wäre ich Ihnen dankbar, wenn Sie sich mit mir sofort in Verbindung setzen könnten.

Ich entschuldige mich noch einmal für die Ihnen verursachten Unannehmlichkeiten und verspreche Ihnen, daß solche Irrtümer nicht wieder vorkommen werden.

Mit besten Grüßen

J. Yipp

1   Note the use of the dative after *versichern* in this sense. 'I assure you of my support': *Ich versichere Sie meiner Unterstützung* (accusative + genitive).

22 Request for payment

Huron Motor Factors
6732 John Street
Markham
Ontario
Canada L3R 1B4

Dear Sir

RE: INVOICE NO. JE/17193

As per our invoice JE/17193 of 13.3.199-, we supplied your Nashlee plant with 500 litres of AVC automotive base paint, payment due 60 days after receipt of our consignment.

This period of time has now elapsed and we request immediate settlement of the above invoice.

Yours faithfully

22 Zahlungsaufforderung

XY Motorwerke
Rennweg 27–29

21864 Hamburg

Sehr geehrte Herren,

gemäß unserer Rechnung JE/17193 vom 13.03.9- belieferten wir Ihr Kieler Werk
mit 500l AVC Fahrzeuggrundierlack, Zahlung 60 Tage nach Erhalt der Lieferung.

Diese Frist ist nun abgelaufen und wir erwarten die sofortige Begleichung der
obigen Rechnung.

Hochachtungsvoll[1]

J. Renner

1 *Hochachtungsvoll* is preferred in view of the overall tone of the letter.

23   Overdue account

First letter

Lota (UK) Ltd
93 Armstrong Road
Dudley
West Midlands DY3 6EJ

Dear Sir

<u>Arrears on Finance Agreement No. 261079</u>

I am writing to advise you that your bankers have failed to remit the April instalment of £8,373 on the above agreement and as a result the account is now in arrears.

This has incurred an additional £460.50 in interest and administration charges.

Please advise your bank to transfer £8,873 to our account to bring your account up to date and enable us to remove it from our arrears listing.

Yours faithfully

23 Überfällige Rechnung

Erste Mahnung

LOTA GmbH
Färberstr. 38

51357 Köln

Betr.: Zahlungsabkommem Nr. 261079 – Rückstände

Sehr geehrte Damen und Herren,

wir teilen Ihnen mit, daß Ihre Bank es verabsäumte, die Aprilrate von 19 257 DM bezügl. des obigen Abkommens zu überweisen, und daß Sie daher im Zahlungsrückstand sind.

Dazu kommen noch DM 1059,15 für Zinsen und Verwaltungsgebühren.

Bitte beauftragen Sie Ihre Bank, DM 19 257 auf unser Konto als Ausgleich zu überweisen,[1] sodaß Sie nicht mehr auf der Liste unserer Rückstände aufscheinen.

Mit vorzüglicher Hochachtung[2]

D. Bursche

1 *Auf unser Konto*: 'to our account'.
2 This expression is very formal, and would be avoided by many writers.

24   Overdue account

Final letter

Lota (UK) Ltd
93 Armstrong Road
Dudley
West Midlands DY3 6EJ

Dear Sir

<u>Arrears on Finance Agreement No. 261079</u>

Our records show that despite our previous reminders, your account remains overdue.

We must now insist that you clear the outstanding arrears by close of business on Friday, 26 June 199-.

Failure to comply with this request by the date specified will result in the termination of the agreement. We will then take steps to recover our property.

Yours faithfully

24 Überfällige Rechnung

Letzte Warnung

LOTA GmbH
Färberstr. 38

51357 Köln

Betreff: Zahlungsabkommen Nr. 261079 – Rückstände

Sehr geehrte Damen und Herren,

aus unseren Unterlagen geht hervor,[1] daß Ihre Rechnung trotz vorhergehender Mahnungen weiterhin überfällig ist.

Wir müssen nun darauf bestehen,[2] daß Sie Ihren Zahlungsrückstand bis Geschäftsschluß am 26. Juni 199- bereinigen.

Sollten Sie dieser Aufforderung bis zum angegebenen Datum nicht Folge leisten, wird dies die Kündigung Ihres Abkommens nach sich ziehen und wir werden Schritte zur Rückzahlung unserer Forderungen in die Wege leiten.

Hochachtungsvoll

D. Bursche

1 Also possible: *wir* (*er*)*sehen aus unseren Unterlagen* ...
2 When used with a noun, *bestehen auf* is used with the dative (*ich bestehe auf sofortiger Begleichung*).

25 Job advertisement

Letter to newspaper

H J Marketing Services
County House
53 Stukely Street
Twickenham TW1 7LA

Dear Sir

Please would you insert the attached job advertisement in the January issues of *East European Marketing Monthly* and *Food Industry Digest*.

As usual we require a quarter-page ad, set according to our house style.

Please invoice payment in the usual way.

Yours faithfully

Enc.

25 Stellenanzeige

Brief an Zeitung

MVS Marketing
Gärtnerweg 18

68523 Wiesbaden

Sehr geehrte Damen und Herren,

bitte setzen die beiliegende Stellenanzeige in die Januar-Ausgabe des
'Osteuropäischen Marktanzeigers' und des 'Informationsblattes für die
Lebensmittelindustrie'.

Wie gewöhnlich benötigen wir ein viertelseitiges Inserat im von unserer Firma
bevorzugten Layout.

Wir erbitten Rechnungsstellung wie üblich.[1]

Mit besten Grüßen

D. Herder

Anlage
Stellenanzeige

1 *Wir erbitten*: *wir bitten um* ... would also be possible.

26   Newspaper advertisement

We are now expanding our operations in Eastern Europe and require experienced people within the food processing industry who are looking for an opportunity to sell in Hungary and Bulgaria products of leading food companies. The products are of good quality and already enjoy a substantial international reputation.

The salary for the above position is negotiable dependent upon experience and qualifications. A competitive benefits package is also offered.

For further details and application form please write to the Personnel Manager, EEF Ltd, Roman Road, Epsom, Surrey, KT72 7EF, quoting reference HB/127.

Closing date: 14 February 199-.

27   Asking for further details and application form

EEF Ltd
Roman Road
Epsom
Surrey KT72 7EF

Dear Sir

Ref. HB/127

I would be grateful if you could send me further details and an application form for the post of sales manager advertised in this month's *East European Marketing Monthly*.

Yours faithfully

26 Stellenanzeige

Zur Erweiterung unserer Geschäftstätigkeit in Osteuropa benötigen wir Mitarbeiter mit Erfahrung in der nahrungsmittelverarbeitenden Industrie für die Suche nach[1] Verkaufsmöglichkeiten von Produkten führender Lebensmittelfirmen in Ungarn und Bulgarien. Es handelt sich dabei um Spitzenprodukte[2] von erheblichem internationalem Ruf.

Gehalt für obige Stellung nach Vereinbarung, abhängig von Erfahrung und Qualifikation. Wir bieten auch ein zusätzliches Leistungspaket, das sich sehen lassen kann.

Für weitere Einzelheiten bzw.[3] Bewerbungsformulare schreiben Sie bitte an die Personalleitung, EEF GmbH, Römerstr.19, 67000 Mainz, unter Angabe von Zeichen HB/127.

Einsendeschluß: 14. Februar 199-

1 *Die Suche nach*: 'the search for'.
2 *Spitzenprodukte*: 'leading products'. cf. *Spitzenpolitiker*: 'leading politician'.
3 *Bzw.*, abbreviation for *beziehungsweise*: 'or'.

27 Bitte um weitere Einzelheiten und Bewerbungsformular

EEF GmbH
Personalabteilung
Römerstr.19

67000 Mainz

Zeichen: HB/127

Sehr geehrte Damen und Herren,

ich wäre Ihnen dankbar für die Übersendung von weiteren Einzelheiten sowie einem Bewerbungsformular für die Stellung als Verkaufsleiter, für die Sie im 'Osteuropäischen Marktanzeiger' dieses Monats inserieren.

Mit freundlichen Grüßen

28 Job application

25 January 199-

Black's (Automotive) Ltd
18 Dawson Street
Birmingham
B24 4SU

Dear Sir

I am applying for the post of market research officer advertised in the *Guardian* on 21.1.9-.

I graduated from Chiltern University in June with an upper second class degree in European Business. The following January I was awarded the Diploma of the Chartered Institute of Marketing. On my degree course I specialized in market research and did a one-year work placement with Cox, Paton and Taylor in London.

Since leaving university I have been employed as a market research assistant in the Quantocks Tourist Agency. I am now seeking an opportunity to apply the knowledge and skills I have acquired in a larger, more market-orientated organization.

I enclose a CV and the names of two referees. I would be grateful if you would not contact my current employer without prior reference to me.

Yours faithfully

Michael Westwood

Enc.

28 Bewerbungsschreiben

25. Januar 199-

Kfz Handel Schwarz
Valentinstr. 76

62345 München

Sehr geehrte Damen und Herren,

ich möchte mich um die Stellung als Mitarbeiter in der Marktforschung bewerben gemäß Ihrer Anzeige in der Süddeutschen Zeitung vom 21.01.9-.[1]

Im Juni schloß ich mein Studium der Europäischen Betriebswirtschaft an der Universität Bochum mit gutem Erfolg ab. Im folgenden Januar erwarb ich das Staatsdiplom in Marketing. Während meines Studiums wählte ich Marktforschung als Spezialfach[2] und machte in diesem Zusammenhang ein einjähriges Praktikum bei der Firma Cox, Paton & Taylor in London.

Seit dem Ende meines Studiums bin ich als Marktforschungsassistent beim Reiseunternehmen DEG tätig. Jetzt suche ich nach einer Gelegenheit, meine erworbenen Kenntnisse und Fähigkeiten in einer größeren, stärker marktorientierten Organisation anzuwenden.

Ich lege einen Lebenslauf sowie die Namen von zwei Referenzen bei und wäre dankbar für Ihre Mitteilung, wenn Sie meinen Arbeitgeber kontaktieren.

Mit besten Grüßen

Michael Oswald

Anlage
Lebenslauf

1 *Bewerben* could have been placed at the end of the sentence.
2 *Spezialfach*: 'specialist subject'. Note also *Hauptfach* ('main subject'); *Nebenfach* ('subsidiary subject').

29 Curriculum vitae

Surname:	Cording
First names:	Donald Maurice
Date of Birth:	18 March 1959

QUALIFICATIONS: BA (Hons) Business Studies (Leeds, 1981)
MBA (Warwick, 1985)

CURRENT EMPLOYMENT:
(Sept. 1988 to the present)   Marketing Manager, Cockpit Industries Ltd,
8 Wendover Road, Accrington, Lancs.
BB7 2RH

PREVIOUS EMPLOYMENT:
(a)   Jan. 1986–Sept. 1988:   Marketing Assistant,
Spurlands Ltd, 71 Misbourne Road,
Northallerton, Yorks. DL5 7YL

(b)   Oct. 1981–Dec. 1985:   Marketing Assistant,
Tutton Enterprises Ltd, Wye House,
Cores End, Wolverhampton WV6 8AE

(c)   Sept. 1979–July 1980:   Sales Assistant,
J V Ansell & Co., Greenaway Avenue,
Leek, Staffs. ST15 4EH

29 Lebenslauf

Familienname:	Cording
Vornamen:	Donald Maurice
Geburtsdatum:	18.03.59

QUALIFIKATIONEN:	BA (Hons) Betriebswirtschaftslehre
	Universität Leeds, 1981
	MBA, Universität Warwick, 1985

GEGENWÄRTIGE STELLUNG:	Marketing Manager, Cockpit Industries Ltd, 8
(seit Sept. 1988)	Wendover Road, Accrington Lancs. BB7 2RH

FRÜHERE STELLUNGEN:

(a) Jan. 1986–Sept. 1988:	Marketing Assistent, Spurlands Ltd, 71 Misbourne Road, Northallerton, Yorks. DL5 7YL
(b) Okt. 1981–Dez. 1985:	Marketing Assistent, Tutton Enterprizes Ltd, Wye House, Cores End, Wolverhampton WV6 8AE
(c) Sept. 1979–Juli 1980:	Verkäufer, J V Ansell & Co., Greenaway Ave, Leek, Staffs. ST15 4EH

30 Unsolicited letter of application

Executive Agency plc
22 Ellison Place
London WC1B 1DP

Dear Sirs

I have recently returned to Britain after working in Canada and the Gulf States for the last 15 years.

I spent five years in Canada as chief financial accountant of Bourges-Canada in Montreal, before moving to the Gulf. I have worked there as financial director for Jenkins-Speller for the last ten years. During this period the company's number of clients and turnover have quadrupled.

I have returned to Britain for family reasons and I am now seeking an appropriate position in a company that can capitalize on my expertise in financial management and strategy.

I enclose a detailed CV for your further information and look forward to hearing from you soon.

Yours faithfully

R Bennett

Enc.

30 Stellenbewerbung ohne vorherige Anzeige

Stellenvermittlung GmbH
Elisenplatz 22

80000 München

Sehr geehrte Damen und Herren,

nach 15 Jahren beruflicher Tätigkeit in Kanada und in den Golfstaaten bin ich seit einiger Zeit wieder zurück in Deutschland.

Ich war fünf Jahre Hauptbuchhalter bei der Firma Bourges-Canada in Montreal und übernahm dann eine Stellung in den Golfstaaten, wo ich die letzten zehn Jahre als Finanzleiter der Firma Jenkins-Speller tätig war. Während dieser Zeit vergrößerten sich Umsatz- sowie Kundenzahlen um ein Vierfaches.[1]

Ich bin aus familiären Gründen nach Deutschland zurückgekehrt und suche nun eine geeignete Stellung bei einem Unternehmen, dem meine Sachkenntnis der Finanzleitung und -planung von Nutzen sein kann.

Zu Ihrer weiteren Information[2] finden Sie in der Anlage einen detaillierten Lebenslauf. Ich würde mich freuen, bald von Ihnen zu hören.

Mit besten Grüßen

R. Binder

Anlage
Lebenslauf

1 *Um ein Vierfaches*: lit. 'fourfold'. Note also *um ein Dreifaches*; *um ein Fünffaches*, etc.
2 *Zu Ihrer weiteren Information*: 'for your further information'. Note the preposition used.

31 Interview invitation

Ms F Jones
23 Park View
Colchester
Essex CO4 3RN

Dear Ms Jones

Ref. PS/2021: Personnel assistant

Interviews for the above position will take place on Friday, 22 February 199-,
beginning at 10 a.m.

We expect to conclude the interviews after lunch, at approximately 2.30 p.m.

Please confirm whether you will be able to attend the interview.

Yours sincerely

Mr C Smith
Personnel Officer

31 Einladung zum Vorstellungsgespräch

Frau
Johanna Richter
Am Park 17

4020 Linz

Betr: Chefsekretärin – Zeichen PS/2021

Sehr geehrte Frau Richter,

Vorstellungsgespräche für die obige Stellung finden am Freitag, 22. Februar 199-
um 10.00 Uhr statt.

Ende der Interviews voraussichtlich um 14.30 Uhr.

Bitte bestätigen Sie Ihre Teilnahme.

Mit besten Grüßen

S. Schmidt
Personalleiter

32 Favourable reply to job application

Mrs L Flint
7 Fisherman's Way
Okehampton
Devon EX12 0YX

Dear Mrs Flint

I am writing to offer you formally the position of personal assistant to the operations director at Farnbury.

As discussed at the interview the normal working hours are 8.30 a.m.–5 p.m., Monday to Friday, although the position requires a flexible approach and on occasions you will be expected to work outside these times. The annual salary is £18,000.

You will receive further details if you accept the position.

Please confirm in writing by first post, Monday 3 April at the latest, whether you accept the offer of the position.

Yours sincerely

32 Positive Antwort auf Bewerbung

Frau Laura Feuerstein
Fischergasse 56

27000 Bremen

Sehr geehrte Frau Feuerstein,

Wir möchten Ihnen hiermit offiziell die Stellung als Chefsekretärin unseres Betriebsleiters in Bremerhaven anbieten.

Wie bereits beim Vorstellungsgespräch erwähnt ist die normale Arbeitszeit 8.30 Uhr – 17.00 Uhr, montags bis freitags, doch da Ihre Position eine gewisse Flexibilität erfordert, wird erwartet, daß Sie gelegentlich außerhalb dieser Zeit tätig sind. Ihr Gehalt beträgt monatlich DM 3450.

Weitere Einzelheiten erhalten Sie, wenn Sie die Stellung angenommen haben.

Bitte schicken Sie uns umgehend, spätestens aber bis Montag, 3. April, Ihre schriftliche Bestätigung, ob Sie unser Angebot annehmen.

Mit freundlichen Grüßen

L. Kenner

33 Unfavourable reply to job application

Mr R Smith
15 Adams Way
Reading
Berks
RG23 6WD

Dear Mr Smith

RE: POSITION AS SALES DIRECTOR

I am writing to inform you that your application was unsuccessful on this occasion.

I thank you for your interest in our company and wish you every success with your career.

Yours sincerely

33 Negative Antwort auf Bewerbung

Herrn
Robert Reiter
Adamgasse 15

28794 Cuxhaven

Sehr geehrter Herr Reiter,

wir möchten Ihnen mitteilen, daß Sie mit Ihrer Bewerbung dieses Mal keinen Erfolg hatten.

Vielen Dank für Ihr Interesse an unserem Unternehmen und unsere besten Wünsche für eine erfolgreiche Berufslaufbahn.[1]

Mit freundlichen Grüßen

L. Kenner

1 *Berufslaufbahn*: 'career'. Also possible: *Karriere*.

34 Requesting a reference for an applicant

Your ref. AS/
Our ref. FG/JL

2 February 199-

The Manager
First Class Bank
1–6, King's Square
BURY

Dear Mr Swift

RE: MISS STEPHANIE BOSSOM

This branch of the Safety First has recently received an application for employment as an accounts clerk from Ms Stephanie Bossom, who has quoted your name as a referee to whom we might address ourselves in the event of our wishing to interview her.

I believe that Ms Bossom has been working in your bank for several years and that her desire to change employment is prompted largely by her intention to marry and settle in this area. From her application it would seem that she would be a valuable asset to us; therefore we should be most grateful if you could confirm our impression in writing (by fax if possible) as soon as is convenient.

Please feel free to comment on any aspect of Ms Bossom's work that you deem to be of likely interest to us.

I thank you in advance for your co-operation.

Yours sincerely

Frank Graham
Branch Manager

34 Ersuchen um Bewerberreferenz

2. Februar 199-

PRIMA Bank
z.H. Herrn F. Rasch
Königsallee 1–6

40000 Düsseldorf

Ihre Zeichen: AS/   Unsere Zeichen: FG/JL

Sehr geehrter Herr Rasch,

die hiesige TOTAL Zweigstelle hat vor kurzem ein Bewerbungsschreiben von
Frau Stefanie Bessemer erhalten. Frau Bessemer bewirbt sich um die Stelle als
Mitarbeiterin in der Buchhaltung und hat Ihren Namen als Referenz angegeben,[1]
sollten wir sie zu einem Einstellungsgespräch einladen.

Soviel ich weiß, war Frau Bessemer einige Jahre in Ihrer Bank beschäftigt, und
ihr beabsichtigter Stellungswechsel rührt daher, daß sie nach ihrer Heirat in
unserem Gebiet ihren Wohnsitz nehmen möchte.

Ihrer Bewerbung nach scheint es, daß sie für uns eine Bereicherung bedeuten
könnte. Wir wären daher äußerst dankbar, wenn Sie uns Ihre Eindrücke so bald
wie möglich schriftlich oder per Fax übermitteln könnten.

Bitte kommentieren Sie uneingeschränkt alle Aspekte von Frau Bessemers
Tätigkeit, die Ihrer Meinung nach für uns von Interesse wären.

Ich darf Ihnen bereits im voraus für Ihr Entgegenkommen vielmals danken.

Mit besten Grüßen

Franz Gruber

1 *Als Referenz*: 'as referee'.

35 Providing a positive reference for an employee

4 February 199-

Your ref. FG/JL
Our ref. AS/MN

Mr F Graham
Safety First Assurance plc
12 Bright Street
Lancaster

Dear Mr Graham

MS STEPHANIE BOSSOM

I hasten to reply to your request for a reference for Ms. Stephanie Bossom. Please accept my apologies for not being able to fax my reply, but at present we are experiencing problems with the machine.

Yes, Stephanie has been an ideal employee who started with us as an office junior straight from school and has been promoted on several occasions in recognition of her work. I understand her reasons for wishing to leave; had she stayed, I would very soon have been promoting her myself.

You will see from her application that she has sat and passed a number of professional examinations over the last two years. In that time she has taken responsibility for supervising the progress of trainees and has been involved in new initiatives relating to our office systems.

You will find Stephanie a pleasant, willing and talented person who can be relied upon in the carrying out of her professional duties to the best of her ability at all times.

I hope you will be able to offer her the post, which you imply is likely in your initial letter.

Yours sincerely

Alan Swift
Manager, Town Centre Branch

35 Positive Referenz

4. Februar 199-

TOTAL Versicherung GmbH
z.H. Herrn F. Gruber
Stadtplatz 12a

88400 Konstanz

Ihr Zeichen: FG/JL
Unser Zeichen: AR/MN

Sehr geehrter Herr Gruber,

umgehend komme ich gerne Ihrem Ersuchen um eine Referenz für Frau Stefanie Bessemer nach. Bitte entschuldigen Sie, daß ich meine Antwort nicht per Fax übermitteln kann, da wir zur Zeit Schwierigkeiten mit unserem Gerät haben.

Stefanie ist tatsächlich eine ausgezeichnete Mitarbeiterin. Sie kam zu uns direkt von der Schule und begann als Bürolehrling. In Anerkennung ihrer Leistung wurde sie mehrmals befördert. Ich verstehe die Gründe, warum sie unsere Organisation verlassen möchte. Wäre sie geblieben, hätte ich sie in nächster Zeit selbst befördert.[1]

Aus ihrer Bewerbung werden Sie entnehmen, daß sie während der letzten beiden Jahre verschiedene Fachprüfungen erfolgreich abgelegt hat.[2] In dieser Zeit übernahm sie auch die Verantwortung für die Fortschrittskontrolle des Trainingsprogramms. Sie war auch mitbeteiligt an büropraktischen Initiativen.

Sie werden in Stefanie eine freundliche, bereitwillige und begabte Mitarbeiterin finden, welche die ihr gestellten fachlichen Aufgaben jederzeit tüchtig und verläßlich ausführen wird.

Ich hoffe, daß Sie, wie in Ihrem Brief angedeutet, in der Lage sein werden, ihr die Stellung zum Angebot zu machen.

Mit besten Grüßen

Andreas Rasch
Filialleiter

1 *Wäre sie geblieben* . . .: this avoids the use of *wenn* . . . with the subsequent change of word order.
2 *Eine Prüfung ablegen*: 'to take an examination'. *Eine Prüfung bestehen*: 'to pass an examination'. *Bei der Prüfung durchfallen*: 'to fail the exam'.

36 Acceptance letter

Melton's Motor Factors Ltd
63 Station Road
Thirsk
N. Yorkshire
YO9 4YN

Dear Sir

Thank you for your letter of 17 July in which you offer me the post of parts manager.

I am delighted to inform you that I accept your offer.

Yours sincerely

W Holland

36 Annahme eines Stellenangebots

WV Motorwerke
Bahnhofstr. 17–20

01653 Meißen

Sehr geehrte Damen und Herren,

ich danke Ihnen für Ihren Brief vom 17. Juli, in dem Sie mir die Stellung des Leiters der Abteilung Ersatzteile anbieten.

Ich freue mich, Ihnen mitteilen zu können, daß ich Ihr Angebot gerne annehme.

Mit besten Grüßen

W. Hofer

37 Contract of employment

Dear

Following recent discussions we are pleased to offer you employment at our Company as Area Manager on the following terms and conditions:-

Remuneration

Your salary will be £15,000 per annum plus commission on the basis we have already discussed with you. As with all our staff your salary will be paid monthly on the last Thursday in each month, your first review being in July 199-.

Notice

As with all our staff, you will be employed for an initial trial period of six months, during which time either you or we may terminate your appointment at any time upon giving seven days' notice in writing to the other. Provided that we are satisfied with your performance during the trial period, we will thereafter immediately confirm your appointment as a permanent member of our staff and the seven days' period of notice referred to above will be increased to one month.

Sickness Pay

During any reasonable absence for illness the Company, at its discretion, will make up the amount of your National Insurance Benefit to the equivalent of your normal salary, although this will be essentially relative to your length of service.

Holidays

Your normal paid holiday entitlement will be 20 working days in a full year, the holiday year running from 1 January to 31 December.

Car

We will provide you with a suitable Company car (cost circa £14,000), which is to be mainly for your business use but also for your private use. The Company will meet all normal running expenses associated with the car such as road tax, insurance, repairs, servicing and petrol.

Pensions

The Company operates its own Pension Plan. You can either decide to join the Company Scheme after six months' service at the Scheme's next anniversary date (July 199-), or alternatively choose a Personal Pension Plan to which the Company would contribute.

Hours

Normal office hours are from 9.00 a.m. to 5.15 p.m. from Monday to Friday with one hour for lunch. However, it is probable that additional calls will be made upon your time.

37 Arbeitsvertrag

Sehr geehrter Herr/geehrte Frau_____,

im Anschluß an unser kürzliches Gespräch freuen wir uns, Ihnen die Stellung als Regionalleiter zu den folgenden Bedingungen anbieten zu können:

Vergütung

Ihr Jahresgehalt beträgt 34500 DM sowie Provision auf der von uns bereits erörterten Basis. Die Auszahlung erfolgt wie für unsere ganze Belegschaft monatlich u. zw.[1] am letzten Donnerstag des Monats. Ihre erste Gehaltserhöhung wird im Juli 199- stattfinden.

Kündigung

Wie für unsere ganze Belegschaft gilt für Sie eine anfängliche Probezeit von sechs Monaten, während dieser eine beiderseitige Aufkündigung des Anstellungsverhältnisses jederzeit binnen sieben Tagen schriftlich erfolgen kann. Vorausgesetzt Ihre Probezeit verlief zu unserer Zufriedenheit, werden wir Ihre Festanstellung unmittelbar danach bestätigen. Die Kündigungsfrist wird sich in diesem Falle von sieben Tagen auf einen Monat verlängern.[2]

Krankengeld

Während berechtigter Abwesenheit aus Krankheitsgründen wird die Firma nach eigenem Ermessen die Krankenversicherungsbeiträge auf Ihr Gehaltsniveau ausgleichen. Dies wird aber im wesentlichen von der Zahl Ihrer Dienstjahre abhängen.

Urlaub

Ihr Anspruch auf bezahlten Urlaub beträgt normalerweise 20 Arbeitstage pro Jahr, mit Beginn am 1. Januar und Ende am 31. Dezember.

Firmenwagen

Wir stellen Ihnen einen geeigneten Firmenwagen (Kosten etwa 32000 DM) hauptsächlich für geschäftliche Zwecke aber auch für Ihren privaten Gebrauch zur Verfügung. Für die üblichen Betriebskosten wie Straßenbenützungsgebühr, Versicherung, Reparatur, Wartung und Treibstoff, werden wir aufkommen.

Altersversorgung

Die Firma hat ihren eigenen Altersversorgungsplan. Es steht Ihnen frei, der betrieblichen Rentenversicherung nach sechsmonatiger Dienstzeit zum nächsten Jahrestermin beizutreten oder einen privaten Pensionsplan zu wählen, zu dem die Firma Beitrag leistet.

Arbeitszeit

Normale Dienstzeit ist von 09.00–17.15 Uhr von Montag bis Freitag mit einer Stunde Mittagspause. Es ist aber durchaus möglich, daß Ihre Zeit zusätzlich in Anspruch genommen werden kann.

Grievance and Disciplinary Procedure
Should you wish to seek redress for any grievance relating to your employment, you should refer, as appropriate, either to the Company Secretary or to the Managing Director. Matters involving discipline will be dealt with in as fair and equitable a manner as possible.

Health & Safety at Work Act
A copy of the Staff Notice issued under the Health & Safety at Work Act 1974 will be given to you on the first day of your employment. Your acceptance of the appointment will be deemed to constitute your willingness to comply with these regulations.

Start Date
The date on which your employment by the Company is to commence remains to be agreed by us. We look forward to establishing a mutually acceptable date as soon as possible.

Will you kindly provide us with your acceptance of this offer of employment by signing and returning to us the enclosed duplicate copy of this letter.

We trust that you will have a long, happy and successful association with our Company.

Yours sincerely

B. Foster
Managing Director

Enc.

Beschwerde- und Disziplinarweg
Zur Bereinigung einer Beschwerdesituation sollten Sie sich entsprechend entweder an den Prokuristen oder an den Geschäftsführer wenden. Disziplinäre Angelegenheiten werden so gerecht und unparteilich wie möglich behandelt.

Arbeitsschutzvorschriften
Bei Dienstantritt erhalten Sie eine Belegschaftsmitteilung, ausgegeben im Zusammenhang mit dem Arbeitschutzgesetz von 1974. Ihre Annahme der Stellung gilt als Bereitschaft, diese Vorschriften einzuhalten.[3]

Beginn Ihrer Tätigkeit
Die Entscheidung über das Datum Ihres Arbeitsantritts bleibt der Firma vorbehalten. Wir hoffen, einen beiderseits geeigneten Zeitpunkt so bald wie möglich festzusetzen.

Zur Annahme unseres Stellenangebots wären wir Ihnen dankbar, wenn Sie die beiliegende Kopie dieses Briefes unterschrieben an uns zurücksenden würden.

Wir hoffen auf eine lange, glückliche und erfolgreiche Zusammenarbeit mit Ihnen.

Mit besten Grüßen

B. Förster
Geschäftsführer

Anlage
Kopie

1 *U. zw.*: 'und zwar'.
2 *Verlängern auf*: 'extend to'. Similarly *erhöhen auf*: 'increase to'.
3 *Vorschriften einhalten*: 'respect/keep to the regulations'. Also *einen Termin einhalten*: 'make/keep an appointment'.

38 Enquiring about regulations for purchase of property abroad (memo)

LUJIPROP SA

<u>Internal memorandum</u>

From: Terry Baddison (Customer Services)
To: Guillermo Estuardos (Legal Department)

Date: 9 September 199-

Message: I urgently need some information on current rules and regulations concerning the purchase and renting of property in Spain. We have some clients interested in the new complex at Carboneras, but we are not sure whether they can sublet part of the premises without paying local tax on the rental. Can you check this out ASAP?

P.S. I'm in the office every afternoon this week.

Terry

38 Anfrage über Vorschriften bezügl.[1] Immobilienkauf im Ausland (Mitteilung)

Hausmitteilung

Von: Herrn T. Petersen (Kundendienst)
An: Herrn G. Estuardos (Rechtsabteilung)

Datum: 09.09.9-

Ich brauche dringend Informationen über die derzeit gültigen Vorschriften und Bestimmungen betreffs Ankauf oder Miete spanischer Immobilien. Einige Kunden haben Interesse an der neuen Anlage in Carboneras, aber wir sind nicht sicher, ob sie Ortstaxe erlegen müssen, wenn sie die Räumlichkeiten weiter vermieten. Könnten Sie die Angelegenheit so bald wie möglich klären?

P.S. Ich bin die ganze Woche nachmittags im Hause.

T.

1 *Bezügl.*: abbreviation for *bezüglich*: 'concerning', 'regarding'.

39   Advising of delay in delivery (telex)

TELEX:	Expofrut (Almería, Spain) to Henshaw Bros. (Wolverhampton, England)
Subject:	Delay in delivery
Sender:	Pablo López
Addressee:	Mary Henshaw
Date:	1 May 199-
Message:	APOLOGIES FOR FAILING TO DELIVER USUAL ORDER THIS WEEK.

DOCKS STRIKE CALLED FROM TODAY THROUGHOUT SPAIN.

YOUR CONSIGNMENT OF FRUIT AND VEGETABLES ON QUAYSIDE. STILL POSSIBLE TO SEND GOODS BY ROAD, BUT COULD NOT GUARANTEE DELIVERY BY WEEKEND.

INFORM BY TELEPHONE (00 3451 947583) THIS P.M. IF TO PROCEED WITH ORDER BY ROAD.

REGARDS

Pablo López
(Export Manager)

39 Mitteilung über Lieferverzögerung (Fernschreiben)

TELEX: Expofrut (Almeria, Spanien)

                An
                Gebrüder Sievers (Bremen, Deutschland)

Betrifft: Lieferverzögerung

Absender: Pablo López
Adressat: Martin Sievers
Datum: 1. Mai 199-

Nachricht: Bedauern Ausfall der normalen Lieferung diese Woche.
                Hafenarbeiterstreik heute für ganz Spanien ausgerufen.
                Ihre Obst- und Gemüseladung z.Zt. im Hafen.[1] Möglichkeit des
                Straßentransports, aber keine Garantie, daß Lieferung bis
                Wochenende eintrifft. Bitte um Telefonbescheid (00 3451 947583)
                heute nachmittag wegen Straßentransport.

                MfG[2]
                Pablo López

1 *Z. Zt.*: *zur Zeit.*
2 *MfG*: abbreviation for *mit freundlichen Grüßen.*

40 Seeking clarification of financial position (fax)

To: Accounts Section, MULTIBANK,
            Prince's Square, Crewe

From: John Turket, PERLOANS
            High Street, Tamworth

Date: 4 November 199-

No. of pages, including this: 2

Dear Sir

This company has been approached today by a Mr Alan Thomas, who wishes to secure a loan in order to finance a family visit to relatives living overseas. He has given his approval to my contacting your branch of Multibank, where he holds two accounts, in order to verify and clarify information he has proffered about his financial position.

Once you have satisfied yourselves that Mr Thomas is willing that you divulge facts about his finances, can you please provide the following information?

1 Has Mr Thomas incurred major overdrafts since 1990?

2 Do both Mr Thomas and his wife have salary cheques paid directly each month into their current account?

3 Does your bank have any reason to believe that Mr Thomas will not be able to repay a £3,000 loan to Perloans over 3 years from July 199-.

We hope you feel able to respond to our request, and thank you for your assistance in this matter.

Yours faithfully

John Turket
Loans Manager

40 Einholung einer Bankreferenz (Fax)

An: Kontenabteilung, Oberbank
            Fürstenplatz, 86345 Augsburg

Von: Walter Türk, Kreditverleih FAMILIA
            Hauptstr. 34, Nürnberg.

Datum: 4. November 199-

Sehr geehrte Herren,

in einem Schreiben an unser Unternehmen bewirbt sich Herr Andreas Thomas um einen Kredit zur Finanzierung einer Reise, um mit seiner Familie Verwandte in Übersee zu besuchen. Er gab mir die Erlaubnis, mich mit Ihrer Filiale, bei der er Inhaber zweier Konten ist,[1] in Verbindung zu setzen, um seine eigene Auskunft über seine Finanzlage zu überprüfen.

Sobald Sie selbst Herrn Thomases Zustimmung zu Ihrer Auskunftserteilung eingeholt haben, wären wir Ihnen dankbar für die folgenden Informationen:

1. Hat Herr Thomas seine Konten seit 1990 in größerem Maße überzogen?

2. Werden die Monatsgehälter von Herrn Thomas sowie seiner Frau direkt auf ihre laufenden Konten überwiesen?

3. Hat Ihre Bank Grund zur Annahme, daß Herr Thomas nicht in der Lage ist, eine Anleihe von 6500 DM innerhalb von drei Jahren beginnend im Juli 199- zurückzuerstatten?

Wir hoffen, daß Sie in der Lage sind, unserem Ersuchen nachzukommen, und danken Ihnen für Ihre Hilfe in dieser Angelegenheit.

Mit besten Grüßen

Walter Türk
Leitung Kreditabteilung

1 *Zweier Konten*: this is very formal style. *Von zwei Konten* is less elevated.
2 *Innerhalb von drei Jahren*: *innerhalb* is used with the genitive if the genitive case can be indicated by an appropriate ending (*innerhalb einer Woche*). If not, then it is used with the dative, as here.

41 Reporting to client on availability of particular property (fax)

To: Ms L Topcopy
            Trendset Printers

From: Mrs D Russell
            Smith & Jones

Date: 6 September 199-

No. of pages, including this: 1

Re: Office for lease

Dear Ms Topcopy

I am faxing you urgently to let you know that office premises have just become available in the area of town you said you liked. The lease on a street-front shop with an office on the first floor has been cancelled early by another client who is moving south. If you would like to see the property, please get back to us this afternoon and we will arrange a visit.

Best wishes

Dorothy Russell

41 Kundeninformation bezügl. Bürovermietung (Fax)

An: Frau L. Gutenberg
Druck 2000

Von: Frau D. Rüßler
Zimmer & Frahm

Datum: 06.09.9-

Betrifft: Bürovermietung

Sehr geehrte Frau Gutenberg,

ich möchte Ihnen dringend mitteilen, daß Büroräume in dem von Ihnen bevorzugten Stadtteil verfügbar wurden. Einer unserer Kunden hat wegen seines beabsichtigten Umzugs nach Süddeutschland die Miete eines straßenseitig gelegenen Geschäftes mit Büro im 1. Stock vorzeitig gekündigt. Sollten Sie die Liegenschaft sehen wollen, bitte setzen Sie sich noch diesen Nachmittag mit uns in Verbindung, und wir vereinbaren eine Besichtigung.

MfG

D. Jensen

42   Complaining about customs delay (fax)

To:	HM Customs and Excise London
From:	Ordenasa, Madrid
Date:	21/2/9-
No. of pages:	1

Dear Sirs

On behalf of my director colleagues of this computer software business I wish to lodge a complaint about customs clearance at British airports.

On several occasions since October 199- materials freighted from Madrid to retailers in Great Britain have been subject to unexplained and unjustifiable delays. This company depends for success on its ability to respond quickly to market demand; furthermore, at all times the requisite export licences have been in order.

This communication by fax is prompted by the latest and most frustrating hold-up, at Gatwick Airport yesterday, which has allowed a market competitor to secure a valuable contract ahead of us.

If the Single Market is to function effectively this is precisely the type of situation that must be avoided. I intend to contact the relevant Chamber of Commerce, but in the meantime I insist on an explanation from your officers of why consignment AT/463 was not permitted immediate entry on 20 February 199-.

Yours faithfully

Dr. Norberto Mateos
(Managing Director)

42   Beschwerde über Zollprobleme (Fax)

An: Deutsche Zollbehörde, Frankfurt

Von: ORDENASA, Madrid

Datum: 21.02.9-

Sehr geehrte Damen und Herren,

im Namen meiner Vorstandskollegen im obigen Computer Software Unternehmen möchte ich mich über die Zollabfertigung am Frankfurter Flughafen beschweren.

Seit Oktober 199- wurden unsere per Luftfracht aus Madrid angelieferten Waren mehrmals unerklärlichen wie auch ungerechtfertigten Verzögerungen ausgesetzt.

Der Erfolg unserer Firma hängt von einem raschen Reagieren auf die Bedürfnisse des Marktes ab; noch dazu entsprachen die erforderlichen Einfuhrgenehmigungen zu jeder Zeit den geltenden Bestimmungen.

Diese Fax-Mitteilung ist eine Reaktion auf die jüngste und äußerst frustrierende gestrige Verzögerung am Frankfurter Flughafen, was einem Konkurrenzunternehmen einen bedeutenden Vorsprung bei einem Geschäftsabschluß zusicherte.

Zur reibungslosen Abwicklung des Gemeinsamen Binnenmarktes[1] sollten Situationen wie diese tunlichst vermieden werden.

Ich beabsichtige auch, mich an die zuständige Handelskammer zu wenden, doch inzwischen muß ich auf einer offiziellen Erklärung darüber bestehen, warum der Lieferung AT/463 am 20. Februar die direkte Einreise verweigert wurde.

Hochachtungsvoll

Dr. Norberto Mateos
Geschäftsführer

---

1   *Binnenmarkt* (here): Single Market. It can also be used to mean simply 'domestic market'.

43 Stating delivery conditions

1 August 199-

Your Reference: AD/LR
Our Reference: TH/PA

Sr José Escalante
Managing Director
Escalante e Hijos
Avenida del Sol
San Sebastián
SPAIN

Dear Mr Escalante

Thank you for your fax communication of yesterday regarding the delivery of the chickens and other poultry ordered by you from this company in early July. As we indicated in our original quote to Mr Salas, who first contacted us, the delivery can only be guaranteed if your bank is able to confirm that debts owed to us will be cleared this week.

Please note that our drivers would much appreciate assistance with overnight accommodation and that any costs they incur should be charged directly to Bridge Farm on completion of the delivery next week.

We look forward to hearing from you on both matters.

Yours sincerely

Tom Holbrook
Transport Manager

43 Versandbedingungen

1. August 199-

IDAL
z.H. Herrn W. Ecker, Geschäftsführer
Sonnenweg 28

D–25041 Kiel

Sehr geehrter Herr Ecker,

besten Dank für Ihre gestrige Faxmitteilung bezüglich der Hühner- und Geflügellieferung, die Sie bei uns Anfang Juli bestellt haben.[1] Wie wir bereits Herrn Stiller, unserem ersten Kontakt mit Ihnen, in unserer ursprünglichen Preisangabe bedeutet haben, können wir die Lieferung nur dann gewährleisten, wenn Ihre Bank noch diese Woche die Begleichung unserer Forderungen bestätigen kann.

Dürften wir Sie auch ersuchen, bei der Beschaffung von Übernachtungsgelegenheiten für unsere Transportfahrer behilflich zu sein, wobei alle in diesem Zusammenhang entstandenen Unkosten uns direkt nach Ausführung der Lieferung nächste Woche in Rechnung zu stellen sind.

Wir freuen uns, von Ihnen in beiden Angelegenheiten zu hören.

Mit besten Grüßen

Tom Holbrook
Transportleiter

1 *Anfang Juli*: 'at the beginning of July'. When used in the temporal sense, *Anfang* does not require a preposition (cf: *Mitte Mai, Ende Oktober*, but *am Ende der Straße*).

44 Confirming time/place of delivery

12 June 199-

Your Reference: RCG/LP
Our Reference: FG/JD

Dr Rosa Castro Giménez
Subdirectora
Departamento de Relaciones Exteriores
Ministerio de Industria
Quito
ECUADOR

Dear Madam

Further to our communication of 9 May in which we outlined to your department the likely oil needs of the companies we represent, it is with some concern that we have heard indirectly that your Ministry may be unable to fulfil its immediate responsibilities. We would be most obliged to hear, at your earliest convenience, that the draft agreement signed recently by our representatives remains valid.

In spite of our concern we are fully committed to the trading relations discussed and as such wish to confirm details of first delivery of manufactured goods being exchanged for the above-mentioned oil imports. Carlton Excavators plc have confirmed this week that the consignment of earthmovers, tractors and diggers bound for Constructores Velasco was loaded on Monday of this week. The consignment should reach the port of Guayaquil by the end of the month. We will, of course, provide you with more precise details nearer the time.

Meanwhile, please accept our best wishes for the continuation of our collaborative venture as we await your confirmation regarding the deliveries of your oil to our New South Wales terminal.

Yours faithfully

Frank Gardner
Senior Partner

44 Versandbestätigung

12. Juni 199-

Dr. Rosa Castro Gimnez
Subdirectora
Departamento de Relaciones Exteriores
Ministerio de Industria
Quito
Ecuador

Sehr geehrte Frau Dr. Castro Giménez,

wir beziehen uns auf unser Schreiben an Ihre Abteilung vom 9. Mai, in dem wir den erwarteten Ölbedarf der von uns vertretenen Unternehmen kurz darlegten. Zu unserer Besorgnis hören wir nun von anderer Seite, daß Ihr Ministerium möglicherweise nicht in der Lage ist, seinen direkten Verpflichtungen nachzukommen. Wir wären Ihnen daher äußerst dankbar, wenn Sie uns so bald wie möglich mitteilen könnten, ob der von Ihren Vertretern kürzlich unterzeichnete Vertragsentwurf weiterhin gültig bleibt.

Trotz unserer Besorgnis möchten wir unseren Einsatz für die abgesprochenen Handelsbeziehungen betonen und in diesem Zusammenhang die Einzelheiten des Versandes von Fertigprodukten im Austausch für obig erwähnte Ölimporte bestätigen.

Karlsson Baumaschinen GmbH haben diese Woche die Verschiffung einer Ladung von Traktoren, Baggern und anderen Maschinen zur Erdbewegung am Montag an die Firma Constructores Velasco bestätigt. Die Ladung wird den Hafen von Guayaquil voraussichtlich am Ende des Monats erreichen. Wir werden Ihnen selbstverständlich vorher noch genauere Einzelheiten zukommen lassen.

In der Zwischenzeit erwarten wir Ihre Bestätigung in bezug auf Ihre Öllieferung nach Hamburg und geben unseren Wünschen für die Fortdauer unserer gemeinsamen Unternehmungen Ausdruck.

Mit besten Grüßen

Friedrich Gärtner
Seniorpartner

45   Checking on mode of transportation

19 February 19-

Your ref. SM/MB
Our ref. TS/PU

Mr Sebastián Morán
Sales Manager
Hermanos García SA
Carretera Luis Vargas, 24
CUENCA
Spain

Dear Mr Morán

Thank you for your letter sent on Tuesday last in which you refer to the kitchen equipment we ordered from García Brothers in December. As you know, our market has been rather depressed, but there are recent signs of improvement, and as a result we now need to receive the cupboard doors and worktops much more promptly than hitherto.

Can you please confirm that where necessary you would be able to deliver some items by road, or even by air if very urgent, rather than by the sea route you currently use?

We have checked that from Valencia it would be possible to airfreight at a reasonable price to East Midlands Airport on a Monday afternoon and a Thursday evening.

I would be grateful if you could send us a reply confirming whether our proposal is viable.

Yours sincerely

Trevor Sharp
Warehouse Manager

45 Transportmittel

19. Februar 199-

Hager Küchen
z.H. Herrn S. Mann, Verkaufsleiter
Postfach 275

D 31856 Hannover

Sehr geehrter Herr Mann,

besten Dank für Ihren Brief vom letzten Dienstag bezüglich der von uns bei Ihnen im Dezember bestellten Kücheneinrichtungen. Wie Sie wissen, ist die Marktsituation bei uns zur Zeit noch ziemlich flau,[1] doch jüngsten Anzeichen von Erholung zufolge liegt uns daran, die Schranktüren und Arbeitsflächen pünktlicher als bisher zu erhalten.

Könnten Sie uns bitte verbindlich zusagen, daß Sie bei Bedarf bestimmte Artikel auf dem Landweg oder im dringenden Falle sogar auf dem Luftweg statt auf dem derzeit benützten Seeweg befördern könnten?

Unseres Wissens[2] gibt es jeden Montag nachmittag und jeden Donnerstag abend eine preisgünstige Luftfrachtverbindung von Hamburg zum Flughafen East Midlands.

Ich wäre Ihnen dankbar für Ihre Antwort, sollten Sie unsere Vorschläge annehmbar finden.

Mit freundlichen Grüßen

Trevor Sharp
Lagerhausleiter

1 *Flau*: 'flat', 'dead', 'lifeless'. Note also: *die Flaute*: 'recession'.
2 *Unseres Wissens*: this is very formal. *Wir glauben* ... would be just as acceptable.

46 Claiming for transportation damage

Claims Department
Lifeguard Assurance plc
Safeside House
High Street
Bromsgove
Worcs.

Dear Sir/Madam

POLICY NO. AL 78/2139B

My letter concerns a claim I wish to make on behalf of this firm, Anchor Lighting. We have had a policy with your company for many years, and rarely have needed to call upon your services. This time, however, we have suffered a serious financial loss due to damage incurred during the transit of goods.

Last week a whole consignment of lamps and other fittings was lost when our delivery truck ran off the road and turned over. The retail value of the merchandise ruined was in the region of £7,000, a sum equivalent to an entire quarter's profit.

I would be most grateful if you could send at your earliest convenience a major claim form and some general information on your settlement procedures.

Our policy number is as follows: AL 78/2139B.

I look forward to hearing from you soon.

Yours faithfully

Brian Tomkinson
Proprietor

46 Schadenersatzforderung für Transport

Adler Versicherung Gmbh
Luegerring 14/II

1010 Wien

Sehr geehrte Damen und Herren,

ich beziehe mich in meinem Schreiben auf einen Antrag auf Schadenersatz, den ich im Namen der Firma Anker Beleuchtungshaus stellen möchte. Wir haben seit Jahren einen Versicherungsvertrag mit Ihrer Gesellschaft und hatten nur wenig Anlaß, Ihre Dienste in Anspruch zu nehmen. Diesmal aber erlitten wir ernsthafte finanzielle Verluste aufgrund von Beschädigung unserer Waren beim Transport.

Eine gesamte Ladung von Lampen und anderen Beleuchtungskörpern wurde letzte Woche zerstört, als unser Lieferwagen von der Straße abkam und umstürzte. Der Verkaufswert der nun unbrauchbaren Waren belief sich auf 700 000, -S, was dem Gewinn eines ganzen Quartals entspricht.

Bitte schicken Sie so bald wie möglich ein Antragsformular sowie allgemeine Informationen über Ihr Auszahlungsverfahren.

Unsere Versicherungspolizze hat die Nummer AL 78/21398.

Ich würde mich freuen, bald von Ihnen zu hören.

Mit besten Grüßen

Andreas Hofer
Inhaber

47 Enquiring about customs clearance

5 November 199-

Your ref.
Our ref. TC/LJ

The Customs and Excise Branch
Chilean Trade Ministry
SANTIAGO
Chile
South America

Dear Sirs

I have been advised to write to you directly by the Commercial Section of the Chilean Embassy in London. My company produces high-tech toys for the world market. At a recent trade fair in Barcelona several Chilean retailers expressed interest in importing our products. They were, however, unable to provide information on customs formalities in your country. Similarly, the London Embassy has recommended that I consult your Branch to seek up-to-date information.

The situation is as follows: our products include computer games, remote-control toy cars and mini-sized televisions. It seems that goods made in the EU are subject to a customs process rather more restrictive than those from Japan or the USA. As my company is a wholly-owned subsidiary of a US parent firm, would it be easier and cheaper to export to Chile from the USA rather than from Britain?

Our intention is not merely to circumvent regulations but to optimize our operations at a time when such matters as customs clearance can result in costly delays.

We thank you for your attention and look forward to an early reply from you.

Yours sincerely

Thomas Carty
Managing Director

47 Erkundigung über Zollabfertigung

5 November 199-

An das
Handelsministerium der Republik Chile
Zollabteilung

Santiago
Chile

Sehr geehrte Damen und Herren,

auf Anraten der chilenischen Botschaft, Sektion Handel, richten wir unser
Schreiben direkt an Sie. Wir sind Hersteller von High-Tech-Spielzeug für den
Weltmarkt. Auf einer Messe in Barcelona zeigten sich unlängst einige chilenische
Einzelhändler sehr interessiert an einer Einfuhr unserer Waren. Leider aber waren
sie nicht in der Lage, Auskunft über die Zollformalitäten Ihres Landes zu geben,
ähnlich wie die Botschaft in Bonn, die uns daher empfahl, Sie um Auskunft über
den neuesten Stand der Dinge zu ersuchen.

Es handelt sich um folgende Situation: Wir führen unter anderem
Computerspiele, Spielzeugautos mit Fernsteuerung und
Miniatur-Fernsehapparate. Dem Anschein nach sind Erzeugnisse der
Europäischen Union einem strengeren Zollverfahren unterworfen als die aus
Japan oder den USA.[1] Da unser Betrieb die Tochterfirma[2] im Alleinbesitz eines
US-Unternehmens ist, möchten wir gerne wissen, ob der Export nach Chile aus
den Vereinigten Staaten problemloser und billiger als aus der Bundesrepublik
wäre.

Es liegt uns nicht so sehr an der Umgehung von Bestimmungen, sondern an
einer bestmöglichen Abwicklung unserer Geschäfte unter Vermeidung von
kostspieligen Verzögerungen in der Zollabfertigung.

Wir wären Ihnen dankbar, wenn Sie diesem Sachverhalt Ihre Aufmerksamkeit
schenken würden, und freuen uns, bald von Ihnen zu hören.

Mit besten Grüßen

Thomas Kettner
Geschäftsleiter

1 Note the construction *aus den USA*; because USA is plural.
2 *Tochterfirma*: 'subsidiary company'. Similarly, *Muttergesellschaft*: 'parent company'.

48 Undertaking customs formalities

27 November 199-

Your ref.
Our ref. RM/AP

HM Customs and Excise
Government Offices
LONDON WC2

Dear Sir/Madam

I write to inform you of a business operation in which my company is to be involved for the first time and to request your advice in the case of any misapprehension on my part.

As sole director of Leatherlux I have recently been able to conclude a deal with a firm of suppliers in Tunisia. I imagine that as a non-EU nation Tunisia cannot trade with complete freedom from import/export levies. I wish therefore to inform you that I intend to import from Nabeul in the next fortnight the following articles:

    150 men's leather jackets
     50 pairs of ladies' leather trousers
    250 leather belts
    100 pairs of leather sandals
     50 pairs of men's leather boots

I anticipate paying approximately £3,000 for the consignment. Can you please provide me with official documentation (if required) or at least confirm by fax that I shall be required to pay some form of duty on these imports?

I thank you in anticipation of your assistance.

Yours faithfully

Royston McAughey
Managing Director

48 Zollformalitäten

27. November 199-

An das Zollamt
Heinestr. 27

40002 Düsseldorf

Sehr geehrte Damen und Herren,

in Zusammenhang mit für meine Firma neuartigen geschäftlichen
Unternehmungen möchte ich mich an Sie um Rat wenden,[1] um
Mißverständnisse meinerseits möglichst zu vermeiden.

Als alleiniger Geschäftsleiter von Lederlux gelang mir kürzlich ein
Geschäftsabschluß mit einer Lieferantenfirma in Tunesien. Da Tunesien als
Nicht-EU-Land gewissen Ein- und Ausfuhrabgaben unterliegen dürfte, möchte
ich Ihnen hiermit zur Kenntnis bringen, daß ich in den nächsten 14 Tagen
folgende Artikel aus Nabeul zu importieren beabsichtige:

150 Lederjacken für Herren
 50 Lederhosen für Damen
250 Ledergürtel
100 Paar Ledersandalen
 50 Lederstiefel für Herren

Der Preis für die Lieferung beträgt etwa 6900,- DM. Könnten Sie mir bitte
nötigenfalls amtliche Papiere zukommen lassen oder zumindest möglichst per
Fax bestätigen, daß ich gewisse Einfuhrabgaben zu entrichten habe.

Ich danke Ihnen im voraus für Ihre Hilfe und verbleibe

mit besten Grüßen

Richard Vandenhove
Geschäftsleiter

1 *Um Rat*: 'for advice'. Note the preposition.

49 Informing of storage facilities

13 June 199-

Your ref. JG/TK
Our ref. JS/PI

Hurd's (International) Removals
34–36, Wesley Avenue
CROYDON
Surrey

Dear Mrs Gordon

I am pleased to inform you that the container of household goods your company contracted us to transport from Australia has now been delivered to our depot here in Kent.

We will need by the end of this week to complete the official formalities, but you are welcome to pick up the unloaded contents for onward delivery to your customer from next Monday.

If you prefer to leave the goods here in store until further notice, please consult our price list (enclosed) for storage facilities and let us know your intention by fax.

As and when your driver does come to pick up the goods, he should enter the terminal by the side entrance which will lead him straight to the relevant loading area, marked DOMESTIC.

I trust these arrangements meet with your approval.

Yours sincerely

Jim Smith
Depot Manager

Enc.

49 Mitteilung zur Warenlagerung

13. Juni 199-

Spedition Hirt
z. H. Frau G. Jäger
Friesenweg 18-20

27456 Bremen

Sehr geehrte Frau Jäger,

wir freuen uns, Ihnen mitteilen zu können, daß der Container mit
Haushaltsgeräten, den wir im Auftrag Ihrer Firma aus Spanien beförderten, nun
in unserem Depot hier in Bremerhaven eingelangt ist.

Die amtlichen Formalitäten müssen bis zum Ende dieser Woche von uns erledigt
werden. Ab nächsten Montag können Sie dann die entladenen Waren zur
Weiterbeförderung an Ihre Kunden hier abholen.

Sollten Sie aber vorziehen, die Waren bis auf weiteres hier zu lagern, entnehmen
Sie bitte die Lagergebühren der beiliegenden Preisliste und faxen Sie uns Ihre
Mitteilung.

Zur Abholung der Waren sollte Ihr Fahrer den Seiteneingang zum
Kontainerterminal benutzen und direkt zum Ladebereich bezeichnet INLAND
weiterfahren.

Mit besten Grüßen

J. Schmidt
Depotleiter

Anlage
Preisliste

50 Assuring of confidentiality of information

1 November 199-

Your ref. EF/LJ
Our ref. HE/PI

Dr Ernesto Furillo
University Hospital
University of Managua
Managua
República de Nicaragua

Dear Dr Furillo

MISS ALICIA BARTOLOMÉ

Thank you for your letter of last month in which you sought confirmation that the reference you provided for Miss Alicia Bartolomé and her personal details would remain confidential.

It is the policy of the Government and of this Ministry to maintain total discretion when dealing with citizens from other countries who come here in order to develop their professional studies. Miss Bartolomé's course begins in three weeks' time. By then, her curriculum vitae will have been duly stored on computer in this Ministry and will be accessible only to those with the due authorization.

You may rest assured that all proper measures will be taken to protect the interests of our students.

Yours sincerely

Hortensia Enríquez Castro
Personnel Supervisor

50 Versicherung der Datengeheimhaltung

1. November 199-

Frau
Dr. E. F. Firth
University Hospital
University of Edinburgh

Edinburg
Großbritannien

Sehr geehrte Frau Dr. Firth,

wir danken Ihnen für Ihren Brief vom letzten Monat, in dem Sie uns ersuchen, die vertrauliche Behandlung Ihrer Referenz für Frl. Angela Bartholomew sowie ihrer persönlichen Daten zu bestätigen.

Der Datenschutz in bezug auf ausländische Studenten wird von unserer Universität grundsätzlich wahrgenommen. Die Vorlesungen für Frl. Bartholomews Studium beginnen in drei Wochen. Bis dahin wird ihr Lebenslauf im Universitätskomputer gespeichert und nur befugten Personen zugänglich sein.

Sie können also sicher sein, daß vollste Diskretion im Interesse unserer Studenten gewahrt bleibt.

Mit besten Grüßen

Dr. G. Radtner

51 Informing a client on conditions of loans/mortgages available

14 July 199-

Your ref. GB/LK
Our ref. PH/VE

Mr G Brookham
Managing Director
MultiCast
Floor 11
Forum House
Dukeries Avenue
Mansfield

Dear Mr Brookham

Since receiving your letter of 23 June we have been making enquiries on the matter of financing that you raised; please accept our apologies, nevertheless, for the delay. You will find enclosed three leaflets containing information about properties you may find interesting. We shall await your reaction to them.

More pressing, perhaps, is the question of finance. Having consulted local banks as well as our own finance broker, we conclude that you would do best to arrange a meeting with the latter. Charles Element will be pleased to outline for you a variety of mortgage as well as short-term loan plans.

All four major banks in town offer facilities for loans, so you may prefer to try them before or after meeting Mr Element. However, it certainly appears that our broker can secure more favourable conditions if you are interested principally in a short-term loan.

Please see our broker's details below:

Element Financial Services, Star Chambers, High Street, Worksop, Nottinghamshire.

Yours sincerely

Percy Hartshorn
Customer Liaison

Encs

51   Auskunft über Anleihen bzw. Hypotheken

14. Juli 199-

TV Becker GmbH
z. H. Herrn G. Bacher, Geschäftsleiter
Hölderlinstr. 59

87401 Kempten i. Allgäu

Sehr geehrter Herr Bacher,

seit dem Erhalt Ihres Briefes von 23. Juni haben wir uns über die von Ihnen erwähnten Finanzierungsmöglichkeiten hier erkundigt. Bitte entschuldigen Sie die daher verspätete Antwort. In der Anlage finden Sie drei Prospekte mit Information über Räumlichkeiten, die Sie interessieren dürften. Sie bedürfen keiner weiteren Erklärung[1] und wir erwarten Ihre Stellungnahme dazu.

Die Frage der Finanzierung ist vielleicht etwas drängender. Als Ergebnis unserer Erkundigungen bei den hiesigen Banken wie auch bei unserem eigenen Finanzmakler möchten wir Ihnen raten,[2] einen Termin mit letzterem zu vereinbaren. Herr Lederer wird Ihnen gerne einen Überblick über verschiedene Hypothekenarten und kurzfristige[3] Darlehen geben.

Da alle vier größeren Banken der Stadt Darlehen gewähren, wäre es vielleicht ratsam, sie vor oder nach Ihrer Besprechung mit Herrn Lederer zu konsultieren. Wenn Sie aber hauptsächlich nur an einem kurzfristigen Darlehen interessiert sind, ist unser Makler bestimmt besser in der Lage, Ihnen günstigere Bedingungen dafür zu vermitteln.

Hier die Adresse unseres Maklers:
Lederer Finanzen, Hauptplatz 26, 88003 Konstanz

Mit besten Grüßen

Paul Formann
Kundendienst

Anlage
Drei Prospekte

---

1   *Bedürfen* is used with the genitive. *Brauchen* and *benötigen* take the accusative.
2   *Raten* takes the dative. *Beraten* is used with the accusative.
3   *Kurzfristig*: 'short-term'. Medium-term: *mittelfristig*; long-term: *langfristig*.

52   Circulating local businesses with property services available

Our ref. CE/MB

To: Directors of all businesses in the
     Castilla-León region

Dear Colleague

I take the opportunity to write to you on behalf of myself and my partner in order to publicize as widely as possible the property services we can make available to businesses in the region.

Since establishing our company here in 1976 we have gradually expanded our range of activities and clients. Most recently we have opened a free advice centre in Puentenorte for any member of the public to obtain up-to-date information on the property market.

As regards the needs of business, we offer the following services:

- a weekly guide to premises for rent and sale
- a direct link to sources of finance
- rent-collection service
- legal and insurance consultancy
- assistance in securing mortgages
- technical support in planning space and furbishment
- computer database linked to the national property network

These and many more services are available from us, and all are on your doorstep. Don't hesitate – call us today, or come in person, when you can be sure of a warm welcome.

Yours sincerely

Carlos Estévez

52 Rundschreiben bezügl. Dienstleistungen einer Immobilienfirma

(Adresse)

Sehr geehrte Damen und Herren,

mein Geschäftspartner und ich möchten hiermit die Gelegenheit ergreifen, Sie auf unsere Dienstleistungen im Bereich Geschäftsimmobilien in Berlin und Umgebung aufmerksam zu machen.[1]

Seit der Gründung unserer Firma im Jahre 1976 haben wir unser Angebot und unseren Kundenkreis allmählich vergrößert. Mit der kürzlichen Eröffnung unseres Beratungszentrums in Berlin ist auch aktuelle Information über den Immobilienmarkt für jedermann kostenlos erhältlich.

Speziell für den unternehmerischen Bedarf bieten wir folgende Leistungen:

- ein wöchentliches Anzeigenblatt für Miet- und Kaufgelegenheiten
- direkte Verbindung zu Finanzquellen
- Mietkassierungsdienst
- Beratung in Rechts- und Versicherungsangelegenheiten
- Hilfe bei der Hypothekenerwerbung
- fachliche[2] Unterstützung bei Raumplanung und Möblierung
- Datenbank mit Anschluß an das überregionale Immobilien-Datennetz

Zu Ihrer weiteren Information stehen wir Ihnen gerne zur Verfügung. Wir würden uns über Ihren Anruf oder Besuch sehr freuen.[3]

Mit den besten Grüßen

Hermann Kunze

1 Alternative to *aufmerksam machen*: *Ihre Aufmerksamkeit auf ... lenken*.
2 *Fachlich*: 'specialist'. Cf: *Fachleute*: 'experts', 'specialists'.
3 *Sich freuen über*: 'be pleased about'. *sich freuen auf*: 'to look forward to'.

53 Advertising maintenance services available for office equipment

30 January 199-

Your ref.
Our ref. TH/JY

To: Office Managers
     Motor Sales businesses
     in South London area

Dear Colleague

You may be aware from press advertising that our firm offers a new service to the motor trade, in particular to maintain equipment used in processing stores supplies. Most large dealerships with service and accessories departments have installed a fully integrated system that reduces drastically the need for large numbers of warehousemen.

The service charge is £350 per quarter, irrespective of visits made or problems solved; this figure also includes a component of insurance that covers both the dealership and ourselves against major breakdowns.

In recent months we have signed such service contracts with more than 40 dealerships whose names we are happy to supply if you are interested in checking our claims.

Thank you for your attention. Please do not hesitate to ring or fax us this week if the enclosed leaflet information is relevant to your needs.

Yours sincerely

Tom Henderson
Managing Director

Enc.

53 Rundschreiben bezügl. Wartung von Lagerhauskontrollsystemen

30. Januar 199-

(Adresse)

Sehr geehrte Damen und Herren,

unsere Firma ist Ihnen möglicherweise aus Pressewerbung bereits bekannt. Wir bieten einen neuartigen Service im Kfz-Handel[1] bezügl. der Wartung von elektronischen Lagerhauskontrollgeräten. Die meisten größeren Handelsunternehmen mit eigenen Kundendienst- und Zubehörabteilungen verfügen über ein einheitliches System, das die Zahl der notwendigen Lagerhausarbeiter wesentlich reduziert.

Die Service-Gebühr beträgt DM 805 pro Quartal unabhängig von Besuchen unserer Mitarbeiter oder Reparaturen. Dieser Betrag enthält auch einen Versicherungsbeitrag gegen Betriebsschäden auf beiden Seiten.

In den letzten Monaten kamen wir mit über 40 Händlern zum Abschluß eines Service-Vertrags. Zur Prüfung unserer Leistungen sind wir gern bereit, Ihnen eine Liste ihrer Namen zu übersenden.

Wir danken Ihnen für Ihr Interesse. Sollte die beiliegende Information auf Ihre Bedürfnisse zutreffen, würden wir uns freuen, von Ihnen telefonisch oder per Fax zu hören.

Mit freundlichen Grüßen

T. Hillinger
Geschäftsleiter

Anlage
Information

1 *Kfz*: abbreviation for *Kraftfahrzeug* ('vehicle').

54 Arranging a meeting for further discussions

28 August 199-

Our ref: TSS/EHK

Mr Angelo Ricasso
Cuscinetti SAS
Via Alessandro Manzoni, 32
20050 Triuggio (MI)
Italy

Dear Mr Ricasso

RE: THRUST BEARINGS

In 1989 we had discussions regarding the addition of our thrust bearings to the Dudley range for sale in your country.

We regret that due to many changes which have occurred in this company and in our parent company no progress was made with our arrangements, and we understand that it must have been disappointing for you not to have heard from us for such a long time.

We are now willing to try again, if you have not made other arrangements and we would like to arrange a meeting with you in Cologne at the Hardware Fair next March.

We look forward to hearing from you.

Yours sincerely

Thomas Stone
SALES DIRECTOR

54 Festsetzung eines weiteren Besprechungstermins

28. August 199-

Firma Steiner & Co
z.H. Herrn F. Steiner
Postfach 259

82400 München

Betrifft: Drucklager

Sehr geehrter Herr Steiner,

wir hatten im Jahre 1989 die Möglichkeit mit Ihnen besprochen, unsere Drucklager in die in Deutschland erhältliche Dudley Produktreihe aufzunehmen.

Es tut uns leid, daß aufgrund von betrieblichen Veränderungen bei uns sowie bei unserer Muttergesellschaft keinerlei Fortschritte in dieser Angelegenheit gemacht wurden, und wir verstehen Ihre Enttäuschung darüber, so lange nicht von uns gehört zu haben.

Falls Sie keine anderen Schritte unternommen haben, würden wir gerne noch einmal mit Ihnen über die Angelegenheit sprechen und möchten ein Treffen in Köln auf der Messe[1] für Eisenwaren im März vorschlagen.

Wir freuen uns, bald von Ihnen zu hören.

Mit besten Grüßen

T. Stone
Verkaufsleiter

1 *Auf der Messe*: 'at the trade fair'. Note the preposition.

55 Reservations

Enquiry about hotel accommodation (fax)

Hotel Lucullus
Amadeusplatz 27
Hannover
Germany

Dear Sirs

I am attending the trade fair in Hanover in May with two colleagues, and we require rooms for three nights. Please could you confirm availability and price of the following:

   three single rooms with bath/shower from 3 to 6 May.

Yours faithfully

Fred Garner

55 Reservierungen

Auskunft bezügl. Hotelunterkunft (Fax)

Hotel Lucullus
Amadeusplatz 27

D–30005 Hannover

Sehr geehrte Herren,

ich beabsichtige, die Hannoveraner Messe im Mai mit zwei meiner Kollegen zu besuchen und benötige daher Zimmer für drei Nächte. Könnten Sie bitte Tarif und Verfügbarkeit für drei Einzelzimmer mit Bad oder Dusche für die Zeit vom 3. bis 6. Mai bestätigen.

Mit freundlichen Grüßen

Fred Garner

56 Reservations

Confirmation of reservation (fax)

Ms G Cole
Ledington Parker plc
Moreton Avenue
Birmingham
B37 9KH

Dear Ms Cole

Room reservation 15–18 November

We confirm that we are able to offer the following accommodation:

> Four single rooms with shower/WC @ £150 per night, inclusive of breakfast and service.

We should be grateful if you could confirm the booking in writing as soon as possible.

Yours sincerely

H Japer

56 Reservierungen

Bestätigung einer Buchung (Fax)

Föttinger & Co
z.H. Frau Gerda Kohl
Ringstr. 19

A 4600 Wels

Betr: Zimmerreservierung 15. – 18. November

Sehr geehrte Frau Kohl,

wir bestätigen, daß folgende Unterkunft verfügbar ist:

4 Einzelzimmer mit Dusche und WC zu DM 345 pro Nacht,[1] einschließlich Frühstück und Bedienung.

Wir wären Ihnen dankbar, wenn Sie Ihre Buchung so bald wie möglich schriftlich bestätigen könnten.

Mit besten Grüßen

H. Japer

1   Note the use of *zu* ('at 345 Marks').

57 Reservations

Change of arrival date

Ms J Hinton
Hotel Bonner
46 Southampton Way
London
SE39 8UH
England

Dear Madam

We have today received your confirmation of our booking of three single rooms from 18 to 23 March.

Unfortunately, we have had to change our plans, and shall not now arrive in London until the morning of 20 March. We would be grateful if you could change the reservation accordingly.

Yours faithfully

57 Reservierungsänderung

Hotel Bonner
z. H. Frau J. Hinton
46 Southampton Way

London
SE39 8UH
Großbritannien

Sehr geehrte Frau Hinton,

wir haben heute Ihre Bestätigung unserer Reservierung von drei Einbettzimmern von 18. bis 23. März erhalten.

Leider mußten wir unsere Pläne ändern und werden daher erst am 20. März vormittags in London ankommen. Bitte können Sie unsere Reservierung dementsprechend abändern.

Mit freundlichen Grüßen

H. Klempner
Personalabteilung

58   Reservations

Request for confirmation of reservation

Ms J Petersen
45 Dorrington Terrace
Bradford
Yorkshire
England

Dear Ms Petersen

You made a telephone reservation one week ago for a single room for two nights (20–22 July). We indicated to you when you made the reservation that we would hold it for one week, but that we required written confirmation.

If you still require the room, could you please confirm within 24 hours, or we shall have to reserve the room for other clients.

Thank you for your co-operation.

Yours sincerely

58 Reservierungen

Ersuchen um Bestätigung

Frau J. Petersen
45 Dorrington Terrace

Bradford
Yorkshire
Großbritannien

Sehr geehrte Frau Petersen,

vor einer Woche reservierten Sie telefonisch ein Einbettzimmer für zwei Nächte
(20. – 22. Juli). Dabei wiesen wir Sie darauf hin, daß wir das Zimmer eine Woche
halten würden, aber eine schriftliche Bestätigung benötigten.

Bitte können Sie in den nächsten 24 Stunden bestätigen, daß Sie die Buchung
noch wünschen, anderenfalls wird das Zimmer an andere Gäste vergeben.

Wir danken Ihnen für Ihr Verständnis.

Mit freundlichen Grüßen

J. Simpel

59 Insurance

Request for quotation for fleet car insurance

Hartson Insurance Services
24 Westbury Way
Sheffield
S12 9JF

Dear Sirs

We understand from colleagues that you specialize in insurance for company fleet cars. We have a large fleet of executive saloons, and are currently obtaining quotations for insurance cover.

If you are interested in giving us a quotation, could you please contact Ms Helen Bridges, our fleet manager, who will give you the appropriate details.

Yours faithfully

D J Spratt

59 Versicherung

Ersuchen um Angebot für Firmenwagenversicherung

Carstorp Versicherung
Westenbergstr. 24

14003 Potsdam

Sehr geehrte Damen und Herren,

von Geschäftsfreunden erfahren wir, daß Sie sich auf die Versicherung von Firmenwagen spezialisieren.[1] Wir verfügen über einen größeren Wagenpark bestehend aus Wagen der gehobenen Klasse, für die wir zur Zeit Versicherungsangebote einholen.

Wenn Sie uns ein Angebot machen wollen, wenden Sie sich bitte an Frau Helene Bruckner, Wagenparkverwaltung, um genauere Einzelheiten.

Mit freundlichen Grüßen

D. Späth

1 *Sich spezialisieren auf*: 'to specialize in'. Note the preposition. (But: *sich interessieren für*: 'to be interested in').

60 Insurance

Reminder of overdue premium

Mr R Collins
45 Delta Road
Stoke-on-Trent

Dear Mr Collins

Your vehicle, registration no H351 AWL is currently insured by us. We sent you several days ago a reminder that the insurance renewal premium was due. As we have still not received this from you, we have to inform you that unless we receive payment within 72 hours, the insurance cover will lapse. Please send payment directly to our office in Gower Street, London.

Yours sincerely

60 Versicherung

Mahnung bezügl. überfälliger Prämie

Herrn R. Koller
Dürerstr. 38

91000 Nürnberg

Sehr geehrter Herr Koller,

Ihr Fahrzeug, Kennzeichen NÜ 351 AW3, ist gegenwärtig bei uns versichert. Vor einiger Zeit schickten wir Ihnen eine Mahnung bezügl. der ausstehenden Zahlung Ihrer Erneuerungsprämie. Da wir diese bis jetzt noch nicht erhalten haben, müssen wir Ihnen mitteilen, daß Ihre Versicherung verfällt, wenn wir nicht binnen 72 Stunden Zahlung von Ihnen erhalten. Bitte überweisen Sie den Betrag direkt an unser Berliner Büro.[1]

Hochachtungsvoll

R. Mansion

1 *Überweisen an*: 'transfer to'. to transfer money to an account: *Geld auf ein Konto überweisen.*

61   Insurance

Submission of documents to support a claim

Darton Insurance Services
59 Tristan Road
Uttoxeter
Staffordshire

Dear Sirs

I submitted to you several days ago a claim form under the terms of my motor vehicle insurance (policy number CDF 9486756 UY 94766). Your head office has since requested from me the original policy document. I regret that this is no longer in my possession, and I enclose herewith a photocopy. I trust that this will meet your requirements.

Yours faithfully

A Lightowlers

Enc.

61   Versicherung

Vorlage von Dokumenten bei Versicherungsanspruch

MBS Versicherungsanstalt
Tristanstr. 41

4020 Linz

Sehr geehrte Herren,

vor einigen Tagen sandte ich Ihnen ein Formular zur Geltungmachung eines Anspruchs aufgrund meiner Kfz-Versicherung (Polizzennr. CDF 9486756 UY 94766). Von Ihrem Hauptbüro erhielt ich nun die Aufforderung, die Polizze im Original vorzulegen, was leider nicht möglich ist, da sich das Dokument nicht mehr in meinem Besitz befindet. Ich hoffe, Sie finden es akzeptabel, wenn ich daher eine Photokopie der Polizze beilege.

Mit freundlichen Grüßen

H. Beyer

<u>Anlage</u>
Photokopie

62 Insurance

Taking out third party vehicle insurance

Uxbridge Insurance
Grosvenor House
12b Weston Terrace
Bournemouth
Hants

Dear Sirs

After receiving your quotation, I confirm that I wish to take out Third Party car insurance, and enclose the appropriate fee in the form of a cheque.

I should be grateful if you could send me confirmation and the policy certificate as soon as possible.

Yours faithfully

Penny Simpkin

62 Versicherung

Abschluß einer Kfz-Haftpflichtversicherung[1]

Liebstock Versicherung
Am Hof 25

23000 Lübeck

Sehr geehrte Damen und Herren

Nach Erhalt Ihres Angebots bin ich bereit, eine Kfz-Haftpflichtversicherung abzuschließen und lege die entsprechende Gebühr in Form eines Schecks bei.

Für die möglichst baldige Übersendung der Polizze sowie einer Bestätigung wäre ich Ihnen dankbar.

Mit freundlichen Grüßen

G. Schubarth

1 *Kfz*: abbreviation for *Kraftfahrzeug* 'motor vehicle'.

63 Insurance

Refusal to meet claim

Ms D Leach
29 Janison Avenue
York

Dear Ms Leach

RE: CLAIM NO. JH 8576/HY

We acknowledge receipt of your claim form (reference JH 8576/HY) for water damage to your stock on the night of 27 March.

We regret, however, that our company is unable to meet your claim, as our policy (section 3, paragraph 5) specifically excludes this form of damage, particularly since the premises were unoccupied for a period of two weeks before the damage occurred.

Yours sincerely

P Hartwell

63 Versicherung

Ablehnung eines Anspruchs

Frau Dorte Becker
Rablstr. 37

44602 Dortmund

Sehr geehrte Frau Becker,

wir bestätigen den Empfang Ihres Antragsformulars (Zeichen JH 8576/HY)
bezügl.[1] des in der Nacht vom 27. Mai an Ihrem Warenlager entstandenen
Wasserschadens.

Leider sind wir nicht in der Lage, Ihrem Anspruch stattzugeben, da diese Art von
Schaden ausdrücklich als Versicherungsbegrenzung in Ihrer Polizze (Abschnitt 3,
Paragraph 5) aufscheint. Noch dazu wurden die Geschäftsräume vor der
Entstehung des Schadens zwei Wochen lang nicht benützt.

Mit freundlichen Grüßen

P. Stark

1 *Bezügl.*: abbreviation of *bezüglich*. Takes the genitive.

64   Considering legal action

24 May 199-

Cabinet Rossignol
4 rue des Glaïeuls
75009 Paris
France

<u>For the attention of Maître Patelin</u>

Dear Maître Patelin

Your name was given to us by Robert Mackenzie of Canine Crunch Ltd for whom you acted last year.

We have a complaint against the newspaper *La Gazette du Samedi* who have, in our opinion, seriously defamed us in the enclosed article dealing with the closure of our plant at Roissy-en-France.

We would wish to take legal action against the said journal but first would like to have your professional advice on the strength of our case. Could you also let us know how long such a case might run and the likely scale of our legal costs.

Yours sincerely

Lionel E Bone
Managing Director

Enc.

64 Erwägung des Rechtsweges

Herrn
Dr. Franz Billig
Rechtsanwalt
Heinrich-Heine-Str. 72

D–53000 Bonn

Sehr geehrter Herr Dr. Billig,

wir wenden uns an Sie auf Vorschlag von Herrn Robert Mackenzie von der Firma Canine Crunch Ltd, für die Sie im letzten Jahr als Rechtsvertreter fungierten.

Wir erheben Beschwerde gegen die Zeitung 'Samstagsblatt', die sich unserer Meinung nach in dem beiliegenden Artikel über die Stillegung unserer Fabrik in Mönchengladbach einer schweren Defamierung unserer Firma schuldig macht.

Wir sind bereit, gegen die besagte Zeitung zu prozessieren, möchten aber vorerst Ihren fachmännischen[1] Rat mit Bezug auf die Stichhaltigkeit unseres Falles einholen. Könnten Sie uns auch gleichzeitig über die erwartete Prozeßdauer und die voraussichtlichen Gerichtskosten unterrichten.

MIt besten Grüßen

Lionel E. Bone
Geschäftsleiter

Anlage

Artikel

---

1 *Fachmännisch*: 'expert'. Note also: *Fachmann* (pl. *Fachleute*); 'expert'. *Fachgebiet*: 'specialist area', 'specialism'.

65 Requesting information on setting up a plant abroad

23 May 199-

Office Notarial
84 rue du Grand Pineau
85000 Olonnes sur Mer
France

Dear Sirs

Our company is proposing to set up a dairy produce processing plant in western France and we would like you to find us a suitable site.

We need either freehold or leasehold premises of 2,000 square metres on a plot with easy access for large vehicles.

Can you help us in finding the site and act for us in its acquisition? This is our first venture into France so we would appreciate all additional information about property purchase or leasing.

Yours faithfully

Arthur Sturrock
Managing Director

65 Erkundigung über Gründung einer Produktionsanlage im Ausland

23. Mai 199-

Notariatskanzlei Dr. S. Grasskamp
Fontaneweg 37

D–17236 Greifswald

Sehr geehrte Damen und Herren,

unser Unternehmen beabsichtigt, in Ostdeutschland eine Anlage zur Konservierung von Molkereiprodukten einzurichten,[1] und wir möchten Sie ersuchen, uns ein geeignetes Gelände zu finden.

Wir benötigen eine gewerbliche Nutzfläche von etwa 2000m^2, entweder zum Verkauf oder zur Pacht, auf einem für große Fahrzeuge leicht zugänglichen Grundstück.

Wir wären Ihnen dankbar für Ihre Hilfe bei der Suche und beim Erwerb einer Anlage. Da dies unser erstes Geschäftsprojekt in Deutschland ist, wäre uns jede zusätzliche Information über Kauf oder Pacht von Liegenschaften äußerst willkommen.

Mit freundlichen Grüßen

Arthur Sturrock
Geschäftsführer

1 *Eine Anlage einrichten*: set up, establish a plant; *gründen* would also be possible.

66 Complaint about delay in administering an account

18 September 199-

Société Bancaire Générale
4 boulevard Leclerc
76200 Dieppe
France

For the attention of the Manager

Dear Sir

RE: ACCOUNT NO. 654231

We have received the July statement of our above account no. 654231 and are surprised that the balance shown is so low.

We have been assured by two of our major customers, Alligand SA and Berthaud Etains, that they settled large outstanding invoices by bank transfer to that account four weeks and five weeks ago respectively.

Will you please check our account very carefully and let us know the exact balance by fax. If as we think, work is being processed by you in a dilatory fashion, please could you let us know the reason for this.

Yours sincerely

Eric Smith
Finance Director

66   Beschwerde über Kontenverwaltung

18. September 199-

An die Direktion
der Allgemeinen Wirtschaftsbank
Stolzingplatz 78

D–90000 Nürnberg

Sehr geehrte Damen und Herren,

wir erhielten soeben den Juli-Auszug unseres Kontos Nr. 654231 und sind
erstaunt über den niedrigen Kontostand.

Zwei wichtige Kunden, Wanninger AG und Kleinwerth & Sohn, haben uns
versichert,[1] daß sie vor vier bzw. fünf Wochen größere Summen als Begleichung
ausstehender Rechnungen auf unser Konto überwiesen haben.

Könnten Sie unser Konto noch einmal überprüfen und uns den genauen Stand
per Fax übermitteln oder uns eine Erklärung für die unserer Ansicht nach
ungebührliche Verzögerung in Ihrer Verwaltung geben.

Mit besten Grüßen

Eric Smith
Finanzleiter

1   *Haben uns versichert*: the *uns* is in the dative – 'they assured us.' Note: *Versichern* +
    accusative: 'to insure'.

67   Complaint about mail delivery

19 November 199-

The Central Post Office
Place Centrale
53000 Laval
France

Dear Sirs

As a result of enquiries we have made in England it appears that delays we have experienced in the delivery of our mail to our subsidiary in Cossé le Vivien are being caused at the Laval sorting office.

Since our business is being seriously inconvenienced by postal delays we would be most grateful if you could look into the matter.

It should not take 10 days for orders and invoices to get from us to our colleagues in Cossé. Enclosed is a sample mailing where you can see the dates clearly marked.

Yours faithfully

Jeremy P Johnson
Director

Enc.

67 Beschwerde über Postzustellung

19. November 199-

Zentralpostamt
Fadingerstr. 38

D 80001 München

Sehr geehrte Damen und Herren,

unseren Erkundigungen in England zufolge scheint es, daß die Verzögerung in
der Postzustellung an unsere Niederlassung in Holzkirchen von der Sortierstelle
in München verursacht wird.

Da unsere Geschäfte durch die langsame Postzustellung ernstlich beeinträchtigt
werden, möchten wir Sie bitten, die Angelegenheit zu untersuchen.

Es sollte nicht vorkommen, daß Aufträge und Rechnungen 10 Tage von uns nach
Holzkirchen unterwegs sind, wie Sie dem Beispiel des beiliegenden Briefes mit
deutlich markierten Daten entnehmen können.[1]

Mit freundlichen Grüßen

Jeremy P. Johnson
Direktor

Anlage

Brief

1 *Entnehmen* does not require a preposition, simply the dative. *Sie entnehmen meinem
Brief* . . .: 'you see from my letter' . . .

68 Complaint about wrong consignment of goods

1 September 199-

Dessous Dessus
14 rue Legrand
80000 Amiens
France

For the attention of Mr A Malraux

Dear Mr Malraux

RE: INVOICE NO. 13322/08/92

We regret to inform you that the garments you sent us in your consignment of 25 August were not what we had ordered.

If you refer to our order (copy enclosed) and to your invoice, you will see that the briefs, slips and bras are mostly the wrong sizes, colours and materials.

We are at a loss to explain this departure from your normally reliable service. Will you please contact us immediately so that we can put matters right?

Yours sincerely

Fred Smith
Manager

Enc.

68 Beschwerde über falsche Lieferung

1. September 199-

Palmer Dessous
Wedekindstr. 39

D–76000 Karlsruhe

Zu Händen von Herrn A. Brecht

Sehr geehrter Herr Brecht,

wir müssen Ihnen leider mitteilen, daß Ihre Lieferung vom 25. August nicht unserem Auftrag entspricht.

Wie Sie aus der beiliegenden Kopie unseres Auftrags und aus Ihrer Rechnung ersehen können, handelt es sich bei den Höschen, Unterkleidern und Büstenhaltern zumeist um die falschen Größen, Farben und das falsche Material.

Wir können uns nicht erklären, warum Ihr normalerweise verläßlicher Geschäftsbetrieb diesmal nicht funktionierte und möchten Sie ersuchen, die Angelegenheit so bald wie möglich richtig zu stellen.

Mit freundlichen Grüßen

Fred Smith
Geschäftsführer

Anlage
Auftrag

69   Complaint about damage to goods

3 April 199-

Transports Transmanche SA
Quai des Brumes
14000 Caen
France

For the attention of Mr Gérard Dispendieux

Dear Monsieur Dispendieux

We have received a complaint from John Ferguson of Amex Insurance concerning their removal to Beauvais. You will remember that we subcontracted this removal to your company.

Mr Ferguson claims that several of the items of furniture and office equipment were damaged on arrival at the premises in Beauvais.

Although he immediately complained to your deliverymen, he has still not heard from your company. In the interests of our future business relations I would be grateful if you could clarify this situation.

Yours sincerely

Gerald Wagstaffe
French Area Manager

69 Beschwerde über Warenschäden

3. April 199-

Spedition Jensen GmbH
Friesendeichstr. 48

D 28207 Bremerhaven

Zu Händen von Herrn W. Wenders

Sehr geehrter Herr Wenders,

wir erhielten eine Beschwerde von Herrn John Ferguson, Firma Amex Versicherung, bezüglich ihrer Übersiedlung nach Magdeburg. Wie Sie wissen, hatten wir Ihre Firma für diese Unternehmung unter Vertrag genommen.

Herr Ferguson behauptet, daß etliche[1] Möbelstücke und Bürogeräte bei der Ankunft in Magdeburg beschädigt waren.

Obwohl er sich sofort beim Transportpersonal beschwert hatte, hat er bis jetzt noch keine weitere Nachricht von Ihrer Firma. Wir möchten Sie daher ersuchen, die Angelegenheit im Interesse unserer zukünftigen Geschäftsbeziehungen zu klären.

Mir freundlichen Grüßen

Gerald Wagstaffe
Gebietsleiter für Deutschland

1 *Etliche*: 'quite a few', 'many'. This word is very formal and not particularly common. It would be little used in spoken German.

70 Informing customers that a company has been taken over

24 July 199-

Produits Chimiques SA
89 rue Jules Barni
80330 Longueau
France

Dear Sirs

Thank you for your order dated 17 July. We have to inform you, however, that our company has recently been taken over by a larger concern, International Chemicals Inc.

As a result of this, we no longer produce the polymers that you request at this site. We have however passed on your order to our parent company and are confident that you will be contacted soon.

In the interests of our future business relations we enclose the latest catalogue of our total range of products, indicating which subsidiary manufactures which product.

Yours faithfully

Frederick Herriot
Plant Director

Enc.

70 Mitteilung über Firmenübernahme

24. Juli 199-

Neckarchemie AG
Postfach 375

68000 Mannheim

Sehr geehrte Herren,

wir danken Ihnen für Ihren Auftrag vom 17.07. und möchten Ihnen gleichzeitig die Übernahme unseres Betriebs durch den Großkonzern International Chemicals Inc. bekanntgeben.

Außerdem müssen wir Ihnen mitteilen, daß wir die von Ihnen benötigten Polymere nicht mehr herstellen. Wir haben jedoch Ihre Bestellung an unsere Mutterfirma[1] weitergeleitet und sind sicher, daß Sie demnächst benachrichtigt werden.

Im Interesse unserer zukünftigen Geschäftsbeziehungen legen wir den neuesten Katalog unserer gesamten Produktpalette bei mit dem Hinweis auf die betreffenden Herstellerfirmen unserer Gruppe.[2]

Mit besten Grüßen

Frederick Herriot
Werksleiter

Anlage
Katalog

1 *Mutterfirma*: 'parent company'. Note also *Tochtergesellschaft*: 'subsidiary'.
2 Note the word order here. *Bei* would be expected to be at the end of the sentence. It is placed here because of the long phrase which follows.

71 Informing customers of change of name and address

EUROPEAN COMMERCIAL INSURANCE Ltd
47 Broad Walk
Preston
Lancashire United Kingdom

(Formerly PRESTON INSURERS Inkerman Street, Preston)

1 June 199-

The Export Manager
Nouveaux Textiles
342 chaussée Baron
59100 Roubaix
France

Dear Sir

RE: CHANGE OF COMPANY NAME AND ADDRESS

We are writing to all our valued customers to inform them that we have changed both our registered name and our address.

We are still located in Preston and operating as commercial insurers as before. However, we have acquired new partners who have invested fresh capital in the business.

It is our intention to increase our European business, hence the new name. Enclosed is our brochure setting out our range of services and tariffs. Do not hesitate to contact us if you have any queries about these changes.

Yours faithfully

Nancy Wilton
Customer Liaison Manager

Enc.

71 Kundenavis – Namens- und Adressenänderung

European Commercial Insurance Ltd
47 Broad Walk
Preston
Lancashire
United Kingdom

(Vormals Preston Insurers, Inkerman Street, Preston)

1. Juni 199-

Epple Maschinenbau AG
Exportabteilung
Postfach 486

D–61007 Frankfurt

Sehr geehrte Damen und Herren,

wir möchten hiermit unsere werten Kunden davon in Kenntnis setzen, daß wir sowohl unseren eingetragenen Namen als auch unsere Adresse geändert haben.

Unsere Firma befindet sich nach wie vor in Preston und fungiert weiterhin als gewerbliche Versicherungsanstalt. Durch die Aufnahme neuer Geschäftspartner floß frisches Investitionskapital in unser Unternehmen.

Unsere Namensänderung rührt von der Absicht, unseren europäischen Geschäftsbereich zu erweitern. In der Anlage[1] finden Sie eine Broschüre mit unseren Dienstleistungen und Tarifen. Sollten Sie irgendwelche Fragen über diese Veränderungen haben, bitte zögern Sie nicht, sich an uns zu wenden.

Mit besten Grüßen

Nancy Wilson
Kundendienstleitung

Anlage
Broschüre

1 *In der Anlage*: enclosed. Also possible would be: *als Anlage; wir legen . . . bei.*

72 Informing customers of increased prices

12 November 199-

Epicerie Fine
9 rue Dutour
72100 Le Mans
France

Dear Monsieur Olivier

In reply to your letter of the 5th I am sending you a new price list.

You will note that all of our prices have increased by some 6.3 per cent. This was unfortunately made necessary by our continuing inflation as well as the British Chancellor's recent decision to increase the general rate of VAT to 17.5 per cent.

I hope, however, that the quality of our produce will continue to engage your loyalty. It is also the case that the pound sterling has reduced in value.

Yours sincerely

Michael McDermott
Marketing Manager

Enc.

72 Kundenavis – Preiserhöhung

12. November 199-

Feinkost Derflinger
Ringstr. 79

D 66000 Saarbrücken

Sehr geehrter Herr Derflinger,

in Antwort auf Ihren Brief vom 5. d. M. sende ich Ihnen eine neue Preisliste.

Sie werden ersehen, daß alle unsere Preise um[1] etwa 6,3% gestiegen sind. Dies ist leider auf die anhaltende Inflation zurückzuführen und auch auf die jüngste Entscheidung des britischen Schatzkanzlers, die Mehrwertsteuer auf 17,5% zu erhöhen.

Ich hoffe aber, daß Sie uns aufgrund der Güte unserer Erzeugnisse Ihre Kundentreue bewahren werden (ungeachtet der Tatsache, daß auch nun das Pfund Sterling an Wert verloren hat).

Mit besten Grüßen

Michael McDermott
Marketingleiter

Anlage
Preisliste

1   *Um*: 'by', is used with all verbs of increasing or decreasing. Such verbs also add *auf*: 'to' (as with *erhöhen auf* below).

73 Requesting information about opening a business account

23 October 199-

The Manager
Crédit Mercantile
89 rue Béranger
69631 VÉNISSIEUX
France

Dear Sir

We are proposing to open an office and refrigerated storage facility at Vénissieux in the new year and would appreciate some information about opening a bank account at your branch.

Initially we would be transferring funds to finance the setting up of our new business premises. Thereafter we would expect to use the account to receive payments from French customers and to pay local suppliers etc.

We would be most grateful if you could inform us of all the formalities that we need to observe, both public and particular, to Crédit Mercantile. Could you also inform us of your charges on business accounts?

Yours faithfully

Eric Wise
Commercial Manager

73 Erkundigung über Eröffnung eines Geschäftskontos

23. Oktober 199-

An die Direktion
Gewerbebank
Hohenzollernplatz 58

D 07370 Neubrandenburg

Sehr geehrte Herren,

wir beabsichtigen, im kommenden Jahre eine Geschäftsstelle sowie Kühlräume in Neubrandenburg zu eröffnen und möchten gerne Auskunft über die Eröffnung eines Kontos bei Ihrer Bank.

Anfänglich würden wir Beträge zur Einrichtung unserer Geschäftsräume überweisen, später würden wir das Konto zur Abrechnung mit unseren deutschen Kunden und Lieferanten verwenden.

Wir wären Ihnen dankbar, wenn Sie uns über alle notwendigen Formalitäten in der Bank und im allgemeinen Auskunft geben könnten. Könnten Sie uns auch gleichzeitig Ihre Gebühren bei Geschäftskonten mitteilen.

Mit freundlichen Grüßen

Eric Wise
Geschäftsleiter

74   Requesting information about opening a personal bank account

4 November 199-

The Manager
Banque Nationale
146 boulevard Haussmann
75016 Paris
France

Dear Sir

My British employers are posting me to their French subsidiary and I will therefore be moving to Paris with my family and expect to be resident in France for two years.

Would you please let me have details about opening a personal current account at your bank. My salary would be paid into the account and I would wish to draw money from it and to pay bills by cheque etc. I may also wish to transfer money to a bank account in England.

I would be grateful for any documentation you can send me.

Yours faithfully

Stuart Smith

74   Erkundigung über Eröffnung eines Privatkontos

4. November 199-

Bank für Hessen
Kontenabteilung
Krönungsallee 37

D–60000 Frankfurt

Sehr geehrte Damen und Herren,

aufgrund meiner Versetzung von England in unsere deutsche Filiale werde ich mit meiner Familie nach Frankfurt übersiedeln und dort voraussichtlich zwei Jahre wohnhaft sein.

Könnten Sie mir bitte Information über die Eröffnung eines Privatgirokontos bei Ihrer Bank zukommen lassen. Das Konto sollte die Funktion eines Gehalts-, Zahlungs- und Scheckkontos haben. Möglicherweise würde es auch zur Geldüberweisung auf ein englisches Konto benützt werden.

Ich wäre Ihnen dankbar für die Übersendung von Informationsmaterial in dieser Angelegenheit.

Mit freundlichen Grüßen

Stuart Smith

75 Letter re overdrawn account

9 March 199-

J H Jameson
47 Narrow Bank
Lichfield
Staffordshire

Dear Mr Jameson

We regret to inform you that your account, number 62467840, is overdrawn by £21.09.

We would appreciate your rectifying this situation as soon as possible since you have no overdraft arrangement with us.

Yours sincerely

F E Jones
Manager

75 Kontoüberziehung

9. März 199-

Herrn
Heinrich Höllerer
Gablerstr. 34

52061 Bochum

Sehr geehrter Herr Höllerer,

wir müssen Ihnen leider mitteilen, daß Ihr Konto, Nr. 62647840, um DM 48,83 überzogen ist.

Da Sie über keinen Dispositionskredit bei uns verfügen, müssen wir Sie ersuchen, diese Angelegenheit ehestens zu bereinigen.

Mit besten Grüßen

F. Jocher
Direktor

76   Bank's letter to customer

2 May 199-

Mr Bernard J Mann
4 Beauchamp Mews
London
England

Dear Mr Mann

We are writing to inform you that we have today received a cheque payable to you for the sum of $124,035.00 and sent by J et P Barraud Notaires, 307 rue du Château, Luxembourg.

Can you please confirm as soon as possible that you were expecting this deposit and let us know your instructions concerning it?

Enclosed is a photocopy of this cheque and its accompanying letter.

Yours sincerely

Amélie Dupont
Head Cashier

Encs

76 Bankschreiben an Kunden

2. Mai 199-

Mr. Bernhard J. Mann
4 Beauchamp Mews

London
Großbritiannien

Sehr geehrter Herr Mann,

wir teilen Ihnen mit, daß wir heute einen auf Ihren Namen ausgestellten Scheck[1] über[2] DM 190 035,- von der Notariatskanzlei P. Lützeler, 307 rue du Château, Luxemburg, erhalten haben.

Könnten Sie so bald wie möglich bestätigen, daß Sie diese Einlage erwarten und uns Ihre diesbezüglichen Anweisungen übermitteln.

In der Anlage finden sie eine Photokopie des Schecks und des Begleitschreibens.

Mit freundlichen Grüßen

Amanda Bruckner
Hauptkassier

Anlage
Zwei Photokopien

1 *Einen Scheck ausstellen*: 'to make out a cheque'. 'Crossed cheque': *Verrechnungsscheck*.
2 *Ein Scheck über*: 'a cheque for' (the amount of) . . .

77   General query about banking

Monsieur J. Delor
Président-Directeur Général
Mouton-Poulenc
7 rue du Trocadéro
Paris 3 Cedex
France

Dear Sir

In response to your general query about banking in England there are two main types of bank, merchant banks and commercial banks. The former are very numerous and deal with companies generally. The latter are mainly the four big groups, Lloyds, National Westminster, Barclays and Midland.

The enclosed leaflet will give you further details, including information about banking in Scotland. The Ombudsman's office is mainly concerned with complaints about banks.

You should note that The Post Office in England also has some banking and money transfer facilities.

Yours faithfully

C D Prettyman
For the Ombudsman

Enc.

77 Allgemeine Bankinformation

Herrn Generaldirektor
Dr. Erich Panther
EXI Werke
Händelstr. 24

D–04862 Halle

Sehr geehrter Herr Generaldirektor,

wir beantworten[1] gerne Ihre Anfrage bezügl. des englischen Bankwesens.
Generell gibt es zwei Arten von Banken, Handelsbanken und allgemeine
Kreditinstitute. Erstere sind zahlreich und sind vornehmlich für
Geschäftsunternehmen tätig; zur letzteren gehören hauptsächlich die vier
Großbanken Lloyds, National Westminster, Barclays und Midland.

Die beiliegende Broschüre gibt Ihnen weitere Einzelheiten sowie Auskunft über
das Bankwesen in Schottland. Unser Amt ist vor allem für Bankbeschwerden
zuständig.

Außerdem möchten wir Sie darauf hinweisen, daß auch die Post gewisse
Geldüberweisungs- und andere Bankgeschäfte übernimmt.

Mit besten Grüßen

C.D.Prettyman
i.A. Ombudsman

Anlage
Broschüre

1 'To answer': *beantworten* or *antworten auf*.

78   Enquiry about post office banking facilities

2 February 199-

La Poste Centrale
Place Général De Gaulle
16000 Angoulême
France

Dear Sirs

I am intending to open a second business in Angoulême and would like to enquire what services you offer to small businesses.

I have in mind giro banking; can you tell me how your post office bank accounts work? Secondly, is it to you that I should apply to have a telephone? Thirdly, do you have special rates for business mail?

I would be most grateful for any information you can send me.

Yours faithfully

Mostyn Evans
Proprietor

78 Anfrage bezügl. Bankdienste der Post

2. Februar 199-

An das Hauptpostamt
Westfalenplatz 48

D 48000 Münster

Sehr geehrte Damen und Herren,

wir beabsichtigen, eine Niederlassung in Münster zu eröffnen und möchten uns über Ihr Dienstleistungsangebot für Kleinunternehmer erkundigen.

Könnten Sie uns bitte genauere Einzelheiten bezügl. eines Postscheckkontos geben? Sollen wir das Ansuchen um einen Telefonanschluß an Ihre Adresse richten? Und schließlich möchten wir wissen, ob es Sondergebühren für geschäftlichen Briefverkehr gibt.

Für Ihre diesbezüglichen Informationen wären wir Ihnen äußerst dankbar.

Mit freundlichen Grüßen

Mostyn Evans
Inhaber

79 Enquiry about opening a post office account

8 March 199-

Bureau Central
Postes et Télécommunications
Paris
France

Dear Sirs

I do not know exactly who to write to and hope that this letter will reach the right service.

I wish to obtain information about opening a Post Office account in France, to facilitate financial transactions with my French customers and suppliers.

Will you please inform me of your formalities and send me the necessary forms?

Yours faithfully

Eric Clifford
Managing Director

79 Erkundigung bezügl. Postscheckkonto

8. März 199-

An das
Bundeszentralamt für Post- und Telekommunikation

D–10000 Berlin

Sehr geehrte Damen und Herren,

mangels einer Kontaktadresse wende ich mich an Sie mit der Bitte, diesen Brief nötigenfalls[1] an die richtige Stelle weiterzuleiten.

Ich ersuche um Auskunft über die Eröffnung eines Postscheckkontos in Deutschland zur Abrechnung mit meinen deutschen Kunden und Lieferanten.

Bitte könnten Sie mir über etwaige Formalitäten Bescheid geben und mir die erforderlichen Formulare zukommen lassen.[2]

Mit besten Grüßen

Eric Clifford
Betriebsleiter

1 Alternative to *nötigenfalls*: *wenn nötig*.
2 *Zukommen lassen* is rather formal. *Schicken* or *senden* would be just as acceptable.

80 Opening poste restante

18 April 199-

La Poste Centrale
Place Bellecour
69001 Lyon
France

Gentlemen

We are in the process of moving our French subsidiary from Villeurbanne to Saint Priest; the move should be completed some time in the next month.

Could we ask you on receipt of this letter, and until further notice, to retain all mail addressed to us poste restante at your central office?

Please inform us if there are any other formalities to observe. Enclosed is an addressed envelope and international reply coupon for your reply.

Thank you in advance.

Arthur T Goldberg
On behalf of Software Supplies Inc.

Enc.

80 Eröffnung einer Aufbewahrungsstelle für postlagernde Sendungen

An das Hauptpostamt
Innufer 40

D–94000 Passau

Sehr geehrte Damen und Herren,

wir sind im Begriff, unsere deutsche Tochterfirma von Dingolfing nach Plattling zu verlegen. In etwa einem Monat dürfte die Übersiedlung abgeschlossen sein.

Wir möchten Sie ersuchen, nach Erhalt dieses Briefes alle an uns adressierten Postsendungen bis auf weiteres in Ihrer Zentrale postlagernd aufzubewahren.

Bitte teilen Sie uns mit, ob andere Formalitäten zu erledigen sind. Für Ihre Antwort liegt ein adressierter Umschlag und ein internationaler Antwortschein bei.

Besten Dank im voraus.

i.A. Arthur T. Goldberg

Anlage
Adressierter Umschlag
Internationaler Antwortschein

Business Practice

1 Addressing people

It is customary to address your business partners by their surname, i.e. Herr Hager, Frau Schmidt and use the *Sie* (formal address) even if you know them quite well and would use first names in a similar situation in an English speaking context.

If someone has an academic qualification it is usually used as part of the person's name i.e. Herr Doktor Meister, Frau Professor Trautner, Herr Diplom Ingenieur Huber, at least in introductions and in letters. In southern Germany, and in particular in Austria, people are sometimes addressed by their job title, i.e. Herr Abteilungsleiter, Frau Direktor etc.

Note that *Fräulein* is only used now for teenage girls and sometimes for waitresses. *Frau* no longer denotes marital status in German.

Apart from the standard greetings *Guten Tag/Morgen/Abend* you will hear the regional variation *Grüß Gott* in southern Germany and Austria. In German Switzerland the greeting is *Grüezi*.

On meeting or taking leave of somebody it is customary to shake hands.

2 Communicating with people

Telephone

When answering the phone in Germany it is customary to give your surname (Bauer, Klein etc.) rather than your telephone number, which is the standard practice in the UK. Switchboard operators will give the name of the firm, as well as the customary greeting (*Guten Morgen, Guten Tag* etc.).

When the conversation is finished, you should use *Auf Wiederhören* instead of *Auf Wiedersehen* when ringing off. Telephone facilities are plentiful and efficient. Much the same services as in Britain are available and can be found at the front of telephone directories.

Post Offices offer a service for long distance and international calls whereby the caller is directed to a booth by the official at the telephone counter and pays for the call afterwards.

Fax/mail

Although German business letters observe certain conventions regarding the layout and the language they are on the whole written in an uncluttered style and to the point.

The subject of the letter is usually given before you address the recipient of the letter. The customary salutation is *Sehr geehrter Herr Dr. Beyer!*, *Sehr geehrte Frau Reingruber*, *Sehr geehrte Damen und Herren!* – NEVER: *Sehr geehrte/r Frau/Herr* without the surname.

Needless to say the polite (*Sie*) form of address must be observed.

Letters are concluded by putting *Mit besten Grüßen, Mit freundlichen Grüßen* (*MfG* in faxes). The more formal *Hochachtungsvoll* is still in use but less so.

If the letter is to go to a specific person, *z. H. Frau S. Gruber* (*zu Händen*: 'for the attention of') is placed under the name of the firm. *Vertraulich* (confidential) or *Dringend* (urgent) appear above the address on the envelope and after the subject matter of the letter.

Following reunification, Germany had to change the postal code system. The postal code now consists of a five-digit number in front of the place of destination. The first two digits refer to one of the 83 postal regions i.e. D–51065 Köln (51: region Köln Ost).

3 Appointments and punctuality

It is important to keep appointments and attend punctually. If a meeting is arranged for 1500 hours (the 24-hour clock is used in business, even in spoken language) that means 1500 hours precisely. Lateness is considered bad manners and bad business practice.

If you cannot keep an appointment or attend a meeting you should ensure that you cancel in writing or by phone.

Business meetings are usually brisk and to the point. Smart dress is advisable.

4 Business cards and gifts

It is usual to exchange business cards (*Geschäftskarte*, *Visitenkarte*) before meetings with clients or business contacts.

It is not customary to exchange gifts in business unless it is a matter of celebrating a special corporate event. Then suitable gifts might be appropriate.

When invited to the home of a business partner flowers either sent in advance or given on arrival to the lady of the house are considered a suitable gift and should be presented without their paper wrapping.

5 Office and shop hours

An average working day lasts eight hours and starts at 8 a.m. or before with an hour's break for lunch. However, an increasing number of businesses have some sort of flexi-time system in operation or arrange their working hours in such a way as to enable the workers to finish earlier on Fridays and enjoy a longer weekend.

Most shops open between 8 and 9 a.m. and shut at 6 or 6.30 p.m. from Mondays to Fridays. On Saturdays the closing times vary: in Germany shops close at 1 or 2 p.m. except for the first Saturday of the month, when most shops in towns are open till 6 p.m. This is the so-called long Saturday (*langer Samstag*). Austria and Switzerland follow a similar pattern but the bigger shops are often open until 4 or 5 p.m. on Saturdays.

In smaller towns and in the country most shops are closed at lunch time and sometimes for a half day during the week. Some may be open on Sunday mornings.

6 Business entertainment

Germans are eager to make their guests and business partners feel welcome. Visitors are usually entertained at the firm or invited out to hotels or restaurants.

In all the major towns and cities there are usually a number of restaurants specializing in every type of cuisine, giving an excellent opportunity to sample local and international fare. Food portions are well-known for their size and it may not always be easy to find a selection of vegetarian dishes.

As work tends to start early (usually between 7 and 8 a.m. or sometimes earlier) in most businesses lunch is often taken at noon or 12.30. Dinner as a rule is also at the earlier time of 7 or 7.30 p.m.

Although it is not the norm, longstanding business associates may be invited to the home of a colleague. This might not always be for a meal but more often to informal drinks after dinner. If invited to drinks or to a meal it is advisable to arrive precisely at the time specified. Arriving late is considered not only bad manners but also a lack of regard for the host.

7 Business organizations

The branches of the Chamber of Commerce and Industry (*Industrie- und Handelskammer*) represent the interests of businesses. These are public corporations and membership is obligatory. They provide an information service for foreign trade, give access to the register of firms in the area, issue certificates of the place of origin for local products, facilitate business or trading links, etc.

These bodies also give guidance to the courts, frame legislation on commercial matters and help in dealings with local authorities.

The umbrella organization for the chambers is the Deutscher Industrie- und Handelstag (Bonn).

Handicrafts are represented by their own chambers (*Handwerkskammer*). The crafts themselves are grouped into *Innungen* (types of guild), which are supervized by the respective chambers; all firms must belong to their local chamber. Their responsibilities include the implementation of legislation concerning, for example, the training and examination of apprentices, journeyman's and master's examination; issuing quality certificates; arbitrating in industrial disputes. The umbrella organization is the Zentralverband des Deutschen Handwerks (Bonn).

Similar organizations in Austria and in Switzerland are the Österreichische Handels- und Gewerbekammer and the Schweizerische Handels- und Industrieverein and the Schweizerische Gewerbeverband.

8 Banks and other financial institutions

A major role in the trade and industry of Germany, Switzerland and Austria is played by their banking systems. In Germany the issuing bank with responsibility for currency and credit policy is the independent Deutsche Bundesbank in Frankfurt, with its Landeszentralbanken in the *Länder* (states).

There is an extensive network of joint stock banks (the equivalent of the high street banks in Britain), for example the Dresdner Bank and the Deutsche Bank. There are also savings banks (*Sparkassen*) on a regional or local basis, rural credit co-operatives (*Raiffeisenkasse, Volksbank*), mortgage banks (*Hypothekenbank*) and building societies (*Bausparkassen*).

In spite of the relatively slow growth of capital in a savings account, putting money into the bank is still preferred in Germany to investing in stocks and shares. The main stock exchange in Frankfurt (Börse) is important, but from the point of view of world trading less so than Tokyo, New York or London.

It is interesting to note that although credit cards and cheques are gaining in popularity throughout the German-speaking countries, people still prefer to pay by cash in shops, restaurants, etc. Telephone banking is, however, widely available.

The financial sector of Austria and Switzerland is similar to that of Germany. Switzerland in particular has a long tradition in international banking due to the relative political and economic stability of the country and the comparatively liberal banking laws, which guarantee clients absolute anonymity. Based in a small country with few natural resources, Swiss business has always looked well beyond its frontiers. This has led to the growth of many of its companies into leading multinational organizations, particularly in banking and insurance. A wide range of financial services is available to clients worldwide.

Although Switzerland is not a member of the European Union, Swiss insurance companies were quick to take advantage of the move towards a single insurance market.

9 Legal practitioners

The underlying feature of the German, Austrian and Swiss political, administrative and legal systems is a strong regionalism. Each country consists of a number of more or less *souverain* states within the constitution. In Germany there are 15 states (*Bundesländer*). Austria consists of 9 *Bundesländer* and the 26 Swiss states are called *Kantone*.

The German, Austrian and Swiss legal systems are based on predominantly written law, which developed from Roman law and old regional sources.

The police has strictly controlled powers and is under the administration of the German states. Austria and Switzerland also have a federal (*Bundespolizei*) as well as a regional police (*Gendarmerie*).

Areas of jurisdiction

There are five areas of jurisdiction each with their three, or in financial law, two stages of appeal:

1 Civil and criminal law (*Straf-* und *Zivilrecht*)
2 Industrial law covers such areas as wage negotiations, unlawful dismissal, worker participation, industrial tribunal (*Arbeitsgericht*), structure of business, etc.
3 Administrative law (*Verwaltungsrecht*)

4 Social law (*Sozialrecht*) deals with disputes over social security or social benefits
5 Finance law (*Finanzrecht*) looks after tax and fiscal matters

Jurisdiction is in the hands of professional judges at independent courts. Magistrates (*Justizbeamte*) and lay judges (*Laienrichter*) preside mainly in regional (*Landesgericht*) and local courts (*Landgericht, Amtsgericht*).

In criminal cases the public prosecutor (*Staatsanwalt*) represents the state. The *Rechtsanwalt* is an independent legal adviser whose work combines aspects of a solicitor's and a barrister's work.

10 Advertising media

The press and the electronic media in Germany, Switzerland and Austria are independent of state control and are much less centralized than in Britain.

The press

In Germany local and regional papers make up the bulk of the daily press. Local papers cover national and international news as well as local issues and some of the regional papers have acquired national importance. Thus the *Frankfurter Allgemeine Zeitung* and the *Süddeutsche Zeitung* have become leading publications on political and economic matters throughout Germany alongside such national papers as *Die Welt* or the *Westdeutsche Allgemeine Zeitung*. The daily paper with the highest circulation is the *Bildzeitung*, which caters for the popular mass market.

Weekly papers such as *Die Zeit, Rheinischer Merkur* and *Deutsches Allgemeines Sonntagsblatt* provide background information, extensive arts coverage and carry a lot of advertisements.

Among the illustrated papers and magazines (e.g. *Stern, Bunte* or *Quick*) the news magazine *Der Spiegel*, which is modelled on *Time*, enjoys an international reputation for reporting on controversial issues and uncovering scandals.

Switzerland's multilingual press boasts one of the highest circulations per head of the population worldwide. The *Neue Zürcher Zeitung* is perhaps the German language paper most widely read by the business community.

Among the 16 daily papers currently published in Austria, the three largest-selling papers, *Kronen Zeitung, Kurier* and *Kleine Zeitung*, account for more than two thirds of the total circulation. The leading quality paper is *Die Presse*. Among the magazines and periodicals *Wochenpresse- Wirtschaftswoche* might be of special interest to the business person.

The electronic media

In Germany there are two public TV broadcasting corporations, ARD (Arbeitsgemeinschaft der öffentlich-rechtlichen Rundfunkanstalten Deutschlands) and ZDF (Zweites Deutsches Fernsehen), which are organized on a regional basis, and a number of private providers, who transmit via satellite or cable. Advertising on public TV is restricted to certain times of the day.

The radio stations DLF (Deutschlandfunk), DS (Deutschlandsender Kultur) and RIAS (Rundfunk im Amerikanischen Sektor Berlins) have become subsidiaries of ARD since reunification and broadcast jointly throughout Germany. The DW (Deutsche Welle) operates under the auspices of the federal administration. It provides a German world service in German and several foreign languages.

The Austrian broadcasting corporation ORF (Österreichischer Fundfunk) is also a politically and economically autonomous institution. At present it broadcasts six programmes, two on television and four on radio. Austrian cable-TV subscribers are also able to watch a satellite channel compiled by ORF, the German ZDF and the Swiss SRG (Schweizerische Radio- und Fernsehgesellschaft). This so-called 3SAT channel is intended to represent the German-speaking world and its culture. Blue Danube Radio offers entertainment in several languages as well as information programmes.

The Swiss SRG broadcasts in the four official languages of Switzerland thus providing ten radio and three TV programmes. Schweizer Radio International (SRI) can be received worldwide in many languages. Since the 1993 broadcasting reforms, there is now a semi-privatized TV channel S+ and the wholly commercial channel Tell TV which offers extensive coverage of business and economic matters.

Btx (*Bildschirmtext*) and Videotext are the Ceefax equivalents of the German speaking world.

11 Holidays

Annual holidays

Annual holidays, on average between three and six weeks in Austria and Germany, tend to be spread over the year and usually coincide with the main school holidays at Christmas, Easter and in the summer.

The working week consists of around 40 hours, although the Swiss appear to be among those countries with the most annual working hours (more than 2,000 hours per year).

Public holidays

Public holidays not only vary between the three countries; they also vary according to the main religion within the regions of the countries, northern Germany and Switzerland being predominantly Protestant, while southern Germany and Austria are mostly Catholic areas and consequently have more public holidays.

Thus Epiphany (6 January), Corpus Christi (May/June, depending on the date of Easter Sunday), Ascension Day (May/June, depending on the date of Easter Sunday), Assumption (15 August), All Saints and All Souls (1 and 2 November) are in addition to the standard holidays of New Year's Day, Easter Monday, May Day (1 May), Whit Monday (depending on Easter date), Christmas and Boxing Day.

The Protestant regions have Good Friday and *Buß- und Bettag* (Day of Prayer and Penitence, Germany only, on 11 November) as a public holiday.

All three countries celebrate National Days, Germany on 3 October, Switzerland on 1 August and Austria on 26 October.

When public holidays fall on a Tuesday or a Thursday it is not unusual for businesses to declare a long weekend and close on the Monday or the Friday respectively. Employees are also permitted time off for special events such as wedding and funerals and there is legislation concerning maternity and paternity leave.

12 Trades unions

The trades unions' reform in the post-war years expressed a consensus approach to Germany labour relations, with employers and employees sharing responsibilities in spite of sometimes conflicting interests. Consequently, relatively few working days were lost due to industrial action.

The largest German trades union organization is the DGB (Deutscher Gewerkschaftsbund). It has over 10 million members organized into 16 individual unions. Unlike Britain, which numbers some 300 unions, each for a particular skill, trade or profession, the German system favours the industry principle. This means that all workers in a particular sector of industry are organized on the basis of their employment. Thus all workers in the steel industry, be they clerks, furnace workers, drivers or engineers, belong to the same trade union, which represents their interests and negotiates on their behalf.

Smaller trades union organizations are the DAG (Deutsche Angestellten-Gewerkschaft) for white-collar workers of all sectors of industry, and the DBB (Deutscher Beamtenbund), an organization for state employees, which does not take part in wage negotiations and therefore does not accept strike action as a legal means of settling a dispute. The CGB (Christlicher Gewerkschaftsbund), based on Christian beliefs, is the smallest of the organizations outside the DGB.

All unions are non-partisan. There is no obligation for any worker to belong to a union, the 'closed shop' system does not exist. Membership in individual unions varies; on average approximately 50 per cent of workers are union members.

Wage negotiations take place as a rule once a year in every sector of industry and only during the negotiating period are strikes legally permitted, provided three-quarters of union members are in favour of strike action.

Although the state does not interfere in collective bargaining, German industrial legislation clearly defines the rights and duties of both the employer and the employee. The *Betriebsverfassungsgesetz* (Firms' Constitution Law) states that every firm with five or more employees is entitled to have a democratically elected Works Council (*Betriebsrat*), which represents the workers' interests vis-à-vis management in the day-to-day running of the business.

The *Mitbestimmungsgesetz* (Co-determination Law) covers worker participation in the management of public companies and is dealt with in the section on types of company.

The Austrian trades union system resembles the German one closely with the ÖGB (Österreichischer Gewerkschaftsbund) as the umbrella organization for 14 industrial member unions.

Social stability and generous social legislation have rendered strikes virtually unknown in Switzerland. In 1937 the so-called *Arbeitsfriede* (industrial peace agreement) was reached, which is renewed regularly and, banning strikes and lock-outs, accepts arbitration as the only lawful means to settle a dispute. Detailed employment contracts also ensure a clear definition of workers' and employers' obligations.

13 Types of company

There are several types of company in Germany, designated by their abbreviations after the name of the firm.

The AG (*Aktiengesellschaft*) is very similar to a public company in Britain. Its shares may, but do not have to be, quoted on the Stock Exchange and there are certain publication requirements. The minimum share capital of an AG is 100,000 DM.

The *Gesellschaft mit beschränkter Haftung* (GmbH), the limited liability company, is similar to a private limited company in the UK. Its shares may not be quoted on the stock exchange and it does not have to publish its accounts. A GmbH must have a minimum of 20,000 DM as a share capital. There are no share certificates. Members' voting rights are determined by the extent of their share in the firm.

Every AG and GmbH must have a *Vorstand* (Board of Management) and an *Aufsichtsrat* (Board of Supervision).

The *Vorstand* is appointed by the *Aufsichtsrat* and has the authority to decide on all company matters. It is responsible to the *Aufsichtsrat* and the shareholders at their general meeting. According to the Co-determination Law (*Mitbestimmungsgesetz*) each of the two Boards must have worker participation.

On the Board of Management the workers' interests are represented by the Labour Director (*Arbeitsdirektor*), who has an equal voice with the other Board members on all company affairs.

On the Board of Supervision of companies in the coal and steel industry half the members represent the workers, the other half the shareholders, with one impartial member.

Companies outside the coal and steel industry with a workforce of over 2,000 have a similar system of co-determination. Their Supervisory Board is divided equally between Capital and Labour. The worker representatives of companies with less than 2,000 employees only make up a third of the Supervisory Board. Although this position might not give them a very powerful voice, what it does provide is access to important information on company matters.

The OHG (*Offene Handelsgesellschaft*) is comparable to a partnership in the UK, in as much as the liability of the partners is unlimited.

The KG (*Kommanditgesellschaft*) is a type of partnership with two different types of partners: the *Komplementär*, whose liability is unlimited and the

Kommanditist, whose liability is limited to his holding in the company. There is no restriction on numbers of either type of partner. The *Kommanditist* is not involved in the conduct of the company's affairs but must receive a copy of the annual accounts for verification.

Company law requires that all companies, whether limited or not, and any individual running a business, must be entered in the Commercial Register (*Handelsregister*) held by the local court (duplicates are usually held by the local Chamber of Commerce).

Reference Grammar

1 Cases

Being an 'inflected' language, like Latin, German has four cases:

NOMINATIVE (which indicates the SUBJECT of the verb)

ACCUSATIVE (which indicates the OBJECT of the verb, and which is also used after some prepositions)

GENITIVE (which is used to indicate possession, and after some prepositions)

DATIVE (which indicates the indirect object, and is also used after certain verbs and prepositions)

This system of cases applies to all nouns, pronouns and adjectives in German.

2 Nouns

There are three genders of noun in German:

Masculine (*der Mann*)
Feminine (*die Frau*)
Neuter (*das Haus*)

Nouns in German are always written with a CAPITAL letter.

There are various ways in which German nouns form their plural forms. Some of the typical plural formations are given below.

(a) Masculine nouns

1 Nouns that form their plural by adding an Umlaut

der Laden	die Läden
der Garten	die Gärten
der Vater	die Väter

2 Nouns that form their plural by adding an Umlaut and -e

der Sohn	die Söhne
der Arzt	die Ärzte
der Bart	die Bärte

3 Nouns that form their plural by adding an Umlaut and -er

| der Mann | die Männer |
| der Wald | die Wälder |

4 No change in the plural form

der Onkel	die Onkel
der Lehrer	die Lehrer
der Klempner	die Klempner

der Kellner	die Kellner
der Rasen	die Rasen
der Zweifel	die Zweifel

Most masculine nouns ending in **-el**, **-er**, or **-en** belong to this group.

(b) Feminine nouns

1 Nouns that add (-)(e)n in the plural for:

die Kartoffel	die Kartoffeln
die Frau	die Frauen
die Reise	die Reisen
die Fahrt	die Fahrten
die Uhr	die Uhren

Most feminine nouns form their plural in this way.

2 Nouns that add an Umlaut and -e in the plural form

die Braut	die Bräute
die Kuh	die Kühe
die Stadt	die Städte
die Wurst	die Würste
die Hand	die Hände

(c) Neuter nouns

1 Nouns that do not change in the plural form

These are neuter nouns ending in **-chen**, **-er**, **-en**, **-lein**.

das Ufer	die Ufer
das Zimmer	die Zimmer
das Muster	die Muster
das Mädchen	die Mädchen
das Fräulein	die Fräulein
das Becken	die Becken

2 Nouns that add -er and an Umlaut in the plural form

If the noun contains an 'a', 'o', or 'u' an Umlaut is added.

das Rad	die Räder
das Bild	die Bilder
das Dorf	die Dörfer
das Lamm	die Lämmer
das Gehalt	die Gehälter

3 Nouns that add -en in the plural form

das Bett   **die Betten**
das Hemd   **die Hemden**

There are of course other patterns, but those indicated above are the most common.

3 Pronouns

Pronouns in German take the gender, number and case of the nouns they are replacing:

Das ist eine große Wohnung.   **Wir kaufen sie bald.**
Wo ist der Bericht?   **Er ist hier, auf dem Tisch.**
Wo ist der Brief?   **Ich schreibe ihn gleich.**
Sehen Sie das Auto dort?   **Ja, ich sehe es.**

The full pattern of pronouns is:

Singular

Nominative	Accusative	Genitive	Dative
ich	mich	meiner	mir
du	dich	deiner	dir
er	ihn	seiner	ihm
sie	sie	ihrer	ihr
es	es	seiner	ihm

Plural

Nominative	Accusative	Genitive	Dative
wir	uns	unser	uns
ihr	euch	euer	euch
sie	sie	ihrer	ihnen
Sie	Sie	Ihrer	Ihnen

4 The definite article

In German the form of the definite article indicates the gender, number and case of the noun:

Singular

	Masculine	Feminine	Neuter
Nominative	der Wagen	die Lampe	das Bild
Accusative	den Wagen	die Lampe	das Bild
Genitive	des Wagens	der Lampe	des Bildes
Dative	dem Wagen	der Lampe	dem Bild

Plural

The definite article in the plural has the same form in all three genders.

	Masculine	Feminine	Neuter
Nominative	die Wagen	die Lampen	die Bilder
Accusative	die Wagen	die Lampen	die Bilder
Genitive	der Wagen	der Lampen	der Bilder
Dative	den Wagen	den Lampen	den Bildern

5 The indefinite article

Like the definite article, the form of the indefinite article changes with the gender, number and case of the noun:

Singular

	Masculine	Feminine	Neuter
Nominative	ein Wagen	eine Lampe	ein Bild
Accusative	einen Wagen	eine Lampe	ein Bild
Genitive	eines Wagens	einer Lampe	eines Bildes
Dative	einem Wagen	einer Lampe	einem Bild

Plural

	Masculine	Feminine	Neuter
Nominative	keine Wagen	keine Lampen	keine Bilder
Accusative	keine Wagen	keine Lampen	keine Bilder
Genitive	keiner Wagen	keiner Lampen	keiner Bilder
Dative	keinen Wagen	keinen Lampen	keinen Bildern

6 Adjectives

Adjectives in German take an ending if they precede a noun:

das Bild ist schön.
die Abteilung ist groß.

but:

das schöne Bild
die große Abteilung

When the adjective precedes the noun, its endings are appropriate to its case, number and gender.

Singular

	Masculine	*Feminine*	*Neuter*
Nominative	der neue Wagen	die neue Lampe	das neue Büro
Accusative	den neuen Wagen	die neue Lampe	das neue Büro
Genitive	des neuen Wagens	der neuen Lampe	des neuen Büros
Dative	dem neuen Wagen	der neuen Lampe	dem neuen Büro

Plural

	Masculine	*Feminine*	*Neuter*
Nominative	die neuen Wagen	die neuen Lampen	die neuen Büros
Accusative	die neuen Wagen	die neuen Lampen	die neuen Büros
Genitive	der neuen Wagen	der neuen Lampen	der neuen Büros
Dative	den neuen Wagen	den neuen Lampen	den neuen Büros

The endings after the INDEFINITE article are as follows:

Singular

	Masculine	*Feminine*	*Neuter*
Nominative	ein neuer Wagen	eine neue Lampe	ein neues Büro
Accusative	einen neuen Wagen	eine neue Lampe	ein neues Büro
Genitive	eines neuen Wagens	einer neuen Lampe	eines neuen Büros
Dative	einem neuen Wagen	einer neuen Lampe	einem neuen Büro

Plural

	Masculine	Feminine	Neuter
Nominative	keine neuen Wagen	keine neuen Lampen	keine neuen Büros
Accusative	keine neuen Wagen	keine neuen Lampen	keine neuen Büros
Genitive	keiner neuen Wagen	keiner neuen Lampen	keiner neuen Büros
Dative	keinen neuen Wagen	keinen neuen Lampen	keinen neuen Büros

Comparison of adjectives

In forming comparatives, German adjectives frequently follow the same pattern as English adjectives, i.e. they add **-er**:

> **Sein Wagen ist neu. Ihr Wagen ist neuer.**
> **Dieser Wagen ist schnell, aber mein Wagen ist schneller.**

Certain adjectives take an Umlaut in the comparative form:

> **Er ist größer als ich.**
> **Ich bin jünger als er.**

If the adjective precedes the noun, it takes the appropriate ending:

> **der größere Wagen**
> **die kleineren Unternehmen**
> **mein älterer Bruder**

7 Verbs

Present tense

The endings that follow are common to most verbs in German in the present tense:

> **ich schreibe**
> **du schreibst**
> **er/sie/es schreibt**
> **wir schreiben**
> **ihr schreibt**
> **sie schreiben**
> **Sie schreiben**

Note however that the verbs **sein** ('to be') and **haben** ('to have') are irregular:

Sein	Haben
ich bin	**ich habe**
du bist	**du hast**
er/sie/es ist	**er/sie/es hat**

wir sind	wir haben
ihr seid	ihr habt
sie sind	sie haben
Sie sind	Sie haben

Word order

In main clauses, the verb is the second 'idea'/'concept' in the clause:

Wir kaufen den Wagen heute.
Heute kaufen wir den Wagen.
Den Wagen kaufen wir heute.

In subordinate clauses, the verb is at the end of the clause:

Weil er spät ankommt, gehen wir nicht aus.
Wenn wir heute hier bleiben, fahren wir morgen nach München.

In sentences in which there are expressions of time, manner and place, the expressions are usually in that sequence:

Wir fahren morgen (time) **mit dem Bus** (manner) **nach Bingen** (place).

Questions

In order to form a question, the position of the verb and the subject are inverted:

Wir arbeiten heute.	**Arbeiten wir heute?**
Er übernachtet in diesem Hotel.	**Übernachtet er in diesem Hotel?**

Negatives

The negative of the verb is formed by the use of **nicht**:

Ihre Arbeit gefällt ihr.	**Ihre Arbeit gefällt ihr nicht.**
Mein Chef ist heute im Büro.	**Mein Chef ist heute nicht im Büro.**
Wir fahren zusammen zur Messe.	**Wir fahren nicht zusammen zur Messe.**

Perfect tense

Weak verbs

These form the perfect tense by using the auxiliary verb **haben** with the past participle. The past participle is formed by removing **-en** from the infinitive form of the verb, and adding **ge-** to the front of the verb, and **-(e)t** to the end:

kaufen	kauf	gekauft
arbeiten	arbeit	gearbeitet
stellen	stell	gestellt
setzen	setz	gesetzt

Thus:

Er kauft.	He buys.

Er hat gekauft.	He has bought.
Sie arbeitet.	She works.
Sie hat gearbeitet.	She has worked.

Strong verbs

Most strong verbs also use **haben** as an auxiliary verb (some use **sein** – see below), but form their past participle by adding **-en** rather than **-et**. The verb also frequently undergoes a vowel change as part of the process:

liegen	**gelegen**
werfen	**geworfen**
trinken	**getrunken**
sitzen	**gesessen**
schreiben	**geschrieben**

Ich werfe	I throw.
Ich habe geworfen	I have thrown.

Sie trinkt	She drinks.
Sie hat getrunken	She has drunk.

Wir schreiben.	We write.
Wir haben geschrieben.	We have written.

The form of the past participle of strong verbs is given in any good dictionary.

Some verbs that indicate a change of position or a change of state take **sein** as an auxiliary verb:

Ich gehe.	**Ich bin gegangen.**
Er fährt.	**Er ist gefahren.**
Sie steigt.	**Sie ist gestiegen.**

Imperfect tense

The imperfect tense of the verbs **sein** and **haben** is as follows:

Sein		*Haben*	
ich war	I was, etc.	**ich hatte**	I had, etc.
du warst		**du hattest**	
er/sie/es war		**er/sie/es hatte**	
wir waren		**wir hatten**	
ihr wart		**ihr hattet**	
sie waren		**sie hatten**	
Sie waren		**Sie hatten**	

Future tense

The future is formed by using the appropriate form of **werden**, in the present tense, together with an infinitive:

Wir arbeiten.	Wir werden arbeiten.
Er kommt.	Er wird kommen.
Sie geht.	Sie wird gehen.

The full form of the verb **werden** in the present tense is as follows:

ich werde
du wirst
er/sie/es wird
wir werden
ihr werdet
sie werden
Sie werden

Separable verbs

Separable verbs have a separable prefix, which in main clauses is separated from the verb and placed at the end of the clause:

abfahren	Wir fahren um 7 Uhr ab.
ankommen	Wir kommen um 9 Uhr an.
ausgehen	Wir gehen um 8 Uhr aus.

In subordinate clauses the separable prefix rejoins the verb:

Wenn wir jetzt ausgehen, sind wir um 9 Uhr zurück.

In forming their past participle, separable verbs insert the **ge-** between the prefix and the rest of the verb:

umsteigen	umgestiegen
ausgehen	ausgegangen
absetzen	abgesetzt

8 Modal verbs

The modal verbs in German

können	to be able to
dürfen	to be allowed to
mögen	to like
müssen	to have to
sollen	to be supposed to
wollen	to want to

often take a dependent infinitive:

Ich will gleich fahren.
Er kann gut spielen.
Sie darf nicht rauchen.

Note that these are highly irregular verbs, and the forms are indicated below:

ich kann	ich darf	ich mag
du kannst	du darfst	du magst
er/sie/es kann	er/sie/es darf	er/sie/es mag
wir können	wir dürfen	wir mögen
ihr könnt	ihr dürft	ihr mögt
sie können	sie dürfen	sie mögen
Sie können	Sie dürfen	Sie mögen

ich muß	ich soll
du mußt	du sollst
er/sie/es muß	er/sie/es soll
wir müssen	wir sollen
ihr müßt	ihr sollt
sie müssen	sie sollen
Sie müssen	Sie sollen

Mögen is frequently used in its imperfect subjunctive form:

Möchten Sie ein Eis?
Ich möchte hier bleiben.
Möchten Sie mit uns fahren?

9 Days of the week

Sonntag	Sunday
Montag	Monday
Dienstag	Tuesday
Mittwoch	Wednesday
Donnerstag	Thursday
Freitag	Friday
Samstag	Saturday
(Sonnabend)	(Saturday)

10 Months of the year

Januar	January
Februar	February
März	March
April	April
Mai	May
Juni	June
Juli	July
August	August
September	September

Oktober	October
November	November
Dezember	December

Im Oktober	In October.
Ende November	At the end of November.
Anfang September	At the beginning of September.

11 Numbers

eins	one	**zwanzig**	twenty
zwei	two	**einundzwanzig**	twenty-one
drei	three	**zweiundzwanzig**	twenty-two
vier	four	**dreißig**	thirty
fünf	five	**vierzig**	forty
sechs	six	**fünfzig**	fifty
sieben	seven	**sechzig**	sixty
acht	eight	**siebzig**	seventy
neun	nine	**achtzig**	eighty
zehn	ten	**neunzig**	ninety
elf	eleven	**hundert**	one hundred
zwölf	twelve	**hunderteins**	101
dreizehn	thirteen	**hunderteinundzwanzig**	121
vierzehn	fourteen	**hundertdreiunddreißig**	133
fünfzehn	fifteen	**zweihundert**	two hundred
sechzehn	sixteen	**tausend**	one thousand
siebzehn	seventeen	**zweitausend**	two thousand
achtzehn	eighteen	**eine Million**	one million
neunzehn	nineteen		

2.5 (two point five)   **zwei Komma fünf 2,5**

(Note the use of the comma in expressing decimals in German.)

6%   **sechs Prozent**

Ordinal numbers are formed by adding **-(s)t** to the cardinal number, and the appropriate adjective ending:

zwei	**die zweite Straße rechts**
sechs	**das sechste Haus**
zwanzig	**die zwanzigste Firma**

Note that two of the ordinal numbers are irregular:

eins	one	**die erste Straße**
drei	three	**der dritte Wagen**

12 Time

The twenty-four hour clock is very frequently used, particularly in business/formal contexts, but also increasingly at a more informal level.

12.48 Uhr	**zwölf Uhr achtundvierzig**
14.34 Uhr	**vierzehn Uhr vierunddreißig**

Various other methods of telling the time are used:

9.45		**neun Uhr fünfundvierzig**
	or	**viertel vor zehn**
	or	**fünfzehn Minuten vor zehn**
	or	**dreiviertel zehn**
		(this is particularly common in the South)
10.50		**zehn Uhr fünfzig**
	or	**zehn Minuten vor elf**
	or	**zehn vor elf**
8.30		**acht Uhr dreißig**
	or	**halb neun**

What time is it?

Wieviel Uhr ist es?
Wie spät ist es?
Wieviel Uhr haben Sie?

13 Dates

To form dates, the ordinal numbers are used:

8 May	**der achte Mai**
4 September	**der vierte September**
20 December	**der zwanzigste Dezember**
on 20 May	**am zwanzigsten Mai**
on 14 July	**am vierzehnten Juli**
on March 15	**am vierzehnten März**

14 Prepositions

Prepositions in German take the accusative, genitive, or dative cases.

Some prepositions that always take the accusative are:

bis	until, up to	**gegen**	towards, to, against, compared with
durch	through, by, across	**ohne**	without
entlang	along	**um**	about, around, for
für	for, instead of, as		

Prepositions that always take the genitive are:

trotz	in spite of
wegen	on account of, owing to
statt	instead of

(Note that there is an increasing tendency in spoken German to use **wegen** with the dative case.)

Er kommt wegen dem schlechten Wetter nicht.

The following prepositions always take the dative:

aus	out of, from	**nach**	to, after
außer	apart from, except	**seit**	for, since
bei	near, by	**von**	from
mit	with	**zu**	to, towards
		gegenüber	one another, opposite

The preposition **in** can take either the accusative or the dative case. If motion 'to' or 'into' is implied, then **in** is used with the accusative:

Er geht in das Zimmer.	He is going into the room.
Wir gehen in das Haus.	We are going into the house.

(Wir gehen in dem Haus would mean that we were walking around inside the house.)

If 'static location' is implied, **in** is used with the dative:

Wir bleiben in dem/im Zimmer.	We are staying in the room.
Wir arbeiten in dem/im Büro.	We are working in the office.

Business Glossary

Key to glossary

Grammatical abbreviations

abbr	abbreviation
adj	adjective
adv	adverb
conj	conjunction
det	determiner
n	noun
nf	feminine noun
nfpl	plural feminine noun
nm	masculine noun
nmpl	plural masculine noun
nn	neuter noun
nnpl	plural neuter noun
pp	past participle
pref	prefix
prep	preposition
vb	verb

Symbols

* denotes slang term
(US) term particular to USA
(GB) term particular to Great Britain

NB: Contexts are given in parentheses after term and part of speech
or before multiple translations

German plurals are given in parentheses after term/translation

Parts of speech are provided for all headwords and for translations
where appropriate. Subterms are only supplied with parts of speech
where it is considered necessary to indicate gender or to avoid
ambiguity

German–English

abbauen *vb* (workforce) trim *vb*

Abdruck *nm* imprint **einen Abdruck machen** (credit card) take an imprint

abdrucken *vb* (credit card) take an imprint *vb*

abfahren *vb* leave *vb*

Abfallprodukte *nnpl* waste products *npl*

abfertigen *vb* clear sth through customs *vb*

Abfindung (-en) *nf* severance pay **großzügige Abfindung** golden parachute **hohe Abfindung** golden handshake

Abfindungszahlung (-en) *nf* severance pay *n*

Abflauen (-) *nn* abatement *n*

Abgabe (-n) *nf* toll *n*

abgabenfrei *adj* zero-rated

Abgabenordnung (-en) *nf* tax code *n*

abgemacht! *adj* it's a deal!

Abgeordnete/r *nmf* Member of parliment *nm* **Abgeordnete/r des Europarlaments** Member of the European Parliament (MEP)

abhalten *vb* **eine Sitzung abhalten** hold a meeting

Abhebungen *nfpl* withdrawal of funds *n*

abhören *vb* listen to *vb* **ein Gespräch abhören** bug a call

Abkommen (-) *nn* formal agreement *n* **internationales Abkommen** international agreement *n*

Abkühlung *nf* cooling *n* **konjunkturelle Abkühlung** economic slowdown

abkürzen *vb* abbreviate *vb*

Abkürzung (-en) *nf* abbreviation *n*

Ablagesystem (-e) *nn* filing system *n*

Ablauf *nm* expiry *n*, expiration (US)

ablegen *vb* file *vb*

ablehnen *vb* (goods) reject *vb* (offer) turn down *vb* **einen Anspruch ablehnen** refuse a claim

Ablehnung (-en) *nf* refusal *n*

abonnieren *vb* subscribe *vb*

Abordnung (-en) *nf* secondment *n*

abrechnen *vb* (cheque) clear a cheque *vb*

Abrechnungszahlung (-en) *nf* clearing payment *n*

abreisen *vb* (hotel) check out *vb*

absagen *vb* (an appointment) cancel *vb*

Absatz *nm* sales *n* **den Absatz steigern** boost sales

Absatzprognose (-n) *nf* sales forecast *n*

Absatzquote (-n) *nf* sales quota *n*

Absatzschwankungen *nfpl* fluctuation in sales *n*

abschaffen *vb* abolish *vb*

Abschaffung *nf* abolition *n*

Abschätzung (-en) *nf* appraisal *n*

Abschied *nm* farewell *n*, parting *n* **von jemanden Abschied nehmen** take leave of sb

abschließen *vb* clinch *vb* **ein Geschäft abschließen** clinch/close a deal

Abschluß *nm* terminal *n*

Abschlußzahlung (-en) *nf* final settlement *n*

abschreiben *vb* (debts) write off *vb*

Abschreibung *nf* write-off *n*

Abschwung (-ünge) *nm* (economic) downturn *n*

absenden *vb* (goods) dispatch *vb*

Absender (-) *nm* consigner/or *n*, dispatcher *n*, sender *n*

absetzbar *adj* marketable *adj*

Absetzgebiet (-e) *nn* market outlet *n*

Absicherung *nf* **Absicherung von Risiken** risk management

absolut *adj* absolute *adj*

absorbieren *vb* absorb *vb*

Absprache (-n) *nf* working agreement *n*

absteigend *adj* downward *adj*

abstimmen *vb* vote *vb*

Abstimmung *nf* voting *n*

Abteilung (-en) *nf* department *n*

Abteilungsleiter (-) *nm* head of department *n*

abverkaufen *vb* sell off *vb*

abwägen *vb* weigh *vb*

Abwertung (-en) *nf* devaluation *n*

abwesend *adj* absent *adj*

Abwesenheit *nf* non-attendance *n* **häufige Abwesenheit** absenteeism *n*

abwiegen *vb* weigh *vb*

abziehbar *adj* deductible *adj*

abziehen *vb* deduct *vb*

Abzug (-üge) *nm* deduction *n*

Adresse *nf* address *nf* **Adresse unbekannt** zero address

Adressenkartei (-en) *nf* mailing list *n*

adressieren *vb* address *vb*

aggressiv *adj* high-powered *adj*

Agrar- *cpd* agrarian *adj*

Agrarerzeugnisse *nfpl* produce *n*

Agrargeschäft (-e) *nn* agribusiness *n*

Agrarsubventionen *nfpl* farming subsidies *npl*

Agronom (-e) *nm* agronomist *n*

Akkordarbeit *nf* contract labour *n*, piecework *n*

Akkreditiv (-e) *nn* letter of credit *n* **unwiderrufliches Akkreditiv** irrevocable letter of credit **widerrufliches Akkreditiv** revocable letter of credit

Akte (-n) *nf* file *n*

Aktenschrank (-änke) *nm* filing cabinet *n*

Aktie (-n) *nf* share *n* **Aktien und Obligationen** stocks and shares **Aktien im Publikumsbesitz** outstanding stock **börsennotierte Aktie** listed share, listed stock (US)

Aktienbezugsrecht (-e) *nn* share option *n*, stock option (US)

Aktienbörse (-n) *nf* stock market *n*

Aktienemission (-en) *nf* share issue *n*, stock issue (US)

Aktiengesellschaft (-en) *nf* joint stock company *n*, incorporated company (US)

Aktienhandel *nm* equity trading *n*

Aktienindex (-e) *nm* share index *n*

Aktienkaduzierung *nf* forfeit *n*

Aktienmakler (auf Provisionsbasis) (-) *nm* commission broker *n*

Aktienmarkt (-märkte) *nm* stock market *n*

Aktienrendite *nf* yield on shares *n*

Aktienzertifikat (-e) *nn* share certificate *n*, stock certificate (US)

Aktionär (-en) *nm* shareholder *n* **vorgeschobener aktionär** nominee shareholder

Aktiva *npl* assets *n* **immaterielle Aktiva** intangible assets

Aktuar (-e) *nm* actuary *n*

aktuell *adj* up-to-date *adj*

Akzept *nn* acceptance *nm* **eingeschränktes Akzept** qualified acceptance

Akzeptbank (-en) *nf* acceptance house *n*

akzessorisch *adj* **akzessorische Sicherheit** collateral security

Alarmzeichen (-) *nn* warning sign *n*

allgemein *adj* general *adj* **allgemeine Personengesellschaft (-en)** general partnership **allgemeine Verwaltung** general management

Altersrente (-n) *nf* retirement pension *n*

Altmetall *nn* scrap metal *n*

Amortisation *nf* amortization *n*

Amortisationsfonds (-) *nm* redemption fund *n*

Amortisationsschuld (-en) *nf* redeemable bond *n*

amortisierbar *adj* redeemable *adj*

amortisieren *vb* amortize *vb*, redeem *vb*

Amortisierung *nf* redemption *n*

Amt *nn* office *n* **im Amt sein** hold office **Amt für Anlagen und Wertpapiere** SIB (Securities and Investment Board) (GB) *abbr*

amtierend *adj* office holder *n*

Amtsperiode (-n) *nf* tour of duty *n*

Amtsschimmel *nm* red tape *n*

Amtszeichen (-) *nn* (phone) dialling tone *n*, dial tone (US)

Amtszeit *nf* tenure *n*, term of office *n*

Analyse *nf* analysis **horizontale Analyse** horizontal analysis

analysieren *vb* analyze *vb*

Anbieter (-) *nm* offeror *n*

ändern *vb* amend *vb* (market) turn *vb*

Änderung (-en) *nf* amendment *n*

anerkennen *vb* validate *vb*

Anfangskapital *nn* initial capital *n*

Anfangslohn (-löhne) *nm* starting wage *n*

Anforderungen *nfpl* requirements *npl* **Ihren Anforderungen entsprechend** in accordance with your requirements

Anfrage (-n) *nf* enquiry *n*

Angabe (-en) *nf* specification *n*

angeben *vb* specify *vb*

Angebot (-e) *nn* bid *n*, tender *n* **ein Angebot einreichen** lodge a tender **endgültiges Angebot** final offer **Angebot gilt bis** offer valid until... **Angebot und Nachfrage** supply and demand **Angebot vorbehaltlich der Bestätigung** offer subject to confirmation **ein Angebot zurückziehen** withdraw an offer **festes Angebot** firm offer **höheres Angebot** higher bid **schriftliches Angebot** offer in writing **unverbindliches Angebot** tentative offer

Angebotspreis (-e) *nm* tender price *n*

Angebotsteller (-) *nm* tenderer *n*

angelernt *adj* semi-skilled *adj*

angemessen *adj* **angemessener Lohn** fair wage

angesammelt *adj* accumulated *adj*

angestellt *adj* **neu angestellt** *adj* newly-appointed *adj*

Angestellte/r *nmf* white-collar worker *n* **Angestellter sein** be an employee **leitender Angestellter** executive

Ankaufskurs *nm* buying rate *n*

anklagen *vb* charge sb with sth *vb*

Ankündigung (-en) *nf* advance notice *n*

Ankurbelung *nf* boost *n*

Anlage (-n) *nf* enclosure *n*, facility *n* (machinery) plant *n*

Anlageberater (-) *nm* investment adviser *n*

Anlagenausschlachtung *nf* asset stripping *n*

Anlagenvermietung *nf* plant hire *n*

Anlagevermögen *nn* fixed capital *n*, fixed assets *npl*

anlegen *vb* (ship) dock *vb*

Anlegeplatz (-plätze) *nm* mooring *n*

Anlegerecht *nn* mooring rights *n*

Anleihe *nf* loan *n*, borrowing *n* **Anleihe ohne Zinseinschluß (-n)** flat bond **gesicherte Anleihe (-n)** debenture bond **zweckgebundene Anleihe (-n)** tied loan

Anleihegläubiger (-e) *nm* bondholder *n*

Anleihekapital *nn* debenture capital *n*, debenture stock (US)

anmelden (sich) *vb* (register in an hotel) check in *vb*

Annahmeverweigerung *nf* non-acceptance *n*

annullieren *vb* cancel *vb*

Annullierung (-en) *nf* annulment *n*

anpassen *vb* adjust *vb* (adapt) tailor *vb*
Anpassung (-en) *nf* adjustment *n*
anrechenbar *adj* chargeable *adj*
Anreiz (-e) *nm* incentive *n*
Anruf (-e) *nm* telephone call
Anrufbeantworter (-) *nm* Ansaphone (R) *n*, answering machine *n*
ansammeln *vb* accumulate *vb*
Anschlag (-äge) *nm* touch *n*
Anschläge *npl* **Anschläge pro Minute** wpm (words per minute)
Anschlüsse *nmpl* **Anschlüsse und unbewegliches Inventar** fixtures and fittings *npl*
Ansehen *nn* kudos *n*
Anspruch (-üche) *nm* claim *n* **Ansprüche geltend machen** put in a claim
Anstalt (-en) *nf* institution *n*
Anstieg (-e) *nm* (in earnings) rise *n*, raise (US) (in unemployment) rise *n*
anstreben *vb* tend toward *vb*
Anteil (-e) *nm* stake *n*
anteilig *adj* pro rata
Anteilseigner (-) *nm* stakeholder *n*, stockholder *n*
antiinflationär *adj* **antiinflationäre Maßnahmen** anti-inflationary measures
Antragsformular (-e) *nn* claim form *n*
Antragsteller (-) *nm* claimant *n*
Antwort (-en) *nf* answer *n*
antworten *vb* answer *vb*
Anwalt (-älte) *nm* solicitor *n*, lawyer (US)
Anweisung (-en) *nf* instruction *n* **Anweisungen befolgen** follow instructions
Anwendung *nf* use *n* **intensive Anwendung** intensive usage
Anwerbung *nf* employee recruitment *n*
Anzahlung *nf* down payment
anzapfen *vb* tap *vb*
Anzeige (-n) *nf* classified advertisement *n*
Apparat *nm* appliance *n*, telephone **am Apparat bleiben** (on telephone) hang on *vb*
Appell (-e) *nm* appeal *n*
Arbeit *nf* employment *n*, labour *n*, work *n*, workload *n* **Arbeit einstellen** (finish work) knock off* **Arbeit suchen** look for work **nach Stunden bezahlte Arbeit** hourly-paid work
arbeiten *vb* work *vb*
arbeitend *adj* **arbeitendes Unternehmen** going concern
Arbeiter (-) *nm* worker *n*, blue-collar worker *n* **manueller Arbeiter** manual worker **ungelernter Arbeiter** labourer
Arbeiterdirektor (-en) *nm* worker-director *n*
Arbeitgeber (-) *nm* employer *n*
Arbeitgeberverband (-ände) *nm* employer's federation *n*
Arbeitnehmer (-) *nm* employee *n*
Arbeitsamt (-ämter) *nn* Job centre *n*, Job shop *n*
Arbeitsanalyse (-n) *nf* Job analysis *n*
Arbeitsaufteilung *nf* division of labour *n*
Arbeitsbedingungen *nfpl* working

conditions *npl*
Arbeitsbereich (-e) *nm* working area *n*
Arbeitsbeschaffung *nf* job creation *n*
Arbeitsbeziehungen *nfpl* labour relations *npl* **industrielle Arbeitsbeziehungen** industrial relations
Arbeitsfreude *nf* job satisfaction *n*
Arbeitsgemeinschaft (-en) *nf* workers' collective *n*, working party *n*
Arbeitsgenehmigung (-en) *nf* work permit *n*
Arbeitsgericht (-e) *nn* industrial tribunal *n*
Arbeitshygiene *nf* industrial health *n*
arbeitsintensiv *adj* labour-intensive *adj*
Arbeitskampf (-kämpfe) *nm* industrial action *n*, industrial dispute *n*, labour dispute *n*
Arbeitskollege (-) *nm* workmate *n*
Arbeitskosten *npl* labour costs *npl*
Arbeitskräfte *nfpl* human resources *npl*
arbeitslos *adj* jobless *adj*, redundant *adj*, unemployed *adj* **arbeitslos sein** be out of work
Arbeitslosen (die) *npl* the jobless *npl*
Arbeitslosengeld *nn* unemployment pay *n*
Arbeitslosenrate (-n) *nf* rate of unemployment *n*
Arbeitslosenunterstützung *nf* unemployment benefit *n*
Arbeitslosenversicherung *nf* unemployment insurance *n*
Arbeitslosenziffer (-n) *nf* level of unemployment *n*
Arbeitslosigkeit *nf* redundancy *n*, unemployment *n*
Arbeitsmarkt *nm* labour market *n*
Arbeitspapier (-e) *nn* working paper *n*
Arbeitsplan (-pläne) *nm* work schedule *n*
Arbeitsplatz *nm* workplace *n*
Arbeitsplatzverlust (-e) *nm* loss of job *n*
Arbeitsrecht (-e) *nn* employment law *n*, labour law *n*
Arbeitsstreitigkeit (-en) *nf* industrial dispute *n*
Arbeitstag (-e) *nm* working day *n*, workday (US)
Arbeitsteilung *nf* work sharing *n*
Arbeitsumwelt *nf* working environment *n*
Arbeitsunfall (-älle) *nm* industrial accident *n*
Arbeitsverhältnis (-isse) *nn* working relationship *n*
Arbeitsverhältnisse *nnpl* working conditions *npl*
Arbeitsvermittlung *nf* employment agency *n*
Arbeitsvertrag (-äge) *nm* employment contract *n*
Arbeitswoche (-n) *nf* working week *n*, work-week (US)
Arbeitswütige/r *nmf* workaholic *n*
Arbeitszeit (-en) *nf* working hours *npl* **festgesetzte Arbeitszeit** fixed hours
Arbeitszeugnis (-se) *nn* certificate of employment *n*

Arbitrage (-n) *nf* arbitrage *n*
Art *nf* (method) mode *n*
Artikel (-) *nm* item *n*
ärztlich *adj* medical *adj*
Aufenthaltserlaubnis (-isse) *nf* Green Card (US) *n*
Aufgabe (-n) *nf* task *n*
Aufgabenbereich *nm* terms of reference *n*
Aufgabenverteilung *nf* task management *n*
aufgeben *vb* abandon *vb* **ein Geschäft aufgeben** close a business **das Geschäft aufgeben** (informal) shut up shop
aufgelaufen *adj* **aufgelaufene Zinsen** accrued interest
aufgeschoben *adj* (tax) deferred *adj*
aufgliedern *vb* itemize *vb*
Aufgliederung *nf* breakdown *n* **Aufgliederung der Zahlen** (of figures) breakdown
aufhalten *vb* (delay) hold up *vb*
aufhängen *vb* (telephone) hang up *vb*
aufheben *vb* close *vb*, lift up *vb* **ein Embargo aufheben** lift an embargo **eine Sitzung aufheben** close a meeting **einen Vertrag aufheben** cancel a contract
Aufkauf (-käufe) *nm* buy-out *n*
aufkaufen *vb* buy out *vb*
auflegen *vb* (currency) float *vb*
auflösen *vb* break up *vb* **ein Konto auflösen** close an account
Auflösung (-en) *nf* breakup *n*
aufnahmefähiger Markt (-märkte) *nm* broad market *n*
aufschieben *vb* (postpone) defer *vb* postpone *vb*
aufschreiben *vb* write down *vb*
Aufschub (-übe) *nm* deferment *n*
Aufschwung (-ünge) *nm* upswing *n*, upturn *n* **Aufschwung nehmen** boom
Aufseher (-) *nm* supervisor *n*
aufsichtsführend *adj* supervisory *adj*
Aufsichtsrat (-räte) *nm* factory board *n*, supervisory board *n*
Aufsichtsratsvorsitzende/r *nmf* (of company) president *n*
Auftrag (-äge) *nm* brief *n* **eiliger Auftrag** rush job *n*
Auftragnehmer (-) *nm* contractor *n*
Auftragsbuch (-bücher) *nn* order book
aufwärts *adv* upwards *adv*
Aufwärts- *cpd* upward *adj* **Aufwärtsentwicklung** *nf* upward trend *n*
Aufwendung *nf* expenditure *n*
Aufwendungen *nfpl* **betriebliche Aufwendungen** operating costs *npl*
aufwerten *vb* (currency) revalue *vb*
Aufwertung (-en) *nf* (of currency) revaluation *n*
Aufzeichnung *nf* record *n* **gemäß unseren Aufzeichnungen** according to our records
Auktionator (-en) *nm* auctioneer *n*
Ausbeute *nf* spoils *npl*
ausbilden *vb* (staff) train *vb*

Ausbildung *nf* training *n* **betriebliche Ausbildung** inhouse training
Ausbildungslehrgang (-gänge) *nm* training course *n*
Ausbildungszentrum (-en) *nn* training centre *n*
ausbreiten *vb* (payments) spread *vb*
ausdiskutieren *vb* (agreement, policy) thrash out *vb*
Außenbezirke *nmpl* outer suburbs *npl*
Außendienstleiter (-) *nm* field manager *n*
Außenhandel *nm* foreign trade *n*
Außenmarkt (-märkte) *nm* foreign market *n*
Außenstände *npl* outstanding debt *n*
außerordentlich *adj* extraordinary *adj* **außerordentliche Reservefonds** funds surplus **außerordentlicher Wert** extraordinary value **außerordentliche Versammlung** extraordinary meeting
ausführen *vb* carry out *vb*
Ausfuhrsteuer (-n) *nf* export tax *n*
Ausgaben *nfpl* expenditure *n*, spending *n* **Ausgaben reduzieren** axe* expenditure
Ausgabenstruktur *nf* spending patterns *npl*
Ausgabesteuern *nfpl* expenditure taxes *n*
Ausgänge *nmpl* outgoings *npl*
ausgeben *vb* spend *vb*
ausgleichen *vb* equalize *vb*
ausländisch *adj* foreign *adj*
Auslands- *cpd* external *adj*
Auslandsabsatz *nm* export sales *n*
Auslandsbank (-en) *nf* foreign bank *n*
Auslandsgelder *nnpl* foreign currency holdings *npl*
Auslandshilfe *nf* foreign aid *n*
Auslandshilfsprogramm *nn* foreign aid programme *n*
Auslandsinvestitionen *nfpl* foreign investment *n*
Auslandskonkurrenz *nf* foreign competition *n*
Auslandskredit (-e) *nm* foreign loan *n*
Auslandsreise (-n) *nf* foreign travel *n*
Auslandsunternehmen (-) *nn* foreign company *n*
auslaufen *vb* expire *vb*
auspacken *vb* unpack *vb*
Ausprobieren *nn* trial and error *n*
ausreichen *vb* tide over *vb*
Ausrüstung *nf* (equipment) kit *n*
ausschließen *vb* exclude *vb*
Ausschlußklausel (-n) *nf* exclusion clause *n*
ausschreiben *vb* put something out for tender *vb* **einen Vertrag ausschreiben** tender for a contract
Ausschreibung *nf* tendering *n*
Ausschuß (-üsse) *nm* committee *n*
Ausschußsitzung (-en) *nf* committee meeting *n*
Aussichten (die) *nfpl* future prospects *npl*
Aussperrung (-en) *nf* (of strikers) lockout *n*
ausstatten *vb* equip *vb*
Ausstattung *nf* equipment *n*

ausstehend *adj* outstanding *adj*
ausstellen *vb* display *vb*, exhibit *vb* (cheque) draw *vb* (policy) issue *vb*
Ausstellung (-en) *nf* (of goods) display *n* show *n*, exhibition *n*
Ausstellungshalle (-n) *nf* exhibition hall *n*
Austauschrelationen *nfpl* terms of trade *npl*
Ausverkauf (-äufe) *nm* clearance sale *n*
ausverkauft *adj* out of stock *adj*
Auswanderung *nf* emigration *n*
ausweichen *vb* evade *vb*
Ausweichklausel (-n) *nf* escape clause *n*
Ausweis (-e) *nm* identity card *n*
Ausweitung *nf* expansion *n* **industrielle Ausweitung** industrial expansion
Auswirkung *nf* consequence *n*
Auswirkungen *nfpl* **die finanziellen Auswirkungen** financial effects
auszahlen *vb* disburse *vb*
Auszahlung *nf* net(t) proceeds *n*, payola (US)
Auszubildende/r *nmf* trainee *n*
Auszug (-üge) *nm* abstract *n*
autark *adj* self-sufficient *adj*
Autoindustrie (-n) *nf* automobile industry *n*, motor industry *n*
Automat (-en) *nm* vending machine *n*
automatisch *adj* automatic *adj*
Automatisierung *nf* automation *n*
autonom *adj* autonomous *adj*
Autoversicherung *nf* car insurance *n*
Bahn *nf* **per Bahn** by rail
Bahntransport *nm* rail transport *n*
Baissemarkt (-märkte) *nm* bear market *n*
Baissier (-s) *nm* (stock exchange) bear *n*
Balkendiagramm (-e) *nn* bar chart *n*
Bankangestellte/r *nmf* bank clerk *n*
Bankdarlehen (-) *nn* bank loan *n*
Bankdirektor (-en) *nm* bank manager *n*
Bankfeiertag (-e) *nm* bank holiday *n*
Bankgebühren *nfpl* bank charges *npl*
Bankguthaben (-) *nn* bank balance *n*
Bankier (-s) *nm* banker *n*
Bankkonto (-konten) *nn* bank account *n*
Bankkredit (-e) *nm* bank loan *n*
Bankkreise *nmpl* banking circles *n*
Banknetz (-e) *nn* banking network *n*
Banknote (-n) *nf* banknote *n*
bankrott *adj* bankrupt *adj* **bankrott sein** be bankrupt
Bankspesen *npl* bank charges *npl*
Banküberweisung (-en) *nf* bank transfer *n*
Bankwechsel (-) *nm* bank draft *n*
bar *adj* cash *adj* **bar zahlen** pay in cash
Barangebot (-e) *nn* cash offer *n*
Bargeld *nn* cash *n*, hard cash *n*
Barrabatt *nm* cash discount *n*
Barrengold *nn* gold bullion *n*
Barriere (-n) *nf* barrier *n*
Barscheck (-s) *nm* open cheque *n*
Barzahlung (-en) *nf* cash payment *n* **Barzahlung bei Erhalt der Ware** cash on receipt of goods **Barzahlung vor Lieferung** cash

before delivery **Barzahlung bei Lieferung** cash on delivery (COD)
Basiseinkommen *nn* basic income *n*
Basiszins (-en) *nm* base rate *n*
Baufirma (-firmen) *nf* building firm *n*
Baugenehmigung (-en) *nf* building permlt *n*
Bauindustrie *nf* building industry/trade *n*, construction industry *n*
Baumaterial *nn* building materials *npl*
Bausparkasse (-n) *nf* building society *n*
Baustelle (-n) *nf* building site *n*
Bauträger (-) *nm* property developer *n*
Bauunternehmer (-) *nm* builder *n*, building contractor *n*
beachtenswert *adj* noteworthy *adj*
Beamte/r *nmf* official *n*
beanspruchen *vb* (demand) claim *vb*
beanstanden *vb* complain about sth *vb*
beantworten *vb* answer *vb*
bearbeiten *vb* machine *vb*, process *vb*
beauftragen *vb* brief *vb*
Bedarf *nm* requirement *n*
Bedarfserfassung *nf* needs assessment *n*
Bedienung *nf* service *n* **inklusive Bedienung** service included
Bedienungsanleitung (-en) *nf* instruction book *n*, instruction sheet *n*
Bedingungen *nfpl* terms and conditions *npl* **günstige Bedingungen** favourable terms
bedingungslos *adj* unconditional *adj*
Bedürfnis *nn* need *n*
Bedürfnishierarchie (-n) *nf* hierarchy of needs *n*
Bedürfnisse *nnpl* **industrielle Bedürfnisse** needs of industry
beeinflußt *adj* weighted *adj*
beendigen *vb* wind up *vb*
Beendigung (-en) *nf* termination *n* **Beendigung des Dienstverhältnisses** termination of employment
befördern *vb* forward *vb*, upgrade *vb* (person) promote *vb*
Beförderung *nf* (road) haulage *n*, freight (US) (of person) promotion *n*
Befrachter (-) *nm* freighter *n*
befreit von *adj* exempt *adj*
Befreiung *nf* exemption *n*
befürworten *vb* advocate *vb*
begebbar *adj* negotiable *adj*
Beginn *nm* start-up *n*
beglaubigen *vb* witness a signature *vb*
begleichen *vb* settle a claim *n* **eine Rechnung begleichen** pay an invoice
begrenzt *adj* limited *adj* **begrenzter Markt (-märkte)** narrow market
behalten *vb* retain *vb*
Behälter (-e) *nm* container *n*
Behörde (-n) *nf* (official) authority *n*
Beibehaltung *nf* retention *n*
beilegen *vb* enclose *vb* (dispute) settle *vb*
Beirat (-äte) *nm* advisory committee *n*
beitragen *vb* contribute *vb*

beitragsfrei *adj* non-contributory *adj* **beitragsfreies Programm** non-contributory scheme

bekannt *adj* well-known *adj*

bekanntgeben *vb* announce *vb* **etwas bekanntgeben** give notice of sth

bekommen *vb* obtain *vb*

belasten *vb* (account) debit *vb* **ein Konto mit etwas belasten** charge sth to an account

Belastung *nf* (of tax) imposition *n* load *n*

Belastungsanzeige (-n) *nf* debit note *n*

Belastungssaldo (-en) *nm* debit balance *n*

belegen *vb* **etwas mit einem Embargo belegen** impose an embargo

Belegschaft *nf* staff *n*, workforce *n*

Bemerkung (-en) *nf* comment *n*

Bemessungsgrundlage (-n) *nf* basis of assessment *n*

benachrichtigen *vb* notify *vb*

Benachrichtigung *nf* notification *n*

benützen *vb* use *vb*

benutzerfreundlich *adj* user-friendly *adj*

beobachten *vb* watch *vb*

Beobachtung *nf* **unter Beobachtung** under observation

beraten *vb* advise *vb*, consult *vb*

beratend *adj* advisory *adj*

Berater (-) *nm* adviser/advisor *n*, consultant *n*

Beratung *nf* consultancy firm *n*, consulting firm (US)

Beratungs- *cpd* advisory *adj*

Beratungsgebühren *nfpl* consultancy fees *npl*, consulting fees (US)

Beratungstätigkeit *nf* consultancy work *n*, consulting work (US)

berechnen *vb* calculate *vb*, charge for sth *vb* **eine Gebühr berechnen** charge a fee

Berechnung (-en) *nf* calculation *n*

Berechtigung (-en) *nf* warranty *n*

Bergbau *nm* mining *n*, mining industry *n*

Bergungsplan (-pläne) *nm* recovery scheme *n*

Bericht (-e) *nm* report *n*

Berichterstattung *nf* reporting *n* **aktuelle Berichterstattung** news coverage

berichtigen *vb* **die Zahlen berichtigen** adjust the figures

Beruf (-e) *nm* occupation *n*, profession *n* **von Beruf** by trade **die gehobenen Berufe** the professions

Berufs- *cpd* vocational *adj*

Berufsberatung *nf* careers advice *n*

Berufserfahrung *nf* employment/work history *n* work experience *n*

Berufskrankheit (-en) *nf* occupational disease *n*

Berufsleben *nn* working life *n*

Berufsrisiko (-iken) *nn* occupational hazard *n*

berufstätig *adj* working *adj*

berufstätig sein *vb* be in work *vb*

Berufsverband (-bände) *nm* functional organization *n*

Berufsvergehen (-) *nn* malpractice *n* (man-

agement) misconduct *n*

beschädigen *vb* damage *vb*

Beschaffung *nf* sourcing *n*

beschäftigen *vb* employ *vb*

beschäftigt *adj* busy *adj*

Beschäftigtenstand *nm* level of employment *n*

Bescheid *nm* information *n* **rechtzeitiger Bescheid** due warning *n*

bescheinigen *vb* certificate *vb*, certify *vb*

Bescheinigung (-en) *nf* attestation *n*, certificate *n*

Beschlagnahme *nf* appropriation *n*

beschlagnahmen *vb* impound *vb*

beschleunigen *vb* accelerate *vb*, expedite *vb*

Beschleunigung *nf* acceleration *n*

beschließen *vb* resolve to do sth *vb*

Beschluß (-üsse) *nm* (decision) resolution *n* **einen Beschluß fassen** make a resolution *vb*

beschlußfähig *adj* (meeting) quorate *adj*

beschränken *vb* restrict *vb*

beschränkend *adj* restrictive *adj*

beschränkt *adj* **beschränkte Haftung** limited liability

Beschränkung (-en) *nf* restriction *n* **Beschränkungen auferlegen** impose restrictions

Beschwerde *nf* complaint *n* **Beschwerde einlegen** make a complaint

Beschwerdeabteilung (-en) *nf* complaints department *n*

Beschwerdepunkt (-e) *nm* grievance *n*

beschweren *vb* complain *vb* **sich beschweren über** complain about sth

Besetztton (-töne) *nm* busy signal (US) *n*

besichtigen *vb* inspect *vb*

Besitz *nm* property *n*

besitzen *vb* own *vb*

Besitzer (-) *nm* owner *n* **Besitzer im eigenen Haus** owner-occupier

Bestand (-ände) *nm* supply *n*

Bestandskontrolle *nf* inventory control *n*

bestätigen *vb* warrant *vb* **den Empfang bestätigen** confirm receipt of sth

Bestätigung (-en) *nf* attestation *n*, confirmation *n*

bestechen *vb* bribe *vb*

Bestechung *nf* bribery *n*

Bestechungsgeld (-er) *nn* bribe *n*

bestehen auf *vb* insist on *vb*

Bestellformular (-e) *nn* order form *n*

Bestellnummer (-n) *nf* order number *n*

Bestellung *nf* order *nf* **eine Bestellung erteilen** place an order

Besteuerung *nf* taxation *n*

Bestseller (-) *nm* best seller *n*

Besuch (-e) *nm* visit *n*

besuchen *vb* visit *vb*

Besucher (-) *nm* visitor *n*

Beteiligung (-en) *nf* holding *n* **eine Beteiligung besitzen** have holdings **finanzielle Beteiligung** vested interests

Betracht *nm* **etwas in Betracht ziehen** take sth into account
betrachten *vb* look at *vb*, view *vb*
Betrag (-äge) *nm* amount *n* **ausstehender Betrag** outstanding amount
betragen *vb* amount to *vb*
Betreff *nm* re *prep*
betreffen *vb* (be of importance to) concern *vb*
betreiben *vb* (manage) run *vb* **ein Hotelgeschäft betreiben** run an hotel
Betreiber (-) *nm* operator *n*
Betrieb (-e) *nm* company *n*, works *n* (of business) operation *n*, running *n* **außer Betrieb** out of action **gewerkschaftspflichtiger Betrieb** closed shop **verstaatlichter Betrieb** state-owned enterprise
Betriebsauschuß (-üsse) *nm* works committee *n*
Betriebsausgaben *nfpl* operating expenditure *n*
Betriebsbilanz (-en) *nf* operating statement *n*
Betriebseinkommen *nn* operating income *n*
Betriebsergebnis *nn* operating profit *n*
Betriebskapital *nn* trading capital *n*, working capital *n*
Betriebskosten *npl* running cost *n*, operating expenses *npl*
Betriebsleiter (-) *nm* plant manager *n*
Betriebsplan (-pläne) *nm* **dreischichtiger Betriebsplan** the three-shift system
Betriebsrat (-räte) *nm* works council *n*
Betriebsschluß *nm* closure of business hours *n* **nach Betriebsschluß** after hours
Betriebsstillegung (-en) *nf* closure of a company *n*
Betriebsverlust (-e) *nm* trading loss *n*
Betriebswirtschaftslehre *nf* business studies *n*
betroffen *adj* affected *adj* **schwer betroffen** hard-hit **von etwas schwer betroffen sein** be hard hit
Betrug *nm* fraud *n*
betrügen *vb* defraud *vb*
betrügerisch *adj* fraudulent *adj*
beurlauben *vb* give/grant leave *vb* **sich beurlauben lassen** take leave
Beurlaubung *nf* leave of absence *n*
Bevölkerung *nf* population *n* **arbeitende Bevölkerung** working population *n*
bewährt *adj* well-tried *adj*
Bewährung *nf* field test *n*
bewerben *vb* **sich bewerben um** apply for
Bewerber (-en) *nm* (for job) candidate *n*
Bewerbungsformular (-e) *nn* application form *n*
Bewerbungsschreiben (-) *nn* letter of application *n*
Bewertungsdurchschnitt (-e) *nm* weighted average *n*
Bewertungsindex (-en) *nm* weighted index *n*
bewirten *vb* entertain a client *vb*
bewohnen *vb* (premises) occupy *vb*

Bewohner (-) *nm* occupant *n*
bezahlt *adj* paid *adj*
bezeugen *vb* witness *vb*
Beziehungen *nfpl* relations *npl* **Beziehungen zwischen Arbeitgebern und Gewerkschaften** industrial relations
Bezug *nm* **mit Bezug auf** with reference to
bezüglich *prep* regarding *prep*
Bezugsrechtsangebot (-e) *nn* rights issue *n*
bieten *vb* (auction) bid *vb*
Bilanz *nf* (financial) balance *n* balance sheet *n*
Bilanzbuchhalter (-) *nm* chartered accountant *n*
billigen *vb* approve *vb*
Billigung *nf* approval *n*
Binnenmarkt (-märkte) *nm* home market *n*, domestic market *n*
Bitte (-n) *nf* appeal *n*, request *n*
bitten *vb* appeal *vb*, request *vb*
Blankokredit *nm* open credit *n*, unlimited credit *n*
Blankoscheck (-s) *nm* blank cheque *n*
Block (-öcke) *nm* block *n*
Blockade (-n) *nf* blockade *n*
blockieren *vb* blockade *vb*
Bodenrechtsreform (-en) *nf* land reform *n*
Bodenschätze *nmpl* natural resources *npl*
Bond-Zertifikat (-e) *nn* bond certificate *n*
Bondmarkt (-märkte) *nm* bond market *n*
Bonität *nf* credit rating *n*
Börse (-n) *nf* stock exchange *n*
Börsenaufsichtsrat *nm* SEC (Securities and Exchange Commission) (GB) *abbr*
Börsenmakler (-) *nm* floor broker *n*, stockbroker *n*
börsennotierte *npl* **börsennotierte Aktien** quoted shares, quoted stocks (US) **börsennotiertes Unternehmen (-)** quoted company **börsennotierte Wertpapiere** quoted investment
Börsentip (-s) *nm* market tip *n*
Bote (-n) *nm* messenger *n*
Botschaft (-en) *nf* embassy *n*
Boykott (-s) *nm* boycott *n*
boykottieren *vb* boycott *vb*
Branchengeheimnis (-isse) *nn* trade secret *n*
Branchenverzeichnis (-isse) *nn* the Yellow pages (R) (GB) *npl*
Brandversicherung *nf* fire insurance *n*
Brauch *nm* usage *n*
brauchen (dringend) *vb* be in (urgent) need *vb*
brechen *vb* break *vb* **einen Vertrag brechen** break an agreement
breit *adj* wide-ranging *adj*
Briefkopf (-köpfe) *nm* letterhead *n*
Briefwechsel *nm* correspondence *n*
bringen *vb* yield *vb* **auf den Markt bringen** (product) bring out
britisch *adj* British *adj*
Broker (-) *nm* broker *n*
Bruch- *cpd* fractional *adj*

Bruchteil (-e) nm fraction n
brutto adj gross adj
Bruttoeinkommen nn gross income n
Bruttogewicht nn gross weight n
Bruttoinlandsprodukt nn GDP (Gross Domestic Product) abbr
Bruttoinvestition nf gross investment n
Bruttoproduktion nf gross output n
Bruttosozialprodukt nn GNP (Gross National Product) abbr.
Bruttospanne (-n) nf gross margin n
Bruttosumme nf gross amount n
Bruttotonnage nf gross tonnage n
Bruttoumsatz nm gross sales n
Bruttoverlust (-e) nm gross loss n
Bruttozins nm gross interest n
buchen vb book vb, reserve vb **einen Flug buchen** book a flight **im voraus buchen** book in advance
Bücher nnpl **die Bücher** the books n **die Bücher führen** keep the books
Buchführung nf accountancy n
Buchgewinn nm book profit n
Buchhalter (-) nm accountant n, book-keeper n
Buchhaltung nf book-keeping n, general accounting n **die doppelte Buchhaltung** (bookkeeping) double-entry
Buchhaltungsnormen nfpl accounting conventions n
Buchhändler nm bookseller n
Buchhandlung (-en) nf bookshop n, book-store (US)
Buchprüfer (-) nm auditor n
Buchprüfung (-en) nf audit n, external audit n
Buchwert (-e) nm book value n
Budget (-s) nn budget n **im Budget einplanen** budget for
Budgetabweichung (-en) nf variance n
Bulletin (-s) nn news bulletin n
Bummelstreik (-s) nm (strike) go-slow n
Bund (Bünde) nm federation n
Bündel (-e) nn bundle n
bündeln vb bundle up vb
Bundes- cpd federal adj
Bundestagsabgeordnete/r nmf Member of Parliament (MP) (GB)
Bundestagswahl (-en) nf general election n
Büro (-s) nn office n
Büroangestellte/r nmf office clerk n
Büroarbeit nf clerical work n
Büroeinrichtung (-en) nf office equipment n
Bürogebäude nn office premises npl
Bürokraft (-kräfte) nf clerical worker n
Bürokrat (-en) nm bureaucrat n
Bürokratie nf bureaucracy n
bürokratisch adj bureaucratic adj
Büropersonal nn office staff n
Bürotätigkeit nf office work n
Büroverwaltung nf office management n
Busbahnhof (-höfe) nm bus station n
Cashflow nm cash flow n

Charter (-s) nm charter n
Charterflug (-üge) nm charter flight n
Chef (-s) nm boss n
Chefbuchhalter (-) nm head accountant n
Chemieindustrie (-n) nf chemical industry n
Chemieprodukte (-e) nn chemical products npl
Clearingbank (-en) nf clearing bank n
Clearingstelle (-n) nf clearing house n
Computer (-) nm computer n
Computergrafik nf computer graphics n
Computerhardware nf computer hardware n
Computernetz (-e) nn computer network n
Computerprogramm (-) nn computer program n
Computersprache (-n) nf computer language n
Computerterminal (-e) nn computer terminal n
Container (-e) nm container n
Containerlager (-) nn container terminal n
Containerschiff (-e) nn container ship n
Dachorganisation nf **Dachorganisation der britischen Gewerkschaften** Trades Union Congress
Dachsorganisation nf parent organisation n
Dankadresse (-n) nf vote of thanks n
Darlehen (-) nn loan n **hartes Darlehen (-)** hard loan
Datei (-en) nf computer file n
Daten nnpl data npl
Datenbank (-en) nf data bank n, database n
Datenerfassung nf data capture n
Datenfernübertragung nf teleprocessing n
Datenhierarchie nf data hierarchy n
Datenspeicherung nf information storage n
Datenverarbeitung nf data handling n
Datum (-en) nn date n
Datumsgrenze (-n) nf International Date Line n
Dauerauftrag (-äge) nm standing order n
Dauerbenutzer (-) nm heavy user n
Dauerbeschäftigung nf permanent employment n
Debit nn debit n
Deckungsbestätigung (-en) nf cover note n
Deckungszusage nf cover note n
Defekt (-e) nm fault n, defect n **schwerer Defekt (-e)** serious fault
Defizit (-e) nn budgetary deficit n, deficit n
Defizitwirtschaft nf deficit financing n
Deflation nf deflation n
deflationär adj deflationary adj
degradieren vb (employee) demote vb
deklarieren vb declare vb **nicht deklariert** (goods) undeclared
Delegation nf delegation n
delegieren vb delegate vb
Delegierte/r nmf delegate n
Demographie nf demography n
Design (-s) nn design n
Designer (-) nm (commercial) designer n

deutsch *adj* German *adj* **deutsche Mark** Deutschmark *n*

Devisen *nfpl* foreign exchange *n*

Devisenbeschränkungen *nfpl* exchange restrictions *npl*

Devisenbestände *nmpl* foreign exchange holdings *npl*

Devisenhandel *nm* foreign exchange dealings *npl*, foreign exchange trading (US)

Devisenhändler (-) *nm* foreign exchange dealer *n*

Devisenkontrolle *nf* exchange control *n*

Devisenmakler (-) *nm* exchange broker *n*

Devisenmarkt (-märkte) *nm* exchange market *n*, foreign exchange market *n*

Devisenverrechnungsabkommen *nn* exchange clearing agreement *n*

Diebstahl *nm* pilferage *n*

Dienst *nm* service *n* **Dienst nach Vorschrift machen** work to rule **öffentlicher Dienst** civil service

Dienstleistung *nf* service *n*

Dienstleistungsbereich (-e) *nm* tertiary sector *n*

Dienstleistungsindustrie *nf* tertiary industry *n*, service industry *n*

digital *adj* digital *adj*

direkt *adj* direct *adj*

direkte *nf* **direkte Steuer (-n)** direct tax *n*

Direktor (-en) *nm* director *n*

Direktorium (-ien) *nn* board of directors *n*

Diskette (-n) *nf* disk *n*, floppy disk *n*, magnetic disk *n*

Diskettenlaufwerk (-e) *nn* disk drive *n*

diskontieren *vb* discount *vb*

diskontiert *adj* **diskontierter Einnahmeüberschuß** discounted cash flow (DCF)

Diskontsatz (-sätze) *nm* bank rate *n*, discount rate *n*

Diversifikation *nf* diversification *n*

diversifizieren *vb* diversify *vb*

Dividende (-n) *nf* dividend *n*

Dividendenerträge *nmpl* income from dividends *n* **Dividenderträge nach Steuern** franked income

docken *vb* (ship) dock *vb*

Dokument (-e) *nn* document *n*

Dokumentenauffindung *nf* document retrieval *n*

Dollar *nm* buck* (US) *n*

Draht *nm* wire *n* **der heiße Draht** hot line

drei *adj* three *adj*

dreifach *adj* triple *adj*

dreifache *nf* **dreifache Ausführung** triplicate *n*

dreißig *adj* thirty *adj* **Dreißig-Aktien-Index** Thirty-Share Index (GB) *n*

Dreiteilung (-en) *nf* three-way split *n*

dringend *adj* urgent *adj* **dringende Angelegenheit (-en)** a matter of urgency

dringlich *adv* urgently *adv*

Dringlichkeit *nf* urgency *n* **höchste Drin-** glichkeit top priority

Dritte/r *nmf* third person *n*

dritte/r *adj* third *adj* **dritte Person** third party **Dritte Welt** the Third World

Drückeberger (-) *nm* shirker* *n*

drücken *vb* (spending) squeeze *vb*

Dumping *nn* dumping *n*

dunkel *adj* (dealings) shady* *adj*

durchbrechen *vb* make a breakthrough *vb*

Durchbruch (-brüche) *nm* breakthrough *n*

durchführbar *adj* feasible *adj*, workable *adj*

Durchführbarkeit *nf* feasibility *n*

Durchführbarkeitsstudie (-n) *nf* feasibility study *n*

durchführen *vb* enforce *vb* **einen Lohnstopp durchführen** (prices, wages) freeze

Durchreise *nf* transit *n*

Durchreisende/r *nmf* (transport) transit passenger *n*

Durchschnitt *nm* general average *n* (average) mean *n*

durchschnittlich *adj* (average) mean *adj*

Durchschnittskosten *npl* average costs **Durchschnittskosten pro Einheit** average unit costs

Durchschnittslohn (-löhne) *nm* average wage *n*

durchsetzen *vb* (policy) enforce *vb*

Durschnitt (-e) *nm* average *n*

Dynamik *nf* dynamics *npl*

dynamisch *adj* dynamic *adj*

Echtzeit *nf* real time *n*

Eckzins *nm* basic rate *n* **Eckzins für Ausleihungen** minimum lending rate **Eckzins der Clearing-Banken für Ausleihungen** base lending rate

ECU (-s) *nm* ECU (European Currency Unit) *abbr*

Edelmetallbarren *nm* bullion *n*

Effektenportefeuille (-s) *nn* investment portfolio *n*

effektiv *adj* actual *adj* **effektiver Preis** real price

Effektivlohn (-löhne) *nm* real wages *npl*

EG *nf* European Community (EC) *n*

EG-Kommission *nf* European Commission *n*

ehrenamtlich *adj* honorary *adj*

Ehrenkodex (-e) *nm* professional code of practice *n*

Eigenfinanzierung *nf* equity financing *n*, self-financing *n*

Eigengewicht *nn* dead weight *n*

Eigenheimerwerber (-) *nm* home buyer *n*

Eigenkapital *nn* equity capital *n*

Eigenkapitalrendite *nf* return on equity *n*

Eigenmittel *nnpl* capital funds *n*

Eigenschaft *nf* quality *n* **in meiner Eigenschaft als** in my capacity as chairman

Eigentum *nn* ownership *n*

Eigentumsschaden *nm* damage to property *n*

Eigentumsurkunde (-n) *nf* certificate of ownership *n*, title deed *n*

Eigentumsvorbehalt *nm* retention of title *n*

Eilauftrag (äge) *nm* rush order *n*

Eildienst *nm* express service *n*

Eiltransporter *nm* express carrier *n*

Eilzustellung (-en) *nf* express delivery *n*

einberufen *vb* summon *vb*, call *vb* **eine Sitzung einberufen** call a meeting

einbringen *vb* net(t) *vb* (motion, paper) table *vb*

einchecken *vb* (at airport) check in *vb*

einfach *adj* single *adj* **einfache Fahrkarte** (rail/flight) single/one-way ticket *n*

Einfuhr *nf* imports *npl*

Einfuhrbeschränkungen *nfpl* import restrictions *n*

einführen *vb* (product) launch *vb* **ein Gesetz einführen** introduce legislation

Einfuhrlizenz (-en) *nf* import licence *n*

Einfuhrquote (-n) *nf* import quota *n*

Einfuhrüberschuß (-üsse) *nm* import surplus *n*

Einführungszeit (-en) *nf* lead time

Einfuhrzoll *nm* import duty *n*

eingebaut *adj* built-in *adj*

eingeben *vb* key in *vb*

eingefroren *adj* frozen *adj* **eingefrorene Guthaben** frozen assets **eingefrorener Kredit** frozen credits

eingeschrieben *adj* registered *adj* **eingeschriebener Brief** registered letter

eingetragen *adj* registered *adj* **eingetragene Anschrift (-en)** registered address **eingetragene Firma (-en)** registered company **eingetragenes Warenzeichen (-)** registered trademark

einhalten *vb* keep *vb* **die Regeln einhalten** observe the rules

Einheit (-en) *nf* unit *n*

Einheitstarif (-e) *nm* flat rate *n*, flat-rate tariff *n*

Einkauf *nm* shopping *n*

einkaufen *vb* buy *vb* **in Mengen einkaufen** buy in bulk

Einkaufszentrum (-en) *nn* shopping mall *n*, shopping centre *n*

Einkommen *nn* income *n* **einheitlicher Einkommenssteuersatz** flat-rate income tax **Einkommen erwirtschaften** generate income

Einkommenselastizität *nf* income elasticity *n*

Einkommenserwirtschaften *nn* generation income *n*

Einkommensteuer (-n) *nf* income tax *n*

Einkommensverlust *nm* loss of earnings *n*

Einkommenszufluß *nm* flow of income *n*

Einkünfte *npl* takings *npl* **Einkünfte aus Kapitalvermögen** unearned income

einladen *vb* invite *vb*

Einladung (-en) *nf* invitation *n*

Einlage *nf* deposit *n* **langfristige Einlage** long deposit

Einlagenkonto (-konten) *nn* deposit account *n*

einlösen *vb* cash *vb*, redeem *vb* **einen Scheck**

einlösen cash a cheque

Einlösung *nf* encashment *n*

Einnahmen *nfpl* revenue *n*

Einnahmeunterdeckung *nf* negative cash flow *n*

Einreisevisum (-a) *nn* entry visa *n*

einrichten *vb* (company) set up *vb*

Einrichtungen *nfpl* amenities *npl*

Einsatzbesprechung (-en) *nf* briefing *n*

einschalten *vb* (machine) turn on *vb*

einschätzen *vb* assess *vb*

Einschätzung (-en) *nf* assessment *n*

einschlagen *vb* hit the market *vb*

Einschränkung *nf* limiting factor *n*

Einschreibpost *nf* registered mail

einseitig *adj* one-sided *adj* **einseitig bindend** (contract) unilateral

Einsparungen *nfpl* savings *npl*

Einspruch (-sprüche) *nm* veto *n*

Einstandsgeld *nn* golden hello *n*

einstellen *vb* appoint sb to a position *vb*, recruit *vb*

Einstellung (-en) *nf* (to a position) appointment recruitment *n*

Einstellungskampagne (-n) *nf* recruitment campaign *n*

einstimmig *adj* unanimous *adj*

Eintragung *nf* entry *n* **letzte Eintragung** final entry

Eintritt *nm* entry *n* **Eintritt frei** free entry

einverstanden *adj* agreed *adj*

Einverständnis *nn* consent *n* **in gegenseitigem Einverständnis** by mutual agreement

Einwand (-wände) *nm* objection *n* **Einwände erheben gegen** make/raise an objection

Einweg- *cpd* non-returnable *adj*

einwerfen *vb* post *vb*

einzahlen *vb* deposit *vb*

Einzahlung (-en) *nf* deposit *n*

Einzelhandel *nm* retail trade **im Einzelhandel verkaufen** sell sth retail

Einzelhandelsgeschäft (-e) *nn* retail outlet *n*

Einzelhandelskette (-n) *nf* retail chain *n*

Einzelhandelsmarkt *nm* retail market *n*

Einzelverkaufssteuer *nf* retail sales tax *n*

einziehen *vb* collect *vb* **eine Schuld einziehen** collect a debt *vb*

Einziehung *nf* collection *n* (of debt) recovery *n*

Einzugsemächtigung *nf* direct debiting *n*

Eisenbahn (-en) *nf* railway *n*, railroad (US)

Elastizität *nf* elasticity *n*

elektronisch *adj* electronic *adj* **elektronische Abwicklung von Bankgeschäften** electronic banking **elektronische Datenverarbeitung** electronic data processing **elektronische Post** email

Elektrotechnik *nf* electrical engineering *n*

Embargo (-s) *nn* embargo *n*

Empfang *nm* receipt *n* **den Empfang bestätigen** acknowledge receipt

Empfänger (-) *nm* addressee *n*, consignee *n*, recipient *n*, sendee *n* **Empfänger eines**

Angebots offeree
empfehlen vb recommend vb
Empfehlung (-en) nf recommendation n,
  reference n
Empfehlungsschreiben (-) nn letter of
  introduction n
en gros at/by wholesale
End- cpd terminal adj
Endabnehmer (-) nm end user n
Endabrechnung nf final accounts n
Endergebnis (-isse) nn net(t) result n
Enderzeugnisse nfpl final products npl
Endprämie nf terminal bonus n
Endverbraucher (-) nm end consumer n
eng adj tight adj
englisch adj English adj **englisches Pfund**
  sterling
Engpaß (-pässe) nm bottleneck n
Engpaßinflation nf bottleneck inflation n
enteignen vb expropriate vb
Enteignung nf expropriation n
Enteignungsausschuß (-üsse) nm land
  tribunal n
entladen vb unload vb
entlassen vb (employee) dismiss vb fire* vb,
  make sb redundant vb, sack vb (workers) lay
  off vb
Entlassung (-en) nf dismissal n **unberechtigte Entlassung** wrongful dismissal
entnationalisieren vb denationalize vb
entschädigen vb compensate for vb,
  indemnify vb
Entschädigung nf compensation n,
  recompense n **Entschädigung verlangen**
  claim compensation **Entschädigung zahlen**
  pay compensation
entsprechend adj relevant adj
entwerfen vb (plans) draw up vb draw up vb
  einen Vertrag entwerfen draw up a contract
Entwicklungsland (-änder) nn developing
  country n, third-world country n, underdeveloped country n
Erbe (-n) nn inheritance n
erben vb inherit vb
Erbschaft (-en) nf legacy n
Erbschaftsgesetze nnpl inheritance laws npl
Erdgas nn natural gas n
Erdölindustrie nf oil industry n
erfahren 1. adj experienced adj 2. vb
  experience vb
erforderlich adj necessary adj
erfüllen vb comply with vb **die Bedingungen
  erfüllen** comply with legislation
ergänzend adj supplementary adj
Ergebnis (-sse) nn outcome n
Ergonomie nf ergonomics n
ergreifen vb grasp vb, seize vb **die Gelegenheit ergreifen** seize an opportunity
erhalten vb receive vb
erheben vb (tax) levy vb
erhöhen vb (value) enhance vb (prices, taxes)
  increase vb mark up vb (price, interest rate)

raise vb (capital, loan) raise vb **Preise
  erhöhen** (prices) bump up vb
Erhöhung (-en) nf (prices) escalation n
  markup n **Erhöhung der Lebenshaltungskosten** increase in the cost of living
erholen vb (improve) pick up vb
Erholung nf (economic) recovery n
erkennen vb (profit) realize vb
erklären vb account for vb
erledigen vb (account) settle vb
Erlös nm proceeds npl
ermächtigen vb authorize vb
ermäßigen vb (taxes) reduce vb
Ermäßigung (-en) nf reduction n
ernennen vb appoint vb **ernennen (als Mitglied des/der....)** nominate sb to a board/
  committee
Ernennung (-en) nf nomination n
erneuerbar adj renewable adj
erneuern vb (policy, contract) renew vb
erneut vb **erneut zuteilen** (funds) reallocate
eröffnen vb open vb **ein Konto eröffnen** open
  an account
Eröffnungskurs (-e) nm opening price n
Erpressung nf extortion n
erreichen vb achieve vb **das Ziel erreichen**
  reach an objective
Ersatzperson (-en) nf (person) replacement n
Ersatzteil (-e) nn (for machine) spare part n
erschließen vb develop vb, open up vb **den
  Markt erschließen** open up the market
Erschließungsunternehmen (-) nn
  developer n
erschöpfen vb (reserves) exhaust vb
Erschöpfung nf depletion n
ersetzen vb replace vb
Ersparnisse nfpl savings npl
erst adj **erste Hypothek** first mortgage n
  erste Klasse (plane) first class n **erster Hand**
  first-hand
erstellen vb draw up vb **den Haushaltsplan
  erstellen** draw up a budget
erstklassig adj (investment) first-rate adj, gilt-
  edged adj, high-class adj **erstklassiger
  Wechsel** first-class paper **erstklassige
  Wertpapiere** blue-chip securities **erstklassiges Unternehmen** blue-chip company
erteilen vb place vb **einen Auftrag erteilen**
  place an order
Erteilung nf (of a patent) grant n
Ertrag nm earnings n, yield n **Ertrag des
  investierten Kapitals** return on investment
Ertragsfähigkeit nf earning capacity n, earning power n
Ertragsrückgang nm diminishing returns npl
Ertragstendenz nf earnings drift n
Erwartung (-en) nf expectation n
erweitern vb expand vb **die Kapazität erweitern** expand capacity **die Reihe erwei-
  tern** extend the range
Erweiterung nf expansion n
Erwerb nm acquisition n

erwerben *vb* acquire *vb*
Erwerbstätigkeit *nf* gainful employment *n*
Erzeugerpreis (-e) *nm* factor price *n*
eskalieren *vb* escalate *vb*
Etat *nm* **den Etat ausgleichen** balance the budget
Etikett (-e) *nn* label *n*
etikettieren *vb* label *vb*
Eurobond (-s) *nm* eurobond *n*
Eurodollar (-s) *nm* eurodollar *n*
Eurofusion (-en) *nf* euromerger *n*
Eurogeld (-er) *nn* euromoney *n*
Eurogeldmarkt (-märkte) *nm* eurocurrency market *n*
Eurokapital *nn* eurocapital *n*, eurofunds *npl*
Eurokrat (-en) *nm* eurocrat *n*
Eurokratie *nf* eurocracy *n*
Eurokredit *nm* eurocredit *n*
Euromarkt (-ärkte) *nm* euromarket *n*
europäisch *adj* European *adj* **Europäische Investitionsbank** European Investment Bank (EIB) *n* **Europäische Rechnungseinheit** European Unit of Account *n* **Europäischer Entwicklungsfonds** European Development Fund (EDF) **Europäischer Gerichtshof** European Court of Justice (ECJ) **Europäischer Regionalentwicklungsfonds** European Regional Development Fund (ERDF) **Europäischer Sozialfonds** European Social fund (ESF) **Europäischer Wiederaufbauplan** European Recovery Plan **Europäisches Währungssystem** European Monetary System (EMS) **Europäische Währungsunion** European Monetary Union (EMU)
Europaparlament *nn* European Parliament *n*
Europarat *nm* European Council *n*
Euroscheck (-s) *nm* eurocheque *n*
Euroskeptiker *nm* eurosceptic *n*
Eurowährung (-en) *nf* eurocurrency *n*
Exmittierung *nf* eviction *n*
expansiv *adj* reflationary *adj*
Expedition *nf* forwarding *n*
Experte (-n) *nm* expert *n*
Expertensystem (-e) *nn* expert system *n*
Export *nm* export *n* **unsichtbare Exporte** invisible exports
Exportabteilung (-en) *nf* export department *n*
Exportartikel *nmpl* export goods *n*
Exporteur (-e) *nm* exporter *n*
Exporthandel *nm* export trade *n*
exportieren *vb* export *vb*
Exportkredit (-e) *nm* export credit *n*
Exportkreditversicherung *nf* export credit insurance *n*
Exportlizenz *nf* export licence *n*
Exportmarketing *nn* export marketing *n*
Exportstrategie (-n) *nf* export strategy *n*
Exporttätigkeiten *nfpl* export operations *npl*
Exportüberschuß *nm* export surplus *n*
Exportzuschüsse *nmpl* export subsidies *npl*
Fabrikarbeit *nf* factory work *n*
Fach- *cpd* expert *adj*

Facharbeiter (-) *nm* skilled worker *n*
Fachgebietsleiter (-) *nm* line manager *n*
Fachgebietsleitung *nf* line management *n*
Fachmann (-leute) *nm* specialist *n*
fachsimpeln *vb* (informal) talk shop *vb*
Fachwissen *nn* expertise *n*
Factoring *nn* (of debts) factoring *n*
Fähigkeit (-en) *nf* ability *n*
Fahrkarte (-n) *nf* ticket *n*
Fahrkartenschalter (-) *nm* ticket office *n*
fahrlässig *adj* negligent *adj*
Fahrlässigkeit *nf* negligence *n* **grobe Fahrlässigkeit** gross negligence
Fahrlässigkeitsklausel (-n) *nf* negligence clause *n*
Fahrplan (-äne) *nm* timetable *n*
fair *adj* fair *adj*
Faktor (-en) *nm* (buyer of debts) factor *n*
fakturieren *vb* (debts) factor *vb*
fallen *vb* slump *vb*
fällig *adj* due *adj* **fällig werden** fall due **fällig werden** (business, economy) mature
falsch *adj* false *adj* **falsche Behandlung** mishandling
fälschen *vb* counterfeit *vb*
Fälschung *nf* counterfeit *n*, forgery *n*
Familie (-n) *nf* family *n* **Familien-Aktiengesellschaft** family corporation
Familieneinkommen *nn* family income *n*
Familiengeschäft (-e) *nn* family business *n*
Familienindustrie *nf* family industry *n*
Familienmarke *nf* family branding *n*
Fax (-e) *nn* fax *n*, telefax *n*
faxen *vb* fax *vb*
Faxgerät (-e) *nn* facsimile (fax) machine *n*
Fehlbetrag (-äge) *nm* deficiency *n*
Fehler (-) *nm* defect *n*, fault *n*, mistake *n* **versteckter Fehler** hidden defect
fehlerfrei *adj* zero defect *adj*
fehlerhaft *adj* defective *adj* **fehlerhafte Ware** faulty goods
Fehlkalkulation (-en) *nf* miscalculation *n*
Feiertag (-e) *nm* holiday *n* **öffentlicher Feiertag** bank holiday (GB)
feilbieten *vb* peddle *vb*
feilschen *vb* bargain *vb*
Feingehaltsstempel (-) *nm* hallmark *n*
Feinmechanik *nf* precision engineering *n*
Feldforschung *nf* field research *n*
Fenster (-) *nn* window *n*
Fernkopierer (-) *nm* telecopier *n*
Fernmeldewesen *nn* telecommunications *npl*
Fernschreiber (-) *nm* telex *n*
Fernsehen *nn* television *n* **im Fernsehen bringen** televise
Fertigerzeugnisse *npl* finished goods *npl*
Fertigkeit *nf* skill *n*
Fertigung *nf* production *n* **Fertigungsgemeinkosten** factory overheads
Fertigungsindustrie *nf* secondary sector *n*
Fertigungskosten *npl* factory costs *npl*
Fertigungsstraße (-n) *nf* production line *n*

Fertigwarenlager (-) *nn* finished stock *n*
fest *adj* firm *adj* **feste Belastung** fixed charges **festes Angebot** firm offer **festes Einkommen** fixed income
festmachen *vb* moor *vb* (capital) tie up *vb*
Festplatte (-n) *nf* hard disk *n*
Festpreis (-e) *nm* firm price *n*, fixed price *n*
Festsatzkredit (-e) *nm* fixed credit *n*
festsetzen *vb* (prices) peg *vb* **eine Höchstgrenze festsetzen** put a ceiling on sth **den Preis festsetzen** fix the price
feststehendes Budget *nn* fixed budget *n*
Festzins (-e) *nm* fixed interest *n*
fett *adj* (type) bold *adj* **fett gedruckt** bold type
Fettschrift *nf* bold type *n*
Fifo-Methode (-n) *nf* FIFO (first in first out) *abbr*
fiktiv *adj* fictitious *adj* **fiktiver Vermögenswert** fictitious assets
Filiale (-n) *nf* branch *n*
Filialgeschäft (-e) *nn* chain store *n*, multiple store *n*
Filialleiter (-) *nm* branch manager *n*
Finanzamt (-ämter) *nn* the Inland Revenue *n*, the Internal Revenue Service (IRS) (US)
Finanzberater (-) *nm* financial consultant *n*
Finanzberatung *nf* financial consultancy *n*
Finanzbericht (-e) *nm* financial report *n*
Finanzbuchhaltung *nf* financial accounting *n*
Finanzdirektor (-en) *nm* company treasurer *n*
Finanzgeschäft *nn* financial operation *n*
Finanzgesetz (-e) *nn* Finance Act *n*
Finanzhilfe *nf* financial aid *n*
finanziell *adj* financial *adj* **finanzielle Aktiva** financial assets **finanzielle Maßnahmen** financial measures **finanzieller Anreiz** financial incentive **finanzielle Schwierigkeit** financial difficulty **finanzielles Engagement** financial exposure
Finanzier (-s) *nm* financier *n*
finanzieren *vb* finance *vb*, fund *vb*
Finanzierung *nf* financing *n*, funding *n*
Finanzierungsgesellschaft (-en) *nf* finance company *n*
Finanzierungsinstitut (-e) *nn* credit company *n*
Finanzinstitut (-e) *nn* financial institution *n*
Finanzinvestition *nf* financial investment *n*
Finanzjahr (-e) *nn* tax year *n*
Finanzkontrolle *nf* financial control *n*
Finanzkrise (-n) *nf* financial crisis *n*
Finanzlage (-n) *nf* financial status *n*, financial situation *n*
Finanzleiter (-) *nm* chief financial officer *n*
Finanzmanagement *nn* financial management *n*
Finanzmarkt (-märkte) *nm* financial market *n*, mart *n*
Finanzmaßnahmen *nfpl* fiscal measures *npl*
Finanzminister (-) *nm* chancellor of the exchequer (GB) *n*
Finanzmittel *nnpl* financial resources *npl*,

financial means *npl*
Finanzplanung *nf* financial planning *n*
Finanzpolitik *nf* budgetary policy *n*, financial policy *n*, monetary policy *n*, fiscal policy *n*
Finanzstrategie (-n) *nf* financial strategy *n*
Finanzstruktur *nf* financial structure *n*
Finanzüberschuß (-üsse) *nm* financing surplus *n*
Finanzverwalter (-) *nm* bursar *n*
Finanzwechsel (-) *nm* finance bill *n*
Finanzwesen *nn* finance *n*
Firma *nf* firm *n*
Firmenbesteuerung *nf* corporate taxation *n*
Firmenname (-n) *nm* trade name *n* **eingetragener Firmenname (-n)** registered trade name
Firmenschulden *nfpl* corporate debt *n*
Firmenverzeichnis (-sse) *nn* trade directory *n*
Firmenzeitschrift (-en) *nf* house journal/magazine *n*
Fixkosten *npl* fixed costs *n*
Flaute (-n) *nf* (economic) depression *n*
fleißig *adj* hard-working *adj*
flexibel *adj* flexible *adj* **flexibler Preis** flexible price **flexibler Wechselkurs** flexible exchange rate **flexibles Budget** flexible budget
Flexibilität *nf* (of prices) flexibility *n*
florieren *vb* thrive *vb*
florierend *adj* booming *adj*, prosperous *adj*
Fluchtkapital *nn* flight capital *n*
Flug (-üge) *nm* (in plane) flight *n*
Fluggesellschaft (-en) *nf* airline *n*
Flughafen (-häfen) *nm* airport *n*
Flughafenterminal (-e) *nm* air terminal *n*
Flugkarte (-n) *nf* ticket *n*
Fluglotse (-n) *nm* air traffic controller *n*
Flugreisen *nfpl* air travel *n*
Flußdiagramm (-e) *nn* flow chart *n*
flüssig *adj* fluid *adj* **flüssige Mittel** quick assets
Flüssigmachung *nf* **Flüssigmachung von Vermögenswerten** realization of assets
Folge (-n) *nf* consequence *n*
Fonds *nm* fund *n*
Förderer (-) *nm* sponsor *n*
Fördergebiet *nn* **wirtschaftliches Fördergebiet (-e)** entreprise zone
fordern *vb* demand *vb*
Förderung (-en) *nf* sponsorship *n*
Forderungsübernehmer (-) *nm* assignee *n*
Formalitäten *nfpl* **die Formalitäten beachten** observe formalities
formbedürftig *adj* **formbedürftiger Vertrag** formal contract
formell *adj* formal *adj*
Formular (-e) *nn* (document) form *n*
Forschung *nf* research *n* **Forschung und Entwicklung** research and development (R&D)
Forschungsteam (-s) *nn* research team *n*
Fortbildung *nf* advanced training *n*

Fortschritt (-e) *nm* progress *n*
Fortschritte machen (research, project) progress *vb*
Fotokopie (-n) *nf* photocopy *n*
fotokopieren *vb* photocopy *vb*, xerox *vb*
Fotokopiermaschine (-n) *nf* (machine) Xerox (R) *n*
Fracht (-en) *nf* cargo *n* **ohne Frachtgebühr** free of freight **palettisierte Fracht** palletized freight **per Frachtnachnahme** carriage forward
Frachtbrief (-e) *nm* forwarding note *n*
frachtfrei *adj* carriage included *adj*, carriage paid *adj*
Frachtgebühr (-en) *nf* carriage charge *n*
Frachtgut *nn* freight *n*
Frachtkosten *npl* carriage costs *npl*
Frachtschiff (-e) *nn* cargo ship *n*
Frachtverkehr *nm* freight traffic *n*
Fragebogen *nm* questionnaire *n*
fragen *vb* enquire *vb*
Franchise *nm* franchise *n*
Franchisegeber (-) *nm* franchisor *n*
Franchisenehmer (-) *nm* franchisee *n*
franchisieren *vb* franchise *vb* **franchisierter Ortshändler**
Franchising *nn* franchising *n*
frankieren *vb* frank *vb*
frankiert *adj* franked *adj*
frei *adj* complimentary *adj*, franco *adj* free **frei an Bord** FOB (free on board) **freie Kapazität** idle capacity **freie Marktwirtschaft** free market economy **freier Handel** free trade **freier Markt** free market **freier Tag** day off work **freier Warenverkehr** free movement of goods **freie Stelle** vacancy **freie Wahl** freedom of choice **freie Wirtschaft** free economy **frei Hafen** free on quay, free port **frei Haus** franco domicile **frei Längsseite Schiff** FAS (free alongside ship) **frei Preis** franco price **frei Zone** franco zone
freiberuflich *adj* freelance *adj*, self-employed *adj*
Freiberufliche/r *nmf* freelance *n*, freelancer *n*
Freihandelszone (-n) *nf* free trade area *n*
freiwillig *adj* optional *adj*, voluntary *adj*, unsolicited *adj*
Freizeichnungsklausel (-n) *nf* exemption from liability clause *n* **Freizeichnungsklausel für Fahrlässigkeit** neglect clause
Fremdenverkehrsbranche *nf* the tourist trade *n*
Fremdwährung (-en) *nf* foreign currency *n*
Frequenz *nf* frequency *n*
freundlich *adj* friendly *adj*
Frührente *nf* early retirement *n* **in Frührente gehen** take early retirement
führen *vb* (stock) carry *vb* be ahead of *vb*, manage *vb*, wage *vb* (goods) keep *vb* **ein Geschäft führen** operate a business **eine Werbekampagne führen** run a campaign
führend *adj* leading *adj*, major *adj*

Führung *nf* leadership *n* **die Führung übernehmen** take the lead
Führungsaufgaben *nfpl* executive duties *n*
Führungskräfte *nfpl* executive personnel *n*
Führungsspitze (-n) *nf* top management *n*
Führungsstress *nm* executive stress *n*
Fülle *nf* abundance *n*
Fundbüro (-s) *nn* lost-property office *n*
fundiert *adj* sound *adj*, funded *adj*
fundierte *npl* **fundierte Schulden** funded debt
Funktion *nf* (role) function *n*
funktionierend *adj* working *adj*
Funktionsanalyse *nf* functional analysis *n*
für *prep (acc)* for *prep*
Für *nn* **Für und Wider** pros and cons *n*
Fusion (-en) *nf* amalgamation *n*, merger *n*
fusionieren *vb* amalgamate *vb*, merge *vb*
galoppierend *adj* galloping *adj*
gängig *adj* going *adj*
Garantie (-n) *nf* guarantee *n*, warranty *n* **unter Garantie** under warranty
Garantiegeber (-) *nm* guarantor *n*
garantieren *vb* warrant *vb*
Garantieversicherung *nf* fidelity insurance *n*
Garantievertreter (-) *nm* del credere agent *n*
Gastarbeiter (-) *nm* guest worker *n*, migrant worker *n*
Gastgeber (-) *nm* host *n*
Gastland (-länder) *nn* host country *n*
GATT *nn* GATT (General Agreement on Tariffs and Trade)
Gauner (-) *nm* racketeer *n*
Gaunereien *npl* racketeering *n*
Gebietsplanung *nf* regional planning *n*
Gebietsvertreter (-) *nm* area representative *n*
Gebrauch *nm* usage *n* **Gebrauch machen von** make use of sth
Gebrauchsgüter *nnpl* durable goods *npl*
Gebühr (-en) *nf* fee *n*
Gedächtnis *nn* (DP) memory *n*
Gefahr (-en) *nf* hazard *n* **natürliche Gefahr** natural hazard
gefährlich *adj* hazardous *adj*
Gefallen (-) *nm* favour *n*
Gefälligkeitswechsel (-) *nm* accommodation bill *n*
gefälscht *adj* phoney* *adj*
gegen *prep (acc)* against *prep* **gegen Barzahlung** for cash
gegenseitig *adj* mutual *adj*, reciprocal *adj*, mutually *adv*
gegenzeichnen *vb* countersign *vb*
Gehalt (-älter) *nn* salary *n*
Gehaltserhöhung (-en) *nf* pay rise *n*
Gehaltsliste (-n) *nf* payroll *n*
Gehaltsskala (-en) *nf* salary scale *n*
gelb *adj* yellow *adj*
Geld *nn* money *n* **Geld einziehen von** recover money from sb **Geld auf dem Konto haben** be in the black **Geldmittel flüssig machen** tap resources **Geld verdienen** make money

Geld zurückhalten (money) keep back
heißes Geld hot money
Geldangebot nn money supply n
Geldautomat (-en) nm automatic cash
dispenser n, cash machine n
Geldgeber nm backer n
Geldhändler (-) nm money trader n
Geldmarkt (-märkte) nm money market n
Gelegenheit (-en) nf opportunity n
Gelegenheitsarbeit nf casual work n
Gelegenheitsarbeiter (-) nm casual worker n
gelernt adj (worker) skilled n
gemäß prep in accordance with
gemäßigt adj moderate adj
Gemeinderat (-räte) nm town council n
Gemeinkosten npl overhead costs npl
gemeinsam adj joint adj, jointly adv,
common adj Gemeinsame Agrarpolitik CAP
(Common Agricultural Policy)
Gemeinsam nm Gemeinsamer Markt Com-
mon Market
Gemeinschaftskonto (-konten) nn joint
account n
Gemeinschaftsprogramm (-e) nn collabora-
tive venture n
Gemeinschaftsunternehmen (-e) nn colla-
borative venture n, joint venture n
genau adj accurate adj
Genauigkeit nf accuracy n
genehmigen vb license vb
Generalstreik (-s) nm general strike n
Generalvertreter (-) nm general agent n
Generalvertretungen nfpl general agencies
(US) n
Genesungsurlaub nm sick leave n
Gepäck nn luggage n
Gepäckaufbewahrung nf left-luggage
office n, left luggage n
Gericht nn court n vor Gericht in court
gerichtlich adj judicial adj gerichtliche Ver-
fügung (-en) injunction, writ gerichtlich
vorgehen take legal action
Gerichtshof (-öfe) nm court n
Gerichtsvollzieher (-) nm bailiff n
Gesamtsumme (-n) nf total n, the grand
total n
Gesamtumsatz nm total sales npl
Gesamtwirtschaft nf national economy n
gesamtwirtschaftlich adj gesamtwirtschaftliche Finanzierung funds flow
Geschäft (-e) nn bargain n, business n, business transaction n, deal n (shop) store n
allgemeine Geschäftskosten overheads allgemeine Geschäftsstunden normal trading
hours das Geschäft führen keep the business running unsaubere Geschäfte sharp
practice
Geschäftbeziehungen nfpl business
relations npl
geschäftlich adj regarding business etwas
Geschäftliches besprechen talk business
geschäftlich tätig sein als (name) trade as

Geschäftsadresse (-n) nf business address n
Geschäftsanzug (-züge) nm business suit n
Geschäftsaussichten npl business outlook n
Geschäftsbank (-en) nf clearing bank n,
commercial bank n
Geschäftsbereich (-e) nm (of company)
division n
Geschäftsbeziehungen nfpl business
connections npl
Geschäftsbilanz nf fiscal balance n
Geschäftsfreund (-e) nm business
acquaintance n, business associate n
Geschäftsfreunde nmpl business contacts npl
Geschäftsführer (-) nm executive secretary n
Geschäftshai (-e) nm shark* n
Geschäftsjahr nn financial year n, fiscal
year n, trading year n
Geschäftsjahresende nn fye (fiscal year end)
Geschäftskarte (-n) nf business card n
Geschäftsleitung nf business management n,
senior management n
Geschäftsräume npl business premises npl
Geschäftsreise (-n) nf business trip n
Geschäftsreisen npl business travel n
Geschäftsreisende/r nmf commercial travel-
ler, commercial traveler (US)
Geschäftsschluß nm closing time n
Geschäftssinn nm business acumen n
Geschäftssitzung (-en) nf business meeting n
Geschäftsstunden nfpl business hours npl,
office hours npl
Geschäftswert nm value of (a) business n
Geschäftszeichen (-) nn reference number n
Geschäftszentrum (-en) nn business centre n
geschlossen adj closed adj geschlossene
Sitzung closed session/meeting
Geschworene/r nmf juror n
Geschworenen (die) npl jury n
Gesellschaft (-en) nf company n Gesellschaft
mit beschränkter Haftung limited company
Gesellschaft mit beschränkter Haftung (in
privater Hand) private limited company
Gesellschaft mit Haftungsbeschränkung
limited company Gesellschaft mit unbe-
schränkter Haftung unlimited company
Gesellschafter (-) nm partner stiller Ge-
sellschafter sleeping partner
Gesellschaftsrecht nn company law n
Gesetz (-e) nn law n Gesetz des abnehmen-
den Ertrags law of diminishing returns
Gesetze erlassen legislate
Gesetzgebung nf legislation n
gesetzlich adj legal adj gesetzliches Zahlungsmittel (-) legal tender
gesichert adj secured adj
Gespräch (-e) nn talk n Gespräch mit Voranmeldung (-e) person-to-person call
Gesundheitsgefahr (-en) nf health hazard n
Gesundheitsministerium (-ien) nn Ministry
of Health n
Gesundheitsweswen nn health care
industry n

gewähren *vb* grant *vb* **einen Rabatt gewähren** grant a rebate
Gewerbe *nn* trade *n*
Gewerbeaufsichtssbeamte/r *nmf* factory inspector *n*
Gewerkschaft (-en) *nf* trade union *n*, union *n*
gewerkschaftsgebunden *adj* **gewerkschaftsgebundene Firma** closed shop
Gewerkschaftsmitglieder *npl* (trade unions) organized labour *n*
Gewerkschaftsmitgliedschaft *nf* union membership *n*
Gewerkschaftsverteter (-) *nm* shop steward *n*, union representative *n*
Gewicht *nn* weight *n*
gewichtig *adj* weighty *adj*
Gewinn *nm* gain *n*, profit *n* **einen Gewinn machen** make a profit **Gewinne reinvestieren** (profits) plough back *vb*, plow back (US) **Gewinn je Stammaktie** earnings yield **Gewinn und Verlust** profit and loss **Gewinnund Verlustrechnung** profit and loss account **unerwarteter Gewinn** windfall profit
Gewinnbeteiligung *nf* gain sharing *n*, profit-sharing scheme *n*, a share in the profits *n*
gewinnen *vb* gain *vb*, win *vb* **an Wert gewinnen** gain in value
Gewinnschwelle (-n) *nf* break-even point *n*
Gewinnspanne (-n) *nf* profit margin *n*, return on sales *n*
Gewohnheitsrecht *nn* common law *n*
gewöhnlich *adj* ordinary *adj* **gewöhnliche Sitzung** ordinary general meeting
gezielt *adj* targeted *adj* **gezielte Aktion** targeted campaign *n*
Girokonto (-konten) *nn* current account *n*
Gläubiger (-) *nm* creditor *n*
Gläubigerquorum (-a) *nn* quorum of creditors *n*
gleich *adj* equal *adj* **gleicher Lohn** equal pay
Gleichgewicht *nn* equilibrium *n*
gleitend *adj* sliding *adj* **gleitende Arbeitszeit** flexitime *n*, flextime (US) **gleitender (Lohn) Tarif** sliding scale
global *adj* global *adj* **globale Risikoversicherung** all-risks insurance
Globalisierung *nf* globalization *n*
Glücksfall (-fälle) *nm* a stroke of luck *n* **unerwarteter Glücksfall** windfall
Gold *nn* gold *n*
Goldmarkt (-märkte) *nm* gold market *n*
Goldmünze (-n) *nf* gold coin *n*
Goldreserven *nfpl* gold reserves *npl*
Goldstandard *nm* gold standard *n*
Gönner (-e) *nm* benefactor *n*
graduieren *vb* graduate *vb*
Graduierte/r *nmf* (of university) graduate *n*
Greenwich Mean Time *nf* Greenwich Mean Time (GMT)
Grenz- *cpd* marginal *adj*
Grenze (-n) *nf* frontier *n*, limit *n*
Grenzertrag *nm* marginal revenue *n*

Grenzkosten *npl* marginal cost *n*
Grenznutzen *nm* final utility *n*, marginal utility *n*
groß *adj* large *adj*, big *adj* **groß angelegt** large-scale
Großbritannien *nn* Britain *n*
Größe (-n) *nf* size *n*
Großgedrucktes *nn* large type *n*
Großhandel *nm* wholesale *n*, wholesale trade *n* **im Großhandel** at/by wholesale **im Großhandel verkaufen** sell sth wholesale
Großhandelsmarkt (-märkte) *nm* wholesale market *n*
Großhandelspreis (-e) *nm* trade price *n*, wholesale price *n*
Großhändler (-) *nm* wholesaler *n*
Großindustrie *nf* big business *n*
Großindustrielle/r *nmf* tycoon *n*
Großrechner (-) *nm* mainframe computer *n*
Großzügigkeit *nf* generosity *n*
grün *adj* green *adj* **grüne Dollarwährung** green currency **grünes Pfund** green pound
Grundausbildung *nf* basic training *n*
Grundbesitzer (-) *nm* landowner *n*
Grundbuch *nn* land register *n*
Gründe *npl* rationale *n*
gründen *vb* establish *vb* **ein Geschäft gründen** set up in business **ein Unternehmen gründen** found a company
Gründer (-) *nm* founder *n*
Grundkapital *nn* registered capital *n*
Grundkentnisse *nfpl* working knowledge *n*
Grundsteuer (-n) *nf* land tax *n*
Grundstoff (-e) *nm* basic commodity *n*
Grundstoffindustrie *nf* primary sector *n*
Grundstückskauf *nm* land purchase *n*
Gründung *nf* establishment *n* (of company) formation *n*
grüne *nn* **grünes Pfund** green pound
Gruppenreise *nf* group travel *n*
Gruppenversicherung *nf* group insurance *n*
Gulden (-) *nm* guilder *n*
gültig *adj* valid *adj*
Gültigkeit *nf* validity *n*
gut *adj* good *adj* **gut beraten** well-advised *adj*
gutbezahlt *adj* well-paid *adj*
Güter *npl* goods *n*, freight *n* **leicht verderbliche Güter** perishable goods
Güterverkehr *nm* goods transport *n*
Güterzug (-üge) *nm* goods train *n*, freight train (US)
Gütezeichen (-) *nn* kite mark (GB) *n*
gutgläubig *adj* bona fide *adj*
Guthaben (-) *nn* balance in hand *n*
Gutschein (-e) *nm* voucher *n*
gutschreiben *vb* credit *vb* **einem Konto gutschreiben** credit sth to an account
Gutschrift(sanzeige) (-n) *nf* credit note *n*, advice note *n*
habgierig *adj* acquisitive *adj*
Hafen (Häfen) *nm* (for berthing) dock *n*, port *n*, harbour *n* **ab Hafen** ex-quay, ex-wharf

Hafenanlagen *nfpl* harbour facilities *npl*
Hafenbehörden *nfpl* harbour authorities *npl*
Hafengebühren *nfpl* harbour fees *npl*
Hafengeld *nn* harbour dues *npl*
haftbar *adj* liable *adj* **haftbar machen für** hold sb liable
Haftpflichtversicherung *nf* third party insurance *n*
Haftung *nf* liability *n* **beschränkte Haftung** limited liability **unbeschränkte Haftung** unlimited liability **volle Haftung** full liability
halb *adj* half *adj* **halber Preis** half-price
halbieren *vb* halve *vb*
Halbjahr (-e) *nn* half-year *n*
Halblohn *nm* half-pay *n*
Halbpension *nf* half-board *n*
Hälfte (-n) *nf* half *n* **um die Hälfte reduzieren** reduce sth by half
haltbar *adj* durable *adj*
halten *vb* comply *vb*, maintain *vb* **sich an die Regeln halten** comply with the rules
Hand (Hände) *nf* hand *n*
Handbuch (-bücher) *nn* handbook *n*
Händedruck (-ücke) *nm* handshake *n*
Handel *nm* commerce *n*, dealing *n*, trade *n* **der bilaterale Handel** bilateral trade **günstige Handelsbilanz** favourable balance of trade
handeln *vb* trade *vb* (deal) handle *vb* **handeln mit** trade with sb
Handels- *cpd* mercantile *adj*
Handelsabkommen (-) *nn* trade agreement *n*, commercial treaty *n*
Handelsbank (-en) *nf* merchant bank *n*
Handelsbeschränkungen *nfpl* trade restrictions *npl*
Handelsbezeichnung (-en) *nf* trade name *n*
Handelsbilanz (-en) *nf* balance of trade, trade balance **ungünstige Handelsbilanz** adverse balance of trade
Handelsbilanzdefizit (-e) *nn* trade gap *n*
Handelsembargo (-s) *nn* trade embargo *n*
Handelserweiterung *nf* expansion of trade *n*
handelsgerichtlich *adj* **handelsgerichtlich eingetragene Gesellschaft** registered company
Handelsgesellschaft (-en) *nf* trading partnership *n*
Handelsgespräche *nnpl* trade talks *npl*
Handelskammer (-n) *nf* Chamber of Commerce *n*
Handelskreise *nmpl* the commercial world *n*
Handelsmarine *nf* merchant marine *n*, merchant navy *n*
Handelsministerium *nn* Board of Trade *n*
Handelsnation (-en) *nf* trading nation *n*
Handelsnormen *nfpl* trading standards *npl*
Handelsnormenausschuß *nm* Trading Standards Office (US)
Handelspartner (-) *nm* trading partner *n*
Handelsrecht *nn* business law *n*
Handelssanktionen *nfpl* trade sanctions *npl*

Handelsschiff (-e) *nn* merchant ship *n*
Handelsschranke (-n) *nf* trade barrier *n*
Handelsspanne (-n) *nf* trading margin *n*
Handelsüberschuß (-üsse) *nm* trade surplus *n*
Handelsvertreter (-) *nm* sales representative *n*
Handelsvertretung (-en) *nf* agency **unabhängige Handelsvertretung** free agent
Handelsvolumen *nn* trading volume *n*
Handelsziffern *nfpl* trade figures *npl*
handgearbeitet *adj* handmade *adj*
handgeschrieben *adj* handwritten *adj*
Händler (-) *nm* dealer *n*, distributor *n*, merchandiser *n*, trader *n*
Handzettel (-) *nm* broadsheet *n*
hart *adj* hard *adj* **harte Währung** hard currency
Haupt- *cpd* main *adj*
Hauptbuch (-bücher) *nn* factory ledger *n*, ledger *n*
Hauptbucheintragung *nf* ledger entry *n*
Hauptbuchhalter *nm* chief accountant *n*
Hauptgewinn (-) *nm* jackpot *n*
Hauptkassierer *nm* chief cashier *n*
Hauptlieferant (-en) *nm* main supplier *n*
Hauptniederlassung (-en) *nf* registered office *n*
Hauptperson (-en) *nf* key person *n*
Hauptprodukt (-e) *nn* leading product *n*
Hauptprodukte *nnpl* staple commodities *npl*
Hauptsitz *nm* headquarters *n*
Hauptverwaltung (-en) *nf* (HO) head office *n*, main office *n*
Hauptzahlungsagent (-en) *nm* fiscal agent *n*
Hausbesitzer (-) *nm* home owner **nicht ortsansässiger Hausbesitzer** absentee landlord
Haushalt (-e) *nm* household *n*
Haushaltsausgaben *nfpl* household expenditure *n*
Haushaltsüberschuß (-üsse) *nm* budget surplus *n*
Haushaltsumfrage (-n) *nf* household survey *n*
Haushaltswaren *nfpl* domestic goods *npl*, household goods *npl*, housewares (US) *npl*
Hausinhaber (-) *nm* householder *n*
Hauspreise *nmpl* house prices *npl*
Haussemarkt (-märkte) *nm* bull market *n*
Haussier (-s) *nm* (stock exchange) bull *n*
Haussteuer (-n) *nf* house duty (US) *n*
Haustelefon (-e) *nn* house telephone *n*
Haustürverkauf *nm* door-to-door selling *n*
Hausverkauf (-äufe) *nm* house sale *n*
Heimarbeit *nf* home/out work *n* **Heimarbeit am Computer** teleworking
Heimat *nf* home country *n*
Heimatanschrift (-en) *nf* home address *n*
herabsetzen *vb* (prices) bring down *vb* (price) knock down *vb* (price, interest rate) lower *vb* (price) mark down *vb*
Herabsetzung *nf* markdown *n*
herausbringen *vb* (product) bring out *vb*
herausstellen *vb* (end) turn out *vb*

hergestellt adj made adj **in Frankreich hergestellt** made in France
Herkunftsland (-länder) nn country of origin n
herrenlos adj abandoned adj **herrenlose Güter** abandoned goods
herstellen vb manufacture vb
Hersteller (-) nm manufacturer n
Herstellung nf manufacture n
Herstellungsfehler (-) nm faulty workmanship n
Herstellungspreis (-e) nm cost price n
Hierarchie (-n) nf (corporate) hierarchy n
Hilfs- cpd auxiliary adj
Hilfsarbeiter (-) nm unskilled worker n
Hilfsfonds nm emergency fund n
Hilfskasse nf Friendly Society n
hinsichtlich prep (gen) in respect of... prep
Hinweis (-e) nm indication n (suggestion) tip n
hinweisen vb **hinweisen auf** indicate vb
hoch adj high adj **hoch im Kurs** at a premium
Hochfinanz nf high finance n
Hochsaison (-s) nf high season n
höchst adj highest adj
höchster nm **höchster Verwaltungsbeamter** company secretary
Höchstpreis (-e) nm maximum price n, threshold price n
Höchstpreise nmpl top prices npl
Hochtechnologie nf high technology n
hochwertig adj high-grade adj
Höhepunkt (-e) nm zenith n
höher adj senior adj **höhere Position** seniority n
Holding-Gesellschaft (-en) nf holding company n
Home-Shopping nn home shopping n
horten vb hoard vb
Hotel (-s) nn hotel n **Hotel mit 5 Sternen** five-star hotel
Hotelindustrie nf hotel industry/trade n
Hotelkette (-n) nf hotel chain n
Hotelunterkunft nf hotel accommodation n
Hotelverwaltung nf hotel management n
Hypothek (-en) nf home loan n, mortage n
Hypothekendarlehen (-) nn mortgage loan n
Hypothekengläubiger (-) nm mortgagee n
Hypothekenschuldner (-) nm mortgagor n
Hypothekenvertrag (-äge) nm mortgage deed n
Hypothese (-n) nf hypothesis n
illegal adj illegal adj
Immobilien npl real estate
Immobiliengesellschaft (-en) nf property company n, estate agency n
Immobilienmakler (-) nm estate agent, realtor (US), real estate agent (US)
Immobilienmarkt nm property market (GB) / real estate market (US) n
Import nm import n, importation n **unsichtbare Importe** invisible imports
Importabteilung (-en) nf import department n
Importagent (-en) nm import agent n

Importamt (-ämter) nn import office n
Importartikel nmpl import goods npl
Importeur (-e) nm importer n
importieren vb import vb
Importkontrolle (-n) nf import control n
Importland (-länder) nn importing country n
Importschranke (-n) nf import barrier n
Inanspruchnahme nf takeup n
Index (-e) nm index n
indirekt adj indirect adj **indirekte Kosten** indirect cost, indirect expenses **Indirekte Steuer** indirect tax
Indossament nn endorsement n
industrialisieren vb industrialise vb **neu industrialisiert** newly-industrialised
Industrie (-n) nf industry n
Industriegebiet (-e) nn industrial region n
Industriegelände (-en) nn trading estate n
Industriegewerkschaft (-en) nf industrial union n
Industriekapazität nf industrial capacity n
industriell adj industrial adj
Industriemüll nm industrial waste n
Industriesiedlung (-en) nf trading estate n
Industriestaat (-en) nm advanced country n
ineffizient adj inefficient adj
Inflation nf inflation n **galoppierende Inflation** galloping inflation **übermäßige Inflation** hyperinflation
inflationär adj inflationary adj
Inflationslücke (-n) nf inflationary gap n
Inflationsrate (-n) nf rate of inflation n, level of inflation n
Inflationssicherung nf hedge against inflation n
Inflationsspirale (-n) nf inflationary spiral n
Information (-en) nf information n **konkrete Information** hard news/information
Informationsbearbeitung nf information processing n
Informationsbüro (-s) nn information office n
Informationsschalter (-) nm information desk n
Informationssysteme npl information systems npl
Informationstechnik (IT) nf information technology n
Informationstechnologie (IT) (-n) nf information technology (IT) n
Informationswiedergewinnung nf information retrieval n
informieren vb inform vb
Infrastruktur (-en) nf infrastructure n
Inhaber (-) nm bearer n, holder n, occupier n, proprietor n
Inhaberaktie (-n) nf bearer share n
Inhaberscheck (-s) nm bearer cheque n
Inhaberschuldverschreibung (-en) nf bearer bond n
Inkasso nn collection n
Inkassoagentur (-en) nf collecting adj
Inkrafttreten nn entry into force n

Inland *nn* inland *adj*
inländisch *adj* domestic *adj*
Inlandsabatz *nm* home sales *n*
Inlandsindustrie (-n) *nf* home industry *n*
Inlandspolitik *nf* domestic policy *n*
Inlandsverkäufe *nmpl* home sales *npl*
inoffiziell *adj* unofficial *adj*
Insider (-) *nm* insider *n*
Insidergeschäfte *nnpl* insider dealing *n*, insider trading (US)
Insiderhandel *nm* insider dealing *n*, insider trading (US)
Inspektor (-en) *nm* inspector *n*
Instabilität *nf* instability *n*
Installation *nf* installation *n*
installieren *vb* instal(l) *vb*
Institut (-e) *nn* institute *n* **Institut für Wirtschaftsforschung** National Bureau of Economic Research (US)
instruieren *vb* brief *vb*
Integration *nf* Integration **horizontale Intergration** horizontal integration **wirtschaftliche Integration** economic integration
intensiv *adj* intensive *adj*
Interimsschein (-e) *nm* scrip *n*
international *adj* international *adj* **internationale Konkurrenz** international competition
intervenieren *vb* intervene *vb*
Intervention (-en) *nf* intervention *n* **staatliche Intervention** state intervention
Inventar (-e) *nn* inventory *n*
Inventur *nf* stocktaking *n*
investieren *vb* (money) invest *vb*
Investition (-en) *nf* investment *n*
Investitionsausgaben *nfpl* capital expenditure *n*
Investitionsgüterleasing *nn* equipment leasing *n*
Investitionskapital *nn* invested capital *n*
Investitionsmangel *nm* lack of investment *n*
Investitionsplan (-pläne) *nm* capital budget *n*
Investitionsprogramm (-e) *nn* investment programme *n*, investment program (US)
Investitionsrate (-n) *nf* rate of investment *n*
Investitionsstrategie (-n) *nf* investment strategy *n*
Investmentfonds *nm* investment fund *n* **offener Investmentfonds** mutual funds (US)
Investor (-en) *nm* investor *n*
Jahr (-e) *nn* year *n*
Jahresabschluß (-üsse) *nm* financial statement *n*
Jahresbericht (-e) *nm* annual report *n*
Jahreseinkommen *nn* yearly income *n*
Jahreshauptversammlung *nf* AGM (Annual General Meeting) *abbr*
Jahresschlußinventar (-e) *nn* year-end inventory *n*
Jahreszeit (-en) *nf* season *n*
jahreszeitlich *adj* seasonal *adj* **jahreszeitlich bedingt** seasonal *adj*

jährlich *adj* yearly *adj*
Jobber (-) *nm* jobber *n*
Journalismus *nm* journalism *n*
jung *adj* young *adj* **junge Wirtschaft (-en)** young economy
Junk *nm* junk *n* **Junk Bond** junk bond
Kabine (-n) *nf* (phone) kiosk *n*
Kaduzierung *nf* forfeit *n*, fortfeiture *n*
Kai (-s) *nm* quay *n*
Kaigebühren *npl* quayage *n*
Kampagne (-n) *nf* campaign *n* **eine Kampagne führen** wage a campaign
Kandidat (-en) *nm* (for job) candidate *n* nominee *n*
Kapital *nn* capital *n*, funds *n* **begrenztes Kapital** limited capital **Kapital aufbringen** raise capital **langfristiges Kapital** long capital **voll eingezahltes Kapital** paid-up capital
Kapitalanlagegesellschaft *nf* investment trust *n*, unit trust *n*
Kapitalaufnahme *nf* **Kapitalaufnahme durch Emission von Aktien** flotation *n*
Kapitalausfuhr *nf* capital exports *npl*, export of capital *n*
Kapitalbeteiligung *nf* equity interests *npl*
Kapitalbildung *nf* capital formation *n*
Kapitalgewinn *nm* capital gain *n*
Kapitalgewinne *nmpl* capital gains *npl*
Kapitalgewinnsteuer (-n) *nf* capital gains tax *n*
Kapitalgüter *nnpl* capital goods *npl*
Kapitalhandel *nm* equity transaction *n*
kapitalintensiv *adj* capital-intensive *adj*
kapitalisieren *vb* capitalize *vb*
Kapitalismus *nm* capitalism *n*
Kapitalist (-en) *nm* capitalist *n*
Kapitalkosten *npl* capital cost *n*, capital outlay *n*
Kapitalmarkt (-märkte) *nm* capital market *n*
Kapitalsteigerung *nf* expansion of capital *n*
Kapitaltransferierung *nf* capital transfer *n*
Kapitalumschlag *nm* capital turnover *n*
Kapitalverkehrssteuer (-n) *nf* transfer tax *n*
Kapitalverlust (-e) *nm* capital loss *n*
Kapitalvermögen *nn* capital assets *npl*
Kapitalverzinsung *nf* return on capital *n*
Kapitalzuwachssteuer (-n) *nf* capital gains tax *n*
Karenzzeit *nf* cooling-off period *n*, period of grace *n*
karitativ *adj* charitable *adj* **karitative Organisation** charitable trust, charity
Karriere (-n) *nf* career *n*
Kartell (-e) *nn* cartel *n*
Kassageschäft (-e) *nn* cash sale *n*, cash transaction *n*
Kassakurs (-e) *nm* spot rate *n*
Kassapreis (-e) *nm* spot price *n*
Kasse (-n) *nf* box office *n*, cash desk *n*, ticket office *n* **Kasse machen** cash up
Kassegeschäft (-e) *nn* cash transaction *n*

Kassenleistungen *nfpl* health benefits *npl*
kassieren *vb* cash up *vb*
Kassierer/in *nm/nf* cashier *n*
Kauf (-äufe) *nm* purchase *n* **Kauf und Verkauf** buying and selling
Kaufbedingungen *nfpl* conditions of purchase *npl*
kaufen *vb* purchase *vb* **aus zweiter Hand kaufen** buy sth second hand **im Großhandel kaufen** buy sth wholesale **auf Kredit kaufen** buy sth on credit
Käufer (-) *nm* buyer *n*, vendee *n*
Käufermarkt (-märkte) *nm* buyer's market
Kaufhaus (-üuser) *nn* department store *n*
Kaufkraft *nf* buying power *n*, purchasing power *n*
kaufmännisch *adj* commercial *adj*
Kaufoption *nf* option to buy *n*
Kaufpreis (-e) *nm* buying price *n*, purchase price *n*
Kaution *nf* bail *n*, caution money *n*
Kautionsverpflichtung (-e) *nf* fidelity bond *n*, fiduciary bond *n*
kennenlernen *vb* make the acquaintance of sb *vb*
kenntnisreich *adj* knowledgeable *adj*
Kettenladen (-läden) *nm* chain store *n*
Kindergeld *nn* family allowance *n*
Klage (-en) *nf* legal action **gegen jemanden Klage erheben** take legal action
Klammer (-n) *nf* bracket *n*
Klausel (-n) *nf* (in contract) clause *n*
Kleiderbranche *nf* (informal) the rag trade *n*
klein *adj* small *adj* **kleine Spanne (-n)** narrow margin
Kleinanzeigen *nfpl* small ads *npl*
Kleinfehler (-) *nm* minor fault *n*
Kleingedrucktes *nn* small type *n*
Kleingeld *nn* (coins) loose/small change *n*
klimatisiert *adj* air-conditioned *adj*
Knappheit (-en) *nf* scarcity *n*
Kohlengrube (-n) *nf* coal mine *n*
Kollege (-n) *nm* colleague *n*
Kollektiv (-e) *nn* collective *n*
Kolloquium (-ien) *nn* colloquium *n*
Kommanditgesellschaft (-en) *nf* limited partnership *n*
kommerziell *adj* commercial *adj*
Kommunalanleihen *nfpl* municipal bonds *npl*
Kommunalsteuern *nfpl* (tax) rates *npl*
Kommunikation *nf* communication *n*
Kommunikationsnetz (-e) *nn* communication network *n*
komparativ *adj* comparative *adj* **komparativer Vorteil** comparative advantage
kompatibel *adj* compatible *adj*
komplex *adj* complex *adj*
kompliziert *adj* complex *adj*
Kompromiß (-sse) *nm* compromise *n* **einen Kompromiß schließen** reach a compromise
Komputer *nm* computer *n* **einen Komputer laden** boot a computer

Konferenz (-en) *nf* conference *n*
Konglomerat (-e) *nn* conglomerate *n*
Kongreß (-sse) *nm* congress *n*
Konjunkturpolitik *nf* policy to prevent economic fluctuation *n* **expansive konjunkturpolitik** reflation
Konjunkturverlauf *nm* economic trend *n*
Konjunkturzyklus (-klen) *nm* trade cycle *n*
Konkurrent (-en) *nm* competing company *n*, competitor *n*
Konkurrenz *nf* competition *n* **harte Konkurrenz** tough competition **Konkurrenz auf dem Markt** market competition
Konkurrenzfähigkeit *nf* competitiveness *n*
konkurrieren (mit) *vb* compete *vb*, compete with a rival *vb*
konkurrierend *adj* competing *adj* **konkurrierende Gesellschaft** competing company
Konkurs *nm* bankruptcy *n* **in Konkurs gehen** go to the wall **Konkurs melden** go out of business
Konkursbeschluß (-üsse) *nm* winding-up order
Konkursverwalter (-) *nm* (bankruptcy) receiver *n*, administrator (US)
Konnossement (-s) *nn* bill of lading, export bill of lading
Konservenfabrik *nf* packing house (US) *n*
Konsignatar (-) *nm* consignee *n*
Konsignationsware (-n) *nf* goods on consignment *n*
konsolidieren *vb* consolidate *vb*
konsolidiert *adj* consolidated *adj* **konsolidierte Bilanz** consolidated figures **konsolidierte Zahlen** consolidated figures
Konsortium (-ien) *nn* consortium *n*
konstruieren *vb* design *vb*
Konsul (-n) *nm* consul *n*
Konsulat (-e) *nn* consulate *n*
konsultieren *vb* consult *vb*
Konsumdenken *nn* consumerism *n*
Konsument (-) *nm* consumer *n*
Konsumforschung *nf* consumer research *n*
Konsumkredit *nm* consumer credit *n*
Konsumnachfrage *nf* consumer demand *n*
Konsumtendenzen *nfpl* consumer trends *npl*
Konsumtrends *nmpl* consumer trends *npl*
Konsumumfrage (-n) *nf* consumer survey *n*
Kontainerdepot (-s) *nn* container depot *n*
Kontakte knüpfen (business, society) network *vb*
kontaktieren *vb* contact *vb*
Kontenfälschung *nf* falsification of accounts *n*
Konto *nn* account *n* **ein Konto eröffnen** open an account **ein Konto überziehen** overdraw on an account **neues Konto (-ten)** new account
Kontoauszug (-üge) *nm* statement of account *n*, bank statement *n*
Kontonummer *nf* account number *n*
Kontostand (-ände) *nm* bank balance *n*
Kontrahent/in (-en/-innen) *nm/nf*

covenantor n
Kontrollabschnitt (-e) nm counterfoil n
konvertierbar adj convertible adj **konvertierbare Währung** convertible currency
Konzession (-en) nf franchise n
konzessionial adj **konzessioniale Bank** chartered bank
Konzessionsinhaber (-) nm licensee n
Kopf nm head n **pro kopf** per head
Kopie (-n) nf copy n
kopieren vb (photocopy) copy vb
Kopierer (-) nm (photocopier) copier n
Kopiergerät (-e) nn photocopier n
Körperschaft (-en) nf corporation n
Körperschaftssteuer (-n) nf corporation tax n
korporativ adj corporate adj
korrekt adj aboveboard adj
Korrespondenz nf correspondence n
Korruption nf corruption n
Kosten npl cost n, expense n **Kosten-Nutzen-Analyse (-n)** nf cost-benefit analysis **laufende Kosten** npl running costs
Kostenaufstellung nf cost breakdown n
Kostendegression nf economies of scale n
Kosteneinsparung nf cost trimming n
Kostenkontrolle (-n) nf expense control n
kostenlos adj complimentary adj, free of charge adj
Kostensenkung nf cost-cutting n
Kraftverkehrspedition (-en) nf haulage contractor n
Kraftverkehrunternehmen (-) nn haulage company n, freight company (US)
krank adj sick adj
Krankengeld (-er) nn sickness benefit n
Krankenurlaub nm sick leave n
Krankenversicherung nf health insurance n, medical insurance n
Krankheit (-en) nf sickness n
Kredit nm credit n, loan n **gesicherter Kredit** secured loan **Kredit aufnehmen** obtain credit **Kredit beantragen** request a loan **Kredit gewähren** extend credit, grant a loan **auf Kredit liefern** supply sth on trust **langfristiger Kredit** long credit **offener Kredit** open note (US)
Kreditanstalt nf credit institution n
Kreditaufnahme nf borrowing n
Kreditauskunft (-ünfte) nf credit reference n
Kreditauskunftei (-en) nf credit agency n
Kreditbeschränkung (-en) nf credit squeeze n
Kreditgeber (-) nm lender n
Kreditkarte (-n) nf bank card n, credit card n
Kreditkonditionen nfpl credit terms npl
Kreditkonto (-konten) nn charge account n
Kreditkontrolle nf credit control n
Kreditlinie (-n) nf credit limit n
Kreditvertrag (-äge) nm loan agreement n
kreditwürdig adj creditworthy adj
Kreditwürdigkeit nf creditworthiness n
Kreditwürdigkeitsprüfung nf credit enquiry n
Kreisdiagramm (-e) nn pie chart n

Krieg (-e) nm war n
Krisenpolitik nf brinkmanship n
kritisieren vb find fault with vb
Krone (-n) nf (Swedish) krona n (Danish, Norwegian) krone n
Kubikmeter nm/nn cubic metre n, meter (US)
Kühlhaus (-häuser) nn cold storage plant n
Kunde (-n) nm client n, customer n **Kunden gewinnen** win customers
Kundenbeziehungen nfpl customer relations npl
Kundendienst nm after-sales service n
Kundenkreditkarte (-n) nf charge card n
Kundentreue nf customer loyalty n
kündigen vb foreclose vb, call in vb **ein Darlehen kündigen** demand the repayment of a loan
Kündigung nf advance notice **ungerechtfertigte Kündigung (-en)** unfair dismissal
Kündigungsfrist (-en) nf notice period, term of notice
Kundschaft nf clientele n, patronage n
künstlich adj man-made adj
Kupon (-s) nm coupon n
Kurier (-e) nm courier n
Kurierdienst nm courrier source n **per Kurierdienst** by courier service
Kurs nm price n **letzter Kurs** market price
Kurse nmpl stock exchange prices npl
Kursgewinn nm profit n **nicht realisierter Kursgewinn (-e)** paper profit
Kursivdruck nm italic type n
Kursrisiko (-iken) nn exchange risk n
Kursverfall nm (on stock market) collapse n
Kursverlust nm loss n **nicht realisierter Kursverlust (-e)** paper loss
kurz adj short adj **kurz arbeiten** be on short time
kürzen vb (reduce) cut vb (investment) trim vb
kurzfristig adj at short notice adj, short term adj
Kurzstrecken- cpd short-haul adj
Kürzung nf trimming n
Kurzwaren nfpl dry goods npl
Ladekosten npl handling charges npl
laden vb load vb
Laden (-äden) nm shop n
Ladenkette (-n) nf chain of shops n
Ladenpreis (-e) nm retail price n
Laderaum nm stowage n
Ladeschein (-e) nm bill of lading n
Ladung (-en) nf load n (of vehicle) payload n
Lager (-) nn (goods) stock n, inventory (US) **ab Lager** ex store/warehouse **auf Lager** in stock **auf Lager haben** hold sth in reserve
Lagerhaltung nf warehousing n
Lagerhaus (-häuser) nn warehouse n
Lagerkapazität nf storage capacity n
Lagerkontrolle nf stock control n, inventory control (US)
Lagerverlust (-e) nm stock shrinkage n
Lagervermögen nn storage capacity n

Lagerwirtschaft *nf* stock control *n*
Land (-änder) *nn* country *n* **Land der Dritten Welt** third-world country
Länderblock (-s) *nm* group of countries *n*
landesweit *adj* nationwide *adj*
Landtagswahl (-en) *nf* local election *n*
Landvermesser (-) *nm* chartered surveyor *n*
Landwirtschaft *nf* agriculture *n*, farming *n*
langfristig *adj* long-term *adj* **langfristige Verbindlichkeiten** fixed liabilities
Langstrecken- *cpd* long-distance *adj*, long-haul *adj*, long-range *adj*
Lastenausgleich *nm* equalization of burdens *n*
Lastkraftwagen (-) *nm* heavy goods vehicle *n*
Leasinggeber (-) *nm* lessor *n*
Leasingnehmer (-) *nm* lessee *n*
Lebenshaltungskosten *npl* cost of living *n*
Lebenshaltungskostenindex (-e) *nm* cost of living index *n*
Lebenslauf (-äufe) *nm* curriculum vitae (CV) *n*, resumé (US)
Lebensstandard (-s) *nm* standard of living *n*
Lebensunterhalt *nm* **sich seinen Lebensunterhalt verdienen** make a living *vb*
Lebensversicherung *nf* endowment insurance *n* life assurance/insurance
Lebensversicherungspolice (-n) *nf* endowment policy *n*
leer *adj* vacant *adj*
Lehre *nf* apprenticeship *n*
Lehrling (-e) *nm* apprentice *n*
leichtverdient *adj* **leichtverdientes Geld** easy-money policy
leihen *vb* borrow *vb*, lend *vb*
Leistung (-en) *nf* accomplishment *n*, achievement *n* (behaviour) performance *n*
Leistungsbewertung *nf* performance appraisal *n*
leistungsfähig *adj* efficient *adj*
Leistungsfähigkeit *nf* efficiency *n*, viability *n*
Leistungsprämie (-n) *nf* performance-related bonus *n*
Leistungszulage (-n) *nf* merit payment *n*
leiten *vb* (department) head *vb* manage *vb*
Leitungsausschuß (-üsse) *nm* executive committee *n*
Leitungspyramide *nf* executive hierarchy *n*
Lernkurve *nf* experience curve *n*
Lieferant (-en) *nm* supplier *n*
Liefergebühren *nfpl* delivery charges *npl*
liefern *vb* (goods) deliver *vb* supply *vb*
Lieferschein (-e) *nm* delivery note *n*
Liefertermin (-e) *nm* delivery date *n*
Lieferung (-en) *nf* delivery *n*, supply *n* **Lieferung bis Morgen** overnight delivery **Lieferung frei Bestimmungsort** free delivery **Lieferung frei Haus** home delivery **Lieferung gratis** free delivery **Lieferung ist im Preis enthalten** our price includes delivery
Lieferzeit (-en) *nf* delivery time *n*
Lifo-Methode (-n) *nf* LIFO (last in first

out) *abbr*
Linie line *nf* **harte Linie** hard-line
Liquidation (-en) *nf* breakup *n*, liquidation *n*, winding-up *n* **in freiwillige Liquidation treten** go into voluntary liquidation
Liquidationsmaßnahmen *nfpl* winding-up arrangements *npl*
Liquidationswert *nm* liquidation value *n*
liquide *adj* liquid *adj* **liquide Mittel** liquid assets **liquides Kapital** liquid capital
liquidieren *vb* liquidate *vb*
Liquidität *nf* liquidity *n*
Liste (-n) *nf* list *n*
Listenpreis (-e) *nm* list price *n*
Lizenz (-en) *nf* licence *n*, permit *n*
Lizenzgeber (-) *nm* licensor *n*
Lizenzgebühr (-en) *nf* licence fee *n*
Lizenzinhaber (-) *nm* licence holder *n*
Lockartikel (-) *nm* loss leader *n*
Logistik *nf* logistics *npl*
Lohn (-öhne) *nm* (salary, wages) pay *n* wage *n*
Lohnanspruch (-sprüche) *nm* wage(s) claim *n*
Lohnbegrenzung *nf* wage restraint **freiwillige Lohnbegrenzung** voluntary wage restraint *n*
Lohnerhöhung (-en) *nf* wage increase *n*, wage rise *n*
Lohnetat *nm* wage(s) bill *n*
Lohnforderung (-en) *nf* wage claim *n*, wage demand *n*
Lohnliste (-n) *nf* payroll *n*
Lohnnebenleistungsn *nfpl* fringe benefits *npl*
Lohnpolitik *nf* wage policy *n*
Lohnsteigerungen *nfpl* wage increase *n* **Verhinderung von Lohnsteigerungen** wage restraint
Lohnstopp (-s) *nm* wage(s) freeze *n*
Lohntarif (-e) *nm* wage scale *n*
Lohntüte (-n) *nf* wage packet *n*, salary package (US)
Lohnverhandlungen *nfpl* wage negotiations *npl*
Lohnvertrag (-äge) *nm* wage agreement *n*
Lohnzuschlag (-äge) *nm* double time *n*
Lombardsatz *nm* Lombard Rate *n*
lösen *vb* (sort out) resolve *vb*
Lösen *nn* severance *n*
Luftfahrtindustrie (-n) *nf* aerospace industry *n*
Luftfracht *nf* air freight *n*
Luftpost *nf* airmail *n*
Lufttransport *nm* air transport *n*
Luftverkehr *nm* air traffic *n*
lukrativ *adj* lucrative *adj*
Luxusartikel *nmpl* luxury goods *npl*
Luxussteuer (-n) *nf* luxury tax *n*
Macht *nf* power *n*
Magnat (-en) *nm* magnate *n*
Magnetband (-bänder) *nn* (DP) magnetic tape *n*
magnetisch *adj* magnetic *adj*
Mahnung (-en) *nf* reminder *n* **letzte Mahnung** final demand, final notice

Makler (-) *nm* broker *n*
Maklerfirma (-firmen) *nf* brokerage firm *n*
Maklergeschäft *nn* brokerage *n*
Makrowirtschaft(slehre) *nf*
macroeconomics *npl*
Management *nn* management *n* **Manage-ment-Ausbildung** management training
mittleres Management middle management
Manager (-) *nm* (general) manager *n* **mitt-lerer Manager (-)** middle manager
Mangel (-ängel) *nm* deficiency *n*, lack *n*, shortage *n*
mangelhaft *adj* deficient *adj*
Mangelrüge (-n) *nf* complaint *n*
Marke (-n) *nf* brand *n*
Marken- *cpd* proprietary *adj*
Markenartikel *nm* proprietary brand *n*
Markenbild (-er) *nn* brand image *n*
Markenführer (-) *nm* brand leader *n*
Markenname (-n) *nm* brand name *n*
Marketing *nn* marketing *n* **Marketing-Mix** marketing mix
Marketingabteilung (-en) *nf* marketing department *n*
Markt (Märkte) *nm* market *n* **fallender Markt** falling market **fester Markt** firm market **freier Markt** open market **Gemeinsamer Markt** Common Market **auf den Markt bringen** (product) introduce *vb* **einen Markt erschließen** tap a market **Markt für Staats-papiere** gilt-edged market **Markt für Ter-mingeschäfte** futures exchange **ruhiger Markt** quiet market **schwarzer Markt** black market **umsatzloser Markt** flat market
Marktakzeptanz *nf* market acceptance *n*
Marktanalyse (-n) *nf* market analysis *n*
Marktanteil (-e) *nm* market share *n*
Markteindringen *nn* market penetration *n*
Marktforschung *nf* information management *n*, market research *n*
Marktforschungsfragebogen (-) *nm* market research questionnaire *n*
Marktfosrchungsstudie (-n) *nf* market research survey *n*
Marktführer (-) *nm* market leader *n*
Marktgelegenheit (-en) *nf* market opportunity *n*
Marktgelegenheiten *nfpl* market opportunities *npl*
Marktkräfte *nf* market forces *npl*
Marktpreis *nm* market price *n* **angemessener Marktpreis (-e)** fair market value
Marktsegmentierung *nf* market segmentation *n*
Markttrend (-s) *nm* market tendencies *npl*, market trend *n*
Marktwachstum *nn* market growth *n*
Marktwert (-e) *nm* market price *n*, market value *n* **ohne Marktwert** of no commercial value
Marktwirtschaft (-en) *nf* market economy *n* **freie Marktwirtschaft (-en)** (system) free market economy

Maschine (-n) *nf* machine *n*
Maschinenbau *nm* engineering *n*, mechan-ical engineering *n*
Maschinerie *nf* machinery *n*
Maße *nmpl* weights *npl* **Maße und Gewichte** weights and measures
mäßigen *vb* moderate *vb*
Mäßigung *nf* moderation *n*
maßlos *adj* exorbitant *adj*
Maßnahme (-n) *nf* measure *n* **finanzielle Maßnahme (-n)** financial measure
Massen- *cpd* bulk *adj*
Massenabsatz *nm* mass marketing *n*
Massenarbeitslosigkeit *nf* mass unemployment *n*
Massenfertigung *nf* mass production *n*
Massengüter *nnpl* bulk goods *npl*
Massengutfrachter *nm* bulk carrier *n*
Massengutladung *nf* bulk cargo *n*
Massenmedien *npl* mass media *npl*
Material *nn* materials *npl*
Mathematik *nf* arithmetic *n*
Matrix (-izen) *nf* matrix *n*
Mauer (-n) *nf* wall *n*
maximieren *vb* maximise *vb*
mechanisch *adj* mechanical *adj*
Medien *npl* media *npl*
mehrfach *adj* multiple *adj*
Mehrgewicht *nn* excess weight *n*
Mehrgewinn *nm* extra profit *n*
Mehrgewinnsteuer *nf* excess profit(s) tax *n*
Mehrheit (-en) *nf* majority *n* **arbeitsfähige Mehrheit** working majority
Mehrheitsbeteiligung *nf* majority holding *n* **Mehrheitsbeteiligung/Minderheitsbeteili-gung** majority/minority holding
Mehrkosten *npl* extra cost *n*
Mehrwertsteuer (-n) *nf* VAT *abbr*, value-added tax *n*, sales tax (US)
mehrwertsteuerfrei *adj* zero-rated for VAT *adj*
Meile (-n) *nf* mile *n*
Meilenzahl *nf* mileage *n*
Mengenrabatt *nm* quantity discount *n*, volume discount *n*
merken *vb* take notice *vb*
Meßbrief (-e) *nm* bill of tonnage *n*
Messe (-n) *nf* trade fair *n*
messen *vb* measure *vb*
Metall (-e) *nn* metal *n*
Meter (-) *nm/nn* metre *n*, meter (US)
metrisch *adj* metric *adj*
Metropole (-n) *nf* metropolis *n*
Miete (-n) *nf* rent *n*, rental *n*
mieten *vb* (person) hire *vb* (house, office) rent *vb*
Mieter (-) *nm* tenant *n*
Mietkosten *npl* hire charges *npl*
Mietvertrag (-äge) *nm* hire contract *n*
Mikrochip (-s) *nn* microchip *n*
Mikrocomputer (-) *nm* microcomputer *n*
Mikrofiche (-s) *nm* microfiche *n*

Mikroprozessor (-en) *nm* microprocessor *n*
Million (-en) *nf* million *n*
Millionär (-en) *nm* millionaire *n*
Minderheit (-) *nf* minority *n*
Minderheitsbeteiligung (-en) *nf* minority holding *n*
minderwertig *adj* shoddy* *adj*
Mindestlohn (-löhne) *nm* minimum wage *n* **indexgekoppelter Mindestlohn** index-linked minimum wage
Mindestzins (-en) *nm* minimum lending rate *n*
Mine (-n) *nf* mine *n*
Mineral (-ien) *nn* mineral *n*
minimal *adj* minimal *adj*
Minister (-) *nm* minister *n*
Ministerium (-ien) *nn* ministry *n*
mißbrauchen *vb* abuse *vb*
Mischkonzern (-e) *nm* conglomerate *n*
Mischwirtschaft (-en) *nf* mixed economy *n*
Mißmanagement *nn* mismanagement *n*
Mißtrauensantrag (-äge) *nm* vote of no confidence *n*
Mitarbeiter (-) *nm* workmate *n* **Mitarbeiter im Außendienst** field personnel
Mitbesitz *nm* joint ownership *n*
Mitbestimmung *nf* industrial democracy *n*, worker participation *n*
Mitglied (-er) *nn* member *n* **Mitglied auf Lebenszeit** life member
Mitinhaber (-) *nm* joint holder *n*
Mitteilung (-en) *nf* memo *n*, memorandum *n*, message *n*
Mitteilungsblatt (-blätter) *nn* newsletter *n*
Mittel *nnpl* means *npl*, resources *npl* **Mittel aufbringen** raise money
mittelfristig *adj* medium term *adj*
Mitunterzeichner (-) *nm* cosignatory *n*
Mitverkäufer *nm* joint vendor *n*
Modell (-e) *nn* (person) model *n* working model *n*
Modellvertrag (-äge) *nm* standard agreement *n*
Modem (-s) *nm* modem *n*
modern *adj* modern *adj*
modernisieren *vb* modernize *vb*
Modernisierung *nf* modernization *n*
Modul (-n) *nm* module *n*
möglichst *adv* **möglichst bald** at your earliest convenience
monatlich *adj* monthly *adj*
monetär *adj* monetary *adj*
Monetarismus *nm* monetarism *n*
Monopol (-e) *nn* monopoly *n*
Monopolkommission *nf* Monopolies and Mergers Commission *n*
Montageband (-bänder) *nn* assembly line *n*
Montanunion *nf* ECSC (European Coal and Steel Community) *abbr*
Moral *nf* morale *n* **die Moral heben** boost morale
multilateral *adj* multilateral *adj*
multinational *adj* multinational *adj*

mündlich *adj* verbal *adj* **mündliche Absprache** gentleman's agreement, verbal agreement
Münzanstalt (-en) *nf* mint *n*
Muster (-) *nn* sample *n*
Musterfall (-fälle) *nm* test case *n*
Muttergesellschaft (-en) *nf* parent company *n*
Nachbestellung (-en) *nf* repeat order *n*
Nachfrage *nf* demand *n* **die Nachfrage ankurbeln** boost demand
Nachfrageboom (-s) *nm* boom in demand *n*
Nachfragenelastizität *nf* elasticity of demand *n*
nachkommen comply with *vb* **den Anordnungen nachkommen** comply with legislation **seinen Verpflichtungen nachkommen** meet one's obligations
nachlässig *adj* hit-or-miss *adj*
Nachlässigkeit *nf* (laxity) slackness *n*
Nachricht (-en) *nf* bulletin *n*
Nachrichten *nfpl* news *n* **finanzielle Nachrichten** financial news **gute Nachrichten** good news **schlechte Nachrichten** bad news
Nachrichtenagentur (-en) *nf* news agency *n*, newsdealer (US)
Nachrichtensendung (-en) *nf* bulletin *n*
nachschicken *vb* (mail) redirect *vb*
Nachwuchsführungskraft (-äfte) *nf* trainee manager
Nachzahlung *nf* back pay *n*
Name *nm* name *n* **im Namen** in the name of **mit Namen** by name
Namensaktie (-n) *nf* registered share *n*
Namensschuldverschreibung (-en) *nf* registered bond *n*
Nation (-en) *nf* nation *n*
Nebenkosten *npl* incidental expenses *npl*
Nebenleistung (-en) *nf* (informal) perk *n* (formal) perquisite *n*
Nebenmarkt (-märkte) *nm* fringe market *n*, secondary market *n*
Nebenprodukt (-e) *nn* by-product *n*, spin-off *n*
Nebensaison (-s) *nf* low season *n*
negieren *vb* negative (US) *vb*
Nennwert (-e) *nm* nominal value *n*, nominal price *n*, face value *n*
netto *adj* net(t) *adj*
Nettoauftragseingang (-änge) *nm* net(t) sales *npl*
Nettobetrag (-äge) *nm* net(t) amount *n*
Nettoeinkommen *nn* disposable income *n*, net(t) income *n*
Nettoersparnisse *nfpl* net(t) saving *n*
Nettogewicht *nn* net(t) weight *n*
Nettoinvestition *nf* net(t) investment *n*
Nettokosten *npl* net(t) cost *n*
Nettolohn (-öhne) *nm* net(t) wage *n*
Nettopreis (-e) *nm* net(t) price *n*
Nettotonnage *nf* net(t) tonnage *n*
Nettoverdienst *nm* net(t) earnings *npl*
Nettoverlust (-e) *nm* clear loss *n*, net(t) loss *n*
Nettovermögen *nn* net(t) assets *npl*

Nettozinsen *nmpl* net(t) interest *n*
Neugeschäft *nn* new business *n*
neutral *adj* neutral *adj*
nicht *adv* not *adv* **nicht einstimmige Abstimmung** split division **nicht erwerbswirtschaftlich** non-profitmaking **nicht übertragbar** non-transferable **nicht wandelbar** non-convertible
Nichtabschluß (-üsse) *nm* non-completion *n*
nichtbegebbar *adj* non-negotiable *adj*
nichtdiskriminierend *adj* non-discriminatory *adj*
Nichteingreifen *nn* non-intervention *n*
Nichtlieferung *nf* non-delivery *n*
Nichtzahlung *nf* non-payment *n*
niedrig *adj* (price) low *adj* **niedrigster Preis** bottom price, knockdown price
Nominalbetrag (-äge) *nm* nominal amount *n*
Nominalinflation *nf* nominal inflation *n*
Nominalvermögen *nn* nominal assets *npl*
nominell *adj* nominal *adj*
Nominierung (-en) *nf* nomination *n*
Norm (-en) *nf* norm *n*
Notar (-en) *nm* notary *n*
Notenausgabe *nf* issue *n* **ungedeckte Notenausgabe** fiduciary issue
Notenbank (-en) *nf* bank of issue *n*, issuing bank *n*
Notfall (-fälle) *nm* emergency *n*
Notizen *npl* notes *npl* **Notizen machen** take notes
Notwendigkeit *nf* (goods) necessity *n*
Null *nf* nil *n*, zero *n* **null und nichtig** null and void
Nullgewinn (-e) *nm* nil profit *n*
Nullwachstum *nn* zero growth *n*
nutzbar *adj* (materials) reclaimable *adj*
Nutzen *nm* utility *n*
nützen *vb* benefit *vb*
Nutzfahrzeug (-e) *nn* commercial vehicle *n*
obenerwähnt *adj* above-mentioned *adj*
Obligation (-en) *nf* bond *n*
Obligationär (-e) *nm* bondholder *n*
Obligationsanleihe (-n) *nf* debenture loan *n*
obligatorisch *adj* obligatory *adj*
offen *adj* open *adj* **offener Kredit** unsecured credit
öffentlich *adj* public *adj* **öffentlicher Verkehr** public transport **öffentlicher Zuschuß** state subsidy **öffentliches Geld** public money
Öffentlichkeitsarbeit *nf* public relations *npl*
Öffnungszeiten *nfpl* opening times *npl*
Offshore-Gesellschaft (-en) *nf* offshore company *n*
Ökonometrie *nf* econometrics *npl*
Öldollar *nm* petrodollar *n*
Ölfeld (-er) *nn* oilfield *n*
Oligopolie (-n) *nf* oligopoly *n*
Ölindustrie *nf* petroleum industry *n*
ölproduzierend *adj* oil-producing *adj* **ölproduzierender Staat** oil state
Option (-en) *nf* option *n*

Optionsklausel (-n) *nf* option clause *n*
Optionsmarkt (-märkte) *nm* options market *n*
Organisation (-en) *nf* organization *n*
organisieren *vb* arrange (a conference) *vb*, organize *vb*
örtlich *adj* local *adj*
Ortsnetzkennzahl (-en) *nf* (telephone) code *n*
Output *nm* output *n*
Pachtbesitz *nm* leasehold *n*
Pächter (-) *nm* leaseholder *n*
packen *vb* pack *vb*
Paket (-e) *nn* bundle *n*, package *n*, packet *n*
Palette (-n) *nf* pallet *n*, (product) range *n*
palettisiert *adj* palletized *adj*
Pannendienst (-e) *nm* breakdown service *n*
Papier *nn* paper *n* **Papier mit Briefkopf** headed notepaper
Papiergeld *nn* paper money *n* **Papiergeld ohne Deckung** fiat money
Papierwährung (-en) *nf* paper currency *n*
Parität *nf* parity *n*
Partie (-n) *nf* (at auction) lot *n*
Partner *nm* associate *n*, partner *n*
Passagier (-e) *nm* passenger *n*
Patent (-e) *nn* patent *n*
patentrechtlich *adj* **patentrechtlich geschützt** patented *adj*
Patt *nn* stalemate *n*
Pauschalentschädigung *nf* lump sum settlement *n*
Pauschalreise (-n) *nf* package tour *n*
Pause *nf* break *n* **Pause machen** take a break
Pendant *nn* opposite number *n*
Pendelverkehr *nm* shuttle *n*
Pensionsplan (-pläne) *nm* pension scheme *n*
Personal *nn* human resources *npl*, personnel *n*
Personalabteilung (-en) *nf* personnel department *n*
Personalausbildung *nf* employee training *n*
Personalbestand *nm* manpower *n*
Personalbeziehungen *npl* human relations *npl*
Personalcomputer (-) *nm* personal computer (PC) *n*
Personalkredit (-e) *nm* personal loan *n*
Personalmanagement *nn* human resource management (HRM) *n*
Personengesellschaft (-en) *nf* partnership *n*
Personenzug (-üge) *nm* passenger train *n*
persönlich *adj* personal *adj*
Pfund *nn* (weight) pound *n* **Pfund Sterling (-)** pound sterling *n*
Pfundguthaben (-) *nn* sterling balance *n*
Pharmazieindustrie *nf* pharmaceutical industry *n*
Pilotanlage (-n) *nf* pilot plant *n*
Pilotprojekt *nn* pilot scheme *n*
Pipeline (-s) *nf* pipeline *n*
Piraterie *nf* (at sea) piracy *n*
Plakat (-e) *nn* (advertising) poster *n*
Plan (-äne) *nm* plan *n* **Pläne machen** make

plans **vorläufiger Plan** tentative plan
planen vb plan vb, schedule vb
plangemäß adv according to plan
Planung nf planning n **langfristige Planung** long-term planning
Planwirtschaft (-en) nf planned economy n
Plastikindustrie nf plastics industry n
platzen vb (cheque) bounce* vb
Plebiszit (-e) nn referendum n
Plenar- cpd (assembly, session) plenary adj
Politik nf politics npl
politisch adj political adj
Portefeuille (-n) nn portfolio n
Posfach (-fächer) nn PO box n
Postamt (-ämter) nn post office n
Postbezirk (-e) nm postal zone n
Postdienste nmpl postal services npl
Postfach (-fächer) nn box number n
Postgebühr nf postal charge/rate n **Postgebühr bar bezahlt** Freepost (R) (GB)
postlagernd adj poste restante, general delivery (US)
Postleitzahl (-en) nf post code n, zip code (US)
prägen vb mint vb
praktisch adj handy adj
Prämie (-n) nf bonus n, premium n
Praxis nf usage n
Preis (-e) nm price n **fester Preis** hard price **günstiger Preis** favourable price **Preis ab Werk** factory price **Preise niedrig halten** keep down prices **Preise treiben** profiteer
Preisangabe (-n) nf (price) quotation n
Preisbildungspolitik nf pricing policy n
Preisbindung nf fair trade n
Preisbindungsabkommen (-) nn fair-trade agreement n
Preisentwicklung (-en) nf price trend n
Preiserhöhung nf price increase n
Preisetikett (-e) nn price ticket n
Preisindex (-e) nm price index n
Preiskampf (-kämpfe) nm price war n
Preisniveau (-s) nn level of prices n
Preisobergrenze nf (on prices) ceiling n
Preispolitik nf pricing policy n
Preissturz (-ürze) nm slump n
preiswert adj good value adj **preiswert kaufen** get value for one's money
Pressekonferenz (-en) nf press conference n
Pressezar (-en) nm press baron n
Primawechsel (-) nm first bill of exchange n
Priorität nf priority n
Privatbereich (-e) nm private sector n
Privateigentum nn private property n
Privateinkommen nn private income n
privatisieren vb privatize vb
Privatisierung nf privatization n
Privatunternehmen (-) nn private enterprise n
pro prep per prep **pro Jahr** per annum **pro Kopf** per capita
Probe nf sampling n **auf Probe** on approval **die Probe bestehen** stand the test **auf die**

Probe stellen put sth to the test
Probeangebot (-e) nn trial offer n
Probezeit nf trial period
probieren vb sample vb, try out vb
Produkt (-e) nn product n **neues Produkt (-e)** new product
Produkteinführung (-en) nf product launch n
Produktion nf output n, production n **Produktion pro Stunde** per hour output **die Produktion steigern** boost production
Produktionseinheit (-en) nf unit of production n
Produktionselastizität nf elasticity of production n
Produktionsfaktor (-en) nm factor of production n
Produktionskapazität nf manufacturing capacity n
Produktionskartell (-e) nn quota agreement n
Produktionskontrolle (-n) nf production control n
Produktionsmethode (-n) nf production method n
Produktionsziel (-e) nn production target n
produktiv adj productive adj
Produktivität nf productivity n
Produktivitätssteigerung nf productivity gains npl
Produktmix nm product mix n
Produzent (-en) nm producer n
produzieren vb produce vb
profitieren vb benefit vb
Prognose (-n) nf forecast n
Programm (-e) nn (DP) program n
Programmfehler (-n) nm (listening device) bug n
Programmieren nn (DP) programming n
Programmierer (-) nm (DP) programmer n
Projekt (-e) nn project n **ein Projekt streichen** kill a project
prolongieren vb (to next month) carry over vb
Prospekt (-e) nm brochure n, prospectus n
Protektionismus nm protectionism n
protektionistisch adj protectionist adj
protestieren vb object vb
Protokoll nn (meeting) the minutes npl
Provision nf commission n **Provision berechnen** charge commission
Provisionsgebühr (-en) nf commission fee n
Provisionsvertreter (-) nm commission agent n
provisorisch adj temporary adj
Prozent nn per cent
Prozentsatz (-ätze) nm percentage n **Prozentsatz des Gewinns** percentage of profit
Prozeß (-sse) nm lawsuit n **einen Prozeß führen** litigate vb
prüfen vb check vb, examine vb, inspect vb, make a check on sth vb
Prüfer examiner n **innerbetrieblicher Prüfer (-)** internal auditor
Prüfung (-en) nf examination n

Publikumsgesellschaft (-en) *nf* public company *n*
Publizität *nf* publicity *n*
Punkt (-e) *nm* point *n*
Quadratmeter (-) *nm/nn* square metre, meter (US)
Qualifikation *nf* qualification *n*, academic qualification *n*, educational qualification *n* **berufliche Qualifikation** professional qualification **erforderliche Qualifikationen** necessary qualifications
qualifiziert *adj* qualified *adj* **qualifizierte Arbeitskräfte** qualified personnel
Qualität *nf* quality *n* **(von) guter Qualität** well-made *adj* **(von) minderer Qualität** (goods) inferior *adj* **(von) niedriger Qualität** (product) down-market
qualitativ *adj* qualitative *adj*
Qualitätsbericht (-e) *nm* quality report *n*
Qualitätsgarantie (-n) *nf* quality guarantee *n*
Qualitätskontrolle (-n) *nf* quality control *n*
Qualitätsnorm (-en) *nf* quality standard *n*
Quantität *nf* quantity *n*
quantitativ *adj* quantitative *adj*
Quantitätstheorie *nf* quantity theory *n* **Quantitätstheorie des Geldes** quantity theory of money
Quasi- *cpd* quasi *adj* **Quasi-Einkommen** quasi-income **Quasi-Vertrag** quasi-contract
Quelle (-n) *nf* source *n*
Quittung *nf* receipt *n* **eine Quittung geben** issue a receipt
Quorum (-a) *nn* quorum *n*
Quote (-n) *nf* quota *n*
Quotenauswahlverfahren *nn* quota sampling *n*
Quotenkauf *nm* quota buying *n*
Quotensystem (-e) *nn* quota system *n*
R-Gespräch (-e) *nn* reverse-charge call *n*, collect call (US) **ein R-Gespräch machen** (call) transfer
Rabatt (-e) *nm* discount *n*, rebate *n* **mit Rabatt** at a discount
Ramsch *nm* **im Ramsch verkaufen** sell sth in bulk
Rand- *cpd* peripheral *adj*
Rang (-änge) *nm* tier *n* **von hohem Rang** high-ranking
Rate (-n) *nf* instalment *n*, installment (US)
Ratenzahlungen *nfpl* staged payments *npl*
Rathaus (-häuser) *nn* town hall
ratifizieren *vb* ratify *vb*
Ratifizierung *nf* ratification *n*
rationalisieren *vb* rationalize *vb*
Rationalisierung *nf* rationalization *n*
Rationalisierungsmaßnahmen *nfpl* rationalization measures *npl*
Ratschlag (-äge) *nm* advice *n*
Raum (-äume) *nm* room *n*
Räumlichkeiten *nfpl* premises *npl*
Räumungsverkauf (-äufe) *nm* closing-down sale *n*, closing-out sale (US)

Reallohn (-löhne) *nm* real wage *n*
Realwert (-e) *nm* real value *n*
Rechenfehler (-) *nm* miscalculation *n*
rechenkundig *adj* numerate *adj*
Rechenzentrum *nn* computer centre *n*, computer center (US)
Rechnen *nn* numeracy *n*
Rechner (-) *nm* calculator *n*
rechnergestützt *adj* computer-aided *adj* **rechnergestützte Fertigung** computer-aided manufacture (CAM) **rechnergestütztes Konstruieren** computer-aided design (CAD) **rechnergestütztes Lernen** computer-aided learning (CAL)
Rechnung (-en) *nf* bill *n*, invoice *n*, tally *n* **eine Rechnung ausstellen** issue an invoice **die Rechnung begleichen** pay a bill, settle an account **in Rechnung stellen** (invoice (informal)) bill
Rechnungsabschnitt (-e) *nm* accounting period *n*
Rechnungsduplikat (-e) *nn* duplicate invoice *n*
Recht (-e) *nn* right *n* **alleiniges Recht** sole rights **erworbene Rechte** vested rights **internationales Recht** international law **öffentliches Recht** public law **das Recht auf etwas** the right to sth
Rechtsanwalt (-älte) *nm* barrister *n*, lawyer (US)
Rechtskosten (-) *npl* legal charges *npl*
Rechtsmittelinstanz *nf* Court of Appeal *n*, Court of Appeals (US)
Rechtsstreit (-e) *nm* litigation *n*
rechtsverbindlich *adj* legally binding *adj*
recycelbar *adj* recyclable *adj*
reduzieren *vb* (prices) bring down *vb*, reduce *vb*
Referenz (-en) *nf* referee *n*, testimonial *n*
Reform (-en) *nf* reform *n*
regieren *vb* govern *vb*
Regierung (-en) *nf* government *n*
Regierungsabteilung (-en) *nf* government department *n*
Regierungsapparat *nm* machinery of government *n*
Regierungsausschuß (-üsse) *nm* government body *n*
Regierungschef (-s) *nm* head of government *n*
Regierungspolitik *nf* government policy *n*
Regierungssektor (-en) *nm* government sector *n*
Regierungsunternehmen (-) *nn* government enterprise *n*
Regierungszuschuß (-üsse) *nm* government subsidy *n*
regional *adj* regional *adj* **regionale Subvention** regional grant
Regionalbüro (-s) *nn* regional office *n*
Regionalleiter (-) *nm* area manager *n*
regulär *adj* regular *adj*
Regulierung (-en) *nf* adjustment *n*

Reichtum *nm* wealth *n*
Reihe (-n) *nf* (of products) range *n*
Reihenfertigung *nf* flow line production *n*, flow production *n*
Reingewinn *nm* net(t) profit *n*
Reinverlust (-e) *nm* net(t) loss *n*
Reisebüro (-s) *nn* travel agency *n*
Reisegepäckversicherung *nf* luggage insurance *n*
Reisekosten *npl* travelling expenses *npl*, travel expenses (US)
Reiseleiter (-e) *nm* courier *n*
Reisen *nn* travelling *n*, traveling (US)
Reisende/r *nmf* traveller *n*, traveler (US)
Reisescheck (-s) *nm* traveller's cheque *n*, traveler's check (US)
Reisespesen *npl* travelling expenses *npl*, travel expenses (US)
Reiseversicherung *nf* travel insurance *n*
Reißwolf (-ölfe) *nm* shredder *n*
Reklamationsabteilung (-en) *nf* claims department *n*
Reklamationsverfahren (-) *nn* claims procedure *n*
Rendite *nf* rate of return *n*
Renditekurve (-n) *nf* yield curve *n*
renovieren *vb* refurbish *vb*
Renovierung (-en) *nf* refurbishment *n*
Rentabilität *nf* profitability *n*
Rente (-n) *nf* annuity *n*, pension *n* **gehaltsabhängige Rente** earnings-related pension
Rentenfonds *nm* pension fund *n*
Reparaturkosten *npl* costs of repair *npl*
reparieren *vb* repair *vb*
Repatriierung (-en) *nf* repatriation *n*
Reservewährung (-en) *nf* reserve currency *n*
reservieren *vb* reserve *vb* **ein Hotelzimmer reservieren** book a hotel room
Reservierung (-en) *nf* (reservation) booking *n* reservation *n*
restlich *adj* residual *adj*
Restschuld (-en) *nf* unpaid balance *n*
retten *vb* salvage *vb*
revidieren *vb* revise *vb*
Revision *nf* revision *n* **innerbetriebliche Revision** internal audit
Rezession (-en) *nf* recession *n*
Richtpreis (-e) *nm* bench mark price *n*
richtungsweisend *adj* pointing the way **richtungsweisend sein** set a trend
Riesengeschäft *nn* **Riesengeschäft machen** make a fortune
riesengroß *adj* king-size(d) *adj*
Riesentanker (-) *nm* supertanker *n*
Risiko (-iken) *nn* risk *n* **finanzielles Risiko** financial risk **vom Käufer übernommenes Risiko** at the buyer's risk
Risikoanalyse (-n) *nf* risk analysis *n*
Risikoeinschätzung (-en) *nf* risk assessment *n*
Risikokapital *nn* risk capital *n*
risikoreich *adj* high-risk *adj*
roh *adj* (unprocessed) raw *adj*

Roheisen *nn* pig iron *n*
Rohstoff (-e) *nm* primary product *n* **Rohstoffe** raw materials
Rolltreppe (-n) *nf* escalator *n*
rot *adj* red *adj*
Route (-n) *nf* itinerary *n*
rückdatieren *vb* backdate *vb*
Rückerstattung (-en) *nf* refund *n*
Rückfahrkarte (-n) *nf* return ticket *n*, round-trip ticket (US)
Rückgabe *nf* return *n*
rückgabepflichtig *adj* (deposit) returnable *adj*
Rückgang (-änge) *nm* (economic) decline *n* decrease *n*, shrinkage *n*
rückgängig *adj* declining *adj* **rückgängig machen** (offer) revoke
Rückgängigmachung (-en) *nf* cancellation *n*
Rückgriffsrecht *nn* right of recourse *n*
Rücklage reserve *n* **die freie Rücklage** earned surplus
Rückmeldung *nf* feedback *n* **negative Rückmeldung** negative feedback **Rückmeldung geben** give feedback
Rückstand arrears *n* **im Rückstand** in arrears **Rückstände** backlog **in Rückstand kommen** fall/get into arrears
Rücktritt (-e) *nm* resignation *n* **seinen Rücktritt erklären** hand in one's resignation
rückvergütbar *adj* refundable *adj*
rückvergüten *vb* reimburse *vb*
Rückvergütung (-en) *nf* reimbursement *n*
rückversichern *vb* reinsure *vb*
Rückversicherung *nf* fronting *n*, reinsurance *n*
Rückzahlung (-en) *nf* (of loan) repayment *n* **ohne Rückzahlung** ex repayment
Ruf *nm* reputation *n*
rufen *vb* call for *vb*
Ruhestand *nm* retirement *n* **in den Ruhestand treten** retire
ruinös *adj* ruinous *adj* **ruinöse Konkurrenz** cut-throat competition
rund *adj* round *adj*
Rundfahrt (-en) *nf* round trip *n*
Rundschreiben *nn* (letter) circular *n*
Sachanlage (-n) *nf* tangible asset *n*
Sache (-en) *nf* thing *n*, object *n* **bewegliche Sachen** *nfpl* chattels *npl*
Sanktion *nf* sanction *nf* **wirtschaftliche Sanktion (-en)** economic sanction
Schaden (-äden) *nm* damage *n* **beträchtlichen Schaden verursachen** cause extensive damage
Schadenersatz *nm* indemnity *n* **nomineller Schadenersatz** nominal damages **Schadenersatz beanspruchen** (legal) claim damages
Schadenersatzansprüche *nmpl* **Schadenersatzansprüche geltend machen** claim for damages *vb*
schadenersatzpflichtig *adj* liable for damages *adj*
Schadenersatzversicherung *nf* indemnity

insurance n

Schadensfreiheitsrabatt nm no-claims bonus n

Schadhaftigkeit nf spoilage n

schaffen vb accomplish vb

Schalterbeamte/r teller n

Schalterstunden nfpl banking hours npl

scharf adj (competition) keen adj sharp adj

Schatzanweisung (-en) nf Treasury bill n, treasurer check (US)

schätzen vb estimate vb

Schätzkosten npl estimate of costs n

Schätzung (-en) nf estimate n

Schauraum (-räume) nm showroom n

Scheck (-s) nm cheque n, check (US) **begebbarer Scheck** negotiable cheque **gekreuzter Scheck** crossed cheque **geplatzter Scheck** dud cheque **per Scheck zahlen** pay by cheque **einen Scheck ausstellen** make out a cheque **einen Scheck an den Austeller zurückgeben** return a cheque to drawer **einen Scheck einlösen** cash a cheque **Scheck in Höhe von** a cheque for the amount of **einen Scheck platzen lassen** bounce* a cheque **einen Scheck rückdatieren** backdate a cheque **einen Scheck sperren** stop a cheque **einen Scheck unterschreiben** sign a cheque **unbezahlter Scheck** unpaid cheque

Scheckbuch (-ücher) nn cheque book n, checkbook (US)

Scheckheft (-e) nn cheque book n

Scheckkarte (-n) nf cheque card n

Scheinkauf (-e) nm fictitious purchase n

Scheinverkauf nm fictitious sale n

Schicht (-en) nf shift n

Schichtarbeit nf shift work n

Schiedsgerichtsverfahren (-) nn industrial arbitration n

Schiedsspruch (-üche) nm arbitrage n

Schiene (-n) nf track n

Schienenverkehr nm rail traffic n

Schiff nn ship n **ab Schiff** ex ship

Schiffahrtslinie (-n) nf shipping line n

Schiffbau nm shipbuilding n

Schiffskörper (-) nm hull n

Schiffskörperversicherung nf hull insurance n

Schiffsmakler (-) nm shipping broker n

Schiffsmaschinenbau nm marine engineering n

Schiffsverkehr nm sea traffic n

Schiffswerft (-en) nf shipyard n

Schlagzeile nf headline n **Schlagzeilen machen** hit the headlines

Schlange (-n) nf queue n

Schleuderpreis (-e) nm giveaway price n

Schleudersitz nm hot seat n

Schlichter (-) nm arbitrator n

Schlichtung nf arbitration n

schließen close vb, shut vb **den Laden schließen** (informal) shut up shop

Schließfach (-fächer) nn left-luggage locker n

Schlußbilanz (-en) nf final balance n

Schlußkurs (-e) nm closing price n

Schlußrechnung (-en) nf final invoice n

Schlüsselfrage (-n) nf key question n

Schlüsselindustrie (-n) nf key industry n

Schlüsselkraft (-kräfte) nf key person n

Schlüsselwährung (-en) nf key currency n

Schmiergeld nn backhander* n (bribe) sweetener* n

schmuggeln vb smuggle vb

Schnelldienst nm express agency n

Schnelldreher npl fast-selling goods npl

Schnellspur nf fast track n

Schnittstelle (-n) nf interface n

Schranke (-n) nf barrier n

Schreibarbeiten npl paperwork n

Schreibfehler (-) nm clerical error n

Schreibmaschine (-n) nf typewriter n

Schrott nm scrap metal n **zu Schrott fahren** (vehicle) write off

schrumpfen vb shrink vb

Schuld (-en) nf debt n **in Schuld geraten** get into debt

Schuldanerkenntnis (-sse) nn **schriftliches Schuldanerkenntnis** acknowledgement of debt

schulden vb owe vb

Schuldendienst (-e) nm debt service n

Schuldeneinziehung nf debt collection n

Schuldenerlaß nm quittance n

Schuldner (-) nm debtor n

Schuldschein nm promissory note n **ungesicherter Schuldschein (-e)** unsecured bond

Schuldverschreibung (-en) nf bond n **gesicherte Schuldverschreibung** debenture

Schutzklausel (-n) nf n, hedge clause (US)

Schwangerschaftsurlaub (-e) nm maternity leave n

schwanken vb fluctuate vb

Schwankung (-en) nf fluctuation n

schwarz adj black adj **schwarz arbeiten** moonlight*

Schwarzhandel nm black economy n

Schwarzmarkt (-märkte) nm black economy n, black market n

Schwerindustrie nf heavy industry n

Schwestergesellschaft (-en) nf affiliated company n, sister company n

Schwindel (-) nm swindle* n

Schwindelgeschäft (-e) nn racket n

Schwindelunternehmen (-) nn phoney* company n

Schwindler (-) nm swindler* n

See- cpd marine adj

Seemeile (-n) nf nautical mile n

Seeversicherung nf marine insurance n

Sekretär/in (-en/-innen) nm/nf secretary n

Sektor (-en) nm sector n

sekundär adj secondary adj

Selbstabholung nf **Selbstabholung gegen Kasse** cash and carry

Selbsteinschätzung nf self-assessment n

Selbstkosten *npl* original cost *n*
Selbstverwaltung *nf* self-management *n*
senden *vb* broadcast *vb*, send *vb*, transmit *vb* **per Eilboten senden** courier *vb*
Sendung (-en) *nf* (of goods) batch *n* broadcast *n*, consignment *n*
senkrecht *adj* vertical *adj*
Seriennummer (-n) *nf* serial number *n*
Serienverarbeitung *nf* (DP) batch processing *n*
sicher *adj* safe *adj*, secure *adj*
Sicherheit *nf* safety *n*, security *n* **als Sicherheit halten** hold sth as security
Sicherheitsbeauftragte/r *nmf* safety officer *n*
Sicherheitsmaßnahme (-n) *nf* safety measure *n*
Sicherungsgegenstand *nm* collateral *n*
Sicht *nf* sight *n*
sichtbar *adj* visible *adj*
Sichtfernsprecher (-) *nm* visual telephone *n*
Sichtgerät (-e) *nn* visual display unit (VDU) *n*
Sichtwechsel (-) *nm* sight draft *n*
Siegel (-) *nn* seal *n*
Simulant (-en) *nm* malingerer *n*
Sitz *nm* seat *n* **den Sitz verlegen** relocate
Sitzstreik *nm* (strike) sit-in *n*
Sitzung (-en) *nf* meeting *n*
Sitzungsperiode (-n) *nf* negotiating session *n*
Sitzungssaal (-äle) *nm* board room *n*
Skala (-en) *nf* scale *n*
Slogan (-s) *nm* slogan *n*
sofortig *adj* immediate *adj* **sofortige Bezahlung** spot cash
Software *nf* software *n*
Softwarepaket (-e) *nn* software package *n*
Solawechsel (-) *nm* promissory note *n*
solide *adj* well-made *adj*
Sonderangebot (-e) *nn* bargain offer *n*, clearance offer *n*
Sonderdividende *nf* **Sonderdividende am Schluß des Jahres (-n)** year-end dividend
Sonderrücklage *nf* excess reserves *npl*
Sonderzahlung (-en) *nf* ex gratia payment *n*
Sonderziehungsrechte *npl* SDRs (special drawing rights) *abbr*
Sorte (-n) *nf* kind *n*
Sortiment (-e) *nn* product line *n*
Sozialhilfeleistung *nf* welfare benefits *npl*
Sozialversicherung *nf* National Insurance (NI) (GB), Social Security (GB)
Sozialversicherungsbeiträge *npl* social security contributions *npl*
sozialwirtschaftlich *adj* socio-economic *adj* **sozialwirtschaftliche Begriffe** socio-economic categories
sozioökonomisch *adj* socio-economic *adj*
spalten *vb* split *vb*
Sparkasse *nf* savings bank *n*
Sparkonto (-konten) *nn* savings account *n*
Sparte (-n) *nf* line of business *n*
Spediteur (-e) *nm* carrier *n*, forwarder *n*, forwarding agent *n*, freight forwarder *n*,

agent, transport agent (US)
Spedition *nf* forwarding agent *n*, road haulage *n*, road haulage company *n* **per Spedition** by road
Speicherkapazität *nf* memory capacity *n*
Spekulant (-en) *nm* speculator *n*
Spekulationskapital *nn* venture capital *n*
spekulieren *vb* speculate *vb*
sperren *vb* block *vb*
Sperrkonto (-konten) *nn* blocked account *n*
Sperrzone (-n) *nf* exclusion zone *n*
Spesen *npl* business expenses *npl*
Spesenkonto (-s) *nn* expense account *n*
spezialisieren *vb* specialize *vb*
Spezialität (-en) *nf* speciality *n*
Spielraum *nm* room for manoeuvre *n*
Spitze (-n) *nf* peak *n* **an der Spitze von** at the head of
Spitzen- *cpd* high-level *adj*, top-level *adj*
Spitzennachfrage *nf* peak demand *n*
Spitzenqualität *nf* top-of-the-range *adj*
Spitzentechnologie (-n) *nf* advanced technology *n*
Spitzenzeit (-en) *nf* peak period *n*
Spitzenzeiten *npl*, busy hours (US)
Spotmarkt (-märkte) *nm* spot market *n*
Spottpreis (-e) *nm* bargain price *n*
Sprache (-n) *nf* language *n* **offizielle Sprache** working language
Sprachexperte (-n) *nm* language specialist *n*
Sprecher (-) *nm* spokesperson *n*
Spur (-en) *nf* track *n*
Staatsangehörigkeit *nf* nationality *n*
Staatsanleihe (-n) *nf* government bond *n*, government loan *n* **Staatsanleihen** public funds
Staatsausgaben *nfpl* state expenditure *n*
Staatsdienst *nm* civil service *n*, public service *n*
Staatspapier (-e) *nn* gilt-edged security *n*, government security *n*
Staatsschuld *nf* national debt *n*
Staatswirtschaft *nf* (system) national economy *n*
stabil *adj* (economy) stable *adj*
stabilität *nf* stability *n*
Stabilität *nf* **finanzielle Stabilität** financial stability
Stadt (-ädte) *nf* town *n*
Stadtausbreitung *nf* urban sprawl *n*
Stadterneuerung *nf* urban renewal *n*
städtisch *adj* urban *adj*
Stadtmitte (-n) *nf* town centre *n*
Stadtplanung *nf* town planning *n*
staffeln *vb* (holidays) stagger *vb*
Stagnierung *nf* stagnation *n*
Stahl (-e) *nm* steel *n*
Stahlindustrie (-n) *nf* steel industry *n*
Stammaktie (-n) *nf* equity share *n*, ordinary share *n*, ordinary stock (US)
Stammkunde (-n) *nm* regular customer *n*
Standard- *cpd* standard *adj*

standhalten *vb* withstand *vb*
Standort (-e) *nm* location *n*
Startkapital *nn* start-up capital *n*
Statistik *nf* statistics *npl*
Status quo *nm* status quo *n*
Statut (-e) *nn* statute *n*
steigen *vb* rise *vb*
steigern *vb* increase *vb* **die Produktion steigern** increase output
Steigerung *nf* (in bank rate) rise *n*
Stelle (-n) *nf* (job) post *n*
Stellenangebot (-e) *nn* job offer *n*
Stellenbeschreibung (-en) *nf* job description *n*
Stellenbesetzung *nf* staffing *n*
Stellenrotation *nf* job rotation *n*
Stellenvermittlung (-en) *nf* employment agency *n*
Stellung position *nf* **befristete Stellung (-en)** temporary employment
stellvertretend *adj* deputy *adj* **stellvertretender Leiter** assistant manager **stellvertretender Direktor** deputy director
Stellvertreter (-) *nm* deputy *n*
stempeln *vb* stamp *vb* **den Arbeitsbeginn stempeln** clock in **das Arbeitsende stempeln** clock out
Sterlinggebiet *nn* sterling area *n*
Steuer (-n) *nf* tax *n* **nach Abzug der Steuern** after tax **vor Abzug der Steuern** before tax **indirekte Steuer** indirect tax **örtliche Steuern** local taxes **eine Steuer auferlegen** impose a tax **Steuern einheben** levy taxes **Steuern im Preis enthalten** taxes are included
Steuerbeleg (-e) *nm* fiscal receipt *n*
Steuerbetrug *nm* tax avoidance *n*
Steuereinkommen *nn* taxable income *n*
Steuerforderung *nf* tax claim *n*
steuerfrei *adj* free of tax *adj*, tax-exempt *adj*, tax-free *adj*, zero-rated (taxation) *adj*
Steuerfreijahre *nnpl* tax holiday *n*
Steuerhinterziehung *nf* tax evasion *n*
Steuerjahr (-e) *nn* fiscal year *n*, tax year *n*
Steuerklasse (-n) *nf* tax bracket *n*
Steuerklassifizierung *nf* fiscal zoning *n*
steuerlich *adj* tax *adj* **steuerlich absetzbar** tax-deductible **steuerliche Belastung** fiscal charges
Steuerpflicht (-en) *nf* tax liability *n*
steuerpflichtig *adj* liable for tax *adj*
Steuersatz (-sätze) *nm* tax rate *n*
Steuerschwelle (-n) *nf* tax threshold *n*
Steuersenkung (-en) *nf* tax cut *n*
Steuervergünstigung (-en) *nf* tax allowance *n*
Steuerzahler *nm* taxpayer *n*
Steuerzuschlag (-äge) *nm* surtax *n*
stichhaltig *adj* (fig) watertight *adj*
Stichprobe *nf* random selection *n*
Stichtag (-e) *nm* target date *n*
Stichwort (-wörter) *nn* (computer) keyword *n*
Stiftung (-en) *nf* endowment *n* **eine Stiftung**

errichten set up a trust
still *adj* silent *adj* **stiller Teilhaber** silent partner
Stillegung (-en) *nf* closure *n*, shutdown *n* (strike) stoppage *n*
stillschweigend *adj* tacit *adj*
Stimme (-n) *nf* vote *n*
Stimmrecht *nn* voting right *n*
Stopp (-s) *nm* (on prices, wages) freeze *n*
stoppen *vb* (inflation) halt *vb*
stören *vb* bug *vb*
stornieren *vb* cancel *vb* **einen Vertrag stornieren** cancel a contract
Stornierung (-en) *nf* cancellation *n*
Stornierungsoption *nf* option to cancel *n*
Stornogebühr (-en) *nf* cancellation charge *n*
Stoßzeit (-en) *nf* rush hour *n*
Strafgericht *nn* criminal court *n*
Strafrecht *nn* criminal law *n*
strapazierfähig *adj* heavy-duty *adj*
Straße (-nn) *nf* road *n*
Straßengüterverkehr *nm* road transport *n*
Straßentransport *nm* road transport *n*
Straßenverkehr *nm* road traffic *n*
Strategie (-n) *nf* strategy *n*
strategisch *adj* strategic *adj*
Streik (-s) *nm* strike *n* **offizieller Streik** official strike **wilder Streik** unofficial strike, wildcat strike
Streikabstimmung (-en) *nf* strike ballot *n*
Streikbrecher (-) *nm* scab* *n*, strikebreaker *n*
streiken *vb* strike *vb*
Streikende/r *nmf* striker *n*
Streikmaßnahmen *nfpl* strike action *n*
Streikposten (-) *nm* (strike) picket *n*
Streit (-e) *nm* dispute *n*
streitende Partei (-en) *nf* litigant *n*
Strichcode (-s) *nm* bar code *n*
Stückkosten *npl* unit cost *n*
Stückpreis (-e) *nm* unit price *n*
stufenweise *adj* in stages *adj*
Stunde (-n) *nf* hour *nf* **pro Stunde** *adj* per hour *adj* **Stunde Null** zero hour
Stundenlohn (-öhne) *nm* hourly rate *n*
Stundenlohnarbeiter *npl* hourly workers *npl*
Stundenplan (-äne) *nm* timetable *n*
stündlich *adj* hourly *adj*
Subunternehmer *nm* subcontractor *n*
Subvention (-en) *nf* subsidy *n*
subventionieren *vb* subsidize *vb*
Supermacht (-mächte) *nf* superpower *n* **wirtschaftliche Supermacht** economic superpower
Supermarkt (-märkte) *nm* supermarket *n*
Syndikat (-e) *nn* syndicate *n*
Synergie (-n) *nf* synergy *n*
Synthese (-n) *nf* synthesis *n*
synthetisch *adj* synthetic *adj*
System (-e) *nn* system *n*
Systemanalyse *nf* systems analysis *n*
Systemanalytiker (-) *nm* systems analyst *n*
tabellarisch *adj* tabulated *adj* **tabellarische**

Datenaufstellung tabulated data
tabellarisieren *vb* (data) tabulate *vb*
Tabelle (-n) *nf* chart *n*
Tabellenkalkulation *nf* spreadsheet *n*
Tagebuch (-bücher) *nn* journal *n*
Tageskurs (-e) *nm* transfer price *n*
Tagesordnung (-en) *nf* agenda *n*
Tageszeitung (-en) *nf* daily newspaper *n*
Tagewerk *nn* day's work *n*
Tagungsbericht (-e) *nm* conference proceedings *npl*
Tagungsort (-e) *nm* conference venue *n*
Taktik *nf* tactic *n*
Tarif (-e) *nm* tariff *n*
Tarifabbau *nm* elimination of tariffs *n*
Tarifabkommen (-) *nn* collective agreement *n*, wage(s) agreement *n*, wage(s) settlement *n*
Tarifverhandlung (-en) *nf* collective bargaining *n*
Tarifzone (-n) *nf* wage zone *n*
Tastatur (-en) *nf* keyboard *n*
Tatsachen *nfpl* the hard facts *npl* **die anerkannten Tatsachen** known facts *npl*
tatsächlich *adj* actual *adj*
Tausch (-e) *nm* swap *n*
tauschen *vb* barter *vb*, swap *vb*
Tauschhandel *nm* barter *n*, barter transaction *n*
Tauschhandelsabkommen (-) *nn* barter agreement *n*
Team (-s) *nn* team *n*
Techniker (-) *nm* technician *n*
technisch *adj* technical **technischer Direktor** technical director
Technologie (-n) *nf* technology *n* **neue Technologie** new technology
Technologietransfer *nm* technology transfer *n*
Teil (-e) *nn* (of a machine) part *n*
teilen *vb* share *vb*, split *vb*
Teillieferung (-en) *nf* part shipment *n*, short delivery *n*
Teilzahlung (-en) *nf* part payment *n*, token payment *n*
Teilzahlungskauf *nm* hire purchase *n*
Teilzeit- *cpd* part-time *adj*
Telefon (-e) *nn* telephone *n*
Telefonbankdienst (-e) *nm* telebanking *n*
Telefonbuch (-bücher) *nn* telephone directory *n*
Telefongebühr *nf* call charge *n* **Telefongebühr bar bezahlt** Freefone (R) (GB) *n*
Telefonist (-en) *nm* switchboard operator *n*
Telefonnummer (-n) *nf* telephone number *n*
Telefonverkauf *nm* telesales *npl*
Telefonzelle (-n) *nf* telephone box *n*, telephone booth (US)
Telefonzentrale (-n) *nf* switchboard *n*
Tendenz (-en) *nf* tendency *n*
tendieren *vb* tend *vb*
Termin (-e) *nm* (to meet) appointment *n* (meeting) engagement *n* **zum festgesetzten**

Termin at term **einen Termin einhalten** keep an appointment **einen Termin vereinbaren** make an appointment
Terminal (-s) *nm* computer terminal *n*
Terminalmarkt (-märkte) *nm* terminal market *n*
Termingeschäft (-e) *nn* forward transaction *n*
Termingeschäfte *npl* futures *nnpl*
Terminhandel *nm* futures trading *n*
Terminierung *nf* timing *n*
Terminkontrakt (-e) *nm* forward contract *n*, futures contract *n*
Terminkontraktmarketing *nn* futures marketing *n*
Terminkontraktmarkt (-märkte) *nm* futures market *n*
Terminkontraktpreis (-e) *nm* futures price *n*
Terminlieferung *nf* future delivery *n*
Terminmarkt (-märkte) *nm* forward market *n*
Terminsicherung *nf* forward cover *n*
Terminware *nf* future goods *npl*
Testament (-e) *nn* will *n* **gerichtliche Testamentsbestätigung** probate *n*
Testdaten *nnpl* test data *npl*
Testmarkt (-märkte) *nm* test-market *vb*
teuer *adj* high-priced *adj*
Textil (-ien) *nn* textile *n*
Textilidustrie (-n) *nf* textile industry *n*
Textverarbeitung *nf* word processing *n*
Textverarbeitungsgerät (-e) *nn* word processor *n*
theoretisch *adj* in theory *adj*
Tiefbau *nm* civil engineering *n*
tilgen *vb* wipe out *vb* **eine Schuld tilgen** pay off a debt
tippen *vb* type *vb*
Tippfehler (-) *nm* typing error *n*
Titel (-) *nm* (to goods) title *n*
Tochtergesellschaft (-en) *nf* subsidiary company *n*, susidiary *n* **hundertprozentige Tochtergesellschaft** wholly-owned subsidiary
Tonnage *nf* tonnage *n*
Tonne (-n) *nf* ton *n* **metrische Tonne** metric ton
total *adj* total *adj*
Totalschaden *nm* write-off *n*
Tourismus *nm* tourism *n*
Tourist (-en) *nm* tourist *n*
tragbar *adj* portable *adj* **tragbarer Computer** portable computer
Träger (-n) *nm* bracket *n*
Transaktion (-en) *nf* transaction *n*
Transaktionsverwaltung *nf* transaction management *n*
Transfer (-s) *nm* transfer *n*
Transfertechnik *nf* transfer technology *n*
Transitgüter *nnpl* goods in process *npl*, transit goods *npl*
Transitlager (-) *nn* bonded warehouse *n*
Transitraum (-räume) *nm* (transport) transfer lounge *n*

Transitschäden *nmpl* damage to goods in transit *n*

Transitschalter (-) *nm* (transport) transfer desk *n*

Transitwaren *nf* goods in progress *npl*

Transport *nm* transport *n*

Transportunternehmen (-) *nn* haulier *n*

Tratte (-n) *nf* (financial) draft *n*

Trauschein (-e) *nm* marriage certificate *n*

treffen *vb* meet *vb*

Trend (-s) *nm* trend *n*

Trendanalyse (-n) *nf* trend analysis *n*

Treuhänder (-) *nm* trustee *n*

treuhänderisch *adj* treuhänderisch verwalten hold sth in trust

Treuhandmittel *nnpl* trust fund *n*

Treuhandschaft *nf* trusteeship *n*

Treuhandvermögen (-) *nn* trust estate *n*

Treuhandvertrag (-äge) *nm* trust agreement *n*

Trinkgeld (-er) *nn* gratuity *n*

Trust (-s) *nm* trust company *n*

Typist/in (-en/-innen) *nm/nf* typist *n*

U.A.w.g. (Um Antwort wird gebeten) *abbr* RSVP (répondez s'il vous plaît) *abbr*

über pari above par

Überangebot *nn* oversupply *vb*

überarbeitet *adj* overworked *adj*

Überbevölkerung *nf* overpopulation *n*

überbewerten *vb* overvalue *vb*

überbieten *vb* outbid *vb*

Überbrückungskredit (-e) *nm* bridging loan, bridge loan (US)

übereinstimmen *vb* concur *vb*, tally *vb* übereinstimmen mit tally with

überfällig *adj* overdue *adj*

Übergewicht *nn* excess luggage *n*, excess weight *n*

Überheizen *nn* (of economy) overheating *n*

überholt *adj* out of date *adj*

Überkapazität *nf* excess capacity *n*

überladen *vb* overload *vb*

Übernachfrageinflation *nf* excess demand inflation *n*

Übernahme (-n) *nf* buy-out *n*, takeover *n*

Übernahmeangebot (-e) *nn* tender offer *n*

Übernahmezahlung (-en) *nf* transfer payments *npl*

übernehmen *vb* take charge of sth (company) take over *vb*

Überproduktion *nf* overproduction *n*

überproduzieren *vb* overproduce *vb*

überreichen *vb* hand over *vb*

überschreiben *vb* (ownership) transfer *vb*

überschreiten *vb* exceed *vb*

Überschrift (-en) *nf* heading *n*

Überschuß (-üsse) *nm* surplus *n*

Überschußwaren *nfpl* surplus stock *n* Überschußwaren aufnehmen absorb surplus stock

Übersee- *cpd* overseas *adj*

Überseegebiet (-e) *nn* overseas territory *n*

Überseehandel *nm* overseas trade *n*

Überseemarkt (-märkte) *nm* overseas market *n*

übersehen *vb* overlook *vb*

überstaatlich *adj* transnational *adj*

Überstunden *nfpl* overtime *n*

übertragbar *adj* transferable *adj*

übertragen *vb* carry forward *vb*, transcribe *vb*

Übertragungsurkunde (-n) *nf* (law) deed *n*

überverkaufen *vb* oversell *vb*

überverkauft *adj* oversold *adj*

Überwachungsausschuß (-üsse) *nm* watchdog committee *n*

Überweisung (-en) *nf* remittance *n* bargeldlose Überweisung credit transfer

Überweisungsanzeige (-n) *nf* remittance advice *n*

überzahlen *vb* overpay *vb*

Überzahlung *nf* overpayment *n*

überzeichnet *adj* oversubscribed *adj*

überziehen *vb* overdraw *vb*

Überziehung *nf* overdraft *n*

Überziehungskredit (-e) *nm* bank overdraft *n* einen Überziehungskredit beantragen request an overdraft

überzogenes Konto *nn* overdrawn account

umfassend *adj* comprehensive *adj*

Umfrage (-n) *nf* field investigation *n*

umgehen handle *vb* umgehen mit handle

Umkehr *nf* turnabout *n*

umkehren *vb* reverse *vb*

umladen *vb* transship *vb*

Umlauf *nm* circulation im Umlauf in circulation

Umlaufkapital *nn* floating assets *n*

Umsatz (-ätze) *nm* turnover *n* Umsatz des Anlagevermögens fixed asset turnover

Umsätze *nmpl* hohe(n) Umsätze heavy trading

Umsatzquote (-n) *nf* turnover ratio *n*

Umsatzrate (-n) *nf* turnover rate *n*

Umsatzsteuer (-n) *nf* turnover tax *n*

Umschichten *nn* (of funds) reallocation *n*

Umschreibungsgebühr (-en) *nf* transfer duty *n*

umschulden *vb* reschedule a debt *vb*

Umschuldungsanleihe *nf* funding bonds *npl*

umschulen *vb* retrain *vb*

Umschulung *nf* retraining *n*

Umschulungsprogramm (-e) *nn* retraining programme *n*

Umsiedlung (-en) *nf* relocation *n*

Umstand (-ände) *nm* circumstance *n* unter keinen Umständen under no circumstances nicht in unserer Hand liegende Umstände circumstances beyond our control unvorhergesehene Umstände unforeseen circumstances

umsteigen *vb* (transport) transfer *vb*

Umstellung *nf* rearrangement *n* Umstellung auf das metrische Maßsystem metrication *n*

umstrukturieren *vb* restructure *vb*

Umtausch exchange *n* günstiger Umtausch

favourable exchange
unabgefertigt *adj* (customs) uncleared *adj*
Unannehmlichkeit *nf* inconvenience *n*
unbedeutend *adj* minor *adj*
unbeschränkt *adj* unlimited *adj*
unbeständig *adj* (prices) volatile *adj*
unbestätigt *adj* unconfirmed *adj*
unbezahlt *adj* unpaid *adj*
undatiert *adj* not dated *adj*
uneinbringlich *adj* **uneinbringliche Schuld**
bad debt
unerwartet *adj* unexpected *adj*, without
warning *adj*
unfachmännisch *adj* unprofessional *adj*
Unfall (-älle) *nm* accident *n*
ungefähr *adj* approximate *adj*,
approximately *adv*
ungelegen *adj* inconvenient *adj*
ungelernt *adj* unskilled *adj*
ungenau *adj* hit-or-miss *adj*
ungenutzt *adj* idle *adj* **ungenutzt sein** go to
waste
ungesichert *adj* unsecured *adj*
ungültig *adj* void *adj* **ungültiger Scheck** bad
cheque
Unkosten costs *npl*, expenses *npl* **laufende
Unkosten** standing charges
Unkostensatz (-sätze) *nm* expenditure rate *n*
unnötig *adj* non-essential *adj*
unpopulär *adj* undersubscribed *adj*
unprofitabel *adj* unprofitable *adj*
unrechtmäßig *adj* wrongful *adj*
unter under *prep* **unter Null** below zero
unter pari below par
unterbeschäftigt *adj* underemployed *adj*
unterbewerten *vb* undervalue *vb*
unterbezahlen *vb* underpay *vb*
unterbieten *vb* undercut *vb*
untergeordnet *adj* junior *adj*
Untergeordnete/r *nmf* subordinate *n*
Unterhalt *nf* maintenance *n* (of machine)
operation *n*
Unterhaltskosten *npl* maintenance costs *npl*
unterkapitalisiert *adj* undercapitalized *adj*
Unterkunft (-ünfte) *nf* accommodation *n*
Unterkunftszuschuß (-üsse) *nm* accommodation allowance *n*
Unternehmen (-) *nn* company *n*, concern,
organization *n*, undertaking *n* (project)
enterprise *n* **multinationales Unternehmen
(-)** multinational corporation
Unternehmens-Image (-s) *nn* corporate
image *n*
Unternehmensberater (-) *nm* business
consultant *n*, management consultant *n*
Unternehmensführung *nf* management *n*
zielgesteuerte Unternehmensführung management by objectives
Unternehmensinvestitionen *nfpl* corporate
investment *n*
Unternehmenspolitik *nf* company policy *n*
Unternehmensspitze *nf* top management *n*

Unternehmer (-) *nm* entrepreneur *n*
unternehmerisch *adj* entrepreneurial *adj*
unterschlagen *vb* embezzle *vb*
Unterschlagung *nf* embezzlement *n*
unterschreiben *vb* sign *vb*
Unterschrift (-en) *nf* signature *n*
unterstützen *vb* support *vb* **eine Initiatve
finanziell unterstützen** back a venture
Unterstützung *nf* backing *n* **Unterstützung
finden** win support
unterwegs *adv* in transit *adv*
unterzeichnen *vb* (cheque) endorse *vb*
sign *vb* **einen Vertrag unterzeichnen** sign a
contract
Unterzeichner (-) *nm* signatory *n*,
underwriter *n* **die Unterzeichner** the signa-
tories to the contract
unverkäuflich *adj* unmarketable *adj*,
unsaleable *adj*
unverkauft *adj* unsold *adj*
unverzüglich *adj* without delay *adj*,
prompt *adj*
unwiderruflich *adj* irrevocable *adj*
unzureichend *adj* inadequate *adj*,
unsatisfactory *adj*
Urheberrecht (-e) *nn* copyright law *n*
Urkunde (-n) *nf* record *n* **eine Urkunde nicht
herausgeben** withhold a document
Urlaub *nm* furlough (US) *n*, leave *n* **bezahlter
Urlaub** paid holiday **auf Urlaub** on holiday,
on vacation (US) **Urlaub machen** furlough
(US) *vb* **Urlaub nehmen** take a break
Urlaubsgeld *nn* holiday pay *n*
Ursprung (-ünge) *nm* (of a product) origin *n*
Ursprungsangabe (-n) *nf* statement of
origin *n*
Ursprungszeugnis (-sse) *nn* certificate of
origin *n*
Verabredung (-en) *nf* (agreement)
arrangement *n*
Veralten *nn* obsolescence *n*
veraltet *adj* out of date *adj*, obsolete *adj*
veränderlich *adj* variable *adj* **veränderliche
Kosten** variable costs **veränderlicher Kurs**
variable rate **veränderlicher Markt** fluid
market
veranstalten *vb* organize *vb* **eine Konferenz
veranstalten** arrange a conference
verantwortlich *adj* accountable *adj*,
responsible *adj* **jemanden für verantwortlich halten** hold sb responsible **verantwortlich sein** be in charge
Verantwortlichkeit (-en) *nf* accountability *n*
Verantwortung responsibility *n* **gemeinsame Verantwortung** joint responsibility **die
Verantwortung übernehmen** take responsibility for sth
verarbeitend *adj* processing *adj* **verarbeitende Industrie (-n)** secondary industry
Veräußerungsgewinne *nmpl* capital gains *npl*
Verband (-bände) *nm* union *n*
verbessern *vb* improve *vb*

verbinden *vb* connect *vb* **könnten Sie mich bitte mit X verbinden?** (telephone) could you connect me to... *vb* **verbinden mit** (phone) put sb through (to sb)
verbindlich *adj* binding *adj*
Verbindlichkeiten *nfpl* current liabilities *npl*, accounts payable *npl* **langfristige Verbindlichkeiten** fixed liability
verbleibend *adj* (sum) remaining *adj*
verboten *adj* out of bounds *adj*
Verbraucher (-) *nm* consumer *n*
Verbraucherakzeptanz *nf* consumer acceptance *n*
Verbrauchererwartungen *nfpl* consumer expectations *npl*
Verbrauchergesellschaft (-en) *nf* consumer society *n*
Verbrauchergroßmarkt (-märkte) *nm* hypermarket *n*
Verbraucherzufriedenheit *nf* consumer satisfaction *n*
Verbrauchsdatum *nn* best-before date *n*
Verbrauchsgewohnheiten *nfpl* consumer habits *npl*
Verbrauchssteuer (-n) *nf* excise duty *n*
verderblich *adj* corrupting *adj* **leicht verderblich** perishable *adj*
verdienen *vb* earn *vb*
Verdiener (-) *nm* wage earner *n*
Verdienstausfall (-fälle) *nm* loss of earnings *n*
verdient *adj* earned *adj* **schwer verdient** hard-earned
verdünnen *vb* water down *vb*
Verein (-e) *nm* guild *n*
Vereinbarung *nf* understanding *n*
vereinheitlichen *vb* standardize *vb*
Vereinheitlichung *nf* standardization *n*
Vereinigung *nf* unification *n*
vereint *adj* united *adj*
Vereinten Nationen *npl* **die Vereinten Nationen** the United Nations
Verfahren (-) *nn* process *n*
Verfall *nm* expiration *n*
Verfallstag (-e) *nm* expiry date *n*, expiration (US)
Verfalltag (-e) *nm* termination date *n*
verfälscht *adj* weighted *adj* ·
Verfälschung *nf* falsification *n*
verfassen *vb* draw up *vb* **einen Bericht verfassen** draw up a report
verfügbar *adj* available *adj* **nicht verfügbar** not available
verfügen *vb* order *vb*, decree *vb*
Verfügung *vb* **eine Verfügung herausgeben** issue a writ
Vergehen (-) *nn* offence *n*, offense (US)
vergrößern *vb* enlarge *vb*
vergüten *vb* remunerate *vb*
Vergütung (-en) *nf* remuneration *n* **Vergütung für leitende Angestellte** executive compensation
Verhaltenskodex (-e) *nm* professional code

of practice *n*
Verhältnis (-sse) *nn* ratio *n*
verhandeln (über) *vb* negotiate *vb*
Verhandlung (-en) *nf* negotiation *n* **durch Verhandlung** by negotiation **unter Verhandlung** under negotiation **Verhandlungen beginnen** begin negotiations
Verhandlungsführer (-) *nm* negotiator *n*
Verhandlungsgeschick *nn* negotiating skills *npl*
Verhandlungspaket (-e) *nn* package deal *n*
Verkauf (-äufe) *nm* sale *n* **Verkauf aufgrund einer Ausschreibung** sale by tender
verkaufen *vb* market *vb*, sell *vb*, sell up *vb* **auf Kredit verkaufen** sell sth on credit **zu verkaufen** for sale
Verkäufer (-) *nm* salesperson *n*, seller *n*, shop assistant *n*, vendor *n*
Verkäufermarkt *nm* seller's market
Verkaufsbedingungen *nfpl* conditions of sale *npl*
Verkaufsfläche (-n) *nf* shop floor *n*
Verkaufsgebiet (-e) *nn* trading area *n*
Verkaufsgespräch *nn* sales talk *n*
Verkaufskampagne (-n) *nf* sales campaign *n*
Verkaufskapital *nn* vendor capital *n*
Verkaufskonferenz (-en) *nf* sales conference *n*
Verkaufsleitung *nf* sales management *n*
Verkaufsmethode (-n) *nf* sales technique *n* **aggressive Verkaufsmethode** hard sell
Verkaufsmethoden *nfpl* selling tactics *npl*
Verkaufspotential *nn* sales potential *n*
Verkaufspunkt (-e) *nm* point of sale *n*
Verkaufsschlager (-) *nm* best seller *n* **Verkaufsschlager sein** be in hot demand
Verkaufssteigerung *nf* sales growth *n*
Verkaufsstelle (-n) *nf* sales outlet *n*, ticket agency *n*
Verkaufstaktik *nf* **aggresive Verkaufstaktik** hard sell **weiche Verkaufstaktik** soft sell
Verkaufsurkunde (-n) *nf* bill of sale *n*, deed of sale *n*
Verkaufsziel (-e) *nn* sales target *n*
Verkaufsziffern *nfpl* sales figures *npl*
Verkehrsbetrieb (-e) *nm* transport company *n*
Verkehrsministerium (-ien) *nn* Ministry of Transport *n*
verkümmern *vb* go to waste *vb*
Verladung *nf* shipping *n*
Verlag (-e) *nm* publishing house *n*
Verlagswesen *nn* publishing *n*
verlangen *vb* call for *vb*
verlängern *vb* extend *vb* **einen Vertrag verlängern** extend a contract
Verlängerung (-en) *nf* (of contract) extension *n*
verlangsamen *vb* slow down *vb*
Verlangsamung *nf* slowdown *n*
verläßlich *adj* reliable *adj*
verletzen *vb* contravene *vb*
Verletzung (-en) *nf* contravention *n*
Verleumdung *nf* slander *n* **schriftliche Ver-**

leumdung libel *n*
verlieren *vb* forfeit *vb* (custom) lose *vb* **an Wert verlieren** depreciate
Verlust (-e) *nm* loss *n* **finanzieller Verlust** financial loss **uneinbringlicher Verlust** irrecoverable loss *n* **Verluste haben** be in the red **Verluste minimieren** minimise losses
Verlustquote (-n) *nf* wastage rate *n*
vermachen *vb* bequeath *vb*, bequest *n*
vermehren *vb* multiply *vb*
vermeiden *vb* avoid *vb*
vermieten *vb* lease *vb* (property) let *vb* **zu vermieten** for hire
vermindert *adj* reduced *adj*
vermitteln *vb* arbitrate *vb*, mediate *vb*
vermittelnd *adj* intermediary *adj*
Vermittler (-) *nm* mediator *n*
Vermittlung *nf* mediation *n*
Vermögen (-) *nn* asset *n*, wealth *n* **verstecktes Vermögen** hidden assets
Vermögenssteuer (-n) *nf* wealth tax *n*
Vernachlässigung *nf* neglect *n*
vernünftig *adj* (price) reasonable *adj*
Verpachtung *nf* lease *n* **Verpachtung von Steuern** farming of taxes
verpacken pack *vb* **in eine(r) Kiste verpacken** box sth up
Verpackung *nf* packaging *n*
verpflichten *vb* commit *vb*
verpflichtet *adj* indebted *adj* **verpflichtet sein** be obliged to do sth
Verpflichtung (-en) *nf* commitment *n*, covenant *n*, obligation *n* **gemeinsame Verpflichtung** joint obligation
verrechnet *adj* (cheque) cleared *adj* miscalculated *adj* **noch nicht verrechnet** (cheque) uncleared
versagen *vb* (negotiations) fail *vb* (attempts) fail *vb*
Versagen *nn* failure *n*
Versand *nm* (consignment) shipment *n* transportation *n*
Versandanzeige (-n) *nf* dispatch note *n*
versandbereit *adj* ready for despatch *adj*
Versanddatum (-en) *nn* date of dispatch *n*
Versandgebühren *nfpl* forwarding charges *npl*
Versandhandel *nm* mail order *n*
Versandhaus (-häuser) *nn* mail-order house *n*
verschieben *vb* (to next period) hold over *vb*
Verschleiß *nm* wastage *n* **geplanter Verschleiß** built-in obsolescence, planned obsolescence
verschleudern *vb* undersell *vb*
verschulden *vb* to be the cause of sth *vb*
Verschulden *nn* fault *n*
verschulden *vb* to get into debt *vb*
Verschulden *nn* **mitwirkendes Verschulden** contributory negligence
verschwenden *vb* squander *vb*, waste *vb*
verschwenderisch *adj* spendthrift *adj*
Verschwendung *nf* waste *n*

Versehen (-) *nn* oversight *n* **aus Versehen** due to an oversight
versichern *vb* insure *vb*
Versicherte/r *nmf* policy holder *n*
Versicherung *nf* c.i.f. (cost insurance and freight) *abbr*, cover insurance *n*, insurance *n* **eine Versicherung abschließen** take out insurance
Versicherungsagent *nm* underwriter *n*
Versicherungsanspruch *nm* claim *n* **einen Versicherungsanspruch regulieren** adjust a claim
versicherungsfähig *adj* insurable *adj* **nicht versicherungsfähig** uninsurable *adj*
Versicherungsfonds (-) *nm* insurance fund *n*
Versicherungsgesellschaft (-en) *nf* insurance company *n*
Versicherungsmakler (-) *nm* insurance broker *n*
Versicherungspolice (-n) *nf* insurance certificate *n*, insurance policy *n*
Versicherungsprämie (-n) *nf* insurance premium *n*
Versicherungsträger (-) *nm* insurance underwriter *n*
Versicherungsvertrag (-äge) *nm* insurance contract *n*
Versicherungsvertreter (-) *nm* insurance agent *n*, insurance representative *n*, insurance salesperson *n*
versiegeln *vb* seal *vb*
versorgen *vb* (supply) provide *vb*
Versorgung *nf* (stipulation) provision *n*
Versorgungsbetrieb (-e) *nm* public utility *n*
Versprechen (-) *nn* pledge *n*
versprechen *vb* give one's word *vb*
verstaatlichen *vb* nationalize *vb*
Verstaatlichung *nf* nationalization *n*
versteigern *vb* auction *vb*, sell sth at auction *vb*
Versteigerung (-en) *nf* auction *n*
vertagen *vb* adjourn *vb*
Vertagung (-en) *nf* adjournment *n*
Verteilernetz (-e) *nn* distribution network
Verteilung *nf* distribution *n*
vertikal *adj* vertical *n*
Vertikalintegration *nf* vertical integration *n*
Vertrag (-äge) *nm* contract *n*, treaty *n* **einen Vertrag abschließen** make a treaty **Vertrag von Rom** the Treaty of Rome
Vertragsarbeit *nf* contract work *n*
Vertragsbedingungen *nfpl* the terms of the contract *npl*
Vertragsberechtigte/r *nmf* covenantee *n*
Vertragsentwurf (-ürfe) *nm* draft contract *n*
vertragsgemäß *adj* as stipulated in the contract *adj* **vertragsgemäß wird verlangt, daß...** it is a requirement of the contract that...
Vertragshändler (-) *nm* authorized dealer *n*
Vertragsparteien *nfpl* the contracting parties *npl*

Vertragspflichten *nfpl* contractual obligations *npl*
Vertragsrecht *nn* law of contract *n*
Vertragsverletzung (-en) *nf* breach *n*, breach of contract *n*
Vertrauen *nn* trust *n*
Vertrauensmißbrauch *nm* abuse of confidence *n*
vertraulich *adj* confidential *adj* **streng vertraulich** in strictest confidence **streng vertrauliche Information** classified information
vertreiben *vb* merchandise *vb*
Vertreter (-) *nm* agent *n*, representative *n*
Vertrieb *nm* distribution *n*, merchandizing *n* **Vertrieb nach dem Schneeballprinzip** pyramid selling
Vertriebsberater (-) *nm* marketing consultant *n*
Vertriebsleiter (-) *nm* marketing director *n*
Veruntreuung *nf* misappropriation *n*
verwalten *vb* administer *vb* (money) handle *vb*
Verwalter (-) *nm* administrator *n*
Verwaltung *nf* administration *n* (of business) operation *n*
Verwaltungskosten *npl* administrative costs *npl*
verwässern *vb* water down *vb*
verwässert *adj* watered *adj*
verwässertes *nn* **verwässertes Aktienkapital** watered capital, watered stock
verweigern *vb* refuse *vb* **die Warenannahme verweigern** refuse goods **die Zahlung verweigern** refuse payment
verwenden *vb* use *n*, utilize *vb*
Verwendung *nf* utilization *n*
verwirken *vb* forfeit *vb*
Verzeichnis (-sse) *nn* register *n*
Verzicht *nm* waiver *n*
verzichten (auf) *vb* waive *vb*
Verzichtsleistungsklausel (-n) *nf* waiver clause *n*
Verzinsung *nf* payment of interest *n* **angemessene Verzinsung** fair rate of return
verzögern delay *vb* (withstand scrutiny) hold up *vb*
Verzögerung (-en) *nf* delay *n*, holdup *n*
Verzögerungstaktik *nf* delaying tactics *npl*
Video (-s) *nn* video *n*
Videofilm (-s) *nm* video *n*
Videogeräte *nnpl* video facilities *npl*
Videorekorder (-) *nm* video *n*
Vielzweck- *cpd* multipurpose *adj*
Viertel (-) *nn* (of year) quarter *n*
Vierteljahreszinsen *nmpl* quarterly interest *n*
vierteljährlich *adj* quarterly *adj* **vierteljährliche Kundenkonten** quarterly trade accounts
vierzehntäglich *adj* biweekly *adj*
visuell *adj* visual *adj*
Visum (-en) *nn* visa *n*
Volkseinkommen *nn* national income *n*
Volksvermögen *nn* national wealth *n*

Volkswirtschaft *nf* economics *n*
voll *adj* full *adj* **voll ausgelastet sein** work to full capacity
Vollbeschäftigung *nf* full employment *n*
vollenden *vb* complete *vb*
Vollhafter (-) *nm* general partner
Vollkaskoversicherung *nf* comprehensive insurance policy *n*, comprehensive insurance *n*
Vollkosten *npl* full cost
Vollmacht *nf* power of attorney *n*, warrant *n* (power) proxy *n*
vollständig *adj* wholly *adv*
Vollzeit- *cpd* full-time *adj*
Vollzeitkraft (-kräfte) *nf* full-time worker *n*
Volumen *nn* volume *n*
vorankommen *vb* make headway *vb*
Vorarbeiter (-) *nm* foreman *n*
Vorauszahlung (-en) *nf* advance payment *n*, prepayment *n*
vorbeugen *vb* forestall *vb*
vordatieren *vb* postdate *vb*
vorenthalten *vb* withhold *vb*
Vorfahrtsrecht *nn* right of way *n*
Vorhersage *nf* forecasting *n*
vorhersehbar *adj* foreseeable *adj* **aus nicht vorhersehbaren Gründen** due to unforeseen circumstances
vorhersehen *vb* forecast *vb*
vorläufig *adj* interim *adj*
vorlegen *vb* present *vb* **einen Bericht vorlegen** submit/present a report
vornehmen *vb* **eine Reservierung vornehmen** make a reservation
Vororte *nmpl* suburbs *npl*
Vorrat (-äte) *nm* stocks **einen geringen Vorrat haben** (stocks) run low
Vorräte *nmpl* stocks *n* **Vorräte abbauen** (stocks) run down
Vorratslager (-) *nn* reserve stock *n*
Vorruhestand *nm* early retirement *n*
vorschlagen *vb* nominate *vb*
Vorschrift (-en) *nf* regulation *n*
vorschriftsgemäß *adj* according to the regulations *adj*
Vorschuß (-üsse) **1.** *nm* (on salary) advance *n* cash advance **2.** *vb* **Vorschuß geben** *vb* (salary) advance *vb*
Vorsicht *nf* care *n* **Vorsicht - zerbrechlich!** handle with care
Vorsitz *nm* chairmanship **(bei einer Sitzung) Vorsitz führen** chair a meeting **den Vorsitz übernehmen** take the chair
Vorstand (-ände) *nm* board *n*, board of directors *n*, factory board *n*
Vorstandssitzung (-en) *nf* board meeting
Vorstandsvorsitzende/r *nmf* managing director *n*
vorstellen (sich) *vb* attend for interview *vb*
Vorstellungsgespräch (-e) *nn* interview *n* **ein Vorstellongsgespräch mit jemandem führen** interview **zum Vorstellungsgespräch einla-**

den invite sb to an interview **ein Vorstellungsgespräch führen** hold an interview
Vorteil (-e) *nm* advantage *n*
vorteilhaft *adj* advantageous *adj*
vorverlegen *vb* bring forward *vb*
Vorzug *nm* preference *n*
Vorzugs- *cpd* preferential *adj*
Vorzugszollsystem *nn* **Vorzugszollsystem in EU** community preference
Wachhund (-e) *nm* (fig) watchdog *n*
Wachstum *nn* growth *n* **durch Export bedingtes Wachstum** export-led growth
Wachstumsindex (-e) *nm* growth index *n*
Wachstumsrate (-n) *nf* growth rate *n*, rate of expansion *n* **jährliche Wachstumsrate** annual growth rate
Wachstumsstrategie (-n) *nf* growth strategy *n*
Waffenhandel *nm* arms trade *n*
Wahl (-en) *nf* election *n*
Währung (-en) *nf* currency *n* **gesetzliche Währung** legal currency **harte Währung** hard currency **konvertierbare Währung** convertible currency **weiche Währung** soft currency
Währungsfonds *nm* Monetary Fund **internationaler Währungsfonds** International Monetary Fund (IMF)
Währungsgebiet (-e) *nn* currency zone *n*
Währungskorb *nm* basket of currencies *n*
Währungsreform (-en) *nf* currency reform *n*
Währungsreserve (-n) *nf* currency reserve *n*
Währungsüberweisung (-en) *nf* currency transfer *n*
Wanze (-n) *nf* (listening device) bug *n*
Waren *nfpl* goods *npl*, wares *npl* **Waren auf Probe** goods on approval
Warenausfuhr *nf* visible exports *npl*
Warenausgangsbuch (-bücher) *nn* sales ledger *n*
Wareneinkaufsbuch (-bücher) *nn* bought ledger *n*
Warenhaus (-häuser) *nn* department store *n*
Warenkennzeichnungsgesetz (-e) *nn* Trade Descriptions Act *n*
Warentermingeschäft *nn* future commodity *n*
Warenverkaufskonto (-konten) *nn* trading account *n*
Warenzeichen (-) *nn* trademark *n*
warnen *vb* warn *vb*
Warnstreik (-s) *nm* token strike *n*
Warnung (-en) *nf* warning *n*
Warteliste (-n) *nf* waiting list
warten *vb* (wait) hang on *vb* (on phone) to be on hold *vb*, hold on *vb*
Warten *nn* waiting *n*
Warteraum *nm* waiting room *n* **Warteraum für Transitpassagiere (-räume)** (transport) transit lounge
Wartezone (-n) *nf* hold area *n*
Wechsel (-) *nm* bill of exchange *n* (financial) draft *n* **durch Indossament übertragbarer**

Wechsel negotiable bill **unbezahlter Wechsel** unpaid bill
Wechselgeld *nn* (from purchase) change *n*
Wechselkurs (-e) *nm* exchange rate *n*, rate of exchange *n* **veränderlicher Wechselkurs** floating exchange rate
Wechselkursmechanismus *nm* exchange rate mechanism (ERM) *n*
Wechselobligo *nn* bills discounted *n*
Wechselstube (-n) *nf* bureau de change *n*
Wegwerf- *cpd* (not for reuse) disposable *adj*
weit *adj* wide-ranging *adj*
weitervergeben *vb* **weitervergeben an** subcontract *vb*
Weiterverkauf *nm* resale *n*
Welle (-n) *nf* (of mergers, takeovers) wave *n*
Wellenlänge (-n) *nf* wavelength *n*
Welt *nf* world *n*
Weltausstellung (-en) *nf* world fair *n*
Weltbank *nf* World Bank *n*
Weltexporte *nmpl* world exports *npl*
Weltgerichtshof (-höfe) *nm* World Court *n*
Welthandel *nm* international trade *n*
Weltmarkt (-märkte) *nm* global market *n*
Weltunternehmen (-) *nn* international organization *n*
Weltverbrauch *nm* world consumption *n*
weltweit *adj* worldwide *adj* **weltweites Marketing** global marketing
Weltwirtschaft (-) *nf* (system) global economy *n*
wenden *vb* turn over *vb*
Werbe- *cpd* promotional *adj*
Werbeagentur (-en) *nf* advertising agency *n*
Werbeeinkommen (-) *nn* advertising revenue *n*
Werbeetat (-s) *nm* advertising budget *n*, promotional budget *n*
Werbekampagne (-n) *nf* advertising campaign *n*, promotional campaign *n*
Werbemittel (-) *nn* advertising medium *n*
werben *vb* advertise *vb* **werben für** (product) promote *vb*
Werbeplan (-pläne) *nm* plan of campaign *n*
Werbespruch (-üche) *nm* advertising jingle *n*
Werbung *nf* advertisement *n* (of product) promotion *n* **übertriebene Werbung** hype
Werft (-en) *nf* dockyard *n*
Werk *nn* work *n* **ab Werk** ex factory/works
Werksleiter (-) *nm* works manager *n*
Werksplanung *nf* facility planning *n*
Werkstatt (-stätte) *nf* shop floor *n*, workshop *n*
Wert (-e) *nm* value *n*, worth *n* **im Wert steigen** (rise in value) appreciate **an Wert verlieren** lose value **an Wert zunehmen** gain value **amtlich notierte Werte** listed securities **nicht notierte Werte** unlisted securities
wert *adj* worth *adj* **wert sein** be worth
Wertpapierbörse (-n) *nf* Stock Exchange *n*
Wertpapiere *npl* commercial paper *n*, securities *npl* **mündelssichere Wertpapiere**

gilt-edged securities
Wertpapiermarkt (-märkte) *nm* stock
market *n*
Wertsteigerung *nf* (in value) appreciation *n*
Wertung (-en) *nf* valuation *n*
Wertverlust *nm* depreciation *n*
wertvoll *adj* valuable *adj*
Westeuropäische Union *nf* WEU (Western
European Union) *abbr*
Wettbewerb *nm* competition *n* **lauterer
Wettbewerb** fair competition **unlauterer
Wettbewerb** unfair competition
Wettbewerbsausschluß *nm* foreclosure *n*
Wettbewerbsbeschränkung *nf* restrictive
practices *npl*
wettbewerbsfähig *adj* competitive *adj*
Wettbewerbsfähigkeit *nf* competitiveness *n*
Wettbewerbsfreiheit *nf* free competition *n*
Wettbewerbsmethode (-en) *nf* **lautere
Wettbewerbsmethode** fair-trade practice
Wettbewerbsvorteil (-e) *nm* competitive
advantage *n*, competitive edge *n*
widerrufen *vb* rescind *vb* **eine Bestellung
widerrufen** cancel an order
Wiedereinfuhr *nf* reimportation *n*
wiederernennen *vb* reappoint *vb*
Wiederernennung (-en) *nf* reappointment *n*
wiedergutmachen *vb* make amends *vb*
Wiederherstellung (-en) *nf* reparation *n*
Wiederinbesitznahme (-n) *nf* repossession *n*
wiederverwerten *vb* recycle *vb*
Wiederwahl (-en) *nf* re-election *n*
willkürlich *adj* arbitrary *adj*, at random
Wirklichkeit *nf* actuality *n*
Wirkung (-en) *nf* effect *n*
Wirt (-e) *nm* landlord *n*
Wirtschaft (-en) *nf* (system) economy *n* **sich
entwickelnde Wirtschaft** developing
economy **fortgeschrittene Wirtschaft**
advanced economy **unterentwickelte
Wirtschaft** underdeveloped economy
wirtschaftlich *adj* economic *adj* **wirtschaft-
liche Infrastruktur** economic infrastructure
Wirtschaftsanalyse (-n) *nf* economic
analysis *n*
Wirtschaftsaufschwung (-ünge) *nm* eco-
nomic boom *n*
Wirtschaftsberater (-) *nm* economic adviser *n*
Wirtschaftsbericht (-e) *nm* economic survey *n*
Wirtschaftsentwicklung *nf* economic
development *n*
Wirtschaftsgeographie *nf* economic
geography *n*
Wirtschaftskrieg (-e) *nm* trade war *n*
Wirtschaftskrise (-n) *nf* economic crisis *n*
Wirtschaftsleistung *nf* economic
performance *n*
Wirtschaftsplan (-äne) *nm* economic plan *n*
Wirtschaftsplanung *nf* economic planning *n*
Wirtschaftspolitik *nf* economic policy *n*
Wirtschaftsprognose (-n) *nf* economic
forecast *n*

Wirtschaftsrückgang (-änge) *nm* economic
decline *n*
Wirtschaftsstrategie *nf* economic strategy *n*
Wirtschaftstrend (-s) *nm* economic trend *n*
Wirtschaftsunion (-en) *nf* economic union *n*
Wirtschaftswachstum *nn* economic
expansion *n*, economic growth *n*
Wirtschaftswissenschaftler (-) *nm*
economist *n*
Wirtschaftsziel (-e) *nn* economic objective *n*
Wirtschaftszyklus (-en) *nm* economic cycle *n*
Wissen *nn* knowledge *n*
Wissensbasis (-basen) *nf* knowledge base *n*
Woche (-n) *nf* week *n*
Wochenlöhne *nmpl* weekly wages *npl*
wöchentlich *adj* weekly *adj*
Wohl *nn* welfare *n*
wohl *adv* well *adv* **wohl informiert** well-
informed
wohlerprobt *adj* well-tried *adj*
Wohlfahrtsstaat (-en) *nm* welfare state *n*
Wohlstandsgesellschaft (-en) *nf* affluent
society *n*
Wohnsiedlung (-en) *nf* housing complex *n*,
housing estate *n*, tenement (US)
Wohnung *nf* dwelling *n*, appartment *n*
Wohnung auf Timesharing-Basis (-en) timeshare
Wohnungsbauindustrie *nf* housing
industry *n*
Wohnungsbauprogramm (-e) *nn* housing
scheme *n*
Wohnungsbauprojekt (-e) *nn* housing
project *n*
Wohnverhältnisse *nnpl* living conditions *npl*
Wort *nn* word *n*
Wortlaut *nm* wording *n*
wörtlich *adv* verbatim *adv*
Wucher *nm* usury *n*
zahlbar *adj* payable *adj* **zahlbar an** pay to the
order of... **zahlbar sofort ohne Abzug** terms
strictly net(t) **zahlbar im voraus** payable in
advance
Zahlen *nfpl* figures *npl*, numbers *npl* **in den
schwarzen Zahlen sein** be in the black
zahlen *vb* pay *vb* **eine Gebühr zahlen** pay a
fee **im voraus zahlen** pay in advance
Zahlenanalyse *nf* numerical analysis *n*
Zahltag (-e) *nm* (stock exchange) Account
Day *n*
Zahlung (-en) *nf* payment *n* **volle Zahlung** full
payment **Zahlung bei Auftragserteilung**
cash with order **Zahlung auf Kredit** payment
on account **Zahlung bei Warenerhalt** COD
(cash on delivery) *abbr*, (collect on delivery)
(US)
Zahlungsanweisung (-en) *nf* money order *n*,
warrant for payment *n*
Zahlungsaufforderung (-en) *nf* request for
payment *n*
Zahlungsbilanz (-en) *nf* balance of
payments *n* **günstige Zahlungsbilanz**

favourable balance of payments
Zahlungsbilanzdefizit (-e) *nn* balance of payments deficit *n*
Zahlungsbilanzüberschuß (-üsse) *nm* balance of payments surplus *n*
Zahlungsempfänger (-) *nm* payee *n*
zahlungsfähig *adj* solvent *adj*
Zahlungsfähigkeit (-en) *nf* ability to pay *n*, solvency *n*
Zahlungsmethode (-n) *nf* method of payment *n*
zahlungsunfähig *adj* insolvent *adj*
Zahlungsunfähigkeit *nf* insolvency *n*
Zahlungsverpflichtungen *nfpl* obligation/liability to pay *n* **Zahlungsverpflichtungen nicht nachkommen** default
Zahlungsverzug (-üge) *nm* default *n*
Zeit (-en) *nf* time *n* **Zeit nehmen** take one's time
Zeitbeschränkung (-en) *nf* time limit *n*
Zeiteinteilung *nf* time management *n*
Zeitkarte (-n) *nf* season ticket *n*
Zeitmaßstab (-stäbe) *nm* timescale *n*
Zeitplan (-pläne) *nm* schedule *n*
zeitraubend *adj* time-consuming *adj*
Zeitraum (-äume) *nm* time frame *n*
Zeitschrift (-en) *nf* (journal) magazine *n*
zeitsparend *adj* time-saving *adj*
Zeitstudie (-n) *nf* work study *n*
Zeitung (-en) *nf* newspaper *n*
Zeitungsanzeige (-n) *nf* newspaper advertisement *n*
Zeitungsbericht (-e) *nm* newspaper report *n*
Zeitvergeudung *nf* waste of time *n*
Zeitzone (-n) *nf* time zone *n*
zentral *adj* central *adj* **zentrale Planwirtschaft** central planned economy
Zentralbank (-en) *nf* central bank *n*
zentralisieren *vb* centralize *vb*
Zentralisierung *nf* centralization *n*
Zentralplanung *nf* central planning *n*
zerstören *vb* wreck *vb*
Zessionsurkunde (-n) *nf* deed of transfer *n*
Zeuge (-n) *nm* witness *n*
Ziel (-e) *nn* objective *n*, target *n* **ein Ziel setzen** set a target
Zielmarkt (-märkte) *nm* target market *n*
Ziffer (-n) *nf* numeric character *n*
Zinsbelastung (eines Sollsaldos) *nf* carrying cost *n*
Zinsen *nmpl* interest *n* **ohne Zinsen** ex interest **Zinsen berechnen** charge interest **Zinsen tragen** bear interest **Zinsen zahlen** pay interest
Zinsezins *nm* compound interest *n*
zinsfrei *adj* non-interest-bearing *adj*
Zinskurs (-e) *nm* interest rate *n*, rate of interest *n*
zinslos *adj* interest-free *adj*
Zinsperiode (-n) *nf* interest period *n*
Zinssatz (-sätze) *nm* rate of interest *n* **günstiger Zinssatz** fine rate of interest **veränderlicher Zinssatz** floating rate of interest
zinstragend *adj* interest-bearing *adj*
zirkulieren *vb* **zirkulieren lassen** (document) circulate *vb*
Zivilrecht *nn* civil law *n*
Zoll (Zölle) *nm* customs *npl* (customs) duty *n* **Zölle erhöhen** raise tariffs
Zollabfertigung (-en) *nf* customs check *n*, customs clearance *n*
Zollabfertigungshafen (-häfen) *nm* port of entry *n*
Zollager (-) *nn* bonded warehouse *n*, customs warehouse *n*
Zollamt (-ämter) *nn* customs office *n*
Zollbeamte/r *nmf* customs officer *n*
Zollerklärung (-en) *nf* customs declaration *n*
Zollerlaubnisschein (-e) *nm* clearance certificate *n*
Zollformalitäten *nfpl* customs formalities *npl*
zollfrei *adj* (goods) duty-free **zollfreie Waren** free goods
Zollgebühren *nfpl* customs charges *npl*
Zollinspektor (-en) *nm* customs inspector *n*
Zollkontingent (-e) *nn* tariff quota *n*
Zollkontrolle (-n) *nf* (customs) inspection *n*
Zollmauer (-n) *nf* tariff wall *n*
Zollreform (-en) *nf* tariff reform *n*
Zollschranke (-n) *nf* tariff barrier *n*
Zollunion (-en) *nf* customs union *n*
Zollverhandlungen *npl* tariff negotiations *npl*
Zollverordnungen *npl* customs regulations *npl*
Zollverschluß *nm* **unter Zollverschluß** in bond
Zone (-n) *nf* zone *n* **Einteilung in Zonen** zoning **in Zonen einteilen** zone *vb*
Zufallschaden (-äden) *nm* accidental damage *n*
Zugang *nm* access *n*
Zugänglichkeit *nf* accessibility *n*
zugehen *vb* **zugehen auf** head for
Zulage *nf* weighting *n*
Zunahme (-n) *nf* (in inflation) rise *n*
Züricher Gnomen (die) *n* the Gnomes of Zurich *npl*
zurückgehen *vb* decrease *vb*
zurückhalten *vb* (not release) hold back *vb*
zurückkehren *vb* revert *vb*
zurückkommen *vb* **zurückkommen auf** revert to
zurücknehmen *vb* (licence) revoke *vb*
zurückrufen *vb* (on phone) call back *vb*
zurücksenden *vb* send back *vb*
zurücktreten *vb* resign *vb* (resign) quit *vb* **zurücktreten von** (resign from) leave, resign from office
zurückweisen *vb* (contract) repudiate *vb*
zurückzahlen *vb* refund *vb*, repay *vb*
zurückziehen *vb* withdraw *vb*
zusammenarbeiten *vb* collaborate *vb* **zusammenarbeiten mit** collaborate with *vb*
Zusammenbruch *nm* (of company, economy)

collapse *n*
zusammenhängen *vb* (argument) hang
together *vb*
zusammenrechnen *vb* tally up *vb*
zusätzlich *adj* extra *adj* **zusätzliche Gebühr**
additional charge
Zusatzsteuer (-n) *nf* supertax *n*
Zuschauer (-) *nm* viewer *n*
Zuschuß (-sse) *nm* allowance *n*
Zuständigkeitsbereich *nm* jurisdiction *n*
Zustelldienst *nm* home service *n*
zustimmen *vb* agree *vb*, consent *vb*
Zustimmung *nf* consent *n*
zuteilen *vb* allocate *vb*
zutreffend *adj* applicable *adj* **nicht zutreffend**
N/A (not applicable) *abbr*
Zuverlässigkeit *nf* reliability *n*
Zuwachsrate (-n) *nf* rate of accrual *n* **natür-
liche Zuwachsrate (-n)** natural rate of

increase
zuweisen *vb* assign *vb*
Zuweisung *nf* assignment *n*
Zwangswährung (-en) *nf* forced currency *n*
zweckmäßig *adj* convenient *adj*
zweibahnig *adj* two-way *adj*
Zweigang- *cpd* two-speed *adj*
Zweigniederlassung (-en) *nf* branch
company *n*
Zweigstelle (-n) *nf* branch office *n*
zweijährlich *adj* biennial *adj*
zweimal *adv* twice *adv* **zweimal jährlich**
biannual *adj* **zweimal wöchentlich** twice a
week
zweimonatlich *adj* bimonthly *adj*
zweistufig *adj* two-tier *adj* **zweistufiges Verwaltungssystem (-e)** two-tier system
Zwischenhändler (-) *nm* middleman *n*
Zwischenlager (-) *nn* entrepôt *n*

English–German

abandon *vb* aufgeben *vb*
abandoned *adj* **abandoned goods** herrenlose Güter *nnpl*
abate *vb* nachlassen *vb*
abatement *n* Abflauen (-) *nn*
abbreviate *vb* abkürzen *vb*
abbreviated *adj* abgekürzt *adj*
abbreviation *n* Abkürzung (-en) *nf*
abeyance *n* **to fall into abeyance** außer Gebrauch kommen
ability *n* Fähigkeit (-en) *nf* **ability to pay** Zahlungsfähigkeit (-en) *nf*
aboard *adv* **to go aboard** an Bord gehen
abolish *vb* abschaffen *vb*
abolition *n* Abschaffung *nf*
above-mentioned *adj* obenerwähnt *adj*
aboveboard *adj* korrekt *adj*
abroad *adv* **to go abroad** ins Ausland gehen
absence *n* **in the absence of information** in Ermangelung weiterer Information
absent *adj* abwesend *adj*
absentee *adj* abwesend *adj* **absentee landlord** nicht ortsansässiger Hausbesitzer
absolute *adj* absolut *adj*
absorb *vb* absorbieren *vb* **to absorb surplus stock** Überschußwaren aufnehmen
abstract *n* Auszug (-üge) *nm*
abundance *n* Fülle *nf*
abuse 1. *n* **abuse of power/trust** Machtmißbrauch/Vertrauensmißbrauch *nm/nm* 2. *vb* mißbrauchen *vb*
accelerate *vb* beschleunigen *vb*
acceleration *n* Beschleunigung *nf*
accept *vb* **accept delivery** die Lieferung annehmen
acceptance *n* **consumer acceptance** Verbraucherakzeptanz *nf* **acceptance house** Akzeptbank (-en) *nf* **market acceptance** Marktakzeptanz *nf*
access 1. *n* Zugang *nm* 2. *vb* Zugriff haben auf
accessibility *n* Zugänglichkeit *nf*
accident *n* Unfall (-älle) *nm* **industrial accident** Arbeitsunfall (-älle) *nm*
accidental *adj* **accidental damage** Zufallsschaden (-äden) *nm*
accommodation *n* Unterkunft (-ünfte) *nf* **accommodation allowance** Unterkunftszuschuß (-üsse) *nm* **accommodation bill** Gefälligkeitswechsel (-) *nm* **to**

come to an accommodation zu einer Einigung kommen
accomplish *vb* schaffen *vb*
accomplishment *n* Leistung (-en) *nf*
accordance *n* **in accordance with** gemäß *prep*
according to *prep* **according to plan** plangemäß **according to the minister** laut Minister
account *n* **bank account** Bankkonto (-konten) *nn* **Account Day** (stock exchange) Zahltag (-e) *nm* **expense account** Spesenkonto (-konten) *nn* **payment on account** Zahlung auf Kredit (-en) *nf* **profit and loss account** Gewinn- und Verlustrechnung (-en) *nf* **savings account** Sparkonto (-konten) *nn* **accounts receivable** ausstehende Forderungen **statement of account** Kontoauszug (-üge) *nm* **to open an account** ein Konto eröffnen **to overdraw on an account** ein Konto überziehen **to settle an account** die Rechnung begleichen **to take sth into account** etwas in Betracht ziehen **trading account** Warenverkaufskonto (-konten) *nn*
account for *vb* erklären *vb*
accountability *n* Verantwortlichkeit (-en) *nf*
accountable *adj* verantwortlich *adj*
accountancy *n* Buchführung *nf*
accountant *n* Buchhalter (-) *nm* **chartered accountant** Bilanzbuchhalter (-) *nm*
accounting *n* **accounting conventions** Buchhaltungsnormen *nfpl* **financial accounting** Finanzbuchhaltung *nf* **management accounting** Rechnungswesen für besondere Betriebsprüfungsbedürfnisse **accounting period** Rechnungsabschnitt (-e) *nm*
accredit *vb* akkreditieren *vb*
accrual *n* Ansammlung *nf* **rate of accrual** Zuwachsrate (-n) *nf*
accrued *adj* **accrued interest** aufgelaufene Zinsen *nmpl*
accumulate *vb* ansammeln *vb*
accumulated *adj* angesammelt *adj*
accuracy *n* Genauigkeit *nf*
accurate *adj* genau *adj*
achieve *vb* erreichen *vb*
achievement *n* Leistung (-en) *nf*
acknowledge *vb* **to acknowledge receipt of sth** den Empfang bestätigen

acknowledgement *n* **acknowledgement of debt** schriftliches Schuldanerkenntnis (-sse) *nn*

acquaintance *n* **business acquaintance** Geschäftsfreund (-e) *nm* **to make the acquaintance of sb** jemanden kennenlernen *vb*

acquire *vb* erwerben *vb*

acquisition *n* Erwerb *nm*

acquisitive *adj* habgierig *adj*

action *n* **industrial action** Arbeitskampf (-kämpfe) *nm* **legal action** Klage (-en) *nf* **out of action** außer Betrieb

actual *adj* tatsächlich *adj*

actuality *n* Wirklichkeit *nf*

actuary *n* Aktuar (-e) *nm*

acumen *n* **business acumen** Geschäftssinn *nm*

additional *adj* **additional charge** zusätzliche Gebühr *nf*

address 1. *n* **home address** Heimatanschrift (-en) *nf* **registered address** eingetragene Anschrift (-en) *nf* **to change address** umziehen *vb* 2. *vb* adressieren *vb*

addressee *n* Empfänger (-) *nm*

adjourn *vb* vertagen *vb* sich vertagen *vb*

adjournment *n* Vertagung (-en) *nf*

adjust *vb* anpassen *vb* **to adjust a claim** einen Versicherungsanspruch regulieren **to adjust the figures** die Zahlen berichtigen

adjustment *n* Anpassung (-en) *nf*, Regulierung (-en) *nf*

administer *vb* verwalten *vb*

administration *n* Verwaltung *nf*

administrative *adj* **administrative costs** Verwaltungskosten *npl*

administrator *n* Verwalter (-) *nm*

advance 1. *adj* **advance notice** Kündigung *nf* **advance payment** Vorauszahlung (-en) *nf* 2. *n* (on salary) Vorschuß (-üsse) *nm* **cash advance** Vorschuß (-üsse) *nm* **payable in advance** zahlbar im voraus 3 *vb* (salary) Vorschuß geben *vb*

advanced *adj* **advanced country** Industriestaat (-en) *nm* **advanced technology** Spitzentechnologie (-n) *nf*

advantage *n* Vorteil (-e) *nm* **comparative advantage** komparativer Vorteil (-e) *nm* **competitive advantage** Wettbewerbsvorteil (-e) *nm*

advantageous *adj* vorteilhaft *adj*

adverse *adj* **adverse balance of trade** ungünstige Handelsbilanz *nf*

advertise *vb* werben (für) *vb*

advertisement *n* Werbung *nf*

advertising *n* **advertising agency** Werbeagentur (-en) *nf* **advertising budget** Werbeetat (-s) *nm* **advertising campaign** Werbekampagne (-n) *nf* **advertising medium** Werbemittel (-) *nn* **advertising revenue** Werbeeinkommen (-) *nn*

advice *n* Rat (Ratschläge) *nm*

advise *vb* beraten *vb* **to advise sb about sth** jemanden über etwas beraten

adviser/advisor *n* Berater (-) *nm*

advisory *adj* beratend *adj*, Beratungs- *cpd*

advocate *vb* befürworten *vb*

aerospace *adj* **aerospace industry** Luftfahrtindustrie (-n) *nf*

affidavit *n* eidesstattliche Versicherung (-en) *nf*

affiliated *adj* **affiliated company** Schwestergesellschaft (-en) *nf*

affluent *adj* **affluent society** Wohlstandsgesellschaft (-en) *nf*

afford *vb* **I can't afford (to buy a new printer)** ich kann mir (einen neuen Drucker) nicht leisten **we cannot afford (to take) the risk** wir können das Risiko nicht eingehen

after-sales service *n* Kundendienst *nm*

agency *n* **advertising agency** Werbeagentur (-en) *nf* **employment agency** Stellenvermittlung (-en) *nf* **travel agency** Reisebüro (-s) *nn*

agenda *n* Tagesordnung (-en) *nf*

agent *n* Vertreter (-) *nm*

AGM (Annual General Meeting) *abbr* Jahreshauptversammlung *nf*

agrarian *adj* Agrar- *cpd*

agree *vb* zustimmen *vb*

agreed *adj* einverstanden *adj*

agreement *n* **by mutual agreement** in gegenseitigem Einverständnis **verbal agreement** mündliche Absprache (-n) *nf* **wage agreement** Lohnvertrag (-äge) *nm*

agribusiness *n* Agrargeschäft (-e) *nn*

agriculture *n* Landwirtschaft *nf*

agronomist *n* Agronom (-e) *nm*

aid *n* **financial aid** Finanzhilfe *nf*

air *n* **by air** auf dem Luftweg **air freight** Luftfracht *nf* **air traffic controller** Fluglotse (-n) *nm*

air-conditioned *adj* klimatisiert *adj*

airline *n* Fluggesellschaft (-en) *nf*

airmail *n* Luftpost *nf*

airport *n* Flughafen (-häfen) *nm*

allocate *vb* zuteilen *vb*

allowance *n* Zuschuß (-üsse) *nm*, Zulage (-n) *nf* **family allowance** Kindergeld *nn*

amalgamate *vb* fusionieren *vb*

amalgamation *n* Fusion (-en) *nf*

amend *vb* ändern *vb*

amendment *n* Änderung (-en) *nf*

amends *npl* **to make amends** wiedergutmachen *vb*

amenities *npl* Einrichtungen *nfpl*

amortization *n* Amortisation *nf*

amortize *vb* amortisieren *vb*

amount *n* Betrag (-äge) *nm*

amount to *vb* betragen *vb*

analysis *n* **cost-benefit analysis** Kosten-Nutzen-Analyse (-n) *nf* **systems analysis** Systemanalyse *nf*

analyze *vb* analysieren *vb*

annual *adj* **annual general meeting (AGM)** Jahreshauptversammlung (-en) *nf* **annual report** Jahresbericht (-e) *nm*
annuity *n* Rente (-n) *nf*
annulment *n* Annullierung (-en) *nf*
Ansaphone (R) *n* Anrufbeantworter (-) *nm*
answer 1. *n* Antwort (-en) *nf* 2. *vb* beantworten *vb* antworten *vb*
answering *adj* **answering machine** Anrufbeantworter (-) *nm*
anti-inflationary *adj* **anti-inflationary measures** antiinflationäre Maßnahmen *nfpl*
antitrust *adj* **antitrust laws** Antitrustgesetze *nnpl*, Kartellgesetze *nnpl*
appeal 1. *n* Appell (-e) *nm*, Bitte (-n) *nf* 2. *vb* bitten *vb*
application *n* **application form** Bewerbungsformular (-e) *nn* **letter of application** Bewerbungsschreiben (-) *nn*
apply for *vb* sich bewerben um *vb*
appoint *vb* **to appoint sb to a position** einstellen *vb*
appointment *n* (to meet) Termin (-e) *nm* (to a position) Einstellung (-en) *nf* **to make an appointment** einen Termin vereinbaren
appraisal *n* Abschätzung (-en) *nf*
appreciate *vb* (rise in value) im Wert steigen *vb*
appreciation *n* (in value) Wertsteigerung *nf*
apprentice *n* Lehrling (-e) *nm*
apprenticeship *n* Lehre *nf*
appropriation *n* Beschlagnahme *nf*
approval *n* Billigung *nf* **on approval** auf Probe
approve *vb* billigen *vb*
approximate *adj* ungefähr *adj*
approximately *adv* ungefähr *adv*
arbitrage *n* Arbitrage (-n) *nf*, Schiedsspruch (-üche) *nm*
arbitrary *adj* willkürlich *adj*
arbitrate *vb* vermitteln *vb*
arbitration *n* Schlichtung *nf*
arbitrator *n* Schlichter (-) *nm*
area *adj* **area manager** Regionalleiter (-) *nm*
arithmetic *n* Mathematik *nf*
arithmetical *adj* **arithmetical mean** arithmetisches Mittel (-) *nn*
arms *npl* **arms trade** Waffenhandel *nm*
arrangement *n* (agreement) Verabredung (-en) *nf*
arrears *npl* Rückstände *nmpl* **in arrears** im Rückstand **to fall/get into arrears** in Rückstand kommen
articulated *adj* **articulated lorry** Sattelschlepper (-) *nm*
asap (as soon as possible) *abbr* so bald wie möglich
asking *adj* **asking price** Angebotspreis (-e) *nm*
assembly *n* **assembly line** Montageband (-bänder) *nn*
assess *vb* einschätzen *vb*

assessment *n* Einschätzung (-en) *nf*
asset *n* Vermögen (-) *nn* **capital assets** Kapitalvermögen *nn* **asset stripping** Anlagenausschlachtung *nf*
assign *vb* zuweisen *vb*
assignee *n* Forderungsübernehmer (-) *nm*
assignment *n* Zuweisung *nf*
assistant *adj* **assistant manager** stellvertrender Leiter *nm*
associate 1. *adj* **associate director** außerordentliches Mitglied des Aufsichtsrats, Gesellschafter (-) *nm* 2. *n* Partner *nm*
attestation *n* Bestätigung (-en) *nf*, Bescheinigung (-en) *nf*
attorney *n* **power of attorney** Vollmacht *nf*
auction 1. *n* Versteigerung (-en) *nf* 2. *vb* versteigern *vb*
auctioneer *n* Auktionator (-en) *nm*
audit *n* Buchprüfung (-en) *nf*
auditor *n* Buchprüfer (-) *nm*
authority *n* (official) Behörde (-n) *nf*
authorize *vb* ermächtigen *vb*
authorized *adj* **authorized dealer** Vertragshändler (-) *nm*
automatic *adj* automatisch *adj* **automatic cash dispenser** Geldautomat (-en) *nm*
automation *n* Automatisierung *nf*
automobile *n* **automobile industry** Autoindustrie (-n) *nf*
autonomous *adj* autonom *adj*
auxiliary *adj* Hilfs- *cpd*
average *adj* Durschnitt (-e) *nm* **average unit** Durchschnittskosten pro Einheit *npl*
avoid *vb* vermeiden *vb*
avoidance *n* **tax avoidance** Steuerbetrug *nm*
axe, ax (US) *vb* **to axe expenditure** Ausgaben reduzieren
back *vb* **to back a venture** eine Initiative finanziell unterstützen
back pay *n* Nachzahlung *nf*
backdate *vb* rückdatieren *vb* **to backdate a cheque** einen Scheck rückdatieren
backer *n* Geldgeber *nm*
backhander* *n* Schmiergeld *nn*
backing *n* Unterstützung *nf*
backlog *n* Rückstände *nmpl*
bad *adj* **bad cheque** ungültiger Scheck (-s) *nm* **bad debt** uneinbringliche Schuld (-en) *nf*
bail *n* Kaution *nf*
bailiff *n* Gerichtsvollzieher (-) *nm*
balance 1. *n* (financial) Bilanz *nf* **bank balance** Kontostand (-ände) *nm* **final balance** Schlußbilanz (-en) *nf* **balance in hand** Guthaben (-) *nn* **balance of payments** Zahlungsbilanz (-en) *nf* **balance of payments deficit** Zahlungsbilanzdefizit (-e) *nn* **balance of payments surplus** Zahlungsbilanzüberschuß (-üsse) *nm* **balance of trade** Handelsbilanz (-en) *nf* **balance sheet** Bilanz (-en) *nf* **trade balance** Handelsbilanz (-en) *nf* 2. *vb* **to balance the books** die Bilanz ziehen *vb* **to balance the**

budget den Etat ausgleichen
bank 1. *n* Bank (-en) *nf* **bank account**
Bankkonto (-konten) *nn* **bank balance**
Bankguthaben (-) *nn* **bank card** Kreditkarte
(-en) *nf* **bank charges** Bankgebühren *nfpl*
bank clerk Bankangestellte/r *nmf* **bank draft**
Bankwechsel (-) *nm* **bank holiday**
Bankfeiertag (-e) *nm* **bank loan**
Bankdarlehen (-) *nn* **bank manager**
Bankdirektor (-en) *nm* **bank overdraft**
Überziehungskredit (-e) *nm* **bank rate**
Diskontsatz (-sätze) *nm* **bank statement**
Kontoauszug (-üge) *nm* 2. *vb* **to bank a**
cheque einen Scheck einzahlen
banker *n* Bankier (-s) *nm* **banker's order**
Dauerauftrag (-äge) *nm*
banking *n* **banking circles** Bankkreise *nmpl*
banking hours Schalterstunden *nfpl*
banknote *n* Banknote (-n) *nf*
bankrupt *adj* bankrott *adj* **to be bankrupt**
bankrott sein
bankruptcy *n* Konkurs *nm*
bar code *n* Strichcode (-s) *nm*
bargain 1. *adj* **bargain offer** *adj*
Sonderangebot (-e) *nn* **bargain price** *adj*
niedriger Preis (-e) *nm*, Spottpreis 2. *n*
Geschäft (-e) *nn* **it's a bargain** günstiges
Kaufobjekt (-e) *nn* 3 *vb* feilschen *vb*
barrier *n* Barriere (-n) *nf*, Schranke *nf* **trade**
barrier Handelsschranke (-n) *nf*
barrister, lawyer (US) *n* Rechtsanwalt (-älte)
nm
barter 1. *adj* **barter agreement**
Tauschhandelsabkommen (-) *nn* **barter**
transaction Tauschhandel *nm* 2. *n*
Tauschhandel *nm* 3 *vb* tauschen *vb*
base *adj* **base lending rate** Eckzins der
Clearing-Banken für Ausleihungen *nm*
basic *adj* **basic commodity** Grundstoff (-e)
nm **basic income** Basiseinkommen *nn* **basic**
rate Eckzins für Ausleihungen *nm* **basic**
training Grundausbildung *nf*
basis *n* **basis of assessment**
Bemessungsgrundlage (-n) *nf*
basket *n* **basket of currencies** Währungskorb
nm
batch *n* (of goods) Sendung (-en) *nf* **batch**
processing (DP) Serienverarbeitung *nf*
bear 1. *n* (stock exchange) Baissier (-s) *nm*
bear market *n* Baissemarkt (-märkte) *nm*
2. *vb* **to bear interest** Zinsen tragen *vb*
bearer *n* Inhaber (-) *nm* **bearer bond**
Inhaberschuldverschreibung (-en) *nf* **bearer**
cheque Inhaberscheck (-s) *nm* **bearer share**
Inhaberaktie (-n) *nf*
bench *n* **bench mark** Maßstab (-stäbe) *nm*
bench mark price Richtpreis (-e) *nm*
benefactor *n* Gönner (-e) *nm*
benefit 1. *n* (social security) Nutzen (-) *nm*
2. *vb* profitieren *vb* nützen *vb*
bequeath *vb* vermachen *vb*
bequest *n* Vermachen (-) *nn*

best *adj* **best-before date** Verbrauchsdatum
nn **best seller** Verkaufsschlager (-) *nm*,
Bestseller (-) *nm*
biannual *adj* zweimal jährlich
bid 1. *n* Angebot (-e) *nn* 2. *vb* (auction)
bieten *vb*
biennial *adj* zweijährlich *adj*
bilateral *adj* **bilateral trade** der bilaterale
Handel
bill 1. *n* (invoice) Rechnung (-en) *nf* **bill of**
exchange Wechsel (-) *nm* **bill of lading**
Konnossement (-s) *nn*, Ladeschein (-e) *nm*
bill of sale Verkaufsurkunde (-n) *nf* **bills**
discounted Wechselobligo *nn* **to pay a bill**
die Rechnung begleichen 2. *vb* (invoice) in
Rechnung stellen *vb*
bimonthly *adj* zweimonatlich *adj*
binding *adj* verbindlich *adj* **legally binding**
rechtsverbindlich *adj*
biweekly *adj* vierzehntäglich *adj*
black *adj* **black economy** Schwarzhandel *nm*,
Schwarzmarkt *nm* **black market**
Schwarzmarkt (-märkte) *nm* **to be in the**
black in den schwarzen Zahlen sein, Geld auf
dem Konto haben
blank *adj* **blank cheque** Blankoscheck (-s) *nm*
block 1. *n* Block (-öcke) *nm* 2. *vb* sperren *vb*
blockade 1. *n* Blockade (-n) *nf* 2. *vb*
blockieren *vb*
blocked *adj* **blocked account** Sperrkonto
(-konten) *nn*
blue *adj* **blue-chip company** erstklassiges
Unternehmen (-) *nn* **blue-collar worker**
Arbeiter (-) *nm* **blue-chip securities** erstklassige Wertpapiere *nn*
board *n* Vorstand (-ände) *nm* **Board of Trade**
(GB) Handelsministerium *nn* **board meeting**
(GB) Vorstandssitzung (-en) *nf* **board of**
directors (GB) Vorstand (-ände) *nm* **board**
room (GB) Sitzungssaal (-äle) *nm*
bona fide *adj* gutgläubig *adj*, guten Glaubens
adj
bond *n* Schuldverschreibung (-en) *nf*,
Obligation (-en) *nf* **bond certificate** Bond-
Zertifikat (-e) *nn* **government bond**
Staatsanleihe (-n) *nf* **in bond** unter Zollverschluß
bonded *adj* **bonded warehouse** Zollager (-)
nn
bondholder *n* Obligationär (-e) *nm*,
Anleihegläubiger (-) *nm*
bonus *n* Prämie (-n) *nf*
book 1. *n* **cheque book** Scheckheft (-e) *nn*
book profit Buchgewinn *nm* **the books** die
Bücher *nnpl* **book value** Buchwert (-e) *nm*
2. *vb* **to book a hotel room** ein Hotelzimmer
reservieren *vb* **to book in advance** im
voraus buchen
book-keeper *n* Buchhalter (-) *nm*
book-keeping *n* Buchhaltung *nf*
booking *n* (reservation) Reservierung (-en) *nf*
bookseller *n* Buchhändler *nm*

bookshop, bookstore (US) *n* Buchhandlung (-en) *nf*

boom 1. *n* **economic boom** Wirtschaftsaufschwung (-ünge) *nm* **boom in demand** Nachfrageboom (-s) *nm* 2. *vb* einen Aufschwung nehmen *vb*

booming *adj* florierend

boost 1. *n* Ankurbelung *nf* 2. *vb* **to boost demand** die Nachfrage ankurbeln *vb* **to boost morale** die Moral heben *vb* **to boost production** die Produktion steigern *vb* **to boost sales** den Absatz steigern *vb*

boot *vb* **to boot a computer** *vb* einen Computer laden *vb*

booth *n* (voting) Stand (-ände) *nm*

borrow *vb* leihen *vb*

borrowing *n* Kreditaufnahme *nf*

boss *n* Chef (-s) *nm*

bottleneck *n* Engpaß (-pässe) *nm* **bottleneck inflation** Engpaßinflation *nf*

bottom 1. *adj* niedrig *adj* **bottom price** niedrigster Preis (-e) *nm* 2. *n* **at the bottom** unten *prep* 3 *vb* **to bottom out** den tiefsten Stand erreichen

bought *adj* **bought ledger** Wareneinkaufsbuch (-bücher) *nn*

bounce* *vb* (cheque) platzen *vb*

bound *n* **out of bounds** verboten *adj*

box 1. *n* **box number** Chiffre (-n) *nf*, Postfach (-fächer) *nn* **box office** Kasse (-n) *nf* **PO box** Postfach (-fächer) *nn* 2. *vb* **to box sth up** in eine(r) Kiste verpacken *vb*

boycott 1. *n* Boykott (-s) *nm* 2. *vb* boykottieren *vb*

bracket *n* Träger (-) *nm*, Klammer (-n) *nf* **tax bracket** Steuerklasse (-n) *nf*

branch *n* Filiale (-n) *nf* **branch company** Zweigniederlassung (-en) *nf* **branch manager** Filialleiter (-) *nm* **branch office** Zweigstelle (-n) *nf*

brand *n* Marke (-n) *nf* **brand image** Markenbild (-er) *nn* **brand leader** Markenführer (-) *nm*

breach *n* Vertragsverletzung (-en) *nf* **breach of contract** Vertragsverletzung (-en) *nf*

break 1. *n* **to take a break** Pause machen, Urlaub nehmen 2. *vb* **to break an agreement** einen Vertrag brechen *vb*

break even *vb* kostendeckend arbeiten *vb*

break up *vb* auflösen *vb*

break-even *adj* **break-even point** Gewinnschwelle (-n) *nf*

breakdown *n* (of figures) Aufgliederung der Zahlen *nf* **breakdown service** Pannendienst (-e) *nm*

breakthrough *n* Durchbruch (-brüche) *nm* **to make a breakthrough** durchbrechen *vb*

breakup *n* Auflösung (-en) *nf*, Liquidation (-en) *nf*

bribe 1. *n* Bestechungsgeld (-er) *nn* 2. *vb* bestechen

bribery *n* Bestechung *nf*

bridging *adj* **bridging loan, bridge loan** (US) Überbrückungskredit (-e) *nm*

brief 1. *n* Auftrag (-äge) *nm* 2. *vb* instruieren *vb*, beauftragen *vb*

briefing *n* Einsatzbesprechung (-en) *nf*

bring down *vb* (prices) herabsetzen *vb*, reduzieren *vb*

bring forward *vb* vorverlegen *vb*

bring out *vb* (product) herausbringen *vb*, auf den Markt bringen *vb*

brinkmanship *n* Krisenpolitik *nf*

Britain *n* Großbritannien *nn*

British *adj* britisch *adj* **British Council** British Council *nm* **British Isles** die Britischen Inseln *n*

broad *adj* **broad market** aufnahmefähiger Markt (-märkte) *nm*

broadcast 1. *n* Sendung (-en) *nf* 2. *vb* senden *vb*

broadsheet *n* Handzettel (-) *nm*

brochure *n* Prospekt (-e) *nm*

broker *n* Makler (-) *nm*, Broker (-) *nm*

brokerage *n* Maklergeschäft *nn* **brokerage firm** Maklerfirma (-firmen) *nf*

buck* **(US)** *n* Dollar *nm* **to pass the buck*** die Verantwortung abschieben

budget *n* Budget (-s) *nn* **to draw up a budget** den Haushaltsplan erstellen

budget for *vb* im Budget einplanen

budgetary *adj* **budgetary deficit** Defizit (-e) *nn* **budgetary policy** Finanzpolitik *nf*

bug 1. *n* (listening device) Wanze (-n) *nf*, Programmfehler *nm* 2. *vb* stören *vb* **to bug a call** ein Gespräch abhören

build *vb* **to build a reputation** sich einen Ruf schaffen

builder *n* Bauunternehmer (-) *nm*

building *n* **building contractor** Bauunternehmer (-) *nm* **building firm** Baufirma (-firmen) *nf* **building industry/trade** Bauindustrie *nf* **building permit** Baugenehmigung (-en) *nf* **building site** Baustelle (-n) *nf* **building society** Bausparkasse (-n) *nf*

built-in *adj* eingebaut *adj*

built-up *adj* **built-up area** bebautes Gebiet (-e) *nn*

bulk *n* Massen- *cpd* **the bulk of** der größte Teil *nm* **to buy in bulk** *vb* in Mengen einkaufen *vb*

bull 1. *n* (stock exchange) Haussier (-s) *nm* **bull market** (stock exchange) Haussemarkt (-märkte) *nm* 2. *vb* (stock exchange) auf Hausse spekulieren *vb*

bulletin *n* Nachricht (-en) *nf*, Nachrichtensendung (-en) *nf* **bulletin board** schwarzes Brett (-er) *nn*

bullion *n* Edelmetallbarren *nm*

bump up *vb* (prices) Preise erhöhen

bundle *n* Paket (-e) *nn*, Bündel (-) *nn*

bundle up *vb* bündeln *vb*

buoyant *adj* **buoyant market** eine feste Börse

(-n) *nf*
bureau *n* **bureau de change** Wechselstube
(-n) *nf* **Federal Bureau (US)** Bundesamt *nn*
bureaucracy *n* Bürokratie *nf*
bureaucrat *n* Bürokrat (-en) *nm*
bureaucratic *adj* bürokratisch *adj*
bursar *n* Finanzverwalter (-) *nm*
bus *n* **bus station** Busbahnhof (-höfe) *nm*
business *n* Geschäft (-e) *nn* **to go out of
business** Konkurs melden **business address**
Geschäftsadresse (-n) *nf* **business associate**
Geschäftsfreund (-e) *nm* **big business**
Großindustrie *nf* **business consultant**
Unternehmensberater (-) *nm* **business
expenses** Spesen *npl* **family business**
Familiengeschäft (-e) *nn* **business hours**
Geschäftsstunden *nfpl* **business premises**
Geschäftsräume *nmpl* **business studies**
Betriebswirtschaftslehre *nf* **business suit**
Geschäftsanzug (-züge) *nm* **to set up in
business** ein Geschäft gründen **business
transaction** Geschäft (-e) *nn* **business trip**
Geschäftsreise (-n) *nf*
businesslike *adj* geschäftstüchtig *adj*
busy *adj* beschäftigt *adj* **busy signal (US)**
Besetztton (-töne) *nm*
buy 1. *n* **a good buy** ein gutes Geschäft 2. *vb*
to buy sth at a high price zu einem hohen
Preis kaufen **to buy sth on credit** auf Kredit
kaufen **to buy sth second hand** aus zweiter
Hand kaufen *vb* **to buy sth wholesale** im
Großhandel kaufen *vb*
buy out *vb* aufkaufen *vb*
buy-out *n* Aufkauf (-käufe) *nm*, Übernahme
(-n) *nf*
buyer *n* Käufer (-) *nm* **buyer's market**
Käufermarkt (-märkte) *nm*
buying *n* **buying and selling** Kauf und
Verkauf *nm* **buying power** Kaufkraft *nf*
buying price Kaufpreis (-e) *nm* **buying rate**
Ankaufskurs *nm*
by-product *n* Nebenprodukt (-e) *nn*
bypass *vb* umgehen *vb*
byte *n* Byte *nn*
c.i.f. (cost, insurance and freight) *abbr* cif
(Kosten, Versicherung, Fracht) *abbr*
**CAD (computer-aided or assisted
design)** *abbr* computerunterstütztes Design
calculate *vb* berechnen *vb*
calculation *n* Berechnung (-en) *nf*
calculator *n* Rechner (-) *nm*
call 1. *n* **call money** Tagesgeld *nn* **person-to-
person call** Gespräch mit Voranmeldung (-e)
nn **reverse-charge call, collect call (US)** R-
Gespräch (-e) *nn* 2. *vb* **to call a meeting** eine
Sitzung einberufen **to call it a deal** eine
Abmachung treffen
call back *vb* (on phone) zurückrufen *vb*
call for *vb* verlangen *vb*, rufen *vb*
call in *vb* (demand the repayment of a loan)
ein Darlehen kündigen
campaign *n* Kampagne (-n) *nf* **advertising**

campaign Werbekampagne (-n) *nf* **publicity
campaign** Werbekampagne (-n) *nf* **sales
campaign** Verkaufskampagne (-n) *nf* **to run
a campaign** eine Werbekampagne führen
cancel *vb* annullieren *vb* **cancel a contract**
einen Vertrag aufheben **cancel an appointment** absagen *vb*
cancellation *n* Stornierung (-en) *nf*,
Rückgängigmachung (-en) **cancellation
charge** Stornogebühr (-en) *nf*
candidate *n* (for job) Kandidat (-en) *nm*,
Bewerber (-) *nm*
cap *vb* **to cap the interest rate** die Zinsen
begrenzen
CAP (Common Agricultural Policy) *abbr*
Gemeinsame Agrarpolitik *nf*
capacity *n* **earning capacity** Ertragsfähigkeit
nf **industrial capacity** Industriekapazität *nf*
in my capacity as chairman in meiner
Eigenschaft als Vorsitzender **manufacturing
capacity** Produktionskapazität *nf* **storage
capacity** Lagerkapazität *nf* **to expand capa-
city** die Kapazität erweitern **to work to full
capacity** voll ausgelastet sein
capital *n* Kapital *nn* **capital assets**
(Kapital)vermögen *nn* **capital budget**
Investitionsplan (-pläne) *nm* **capital cost**
Kapitalkosten *npl* **capital expenditure**
Investitionsausgaben *nfpl* **capital exports**
Kapitalausfuhr *nf* **fixed capital**
Anlagevermögen *nn* **capital funds**
Eigenmittel *nnpl* **capital gains**
Kapitalgewinne *nmpl*,
Veräußerungsgewinne *nmpl* **capital gains
tax** Kapitalgewinnsteuer (-n) *nf* **capital
goods** Kapitalgüter *nnpl* **initial capital**
Anfangskapital *nn* **invested capital**
Investitionskapital *nn* **capital loss**
Kapitalverlust (-e) *nm* **capital market**
Kapitalmarkt (-märkte) *nm* **to raise capital**
Kapital aufbringen **capital turnover**
Kapitalumschlag *nm* **venture capital**
Spekulationskapital *nn* **working capital**
Betriebskapital *nn*
capitalism *n* Kapitalismus *nm*
capitalist *n* Kapitalist (-en) *nm*
capitalize *vb* kapitalisieren *vb*
card *n* **bank card** Kreditkarte (-n) *nf* **business
card** Geschäftskarte (-n) *nf* **chargecard**
Kundenkreditkarte (-n) *nf* **cheque card**
Scheckkarte (-n) *nf* **credit card** Kreditkarte
(-n) *nf* **identity card** Ausweis (-e) *nm* **smart
card** Smart-Card *nf*
career *n* Karriere (-n) *nf* **careers advice**
Berufsberatung *nf*
cargo *n* Fracht (-en) *nf* **bulk cargo**
Massengutladung *nf* **cargo ship** Frachtschiff
(-e) *nn*
carriage *n* **carriage charge** Frachtgebühr (-en)
nf **carriage costs** Frachtkosten *npl* **carriage
forward** per Frachtnachnahme **carriage
included** frachtfrei **carriage paid** frachtfrei

carrier *n* Spediteur (-e) *nm* **bulk carrier**
Massengutfrachter *nm* **express carrier**
Eiltransporter *nm*
carry *vb* (stock) führen *vb*
carry forward *vb* übertragen *vb*
carry out *vb* ausführen *vb*
carry over *vb* (to next month) prolongieren *vb*
carrying *adj* **carrying cost** Zinsbelastung
(eines Sollsaldos) *nf*
cartel *n* Kartell (-e) *nn*
cash 1. *n* Bargeld *nn* **cash and carry**
Selbstabholung gegen Kasse *nf* **cash before
delivery** Barzahlung vor Lieferung *nf* **cash
crop** zum Verkauf bestimmte Ernte *nf* **cash
desk** Kasse (-n) *nf* **cash discount** Barrabatt
nm **cash flow** Cashflow *nm*, Kapitalfluß *nm*
for cash gegen Barzahlung **cash machine/
dispenser** Geldautomat (-en) *nm* **cash offer**
Barangebot (-e) *nn* **cash on delivery (COD)**
Barzahlung bei Lieferung *nf* **cash on receipt
of goods** Barzahlung bei Erhalt der Ware *nf*
cash payment Barzahlung (-en) *nf* **cash sale**
Kassageschäft (-e) *nn* **to pay in cash** bar
zahlen **cash transaction** Kassageschäft (-e)
nn **cash with order** Zahlung bei
Auftragserteilung *nf* **2.** *vb* einlösen *vb*,
kassieren **to cash a cheque** einen Scheck
einlösen
cash up *vb* Kasse machen *vb*, kassieren *vb*
cashier *n* Kassierer/in *nm/nf*
cater for *vb* eingestellt sein auf *vb*
caution *n* **caution money** Kaution *nf*
ceiling *n* (on prices) Preisobergrenze *nf* **to
put a ceiling on sth** eine Höchstgrenze
festsetzen
central *adj* **central bank** Zentralbank (-en) *nf*
central planned economy zentrale
Planwirtschaft (-en) *nf* **central planning**
Zentralplanung *nf* **central processing unit
(CPU)** (DP) Zentraleinheit (-en) *nf*, CPU (-s) *nf*
centralization *n* Zentralisierung *nf*
centralize *vb* zentralisieren *vb*
centre *n* **business centre** Geschäftszentrum
(-en) *nn* **Jobcentre** Arbeitsamt (-ämter) *nn*
certificate 1. *n* Bescheinigung (-en) *nf*,
Zeugnis (-se) *nn* **clearance certificate**
Zollerlaubnisschein (-e) *nm* **marriage certificate** Trauschein (-e) *nm* **certificate of
employment** Arbeitszeugnis (-se) *nn* **certificate of origin** Ursprungszeugnis (-se) *nn*
certificate of ownership Eigentumsurkunde
(-n) *nf* **share certificate, stock certificate**
(US) Aktienzertifikat (-e) *nn* **2.** *vb*
bescheinigen *vb*
certified *adj* **certified cheque** gedeckter
Scheck (-s) *nm*
certify *vb* bescheinigen *vb*
chain *n* **chain of shops** Ladenkette (-n) *nf*
retail chain Einzelhandelskette (-n) *nf* **chain
store** Filialgeschäft (-e) *nn*
chair *vb* **to chair a meeting** (bei einer Sitzung)
Vorsitz führen

chamber *n* **Chamber of Commerce**
Handelskammer (-n) *nf*
chancellor *n* **Chancellor of the Exchequer
(GB)** Finanzminister (-) *nm*
change *n* (from purchase) Wechselgeld *nn*
bureau de change Wechselstube (-n) *nf*
loose/small change (coins) Kleingeld *nn*
charge 1. *n* **charge account** Kreditkonto
(-konten) *nn* **bank charges** Bankspesen *npl*
delivery charges Liefergebühren *nfpl* **handling charges** Ladekosten (-) *npl* **legal charge**
Rechtskosten *npl* **to be in charge** verantwortlich sein **2.** *vb* **charge a price**
berechnen **to charge commission** Provision
berechnen **to charge for sth** berechnen **to
charge sth to an account** ein Konto mit
etwas belasten **to take charge of sth** etwas
übernehmen **to charge sb with sth** jemanden anklagen (wegen)
chargeable *adj* anrechenbar *adj*
charitable *adj* **charitable trust** karitative
Organisation (-en) *nf*
charity *n* karitative Organisation (-en) *nf*
chart *n* Tabelle (-n) *nf* **bar chart**
Balkendiagramm (-e) *nn* **flow chart** Flow-
Chart (-s) *nm* **pie chart** Kreisdiagramm (-e)
nn
charter *n* Charter (-s) *nm* **charter flight**
Charterflug (-üge) *nm*
chartered *adj* **chartered accountant**
Bilanzbuchhalter (-) *nm* **chartered bank**
konzessionale Bank (-en) *nf* **chartered surveyor** Landvermesser (-) *nm*
chattels *npl* bewegliche Sachen *nfpl*
check 1. *n* **customs check** Zollabfertigung
(-en) *nf* **to make a check on sth** prüfen *vb*
2. *vb* prüfen *vb*
check in *vb* (at airport) einchecken *vb* (register in an hotel) sich anmelden *vb*
check out *vb* (pay the hotel bill) abreisen *vb*
checkbook (US) *n* Scheckbuch (-ücher) *nn*
chemical *adj* **chemical industry**
Chemieindustrie (-n) *nf* **chemical products**
Chemieprodukte *nnpl*
cheque, check (US) *n* Scheck (-s) *nm* **to
return a cheque to drawer** einen Scheck an
den Austeller zurückgeben **blank cheque**
Blankoscheck (-s) *nm* **cheque book**
Scheckbuch (-bücher) *nn* **crossed cheque**
gekreuzter Scheck (-s) *nm* **dud cheque**
geplatzter Scheck (-s) *nm* **a cheque for the
amount of £100** Scheck in Höhe von £100 (-s)
nm **to bounce a cheque** einen Scheck
platzen lassen **to cash a cheque** einen
Scheck einlösen **to make out a cheque**
einen Scheck ausstellen **to pay by cheque**
per Scheck zahlen **to sign a cheque** einen
Scheck unterschreiben **to stop a cheque**
einen Scheck sperren **traveller's cheque,
traveler's cheque (US)** Reisescheck (-s) *nm*
chief *adj* **chief accountant** Hauptbuchhalter
nm **chief cashier** Hauptkassierer (-) *nm*

chief executive Chief Executive Officer (-s) *nm* **chief financial officer** Finanzleiter (-) *nm*
circular *n* (letter) Rund- *cpd*
circulate *vb* (document) zirkulieren lassen *vb*
circulation *n* **in circulation** im Umlauf
circumstance Umstand (-ände) *nm* **circumstances beyond our control** nicht in unserer Hand liegende Umstände **due to unforeseen circumstances** aus nicht vorhersehbaren Gründen **under no circumstances** unter keinen Umständen
civil *adj* **civil engineering** Tiefbau *nm* **civil servant** Beamte/r *nmf* **civil service** Staatsdienst *nm*
claim 1. *n* **claim form** Antragsformular (-e) *nn* **claims department** Reklamationsabteilung (-en) *nf* **claims procedure** Reklamationsverfahren (-) *nn* **to put in a claim** Ansprüche geltend machen **to settle a claim** begleichen *vb* **wage claim** Lohnforderung (-e) *nf* 2. *vb* (demand) beanspruchen *vb* **to claim for damages** Schadenersatzansprüche geltend machen
claimant *n* Antragsteller (-) *nm*
class *n* **business class** (plane) Business-Class **first class** (plane) erste Klasse *nf*
classified *adj* **classified advertisement** Anzeige (-n) *nf* **classified information** streng vertrauliche Information *nf*
clause *n* (in contract) Klausel (-n) *nf* **escape clause** Ausweichklausel (-n) *nf* **option clause** Optionsklausel (-n) *nf*
clear 1. *adj* **clear loss** Nettoverlust *nm* **to make oneself clear** sich klar ausdrücken 2. *vb* (cheque) abrechnen *vb* **to clear sth through customs** abfertigen *vb*
clearance *n* **clearance offer** Sonderangebot (-e) *nn* **clearance sale** Ausverkauf (-äufe) *nm*
clearing *adj* **clearing bank** Clearingbank (-en) *nf*, Geschäftsbank (-en) *nf* **clearing house** Clearing House (-s) *nn*, Clearingstelle (-n) *nf* **clearing payment** Abrechnungszahlung (-en) *nf*
clerical *adj* **clerical error** Schreibfehler (-) *nm* **clerical work** Büroarbeit *nf*
clerk *n* Büroangestellte/r *nmf*
client *n* Kunde (-n) *nm*
clientele *n* Kundschaft *nf*
clinch *vb* abschließen *vb* **clinch a deal** ein Geschäft abschließen
clock in *vb* den Arbeitsbeginn stempeln
clock out *vb* das Arbeitsende stempeln
close *vb* **to close a business** ein Geschäft aufgeben **to close a deal** ein Geschäft abschließen, stillegen **to close a meeting** eine Sitzung aufgeben **to close an account** ein Konto auflösen
closed *adj* geschlossen *adj* **closed session/meeting** geschlossene Sitzung (-en) *nf* **closed shop** gewerkschaftsgebundene Firma (-en) *nf*
closing *adj* **closing bid** Höchstgebot (-e) *nn*

closing price Schlußkurs (-e) *nm* **closing time** Geschäftsschluß *nm*
closure *n* Stillegung (-en) *nf* **closure of a company** Betriebsstillegung (-en) *nf*
COD (cash on delivery), (collect on delivery) (US) *abbr* Zahlung bei Warenerhalt
code *n* **bar code** Strichcode (-s) *nf* **professional code of practice** Ehrenkodex (-e) *nm*, Verhaltenskodex (-e) *nm* **post code, zip code** (US) Postleitzahl (-en) *nf* **telephone code** Ortsnetzkennzahl (-en) *nf* **tax code** Abgabenordnung (-en) *nf*
collaborate *vb* zusammenarbeiten mit *vb*
collaborative *adj* **collaborative venture** Gemeinschaftsprogramm (-e) *nn*, Gemeinschaftsunternehmen (-) *nn*
collapse *n* (of economy, company) Zusammenbruch (-üche) *nm* (on stock market) Kursverfall *nm*
collateral 1. *adj* **collateral security** akzessorische Sicherheit *nf* 2. *n* Sicherungsgegenstand *nm*, akzessorische Sicherheit *nf*
colleague *n* Kollege (-n) *nm*
collect *vb* einziehen *vb* **to collect a debt** eine Schuld einziehen *vb*
collecting *adj* **collecting agency** Inkassoagentur (-en) *nf*, Inkassobüro (-s) *nn*
collection *n* Inkasso *nn*, Einziehung *nf* **debt collection** Schuldeneinziehung *nf*
collective 1. *adj* **collective agreement** Tarifabkommen (-) *nn* **collective bargaining** Tarifverhandlung (-en) *nf* 2. *n* Kollektiv (-e) *nn* **workers' collective** Arbeitsgemeinschaft (-en) *nf*
colloquium *n* Kolloquium (-ien) *nn*
comment *n* Bemerkung (-en) *nf*
commerce *n* Handel *nm*
commercial *adj* kaufmännisch *adj*, kommerziell *adj* **commercial bank** Geschäftsbank (-en) *nf* **commercial traveller, commercial traveler** (US) Geschäftsreisende/r *nmf* **commercial vehicle** Nutzfahrzeug (-e) *nn*
commission *n* Provision *nf* **commission agent** Provisionsvertreter (-) *nm* **commission broker** Aktienmakler (auf Provisionsbasis) (-) *nm* **commission fee** Provisionsgebühr (-en) *nf* **to charge commission** Provision berechnen
commit *vb* (sich) verpflichten *vb*
commitment *n* Verpflichtung (-en) *nf*
committee *n* Ausschuß (-üsse) *nm* **advisory committee** Beirat (-äte) *nm* **committee meeting** Ausschußsitzung (-en) *nf*
common *adj* **Common Agricultural Policy (CAP)** Gemeinsame Agrarpolitik *nf* **Common Market** Gemeinsamer Markt *nm* **common law** Gewohnheitsrecht *nn*
communication *n* Kommunikation *nf* **communication network** Kommunikationsnetz (-e) *nn*

company n Gesellschaft (-en) nf,
Unternehmen (-) nn, Betrieb (-e) nm **holding
company** Holding-Gesellschaft (-en) nf
incorporated company (US)
Aktiengesellschaft (-en) nf **joint-stock company** Aktiengesellschaft (-en) nf **company
law** Gesellschaftsrecht nn **limited company**
Gesellschaft mit beschränkter Haftung (-en)
nf **parent company** Muttergesellschaft (-en)
nf **company policy** Unternehmenspolitik nf
private limited company Gesellschaft mit
beschränkter Haftung (in privater Hand) (-en)
nf **public limited company** Gesellschaft mit
beschränkter Haftung (-en) nf **registered
company** eingetragene Firma (-en) nf **company secretary** höchster
Verwaltungsbeamter (-en) nm **sister company** Schwestergesellschaft (-en) nf **subsidiary company** Tochtergesellschaft (-en) nf
comparative adj vergleichend adj
compatible adj kompatibel adj
compensate for vb entschädigen vb
compensation n Entschädigung nf **to claim
compensation** Entschädigung verlangen **to
pay compensation** Entschädigung zahlen
compete vb konkurrieren (mit) vb **to compete with a rival** konkurrieren (mit)
competing adj **competing company** konkurrierende Gesellschaft (-en) nf, Konkurrent
(-en) nm
competition n Konkurrenz nf, Wettbewerb
nm **cut-throat competition** ruinöse
Konkurrenz nf **market competition** Konkurrenz auf dem Markt nf **unfair competition**
unlauterer Wettbewerb nm
competitive adj wettbewerbsfähig adj
competitiveness n Wettbewerbsfähigkeit nf,
Konkurrenzfähigkeit nf
competitor n Konkurrent (-en) nm
complain vb **to complain about sth**
beanstanden vb, sich beschweren über vb
complaint n Mangelrüge (-n) nf **to make a
complaint** Beschwerde einlegen **complaints
department** Beschwerdeabteilung (-en) nf
complete vb vollenden vb
complex 1. adj komplex adj, kompliziert adj
2. n Komplex (-e) nm **housing complex**
Wohnsiedlung (-en) nf
complimentary adj frei adj, kostenlos adj
comply vb **to comply with legislation** die
Bedingungen erfüllen, den Anordnungen
nachkommen **to comply with the rules** sich
an die Regeln halten
compound adj **compound interest**
Zinseszins nm
comprehensive adj umfassend adj **comprehensive insurance policy**
Vollkaskoversicherung nf
compromise n Kompromiß (-sse) nm **to
reach a compromise** einen Kompromiß
schließen
computer n Computer (-) nm **computer-**

aided design (CAD) computerunterstütztes
Design nn, CAD nn **computer-aided learning
(CAL)** computergestütztes Lernen nn, CAL
nn **computer-aided manufacture (CAM)**
computergestützte Fertigung nf, CAM nf
computer centre, center (US)
Computerzentrum (-en) nn **computer file**
Datei (-en) nf **computer language**
Computersprache (-n) nf **laptop computer**
Laptop-Computer (-) nm **computer literate**
sich mit Computern auskennen **mainframe
computer** Großrechner (-) nm **computer
operator** Computer-Operator (-en) nm **personal computer (PC)** Personalcomputer (-)
nm, PC (-s) nm **portable computer** tragbarer
Computer (-) nm, portable Computer (-) nm
computer program Computerprogramm (-)
nn **computer programmer** Programmierer
(-) nm **computer terminal** Terminal (-s) nn
concern 1. n Unternehmen (-) nn **going
concern** arbeitendes Unternehmen nn 2. vb
(be of importance to) betreffen vb
concur vb übereinstimmen vb
condition npl **living conditions**
Wohnverhältnisse nnpl **conditions of purchase** Kaufbedingungen nfpl **conditions of
sale** Verkaufsbedingungen nfpl **working
conditions** Arbeitsverhältnisse nnpl,
Arbeitsbedingungen nfpl
conference n Konferenz (-en) nf **conference
proceedings** Tagungsbericht (-e) nm **to
arrange a conference** eine Konferenz veranstalten, organisieren **conference venue**
Tagungsort (-e) nm
confidence n **in strictest confidence** streng
vertraulich
confidential adj vertraulich adj
confirm vb **to confirm receipt of sth** den
Empfang bestätigen
confirmation n Bestätigung nf
conglomerate n Konglomerat (-e) nn,
Mischkonzern (-e) nm
congress n Kongreß (-sse) nm
connect vb **could you connect me to...**
(telephone) könnten Sie mich bitte mit X
verbinden?
connection n **business connections**
Geschäftsbeziehungen nfpl
consent 1. n Zustimmung nf 2. vb
zustimmen vb
consequence n Folge (-n) nf
consideration n (for contract) Überlegung
(-en) nf
consignee n Empfänger (-) nm, Konsignatar
(-e) nm
consigner/or n Absender (-) nm
consignment n Sendung (-en) nf
consolidate vb konsolidieren vb
consolidated adj konsolidiert adj **consolidated figures** konsolidierte Zahlen nfpl, konsolidierte Bilanz nf
consortium n Konsortium (-ien) nn

construction n **construction industry**
Bauindustrie (-n) nf
consul n Konsul (-n) nm
consulate n Konsulat (-e) nn
consult vb beraten vb, konsultieren vb **to
consult with sb** sich mit jemandem beraten
consultancy, consulting (US) adj **consultancy firm** n Beratung nf **consultancy fees**
Beratungsgebühren nfpl **consultancy work**
Beratungstätigkeit nf
consultant n Berater (-) nm
consumer n Verbraucher (-) nm, Konsument
(-en) nm **consumer credit** Konsumkredit nm
consumer demand Konsumnachfrage nf
consumer habits Verbrauchsgewohnheiten
nfpl **consumer research** Konsumforschung
nf **consumer satisfaction**
Verbraucherzufriedenheit nf **consumer survey** Konsumumfrage (-n) nf **consumer
trends** Konsumtrends nmpl,
Konsumtendenzen nfpl
consumerism n Konsumdenken nn
contact 1. n **to get in contact with sb** sich
mit jemandem in Verbindung setzen **business contacts** Geschäftsfreunde nmpl **2.** vb
kontaktieren vb
container n Container (-e) nm, Behälter (-e)
nm **container depot** Containerdepot (-s) nn
container ship Containerschiff (-e) nn **container terminal** Containerlager (-) nn
contract n Vertrag (-äge) nm **breach of
contract** Vertragsverletzung (-en) nf **draft
contract** Vertragsentwurf (-ürfe) nm **contract labour** Akkordarbeit nf **law of contract**
Vertragsrecht nn **the terms of the contract**
die Vertragsbedingungen nfpl **the signato-
ries to the contract** die Unterzeichner nmpl
to cancel a contract einen Vertrag stornieren
to draw up a contract einen Vertrag
entwerfen **to sign a contract** einen Vertrag
unterzeichnen **to tender for a contract** einen
Vertrag ausschreiben **under the terms of the
contract** nach den Vertragsbedingungen
contract work Vertragsarbeit nf
contracting adj **the contracting parties** die
Vertragsparteien nfpl
contractor n Auftragnehmer (-) nm **building
contractor** Bauunternehmer (-) nm **haulage
contractor** Kraftverkehrspedition (-en) nf
contractual adj **contractual obligations**
Vertragspflichten nfpl
contravene vb verletzen vb
contravention n Verletzung (-en) nf
contribute vb beitragen vb
contribution n **social security contributions**
Sozialversicherungsbeiträge nmpl
control n **financial control** Finanzkontrolle nf
production control Produktionskontrolle (-n)
nf **quality control** Qualitätskontrolle (-n) nf
stock control Lagerwirtschaft nf
convene vb **to convene a meeting** eine
Sitzung einberufen

convenience n **at your earliest convenience**
möglichst bald
convenient adj zweckmäßig adj
convertible adj **convertible currency** konvertierbare Währung (-en) nf
copier n (photocopier) Kopierer (-) nm
copy 1. n Kopie (-n) nf **2.** vb (photocopy)
kopieren vb
copyright n Copyright nn **copyright law**
Urheberrecht (-e) nn
corporate adj korporativ adj **corporate image**
Unternehmens-Image (-s) nn **corporate
investment** Unternehmensinvestitionen nfpl
corporation n Körperschaft (-en) nf **corporation tax** Körperschaftssteuer (-n) nf
correspondence n Korrespondenz nf,
Briefwechsel nm
corruption n Korruption nf
cosignatory n Mitunterzeichner (-) nm
cost 1. n Kosten npl **cost breakdown**
Kostenaufstellung nf **cost centre**
Kostenstelle (-n) nf **cost-cutting**
Kostensenkung nf **cost of living**
Lebenshaltungskosten npl **operating cost**
betriebliche Aufwendungen nfpl **cost price**
Herstellungspreis (-e) nm **running cost**
Betriebskosten npl **2.** vb **to cost a job** die
Kosten einer Arbeit ermitteln
counterfeit 1. n Fälschung nf **2.** vb fälschen
vb
counterfoil n Kontrollabschnitt (-e) nm
countersign vb gegenzeichnen vb
country n Land (-änder) nn **developing
country** Entwicklungsland (-änder) nn **third-
world country** Land der Dritten Welt (-änder)
nn, Entwicklungsland (-änder) nn
coupon n Kupon (-s) nm
courier 1. n Kurier (-e) nm, Reiseleiter (-) nm
by courier service per Kurierdienst **2.** vb per
Eilboten senden
court n Gerichtshof (-öfe) nm **Court of
Appeal, Court of Appeals** (US)
Rechtsmittelinstanz nf **criminal court**
Strafgericht nn **in court** vor dem Gericht
covenant n Verpflichtung (-en) nf
covenantee n Vertragsberechtigte/r nmf
covenantor n Kontrahent/in (-en/-innen) nm/
nf
cover n **insurance cover** Versicherung nf
cover note Deckungszusage nf
credit 1. n Kredit nm **credit agency**
Kreditauskunftei (-en) nf **to buy sth on credit**
auf Kredit kaufen **credit card** Kreditkarte (-n)
nf **credit company** Finanzierungsinstitut (-e)
nn **credit control** Kreditkontrolle nf **credit
enquiry** Kreditwürdigkeitsprüfung nf **in credit** in den schwarzen Zahlen **letter of credit**
Akkreditiv (-e) nn **long credit** langfristiger
Kredit nm **credit note** Gutschriftsanzeige
(-n) nf **credit rating** Bonität nf **credit terms**
Kreditkonditionen nfpl **2.** vb **to credit sth to
an account** einem Konto gutschreiben

creditor *n* Gläubiger (-) *nm*
creditworthiness *n* Kreditwürdigkeit *nf*
creditworthy *adj* kreditwürdig *adj*
crossed *adj* **crossed cheque** gekreuzter Scheck (-s) *nm*
currency *n* Währung (-en) *nf* **convertible currency** konvertierbare Währung (-en) *nf* **foreign currency** Fremdwährung (-en) *nf* **hard currency** harte Währung (-en) *nf* **legal currency** gesetzliche Währung (-en) *nf* **paper currency** Papierwährung (-en) *nf* **soft currency** weiche Währung (-en) *nf* **currency transfer** Währungsüberweisung (-en) *nf*
current *adj* **current account** Girokonto (-konten) *nn*
curriculum vitae (CV), résumé (US) *n* Lebenslauf (-äufe) *nm*
customer *n* Kunde (-n) *nm* **customer loyalty** Kundentreue *nf* **regular customer** Stammkunde (-n) *nm* **customer relations** Kundenbeziehungen *nfpl*
customs *npl* Zoll *nm* **customs charges** Zollgebühren *nfpl* **customs clearance** Zollabfertigung *nf* **customs declaration** Zollerklärung (-en) *nf* **customs office** Zollamt (-ämter) *nn* **customs officer** Zollbeamte/r *nmf* **customs regulations** Zollverordnungen *nfpl* **to clear sth through customs** abfertigen *vb* **customs union** Zollunion (-en) *nf* **customs warehouse** Zollager (-) *nn*
cut 1. *n* **tax cut** Steuersenkung (-en) *nf* **2.** *vb* (reduce) kürzen *vb*
damage 1. *n* Schaden (-äden) *nm* **to cause extensive damage** beträchtlichen Schaden verursachen **to claim damages** (legal) Schadenersatz beanspruchen **damage to goods in transit** Transitschäden *nmpl* **damage to property** Eigentumsschaden *nm* **2.** *vb* beschädigen *vb*
data *npl* Daten *nnpl* **data bank** Datenbank (-en) *nf* **database** Datenbank (-en) *nf* **data capture** Datenerfassung *nf* **data processing** Datenverarbeitung *nf*
date *n* Datum (-en) *nn* **delivery date** Liefertermin (-e) *nm* **out of date** veraltet *adj*, überholt *adj* **up to date** aktuell *adj*
deal *n* Geschäft (-e) *nn* **it's a deal!** abgemacht!
dealer *n* Händler (-) *nm* **foreign exchange dealer** Devisenhändler (-) *nm*
dealing, trading (US) *n* Handel *nm* **foreign exchange dealings** Devisenhandel *nm* **insider dealing** Insiderhandel *nm*
debenture *n* gesicherte Schuldverschreibung (-en) *nf* **debenture bond** gesicherte Anleihe (-n) *nf* **debenture capital, debenture stock** (US) Anleihekapital *nn* **debenture loan** Obligationsanleihe (-n) *nf*
debit 1. *n* Debit *nn* **debit balance** Belastungssaldo (-en) *nm* **2.** *vb* (account) belasten *vb*

debiting *n* **direct debiting** Einzugsermächtigung *nf*
debt *n* Schuld (-en) *nf* **corporate debt** Firmenschulden *nfpl* **to get into debt** in Schuld geraten **to pay off a debt** eine Schuld tilgen **to reschedule a debt** umschulden *vb* **debt service** Schuldendienst (-e) *nm*
debtor *n* Schuldner (-) *nm*
decline *n* (economic) Rückgang (-änge) *nm*
decrease 1. *n* Rückgang (-änge) *nm* **2.** *vb* zurückgehen *vb*
deduct *vb* abziehen *vb*
deductible *adj* abziehbar *adj*
deduction *n* Abzug (-üge) *nm*
deed *n* (law) Übertragungsurkunde (-n) *nf* **deed of sale** Verkaufsurkunde (-n) *nf* **deed of transfer** Zessionsurkunde (-n) *nf*
default 1. *n* Zahlungsverzug (-üge) *nm* **2.** *vb* Zahlungsverpflichtungen nicht nachkommen
defect *n* Fehler (-) *nm*
defective *adj* fehlerhaft *adj*
defer *vb* (postpone) aufschieben *vb*
deferment *n* Aufschub (-übe) *nm*
deferred *adj* (tax) aufgeschoben *adj*
deficiency *n* Fehlbetrag (-äge) *nm*, Mangel (Mängel) *nm*
deficient *adj* mangelhaft *adj*
deficit *n* Defizit (-e) *nn* **deficit financing** Defizitwirtschaft *nf*
deflation *n* Deflation *nf*
deflationary *adj* deflationär *adj*
defraud *vb* betrügen *vb*
del credere *adj* **del credere agent** Garantievertreter (-) *nm*
delay 1. *n* Verzögerung (-en) *nf* **without delay** unverzüglich *adj* **2.** *vb* verzögern *vb*
delegate 1. *n* Delegierte/ r *nmf* **2.** *vb* delegieren *vb*
delegation *n* Delegation *nf*
deliver *vb* (goods) liefern *vb*
delivery *n* Lieferung (-en) *nf* **cash on delivery** Barzahlung bei Lieferung **delivery date** Liefertermin (-e) *nm* **free delivery** Lieferung gratis **general delivery (US)** postlagernd *adj* **recorded delivery** Bestätigung der Auslieferung einer Sendung *nf* **delivery time** Lieferzeit (-en) *nf*
demand 1. *n* Nachfrage *nf* **supply and demand** Angebot und Nachfrage *nn* **2.** *vb* fordern *vb*
demography *n* Demographie *nf*
demote *vb* (employee) degradieren *vb*
denationalize *vb* entnationalisieren *vb*
department *n* Abteilung (-en) *nf* **government department** Regierungsabteilung (-en) *nf* **personnel department** Personalabteilung (-en) *nf* **department store** Kaufhaus (-äuser) *nn*
depletion *n* Erschöpfung *nf*
deposit *n* Einzahlung (-en) *nf* einzahlen *vb*

deposit account Einlagenkonto (-konten) *nn*
depository *n* einlagennehmendes Institut (-e) *nn*
depreciate *vb* an Wert verlieren *vb*
depreciation *n* Wertverlust *nm*
depression *n* (economic) Flaute (-n) *nf*
deputy 1. *adj* stellvertretend *adj* **deputy director** stellvertretender Direktor *nm* 2. *n* Stellvertreter (-) *nm*
design 1. *n* Design (-s) *nn* **a machine of good/bad design** eine gut/schlechte konstruierte Maschine *nf* 2. *vb* konstruieren *vb*
designer *n* (commercial) Designer (-) *nm*
devaluation *n* Abwertung (-en) *nf*
developer *n* Erschließungsunternehmen (-) *nn*
digital *adj* digital *adj*
diminishing *adj* **diminishing returns** Ertragsrückgang *nm*
director *n* Direktor (-en) *nm* **board of directors** Vorstand (-ände) *nm*, Direktorium (-ien) *nn* **managing director** Vorstandsvorsitzende/r *nmf*
disburse *vb* auszahlen *vb*
discount *n* Rabatt (-e) *nm* **at a discount** mit Rabatt **discount rate** Diskontsatz (-ätze) *nm*
discounted *adj* **discounted cash flow (DCF)** diskontierter Einnahmeüberschuß (-üsse) *nm*
disk *n* Diskette (-n) *nf* **disk drive** (Disketten)laufwerk (-e) *nn* **floppy disk** Diskette (-n) *nf* **hard disk** Festplatte (-n) *nf* **magnetic disk** Diskette (-n) *nf*
dismiss *vb* (employee) entlassen *vb*
dispatch 1. *n* **date of dispatch** Versanddatum (-en) *nn* 2. *vb* (goods) absenden *vb*
dispatcher *n* Absender (-) *nm*
display 1. *n* (of goods) Ausstellung (-en) *nf* 2. *vb* ausstellen
disposable *adj* (not for reuse) Wegwerf- *cpd* **disposable income** Nettoeinkommen *nn*
dispute *n* Streit (-e) *nm* **industrial dispute** Arbeitsstreitigkeit (-en) *nf*
distribution *n* Vertrieb *nm*, Verteilung *nf*
distributor *n* Händler (-) *nm*
diversification *n* Diversifikation *nf*
diversify *vb* diversifizieren *vb*
dividend *n* Dividende (-n) *nf*
division *n* (of company) Geschäftsbereich (-e) *nm* **division of labour** Arbeitsaufteilung *nf*
dock 1. *n* (for berthing) Hafen (Häfen) *nm* 2. *vb* (ship) anlegen *vb*, docken *vb*
dockyard *n* Werft (-en) *nf*
document *n* Dokument (-e) *nn* **document retrieval** Dokumentenauffindung *nf*
domestic *adj* inländisch *adj* **domestic policy** Inlandspolitik *nf*
door *n* **door-to-door selling** Haustürverkauf *nm*
double *adj* **double-entry** (bookkeeping) doppelte Buchhaltung *nf*

Dow-Jones average (US) *n* Dow-Jones Durchschnitt *nm*
down *adj* **down payment** Anzahlung (-en) *nf*
downturn *n* (economic) Abschwung (-ünge) *nm*
downward 1. *adj* absteigend *adj* 2. *adv* nach unten *adv*
draft *n* (financial) Tratte (-n) *nf*, Wechsel (-) *nm*
draw *vb* (cheque) ausstellen *vb*
dry *adj* **dry goods** Kurzwaren *nfpl*
dumping *n* Dumping *nn*
durable *adj* haltbar *adj* **durable goods** Gebrauchsgüter *nnpl*
duty *n* (customs) Zoll *nm* **duty-free** (goods) zollfrei *adj*
dynamic *adj* dynamisch *adj*
dynamics *npl* Dynamik *nf*
early *adj* **early retirement** Vorruhestand *nm*
earn *vb* verdienen *vb*
earned *adj* **earned income** Arbeitseinkommen *nn* **earned surplus** freie Rücklage (-n) *nf*
earnest *adj* **earnest money** Angeld (-er) *nn*
earning *adj* **earning capacity** Ertragsfähigkeit *nf* **earning power** Ertragsfähigkeit *nf*
earnings *npl* Ertrag *nm* **earnings drift** Ertragstendenz *nf* **loss of earnings** Einkommensverlust *nm* **earnings-related pension** gehaltsabhängige Rente (-n) *nf* **earnings yield** Gewinn je Stammaktie *nm*
easy *adj* **easy-money policy** leichtverdientes Geld *nn*
EC (European Community) *abbr* EG (Europäische Gemeinschaft) *nf*
econometrics *npl* Ökonometrie *nf*
economic *adj* **economic adviser** Wirtschaftsberater (-) *nm* **economic analysis** Wirtschaftsanalyse (-n) *nf* **economic crisis** Wirtschaftskrise (-n) *nf* **economic cycle** Wirtschaftszyklus (-en) *nm* **economic decline** Wirtschaftsrückgang (-änge) *nm* **economic development** Wirtschaftsentwicklung *nf* **Economic and Monetary Union** Wirtschafts- und Währungsgemeinschaft *nf* **economic expansion** Wirtschaftswachstum *nn* **economic forecast** Wirtschaftsprognose (-n) *nf* **economic geography** Wirtschaftsgeographie *nf* **economic growth** Wirtschaftswachstum *nn* **economic infrastructure** wirtschaftliche Infrastruktur *nf* **economic integration** wirtschaftliche Integration *nf* **economic objective** Wirtschaftsziel (-e) *nn* **economic performance** Wirtschaftsleistung *nf* **economic planning** Wirtschaftsplanung *nf* **economic policy** Wirtschaftspolitik *nf* **economic sanction** wirtschaftliche Sanktion (-en) *nf* **economic slowdown** konjunkturelle Abkühlung *nf* **economic strategy** Wirtschaftsstrategie *nf* **economic superpower** wirtschaftliche Supermacht (-mächte) *nf* **economic survey** Wirtschaftsbericht (-e) *nm*

economic trend Wirtschaftstrend (-s) *nm*
economic union Wirtschaftsunion (-en) *nf*
economical *adj* wirtschaftlich *adj*
economics *npl* Volkswirtschaft *nf*
economist *n* Wirtschaftswissenschaftler (-)
nm
economy *n* Wirtschaft (-en) *nf* **advanced
economy** fortgeschrittene Wirtschaft *nf*
developing economy sich entwickelnde
Wirtschaft *nf* **free market economy** freie
Marktwirtschaft (-en) *nf* **global economy**
Weltwirtschaft (-) *nf* **economies of scale**
Kostendegression *nf* **national economy**
Staatswirtschaft *nf* **planned economy**
Planwirtschaft (-en) *nf* **underdeveloped
economy** unterentwickelte Wirtschaft (-en)
nf
**ECSC (European Coal and Steel
Community)** *abbr* Montanunion *nf*
ECU (European Currency Unit) *abbr* ECU
(Europäische Währungseinheit) (-s) *nm*
edge *n* **competitive edge** Wettbewerbsvorteil
(-e) *nm*
effect *n* Wirkung (-en) *nf* **financial effects** die
finanziellen Auswirkungen *nfpl*
efficiency *n* Leistungsfähigkeit *nf*
efficient *adj* leistungsfähig *adj*
EFT (electronic funds transfer) *abbr* EFT
(Europäischer Elektronischer Geldverkehr)
nm
**EFTA (European Free Trade
Association)** *abbr* EFTA (Europäische Freie
Handelsgemeinschaft) *nf*
elasticity *n* Elastizität *nf* **income elasticity**
Einkommenselastizität *nf* **elasticity of
demand** Nachfragenelastizität *nf* **elasticity
of production** Produktionselastizität *nf*
election *n* Wahl (-en) *nf* **general election**
Bundestagswahl (-en) *nf* **local election**
Landtagswahl (-en) *nf*, Gemeinderatswahl
(-en) *nf*
electronic *adj* elektronisch *adj* **electronic
banking** elektronische Abwicklung von
Bankgeschäften *nf* **electronic data processing** elektronische Datenverarbeitung *nf*
electronic mail elektronische Post *nf*
elimination *n* **elimination of tariffs**
Tarifabbau *nm*
email *n* elektronische Post *nf*
embargo *n* Embargo (-s) *nn* **to impose an
embargo** etwas mit einem Embargo belegen
to lift an embargo ein Embargo aufheben
trade embargo Handelsembargo (-s) *nn*
embassy *n* Botschaft (-en) *nf*
embezzle *vb* unterschlagen *vb*
embezzlement *n* Unterschlagung *nf*
embezzler *n* (jemand, der eine Unterschlagung begeht)
emergency *n* Notfall (-fälle) *nm* **emergency
fund** Hilfsfonds *nm*
emigration *n* Auswanderung *nf*
employ *vb* beschäftigen *vb*

employee *n* Arbeitnehmer (-) *nm* **employee
recruitment** Anwerbung *nf* **employee training** Personalausbildung *nf*
employer *n* **employers' liability insurance**
Arbeitgeberhaftpflichtversicherung *nf*
Arbeitgeber (-) *nm* **employers' federation**
Arbeitgeberverband (-ände) *nm*
employment *n* Arbeit *nf* **employment
agency** Arbeitsvermittlung *nf* **employment
contract** Arbeitsvertrag (-äge) *nm* **full employment** Vollbeschäftigung *nf* **employment
law** Arbeitsrecht (-e) *nn*
encashment *n* Einlösung *nf*
enclose *vb* beilegen *vb*
enclosure *n* Anlage (-n) *nf*
end *n* **end consumer** Endverbraucher (-) *nm*
end user Endabnehmer (-) *nm*
endorse *vb* (cheque) unterzeichnen *vb*
endorsement *n* Indossament *nn*
endowment *n* Stiftung (-en) *nf* **endowment
insurance** Lebensversicherung *nf* **endowment policy** Lebensversicherungspolice (-n)
nf
enforce *vb* (policy) durchsetzen *vb*
enforcement *n* Durchführung *nf*
engagement *n* (meeting) Termin (-e) *nm*
engineering *n* Maschinenbau *nm* **civil engineering** Tiefbau *nm* **electrical engineering**
Elektrotechnik *nf* **mechanical engineering**
Maschinenbau *nm* **precision engineering**
Feinmechanik *nf*
enhance *vb* (value) erhöhen *vb*
enlarge *vb* vergrößern *vb*
enquire *vb* fragen *vb*
enquiry *n* Anfrage (-n) *nf*
enterprise *n* (project) Unternehmen (-) *nn*
private enterprise Privatunternehmen (-) *nn*
entertain *vb* **to entertain a client** bewirten *vb*
entrepôt *n* Zwischenlager (-) *nn*
entrepreneur *n* Unternehmer (-) *nm*
entrepreneurial *adj* unternehmerisch *adj*
entry *n* **entry for free goods** Deklaration für
zollfreie Waren **entry into force** Inkrafttreten
nn **port of entry** Zollabfertigungshafen
(-häfen) *nm* **entry visa** Einreisevisum (-a) *nn*
equalization *n* **equalization of burdens**
Lastenausgleich *nm*
equalize *vb* ausgleichen *vb*
equilibrium *n* Gleichgewicht *nn*
equip *vb* ausstatten *vb*
equipment *n* Ausstattung *nf* **equipment
leasing** Investitionsgüterleasing *nn*
equity *n* Eigenkapital *nn* **equity capital**
Eigenkapital *nn* **equity financing**
Eigenfinanzierung *nf* **equity interests**
Kapitalbeteiligung *nf* **equity share**
Stammaktie (-n) *nf* **equity trading**
Aktienhandel *nm* **equity transaction**
Kapitalhandel *nm*
ergonomics *npl* Ergonomik *nf*
escalate *vb* eskalieren *vb*
escalation *n* (prices) Erhöhung (-en) *nf*

escalator *n* Rolltreppe (-n) *nf*
escudo *n* Escudo *nm*
establish *vb* gründen *vb*
establishment *n* Gründung *nf*
estate *n* estate agency, real estate agency
(US) Immobiliengesellschaft (-en) *nf* estate
agent, real estate agent (US)
Immobilienmakler (-) *nm*
estimate 1. *n* Schätzung (-en) *nf* estimate of
costs Schätzkosten *npl* **2.** *vb* schätzen *vb*
eurobond *n* Eurobond (-s) *nm*
eurocapital *n* Eurokapital *nn*
eurocheque *n* Euroscheck (-s) *nm*
eurocracy *n* Eurokratie *nf*
eurocrat *n* Eurokrat (-en) *nm*
eurocredit *n* Eurokredit (-e) *nm*
eurocurrency *n* Eurowährung (-en) *nf* eurocurrency market Eurogeldmarkt (-märkte)
nm
eurodollar *n* Eurodollar (-s) *nm*
eurofunds *npl* Eurokapital *nn*
euromarket *n* Euromarkt (-märkte) *nm*
euromerger *n* Eurofusion (-en) *nf*
euromoney *n* Eurogeld (-er) *nn*
European *adj* europäisch *adj* **European
Advisory Committee** Europäischer
Beratungsausschuß (-üsse) *nm* **European
Commission** EG-Kommission *nf* **European
Community (EC)** Europäische Gemeinschaft
(EG) *nf* **European Council** Europarat (-äte)
nm **European Court of Justice (ECJ)** Euro-
päischer Gerichtshof *nm* **European Deve-
lopment Fund (EDF)** Europäischer
Entwicklungsfonds *nm* **European Invest-
ment Bank (EIB)** Europäische
Investitionsbank *nf* **European Monetary
Agreement (EMA)** Europäisches
Währungsabkommen *nn* **European Mone-
tary Cooperation Fund (EMCF)** Europäischer
Fonds (in währungspolitischer
Zusammenarbeit) *nm* **European Monetary
System (EMS)** Europäisches
Währungssystem *nn* **European Monetary
Union (EMU)** Europäische Währungsunion
nf **European Parliament** Europaparlament
nn **European Recovery Plan** Europäischer
Wiederaufbauplan *nm* **European Regional
Development Fund (ERDF)** Europäischer
Regionalentwicklungsfonds *nm* **European
Social Fund (ESF)** Europäischer Sozialfonds
nm **European Unit of Account (EUA)** Europäische Rechnungseinheit (-en) *nf*
eurosceptic *n* Euroskeptiker *nm*
evade *vb* ausweichen (+ dat) *vb*
evasion *n* tax evasion Steuerhinterziehung *nf*
eviction *n* Exmittierung *nf*
ex *prep* ex factory/works ab Werk ex gratia
payment Sonderzahlung (-en) *nf* ex interest
payment ohne Zinsen ex quay ab Hafen ex repayment ohne Rückzahlung ex ship ab Schiff
ex stock ab Lager ex store/warehouse ab
Lager ex wharf ab Hafen

examination *n* Prüfung (-en) *nf*
examine *vb* prüfen *vb*
exceed *vb* überschreiten *vb*
excess *adj* excess capacity Überkapazität *nf*
excess demand inflation
Übernachfrageinflation *nf* excess profit(s)
tax Mehrgewinnsteuer *nf* excess reserves
Sonderrücklage *nf*
exchange *n* exchange broker Devisenmakler
(-) *nm* exchange cheque Austauschscheck
(-s) *nm* exchange clearing agreement
Devisenverrechnungsabkommen *nn*
exchange control Devisenkontrolle *nf*
foreign exchange Devisen *nfpl* exchange
market Devisenmarkt (-märkte) *nm*
exchange rate Wechselkurs (-e) *nm*
exchange rate mechanism (ERM)
Wechselkursmechanismus *nm* exchange
restrictions Devisenbeschränkungen *nfpl*
exchange risk Kursrisiko (-iken) *nn* Stock
Exchange Wertpapierbörse (-n) *nf*
excise *n* excise duty Verbrauchssteuer (-n) *nf*
the Board of Customs and Excise Minister-
ialabteilung für Zölle und Verbrauchssteuern
nf
exclude *vb* ausschließen *vb*
exclusion *n* exclusion clause
Ausschlußklausel (-n) *nf* exclusion zone
Sperrzone (-n) *nf*
executive 1. *adj* executive committee
Leitungsausschuß (-üsse) *nm* executive
compensation Vergütung für leitende
Angestellte *nf* executive duties
Führungsaufgaben *nfpl* executive hierarchy
Leitungspyramide *nf* executive personnel
Führungskräfte *nfpl* **2.** *n* leitender
Angestellte *nm*
exempt *adj* befreit von *adj* tax-exempt
steuerfrei *adj*
exemption *n* Befreiung *nf*
exhaust *vb* (reserves) erschöpfen *vb*
exhibit *vb* ausstellen *vb*
exhibition *n* Ausstellung (-en) *nf*
exorbitant *adj* maßlos *adj*
expand *vb* erweitern *vb*
expansion *n* Erweiterung *nf* expansion of
capital Kapitalsteigerung *nf* expansion of
trade Handelserweiterung *nf*
expectation *n* Erwartung (-en) *nf* consumer
expectations Verbrauchererwartungen *nfpl*
expedite *vb* beschleunigen *vb*
expenditure *n* Ausgaben *nfpl* expenditure
rate Unkostensatz (-sätze) *nm* state expenditure Staatsausgaben *nfpl* expenditure
taxes Ausgabesteuern *nfpl*
expense *n* Kosten *npl* expense account
Spesenkonto (-s) *nn* expense control
Kostenkontrolle (-n) *nf* entertainment
expenses Unterhaltungskosten *npl* travelling expenses, travel expenses (US)
Reisekosten *npl*
experience 1. *n* Erfahrung (-en) *nf* expe-

rience curve Lernkurve *nf* 2. *vb* erfahren *vb*
experienced *adj* erfahren *adj*
expert 1. *adj* Fach- *cpd* 2. *n* Experte (-n) *nm*
expertise *n* Fachwissen *nn*
expiration *n* Verfall *nm*
expire *vb* auslaufen *vb*
expiry, expiration (US) *n* Ablauf *nm* **expiry date, expiration** (US) Verfallstag (-e) *nm*
export 1. *adj* **export bill of lading** Konnossement (-s) *nn* **export credit** Exportkredit (-e) *nm* **export credit insurance** Exportkreditversicherung *nf* **export department** Exportabteilung (-en) *nf* **export-led growth** durch Export bedingtes Wachstum *nn* **export licence** Exportlizenz *nf* **export marketing** Exportmarketing *nn* **export operations** Exporttätigkeiten *nfpl* **export strategy** Exportstrategie (-n) *nf* **export subsidies** Exportzuschüsse *nmpl* **export surplus** Exportüberschuß *nm* **export tax** Ausfuhrsteuer (-n) *nf* **export trade** Exporthandel *nm* 2. *n* Export *nm* **export of capital** Kapitalausfuhr *nf* 3 *vb* exportieren *vb*
exporter *n* Exporteur (-e) *nm*
express *adj* **express agency** Schnelldienst *nm* **express delivery** Eilzustellung (-en) *nf* **express service** Eildienst *nm*
expropriate *vb* enteignen *vb*
expropriation *n* Enteignung *nf*
extend *vb* **to extend a contract** einen Vertrag verlängern **to extend credit** Kredit gewähren **to extend the range** die Reihe erweitern
extension *n* (of contract) Verlängerung (-en) *nf*
extent *n* **extent of cover** Versicherungsausmaß *nn*
external *adj* Auslands- *cpd* **external audit** Buchprüfung *nf*
extortion *n* Erpressung *nf*
extra *adj* zusätzlich *adj* **extra cost** Mehrkosten *npl* **extra profit** Mehrgewinn *nm*
extraordinary *adj* **extraordinary meeting** außerordentliche Versammlung (-en) *nf* **extraordinary value** außerordentlicher Wert (-e) *nm*
facility *n* Anlage (-n) *nf* **facility planning** Werksplanung *nf*
facsimile (fax) *n* Faxgerät (-e) *nn*
factor 1. *adj* **factor income** Factoring-Einkommen *nn* **factor market** Factoring-Markt (-märkte) *nm* **factor price** Erzeugerpreis (-e) *nm* 2. *n* (buyer of debts) Faktor (-en) *nm* **limiting factor** Einschränkung *nf* **factor of production** Produktionsfaktor (-en) *nm* 3 *vb* (debts) fakturieren *vb*
factoring *n* (of debts) Factoring *nn*
factory *n* **factory board** Vorstand (-ände) *nm*, Aufsichtsrat (-räte) *nm* **factory costs** Fertigungskosten *npl* **factory inspector** Ge-

werbeaufsichtsbeamte/r *nmf* **factory ledger** Hauptbuch (-bücher) *nn* **factory overheads** Fertigungsgemeinkosten *npl* **factory price** Preis ab Werk (-e) *nm*
fail *vb* (negotiations) versagen *vb* (attempts) versagen *vb*
failure *n* Versagen *nn*
fair *adj* fair *adj* **fair competition** lauterer Wettbewerb *nm* **fair market value** angemessener Marktpreis (-e) *nm* **fair rate of return** angemessene Verzinsung *nf* **fair-trade agreement** Preisbindungsabkommen (-) *nn* **fair-trade policy** Außenhandelspolitik auf der Basis gegenteiliger Vorteile *nf* **fair-trade practice** lautere Wettbewerbsmethode (-n) *nf* **fair trading** vertikale Preisbindung *nf* **fair wage** angemessener Lohn *nm*
fall due *vb* fällig werden *vb*
falling *adj* **falling prices** fallende Preise *nmpl* **falling rate of profit** fallende Gewinnspanne *nf*
false *adj* **false representation** Vorspiegelung falscher Tatsachen *nf*
falsification *n* Verfälschung *nf* **falsification of accounts** Kontenfälschung *nf*
family *n* Familie (-n) *nf* **family allowance** Kindergeld *nn* **family branding** Familienmarke *nf* **family corporation** Familien-Aktiengesellschaft (-en) *nf* **family income** Familieneinkommen *nn* **family industry** Familienindustrie *nf*
farm out *vb* an Subunternehmer vergeben *vb*
farming *n* Landwirtschaft *nf* **farming of taxes** Verpachtung von Steuern *nf* **farming subsidies** Agrarsubventionen *nfpl*
FAS (free alongside ship) *abbr* frei Längsseite Schiff
fast *adj* **fast-selling goods** Schnelldreher *npl* **fast track** Schnellspur *nf*
fault *n* Fehler (-) *nm* **minor fault** Kleinfehler (-) *nm* **serious fault** schwerer Defekt (-e) *nm* **to find fault with** kritisieren *vb*
faulty *adj* **faulty goods** fehlerhafte Ware (-n) *nf* **faulty workmanship** Herstellungsfehler (-) *nm*
favour *n* Gefallen (-) *nm* **to do sb a favour** jemandem einen Gefallen tun
favourable *adj* **favourable balance of payments** günstige Zahlungsbilanz *nf* **favourable balance of trade** günstige Handelsbilanz *nf* **favourable exchange** günstiger Umtausch *nm* **favourable price** günstiger Preis (-e) *nm* **favourable terms** günstige Bedingungen *nfpl*
fax 1. *n* Fax (-e) *nm* 2. *vb* faxen *vb*
feasibility *n* Durchführbarkeit *nf* **feasibility study** Durchführbarkeitsstudie (-n) *nf*
feasible *adj* durchführbar *adj*
federal *adj* Bundes- *cpd*
federation *n* Bund (Bünde) *nm*
fee *n* Gebühr (-en) *nf* **to charge a fee** eine Gebühr berechnen **to pay a fee** eine Gebühr

zahlen
feedback *n* Rückmeldung *nf* **to give feedback** Rückmeldung geben
fiat *n* **fiat money** Papiergeld ohne Deckung *nn*
fictitious *adj* **fictitious assets** fiktiver Vermögenswert *nm* **fictitious purchase** Scheinkauf (-e) *nm* **fictitious sale** Scheinverkauf *nm*
fidelity *n* **fidelity bond** Kautionsverpflichtung (-e) *nf* **fidelity insurance** Garantieversicherung *nf*
fiduciary *adj* **fiduciary bond** Kautionsverpflichtung *nf* **fiduciary issue** ungedeckte Notenausgabe *nf*
field *n* **field investigation** Umfrage (-n) *nf* **field manager** Außendienstleiter (-) *nm* **field personnel** Mitarbeiter im Außendienst *nmpl* **field research** Feldforschung *nf* **field test** Bewährung *nf* **field work** Außdienstarbeit *nf*
FIFO (first in first out) *abbr* Fifo-Methode (-n) *nf*
file **1.** *n* Akte (-n) *nf* **2.** *vb* ablegen *vb*
filing *n* **filing cabinet** Aktenschrank (-änke) *nm* **filing system** Ablagesystem (-e) *nn*
final *adj* **final accounts** Endabrechnung *nf* **final demand** letzte Mahnung (-en) *nf* **final entry** letzte Eintragung *nf* **final invoice** Schlußrechnung (-en) *nf* **final offer** endgültiges Angebot (-e) *nn* **final products** Enderzeugnisse *nnpl* **final settlement** Abschlußzahlung (-en) *nf* **final utility** Grenznutzen *nm*
finance **1.** *n* Finanzwesen *nn* **Finance Act** Finanzgesetz (-e) *nn* **finance bill** Finanzwechsel (-) *nm* **finance company** Finanzierungsgesellschaft (-en) *nf* **2.** *vb* finanzieren *vb*
financial *adj* finanziell *adj* **financial accounting** Finanzbuchhaltung *nf* **financial assets** finanzielle Aktiva *npl* **financial balance** Bilanz *nf* **financial company** Finanzierungsgesellschaft (-en) *nf* **financial consultancy** Finanzberatung *nf* **financial consultant** Finanzberater (-) *nm* **financial control** Finanzkontrolle *nf* **financial crisis** Finanzkrise (-n) *nf* **financial difficulty** finanzielle Schwierigkeit (-en) *nf* **financial exposure** finanzielles Engagement *nn* **financial incentive** finanzieller Anreiz (-e) *nm* **financial institution** Finanzinstitut (-e) *nn* **financial investment** Finanzinvestition *nf* **financial loan** Darlehen (-) *nn* **financial management** Finanzmanagement *nn* **financial market** Finanzmarkt (-märkte) *nm* **financial measures** finanzielle Maßnahmen *nfpl* **financial operation** Finanzgeschäft (-e) *nn* **financial planning** Finanzplanung *nf* **financial policy** Finanzpolitik *nf* **financial report** Finanzbericht (-e) *nm* **financial resources** Finanzmittel *nnpl* **financial risk** finanzielles Risiko (-iken) *nn* **financial**

situation Finanzlage *nf* **financial stability** finanzielle Stabilität *nf* **financial statement** Jahresabschluß (-üsse) *nm* **financial strategy** Finanzstrategie (-n) *nf* **financial structure** Finanzstruktur *nf* **financial year** Geschäftsjahr *nn*
financier *n* Finanzier (-s) *nm*
financing *n* Finanzierung *nf* **financing surplus** Finanzüberschuß (-üsse) *nm*
fine *adj* **fine rate of interest** günstiger Zinssatz *nm*
finished *adj* **finished goods** Fertigerzeugnisse *nnpl* **finished stock** Fertigwarenlager (-) *nn* **finished turnover** Umschlaghäufigkeit des Warenbestandes *nf*
fire* *vb* entlassen *vb*
firm *adj* fest *adj* **firm offer** festes Angebot (-e) *nn* **firm price** Festpreis (-e) *nm*
first *adj* **first bill of exchange** Primawechsel (-) *nm* **first class** erste Klasse *nf* **first-class paper** erstklassiger Wechsel (-) *nm* **first customer** erster Kunde (-n) *nm* **first-hand** erster Hand *nf* **first mortgage** erste Hypothek *nf* **first-rate** (investment) erstklassig *adj*
fiscal *adj* **fiscal agent** Hauptzahlungsagent (-en) *nm* **fiscal balance** Geschäftsbilanz *nf* **fiscal charges** steuerliche Belastung *nf* **fiscal measures** Finanzmaßnahmen *nfpl* **fiscal policy** Finanzpolitik *nf* **fiscal receipt** Steuerbeleg (-e) *nm* **fiscal year** Geschäftsjahr *nn* **fiscal year end (fye)** Geschäftsjahresende *nn* **fiscal zoning** Steuerklassifizierung *nf*
fix *vb* **to fix the price** den Preis festsetzen
fixed *adj* **fixed assets** Anlagevermögen *nn* **fixed asset turnover** Umsatz des Anlagevermögens *nm* **fixed budget** feststehendes Budget *nn* **fixed charges** feste Belastung (-en) *nf* **fixed costs** Fixkosten *npl* **fixed credit** Festsatzkredit (-e) *nm* **fixed income** festes Einkommen *nn* **fixed interest** Festzins (-e) *nm* **fixed liabilities** langfristige Verbindlichkeiten *nfpl* **fixed price** Festpreis (-e) *nm*
fixture *n* **fixtures and fittings** Anschlüsse und unbewegliches Inventar *npl*
flat *adj* **flat bond** Anleihe ohne Zinseinschluß (-n) *nf* **flat market** umsatzloser Markt (-märkte) *nm* **flat rate** Einheitstarif (-e) *nm* **flat-rate income tax** einheitlicher Einkommenssteuersatz (-sätze) *nm* **flat-rate tariff** Einheitstarif (-e) *nm*
flexibility *n* (of prices) Flexibilität *nf*
flexible *adj* **flexible budget** flexibles Budget (-s) *nn* **flexible exchange rate** flexibler Wechselkurs (-e) *nm* **flexible price** flexibler Preis (-e) *nm*
flexitime, flextime (US) *n* gleitende Arbeitszeit *nf*
flight *n* (in plane) Flug (-üge) *nm* **flight capital** Fluchtkapital *nn* **to book a flight** einen Flug buchen

float *vb* (currency) floaten *vb*, freigeben *vb*
floating *adj* **floating assets** Umlaufkapital *nn*
  floating exchange rate veränderlicher
  Wechselkurs (-e) *nm* **floating rate interest**
  veränderlicher Zinssatz (-sätze) *nm*
floor *n* **floor broker** Börsenmakler (-) *nm*
  shopfloor Verkaufsfläche (-n) *nf*, Werkstatt
  (-stätte) *nf*
flotation *n* Kapitalaufnahme durch Emission
  von Aktien *nf*
flow *n* **cash flow** Cashflow *nm* **flow chart**
  Flußdiagramm (-e) *nn* **flow line production**
  Reihenfertigung *nf* **flow of income**
  Einkommenszufluß *nm* **flow production**
  Reihenfertigung *nf*
fluctuate *vb* schwanken *vb*
fluctuation *n* Schwankung (-en) *nf* **fluctuation in sales** Absatzschwankungen *nfpl*
fluid *adj* flüssig *adj* **fluid market** veränderlicher Markt (-Märkte) *nm*
FOB (free on board) *abbr* frei an Bord
for *prep* **for sale** zu verkaufen
forced *adj* **forced currency** Zwangswährung
  (-en) *nf*
forecast 1. *n* Prognose (-n) *nf* 2. *vb*
  vorhersehen *vb*
forecasting *n* Vorhersage *nf*
foreclose *vb* kündigen *vb*
foreclosure *n* Wettbewerbsausschluß *nm*
foreign *adj* ausländisch *adj* **foreign aid**
  Auslandshilfe *nf* **foreign aid programme**
  Auslandshilfsprogramm *nn* **foreign bank**
  Auslandsbank (-en) *nf* **foreign company**
  Auslandsunternehmen (-) *nn* **foreign competition** Auslandskonkurrenz *nf* **foreign
  currency** Fremdwährung (-en) *nf* **foreign
  exchange** Devisen *nfpl* **foreign exchange
  dealer** Devisenhändler (-) *nm* **foreign
  exchange market** Devisenmarkt (-märkte)
  nm **foreign currency holdings**
  Auslandsgelder *nnpl* **foreign investment**
  Auslandsinvestitionen *nfpl* **foreign loan**
  Auslandskredit (-e) *nm* **foreign travel**
  Auslandsreise (-n) *nf*
foreman *n* Vorarbeiter (-) *nm*
forestall *vb* vorbeugen *vb*
forestalling *adj* **forestalling policy** produk-
  tionsorientierte Wirtschaftspolitik *nf*
forfeit 1. *n* Kaduzierung *nf* (shares)
  Aktienkaduzierung *nf* 2. *vb* verlieren *vb*,
  verwirken *vb*
forfeiture *n* Kaduzierung *nf*
forgery *n* Fälschung *nf*
form *n* (document) Formular (-e) *nn*
formal *adj* formell *adj* **formal agreement**
  Abkommen *nn* **formal contract** offizieller
  Vertrag (-äge) *nm*
formality *n* **customs formalities**
  Zollformalitäten *nfpl* **to observe formalities**
  die Formalitäten beachten
formation *n* (of company) Gründung (-en) *nf*
  capital formation Kapitalbildung *nf*

forward 1. *adj* **forward contract**
  Terminkontrakt (-e) *nm* **forward cover**
  Terminsicherung *nf* **forward market**
  Terminmarkt (-märkte) *nm* **forward transaction** Termingeschäft (-e) *nn* 2. *vb* befördern
  vb
forwarder *n* Spediteur (-e) *nm*
forwarding *n* Expedition *nf* **forwarding
  agency** Spedition (-en) *nf* **forwarding agent**
  Spediteur (-e) *nm* **forwarding charges**
  Versandgebühren *nfpl* **forwarding note**
  Frachtbrief (-e) *nm*
found *vb* **to found a company** ein Unternehmen gründen
founder *n* Gründer (-) *nm*
fraction *n* Bruchteil (-e) *nm*
fractional *adj* Bruch- *cpd* **fractional money**
  Scheidemünzen *nfpl* **fractional shares** vor-
  geschriebene Mindestreserven *nfpl*
franc *n* **Belgian franc** Belgischer Franken (-)
  nm **French franc** Französischer Franken (-)
  nm **Swiss franc** Schweizer Franken (-) *nm*
franchise 1. *adj* **franchise outlet** franchisierter Ortshändler (-) *nm* 2. *n* Konzession
  (-en) *nf* 3 *vb* franchisieren *vb*
franchisee *n* Franchisenehmer (-) *nm*
franchising *n* Franchising *nn*
franchisor *n* Franchisegeber (-) *nm*
franco *adj* frei *adj* **franco domicile** frei Haus
  franco price frei Preis **franco zone** frei Zone
frank *vb* frankieren *vb*
franked *adj* frankiert *adj* **franked income**
  Dividendenerträge nach Steuern *nmpl*
franking *n* **franking machine**
  Frankiermaschine (-n) *nf*
fraud *n* Betrug *nm*
fraudulent *adj* betrügerisch *adj*
free *adj* **free agent** unabhängige
  Handelsvertretung (-en) *nf* **free alongside
  ship (FAS)** frei Kai **free competition**
  Wettbewerbsfreiheit *nf* **free delivery** Lieferung frei Bestimmungsort *nf* **duty free**
  zollfrei *adj* **free economy** freie Wirtschaft *nf*
  free entry Eintritt frei *nm* **free goods** zollfreie
  Waren *nfpl* **free market** freier Markt (Märkte)
  nm **free market economy** freie
  Marktwirtschaft (-en) *nf* **free movement of
  goods** freier Warenverkehr *nm* **free of
  charge** kostenlos *adj* **free of freight** ohne
  Frachtgebühr **free of tax** steuerfrei *adj* **free
  on board (FOB)** frei Schiff **free on quay** frei
  Hafen **free port** frei Hafen **free trade** freier
  Handel *nm* **free trade area** Freihandelszone
  (-n) *nf*
freedom *n* **freedom of choice** freie Wahl *nf*
Freefone (R) (GB) *n* Telephongebühr bar
  bezahlt *nf*
freelance *adj* freiberuflich *adj*
freelancer (GB) *n* Freiberufliche/r *nmf*
Freepost (R) (GB) *n* Postgebühr bar bezahlt
  nf
freeze 1. *n* (prices, wages) Stopp (-s) *nm*

2. *vb* (prices, wages) einen Lohnstopp durchführen

freight *n* Frachtgut *nn* **freight forwarder** Spediteur (-e) *nm* **freight traffic** Frachtverkehr *nm*

freighter *n* Befrachter (-) *nm*

frequency *n* Frequenz *nf*

friendly *adj* freundlich *adj* **Friendly Society** Hilfskasse *nf*

fringe *adj* **fringe benefits** Lohnnebenleistungen *nfpl* **fringe market** Nebenmarkt (-märkte) *nm*

frontier *n* Grenze (-n) *nf*

fronting *n* Rückversicherung *nf*

frozen *adj* **frozen assets** eingefrorene Guthaben *nnpl* **frozen credits** eingefrorener Kredit *nm*

FT Index (Financial Times Index) *n* Index der Financial Times *nm*

full *adj* **full cost** Vollkosten *npl* **full liability** volle Haftung *nf* **full payment** volle Zahlung (-en) *nf*

full-time *adj/adv* Vollzeit- *cpd* **full-time worker** Vollzeitkraft (-kräfte) *nf*

function *n* (role) Funktion *nf*

functional *adj* **functional analysis** Funktionsanalyse *nf* **functional organization** Berufsverband (-bände) *nm*

fund **1.** *n* Fonds *nm* **2.** *vb* finanzieren *vb*

funded *adj* **funded debt** fundierte Schulden *nfpl*

funding *n* Finanzierung *nf* **funding bonds** Umschuldungsanleihe *nf*

funds *npl* Kapital *nn* **funds flow** gesamtwirtschaftliche Finanzierung *nf* **funds surplus** außerordentliche Reservefonds *nm*

furlough (US) **1.** *n* Urlaub *nm* **2.** *vb* Urlaub machen

future *adj* **future commodity** Warentermingeschäft *nn* **future delivery** Terminlieferung *nf* **future goods** Terminware *nf*

futures *npl* Termingeschäfte *nnpl* **futures contract** Terminkontrakt (-e) *nm* **futures exchange** Markt für Termingeschäfte *nm* **futures market** Terminkontraktmarkt *nm* **futures marketing** Terminkontraktmarketing *nn* **futures price** Terminkontraktpreis (-e) *nm* **futures trading** Terminhandel *nm*

fye (fiscal year end) *abbr* Geschäftsjahresende *nn*

gain **1.** *n* Gewinn *nm* **capital gain** Kapitalgewinn *nm* **capital gains tax** Kapitalgewinnsteuer *nf* **gain in value** Wertgewinn (-e) *nm* **gain sharing** Gewinnbeteiligung *nf* **2.** *vb* gewinnen *vb*

gainful *adj* **gainful employment** Erwerbstätigkeit *nf*

galloping *adj* galoppierend *adj* **galloping inflation** galoppierende Inflation *nf*

Gallup *n* **Gallup poll (R)** Meinungsumfrage (-n) *nf*

gap *n* **population gap** geburtenschwache Jahrgänge *nmpl* **trade gap** Handelsbilanzdefizit (-e) *nn*

gas *n* **natural gas** Erdgas *nn*

GATT (General Agreement on Tariffs and Trade) *abbr* GATT *nn*

gazump *vb* an einen Höherbietenden verkaufen

GDP (Gross Domestic Product) *abbr* Bruttoinlandsprodukt *nn*

general *adj* **general accounting** Buchhaltung *nf* **general agencies (US)** Generalvertretungen *nfpl* **general agent** Generalvertreter (-) *nm* **general average** Durchschnitt *nm* **general election** Bundestagswahl (-en) *nf* **general management** allgemeine Verwaltung *nf* **general manager** Manager (-) *nm* **general partner** Vollhafter (-) *nm* **general partnership** allgemeine Personengesellschaft (-en) *nf* **general strike** Generalstreik (-s) *nm*

generate *vb* **to generate income** Einkommen erwirtschaften

generation *n* **income generation** Einkommenserwirtschaften *nn*

generosity *n* Großzügigkeit *nf*

gentleman *n* **gentleman's agreement** Gentlemen's Agreement (-s) *nn*, mündliche Absprache (-n) *nf*

gilt-edged *adj* erstklassig *adj* **gilt-edged market** Markt für Staatspapiere (Märkte) *nm* **gilt-edged security** Staatspapier (-e) *nn*

gilts *npl* Staatspapiere *nnpl*

giveaway *n* Schleuderpreis (-e) *nm*

global *adj* global *adj* **global economy** Weltwirtschaft *nf* **global market** Weltmarkt (-märkte) *nm* **global marketing** weltweites Marketing *nn*

globalization *n* Globalisierung *nf*

GMT (Greenwich Mean Time) *abbr* Greenwich Mean Time

gnome *n* **the Gnomes of Zurich** die Züricher Gnomen *nmpl*

GNP (Gross National Product) *abbr* Bruttosozialprodukt *nn*

go-slow *n* (strike) Bummelstreik (-s) *nm*

going *adj* gängig *adj* **going concern** arbeitendes Unternehmen (-) *nn*

gold *n* Gold *nn* **gold bullion** Barrengold *nn* **gold coin** Goldmünze (-n) *nf* **gold market** Goldmarkt (-märkte) *nm* **gold reserves** Goldreserven *nfpl* **gold standard** Goldstandard *nm*

golden *adj* **golden handcuffs** Vergünstigungen *nfpl* **golden handshake** hohe Abfindung (-en) *nf* **golden hello** Einstandsgeld *nn* **golden parachute** großzügige Abfindung (-en) *nf*

goods *npl* Waren *nfpl* **bulk goods** Massengüter *nnpl* **domestic goods** Haushaltswaren *nfpl* **export goods** Exportartikel *nmpl* **import goods**

Importartikel *nmpl* **goods on approval** Waren auf Probe *nfpl* **goods in process** Transitgüter *nnpl* **goods in progress** Transitwaren *nfpl* **goods on consignment** Konsignationswaren *nfpl* **goods transport** Güterverkehr *nm*

goodwill *n* Goodwill *nm*

govern *vb* regieren *vb*

government *n* Regierung (-en) *nf* **government body** Regierungsausschuß (-üsse) *nm* **government bond** Staatsanleihe (-n) *nf* **government enterprise** Regierungsunternehmen (-) *nn* **government loan** Staatsanleihe (-n) *nf* **government policy** Regierungspolitik *nf* **government sector** Regierungssektor (-en) *nm* **government security** Staatspapiere *nnpl* **government subsidy** Regierungszuschuß (-üsse) *nm*

graduate 1. *n* (of university) Graduierte/r *nmf* 2. *vb* graduieren *vb*

grant 1. *n* (of a patent) Erteilung *nf* **regional grant** regionale Subvention *nf* 2. *vb* gewähren *vb*

graphics *npl* **computer graphics** Computergrafik *nf*

gratuity *n* Trinkgeld (-er) *nn*

green *adj* **Green Card** Aufenthaltserlaubnis (-sse) *nf* **green currency** grüne Dollarwährung *nf* **green pound** grünes Pfund *nn*

Greenwich *n* **Greenwich Mean Time (GMT)** Greenwich Mean Time *nf*

grievance *n* Beschwerdepunkt (-e) *nm*

gross *adj* brutto *adj* **gross amount** Bruttosumme *nf* **gross domestic product (GDP)** Bruttoinlandsprodukt *nn* **gross interest** Bruttozins *nm* **gross investment** Bruttoinvestition *nf* **gross loss** Bruttoverlust (-e) *nm* **gross margin** Bruttospanne (-n) *nf* **gross national product (GNP)** Bruttosozialprodukt *nn* **gross negligence** grobe Fahrlässigkeit *nf* **gross output** Bruttoproduktion *nf* **gross sales** Bruttoumsatz *nm* **gross weight** Bruttogewicht *nn*

group *n* **group insurance** Gruppenversicherung *nf* **group of countries** Länderblock (-s) *nm* **group travel** Gruppenreise *nf*

growth *n* Wachstum *nn* **annual growth rate** jährliche Wachstumsrate (-n) *nf* **economic growth** Wirtschaftswachstum *nn* **export-led growth** durch Export bedingtes Wachstum *nn* **market growth** Marktwachstum *nn* **growth rate** Wachstumsrate (-n) *nf* **sales growth** Verkaufssteigerung *nf* **growth strategy** Wachstumsstrategie (-n) *nf*

guarantee *n* Garantie (-n) *nf* **quality guarantee** Qualitätsgarantie (-n) *nf*

guarantor *n* Garantiegeber (-) *nm*

guest *n* **guest worker** Gastarbeiter (-) *nm*

guild *n* Verein (-e) *nm*

guilder *n* Gulden (-) *nm*

h *abbr* (hour) St. (Stunde) *abbr*

half *n* Hälfte (-n) *nf* **half-an-hour** eine halbe Stunde *nf* **half-board** Halbpension *nf* **half-pay** Halblohn *nm* **half-price** halber Preis *nm* **to reduce sth by half** um die Hälfte reduzieren **half-year** Halbjahr (-e) *nn*

hall *n* **exhibition hall** Ausstellungshalle (-n) *nf*

hallmark *n* Feingehaltsstempel (-) *nm*

halt *vb* (inflation) stoppen *vb*

halve *vb* halbieren *vb*

hand *n* **in hand** noch nicht fertiggestellt **to hand** zur Hand

hand over *vb* überreichen *vb*

handbook *n* Handbuch (-bücher) *nn*

handle *vb* (deal) handeln mit *vb* (money) verwalten *vb* umgehen mit *vb* **handle with care** Vorsicht - zerbrechlich!

handling *n* **handling charges** Ladekosten *npl* **data handling** Datenverarbeitung *nf*

handmade *adj* handgearbeitet *adj*

handshake *n* Händedruck (-ücke) *nm*

handwritten *adj* handgeschrieben *adj*

handy *adj* praktisch *adj*

hang on *vb* (wait) warten *vb* (on telephone) am Apparat bleiben *vb*

hang together *vb* (argument) zusammenhängen *vb*

hang up *vb* (telephone) aufhängen *vb*

harbour *n* Hafen (Häfen) *nm* **harbour authorities** Hafenbehörden *nfpl* **harbour dues** Hafengeld *nn* **harbour facilities** Hafenanlagen *nfpl* **harbour fees** Hafengebühren *nfpl*

hard *adj* **hard bargain** harte Forderungen *nfpl* **hard cash** Bargeld *nn* **hard currency** harte Währung (-en) *nf* **hard disk** Festplatte (-n) *nf* **hard-earned** schwer verdient **hard-hit** schwer betroffen **hard-line** harte Linie *nf* **hard loan** hartes Darlehen (-) *nn* **hard news/information** konkrete Information *nf* **hard price** fester Preis *nm* **hard sell** aggressive Verkaufsmethode *nf* **the hard facts** die Tatsachen *nfpl* **hard-working** fleißig *adj*

hardware *n* **computer hardware** Computerhardware *nf*

haul *n* **long-haul** Langstrecken- *cpd* **short-haul** Kurzstrecken- *cpd*

haulage, freight (US) *n* **road haulage** Beförderung *nf* **haulage company** Kraftverkehrsunternehmen (-) *nn*, Spedition (-en) *nf*

haulier *n* Transportunternehmen (-) *nn*

hazard *n* Gefahr (-en) *nf* **natural hazard** natürliche Gefahr *nf* **occupational hazard** Berufsrisiko (-iken) *nn*

hazardous *adj* gefährlich *adj*

head 1. *adj* **head accountant** Chefbuchhalter (-) *nm* **head office** Hauptverwaltung (-en) *nf* 2. *n* **at the head of** an der Spitze von **head of department** Abteilungsleiter (-) *nm* **head of**

government Regierungschef (-s) *nm* **per head** pro Kopf **to be head of** führen **3** *vb* (department) leiten *vb*

head for *vb* zugehen auf *vb*

headed *adj* **headed notepaper** Papier mit Briefkopf *nn*

heading *n* Überschrift (-en) *nf*

headquarters *n* Hauptsitz *nm*

headway *n* **to make headway** vorankommen *vb*

health *n* **health benefits** Kassenleistungen *nfpl* **health care industry** Gesundheitswesen *nn* **health hazard** Gesundheitsgefahr (-en) *nf* **industrial health** Arbeitshygiene *nf* **health insurance** Krankenversicherung *nf* **Ministry of Health** Gesundheitsministerium (-ien) *nn*

healthy *adj* **finances** solide *adj*

heavy *adj* **heavy-duty** strapazierfähig *adj* **heavy goods vehicle** Lastkraftwagen (-) *nm* **heavy industry** Schwerindustrie *nf* **heavy trading** hohe(n) Umsätze *npl* **heavy user** Dauerbenutzer (-) *nm*

hedge *n* **hedge against inflation** Inflationssicherung *nf* **hedge clause (US)** Schutzklausel (-n) *nf*

hidden *adj* **hidden assets** verstecktes Vermögen *nn* **hidden defect** versteckter Fehler (-) *nm*

hierarchy *n* (corporate) Hierarchie (-n) *nf* **data hierarchy** Datenhierarchie *nf* **hierarchy of needs** Bedürfnishierarchie (-n) *nf*

high *adj* **high-class** erstklassig *adj* **high finance** Hochfinanz *nf* **high-grade** hochwertig *adj* **high-income** mit hohem Einkommen **high-level** Spitzen- *cpd* **high-powered** einflußreich *adj* **high-priced** teuer *adj* **high-ranking** von hohem Rang **high-risk** risikoreich *adj* **high season** Hochsaison (-s) *nf* **hi-tech** Hochtechnologie- *cpd*

higher *adj* **higher bid** höheres Angebot (-e) *nn*

hire **1.** *n* Mieten *nn* **hire charges** Mietkosten *npl* **hire contract** Mietvertrag (-äge) *nm* **for hire** zu vermieten **hire purchase** Teilzahlungskauf *nm* **2.** *vb* (person) mieten *vb*

history *n* **employment/work history** Berufserfahrung *nf*

hit *vb* **hit-or-miss** ungenau *adj*, nachlässig *adj* **to hit the headlines** Schlagzeilen machen **to hit the market** einschlagen *vb* **to be hard hit by** von etwas schwer betroffen sein

HO (head office) *abbr* Hauptverwaltung (-en) *nf*

hoard *vb* horten *vb*

hold *vb* **to hold a meeting** eine Sitzung abhalten **hold area** Wartezone (-n) *nf* **to hold sth as security** als Sicherheit halten **to hold sb liable** haftbar machen für **on hold** (on phone) warten **hold queue, hold line (US)** Warteschlange (-n) *nf* **to hold sb**

responsible jemanden für etwas verantwortlich halten/machen

hold back *vb* (not release) zurückhalten *vb*

hold on *vb* (on phone) warten *vb*

hold over *vb* (to next period) verschieben *vb*

hold up *vb* (delay) aufhalten *vb* (withstand scrutiny) verzögern *vb*

holder *n* Inhaber (-) *nm* **joint holder** Mitinhaber (-) *nm* **licence holder** Lizenzinhaber (-) *nm* **office holder** amtierend *adj* **policy holder** Versicherte/r *nmf*

holding *n* Beteiligung (-en) *nf* **holding company** Holding-Gesellschaft (-en) *nf* **foreign exchange holdings** Devisenbestände *nmpl* **majority/minority holding** Mehrheitsbeteiligung/Minderheitsbeteiligung *nf* **to have holdings** eine Beteiligung besitzen

holdup *n* Verzögerung (-en) *nf*

holiday, vacation (US) *n* **bank holiday (GB)** öffentlicher Feiertag (-e) *nm* **on holiday, on vacation (US)** auf Urlaub **holiday pay** Urlaubsgeld *nn* **tax holiday** Steuerfreijahre *nnpl*

home *n* **home address** Heimatanschrift *nf* **home buyer** Eigenheimerwerber (-) *nm* **home country** Heimat *nf* **home delivery** Lieferung frei Haus *nf* **home industry** Inlandsindustrie (-n) *nf* **home loan** Hypothek (-en) *nf* **home market** Binnenmarkt (-märkte) *nm* **home owner** Hausbesitzer (-) *nm* **home sales** Inlandsverkäufe *nmpl* **home service** Zustelldienst *nm* **home shopping** Home-Shopping *nn*

honorary *adj* ehrenamtlich *adj*

horizontal *adj* **horizontal analysis** horizontale Analyse *nf* **horizontal integration** horizontale Integration *nf*

host *n* Gastgeber (-) *nm* **host country** Gastland (-länder) *nn*

hot *adj* **hot line** heißer Draht *nm* **hot money** heißes Geld *nn* **hot seat** Schleudersitz *nm* **to be in hot demand** Verkaufsschlager sein

hotel *n* Hotel (-s) *nn* **hotel accommodation** Hotelunterkunft *nf* **hotel chain** Hotelkette (-n) *nf* **five-star hotel** Hotel mit 5 Sternen (-s) *nn* **hotel industry/trade** Hotelindustrie *nf* **hotel management** Hotelverwaltung *nf* **to run a hotel** ein Hotelgeschäft betreiben

hour *n* **after hours** nach Betriebsschluß **business hours** Geschäftsstunden *nfpl* **busy hours (US)** Spitzenzeiten *nfpl* **fixed hours** festgesetzte Arbeitszeit (-en) *nf* **office hours** Geschäftsstunden *nfpl* **per hour** pro Stunde **per hour output** Produktion pro Stunde *nf*

hourly *adj* stündlich *adj* **hourly-paid work** nach Stunden bezahlte Arbeit *nf* **hourly rate** Stundenlohn (-öhne) *nm* **hourly workers** Stundenlohnarbeiter *npl*

house *n* **clearing house** Clearingstelle (-n) *nf* **house duty (US)** Haussteuer (-n) *nf* **house journal/magazine** Firmenzeitschrift (-en) *nf* **mail-order house** Versandhaus (-häuser) *nn*

packing house (US) Konservenfabrik *nf*
house prices Hauspreise *nmpl* **publishing house** Verlag (-e) *nm* **house sale** Hausverkauf (-äufe) *nm* **house telephone** Haustelefon (-e) *nn*
household *n* Haushalt (-e) *nm* **household expenditure** Haushaltsausgaben *nfpl* **household goods** Haushaltswaren *nfpl* **household survey** Haushaltsumfrage (-n) *nf*
householder *n* Hausinhaber (-) *nm*
housewares (US) *npl* Haushaltswaren *nfpl*
housing *n* **housing estate, tenement** (US) Wohnsiedlung (-en) *nf* **housing industry** Wohnungsbauindustrie *nf* **housing project** Wohnungsbauprojekt (-e) *nn* **housing scheme** Wohnungsbauprogramm (-e) *nn*
hull *n* Schiffskörper (-) *nm* **hull insurance** Schiffskörperversicherung *nf*
human *adj* **human relations** Personalbeziehungen *nfpl* **human resource management (HRM)** Personalmanagement *nn* **human resources** Personal *nn*, Arbeitskräfte *nfpl*
hundred *adj* **one hundred per cent** hundert Prozent
hydroelectricity *n* durch Wasserkraft erzeugte Energie
hype *n* übertriebene Werbung *nf*
hyperinflation *n* übermäßige Inflation *nf*
hypermarket *n* Verbrauchergroßmarkt (-märkte) *nm*
hypothesis *n* Hypothese (-n) *nf*
idle *adj* ungenutzt *adj* **idle capacity** freie Kapazität *nf*
illegal *adj* illegal *adj*
implication *n* **this will have implications for our sales** das hat Folgen für unseren Absatz
import 1. *n* Import *nm*, Einfuhr *nf* **import agent** Importagent (-en) *nm* **import barrier** Importschranke (-n) *nf* **import control** Importkontrolle (-n) *nf* **import department** Importabteilung (-en) *nf* **import duty** Einfuhrzoll *nm* **import licence** Einfuhrlizenz (-en) *nf* **import office** Importamt (-ämter) *nn* **import quota** Einfuhrquote (-n) *nf* **import restrictions** Einfuhrbeschränkungen *nfpl* **import surplus** Einfuhrüberschuß (-üsse) *nm* 2. *vb* importieren *vb*
importation *n* Import *nm*
importer *n* Importeur (-e) *nm*
importing *adj* **importing country** Importland (-länder) *nn*
impose *vb* **to impose a tax** eine Steuer auferlegen **to impose restrictions** Beschränkungen auferlegen
imposition *n* (of tax) Belastung *nf*
impound *vb* beschlagnahmen *vb*
imprint *n* **to take an imprint** (credit card) einen Abdruck machen, abdrucken
improve *vb* verbessern *vb* **we must improve our performance** wir müssen unsere Leistung verbessern

inadequate *adj* unzureichend *adj*
incentive *n* Anreiz (-e) *nm*
incidental *adj* **incidental expenses** Nebenkosten *npl*
include *vb* **our price includes delivery** Lieferung ist im Preis enthalten **taxes are included** Steuern sind im Preis enthalten
inclusive *adj* **inclusive of tax and delivery costs** einschließlich Steuern und Lieferkosten **the prices quoted are inclusive** die angegebenen Preise sind Gesamtpreise
income *n* Einkommen *nn* **gross income** Bruttoeinkommen *nn* **net income** Nettoeinkommen *nn* **private income** Privateinkommen *nn* **income tax** Einkommensteuer (-n) *nf*
inconvenience *n* Unannehmlichkeit *nf*
inconvenient *adj* ungelegen *adj*
increase 1. *n* **increase in the cost of living** Erhöhung der Lebenshaltungskosten **price increase** Preiserhöhung *nf* **wage increase** Lohnerhöhung (-en) *nf* 2. *vb* (prices, taxes) erhöhen *vb*
incur *vb* (expenses) machen *vb*
indebted *adj* verpflichtet *adj*
indemnify *vb* entschädigen *vb*
indemnity *n* Schadenersatz *nm* **indemnity insurance** Schadenersatzversicherung *nf*
index *n* Index (-e) *nm* **cost of living index** Lebenshaltungskostenindex (-e) *nm* **growth index** Wachstumsindex (-e) *nm* **price index** Preisindex (-e) *nm* **share index** Aktienindex (-e) *nm*
indicate *vb* hinweisen auf *vb*
indication *n* Hinweis (-e) *nm*
indirect *adj* indirekt *adj* **indirect cost** indirekte Kosten *npl* **indirect expenses** indirekte Kosten *npl* **indirect tax** indirekte Steuer (-n) *nf*
industrial *adj* industriell *adj* **industrial accident** Arbeitsunfall (-fälle) *nm* **industrial arbitration** Schiedsgerichtsverfahren (-) *nn* **industrial democracy** Mitbestimmung *nf* **industrial dispute** Arbeitskampf (-kämpfe) *nm* **industrial expansion** industrielle Ausweitung *nf* **industrial region** Industriegebiet (-e) *nn* **industrial relations** industrielle Arbeitsbeziehungen *nfpl* **industrial tribunal** Arbeitsgericht (-e) *nn* **industrial union** Industriegewerkschaft (-en) *nf*
industry *n* Industrie (-n) *nf*
inefficient *adj* ineffizient *adj*
inferior *adj* (goods) (von) minderer Qualität, minderwertig *adj*
inflation *n* Inflation *nf* **rate of inflation** Inflationsrate (-n) *nf*
inflationary *adj* inflationär *adj* **inflationary gap** Inflationslücke (-n) *nf* **inflationary spiral** Inflationsspirale (-n) *nf*
inform *vb* informieren *vb*
information *n* Information (-en) *nf* **information desk** Informationsschalter (-) *nm* **infor-**

mation management Marktforschung *nf*
information office Informationsbüro (-s) *nn*
information processing Datenverarbeitung
nf **information retrieval**
Informationswiedergewinnung *nf* **information storage** Datenspeicherung *nf* **information systems** Informationssysteme *nnpl*
information technology (IT)
Informationstechnologie (-n) *nf*
infrastructure *n* Infrastruktur (-en) *nf*
inherit *vb* erben *vb*
inheritance *n* Erbe (-n) *nn* **inheritance laws**
Erbschaftsgesetze *nnpl*
inhouse *adj* **inhouse training** *n* betriebliche
Ausbildung *nf*
injunction *n* gerichtliche Verfügung (-en) *nf*
to take out an injunction eine gerichtliche
Verfügung erwirken
inland *adj* Inlands- *cpd* **the Inland Revenue,
the Internal Revenue Service (IRS)** (US)
Finanzamt (-ämter) *nn*
insider *n* Insider (-) *nm* **insider dealing,
insider trading** (US) Insidergeschäfte *nnpl*
insist on *vb* bestehen auf (dat) *vb*
insolvency *n* Zahlungsunfähigkeit *nf*
insolvent *adj* zahlungsunfähig *adj*
inspect *vb* besichtigen *vb*, prüfen *vb*
inspection *n* (customs) (Zoll-)Kontrolle (-n) *nf*
inspector *n* Inspektor (-en) *nm* **customs
inspector** Zollinspektor (-en) *nm*
instability *n* Instabilität *nf*
instal(l) *vb* installieren *vb*
installation *n* Installation *nf*
instalment, installment (US) *n* Rate (-n) *nf*
institute *n* Institut (-e) *nn*
institution *n* Anstalt (-en) *nf* **credit institution**
Kreditanstalt (-en) *nf*
instruction *n* Anweisung (-en) *nf* **instruction
book** Bedienungsanleitung (-en) *nf* **instruction sheet** Bedienungsanleitung (-en) *nf* **to
follow instructions** Anweisungen befolgen
insurable *adj* **insurable risk**
Versicherungsrisiko (-iken) *nn*
insurance *n* Versicherung *nf* **insurance agent**
Versicherungsvertreter (-) *nm* **insurance
broker** Versicherungsmakler (-) *nm* **car
insurance** Autoversicherung *nf* **insurance
certificate** Versicherungspolice (-n) *nf* **insurance company** Versicherungsgesellschaft
(-en) *nf* **comprehensive insurance**
Vollkaskoversicherung *nf* **insurance contract** Versicherungsvertrag (-äge) *nm* **fire
insurance** Brandversicherung *nf* **insurance
fund** Versicherungsfonds (-) *nm* **National
Insurance (GB)** Sozialversicherung *nf* **insurance policy** Versicherungspolice (-n) *nf*
insurance premium Versicherungsprämie
(-n) *nf* **insurance representative**
Versicherungsvertreter (-) *nm* **insurance
salesperson** Versicherungsvertreter (-) *nm*
third party insurance
Haftpflichtversicherung *nf* **to take out insu-**

rance eine Versicherung abschließen **insurance underwriter** Versicherungsträger (-)
nm **unemployment insurance**
Arbeitslosenversicherung *nf*
insure *vb* versichern *vb*
intangible *adj* **intangible asset** immaterielle
Aktiva *npl*
intensive *adj* intensiv *adj* **capital-intensive**
kapitalintensiv *adj* **labour-intensive**
arbeitsintensiv *adj*
interest *n* Zinsen *nmpl* **interest-bearing**
zinstragend *adj* **interest-free** zinslos *adj*
interest period Zinsperiode (-n) *nf* **interest
rate** Zinskurs (-e) *nm* **to bear interest** Zinsen
tragen **to charge interest** Zinsen berechnen
to pay interest Zinsen zahlen
interface *n* Schnittstelle (-n) *nf*
interim *adj* vorläufig *adj*
intermediary *adj* vermittelnd *adj*, Zwischen-
cpd
internal *adj* **internal audit** innerbetriebliche
Revision *nf* **internal auditor** innerbetrieblicher Prüfer (-) *nm* **the Internal Revenue
Service (IRS) (US)** Finanzamt (-ämter) *nn*
international *adj* international *adj* **international agreement** internationales
Abkommen (-) *nn* **international competition**
internationale Konkurrenz *nf* **International
Date Line** Datumsgrenze (-n) *nf* **international organization** Weltunternehmen (-) *nn*
international trade Welthandel *nm*
intervene *vb* intervenieren *vb*
intervention *n* Intervention (-en) *nf* **state
intervention** staatliche Intervention *nf*
interview 1. *n* Vorstellungsgespräch (-e) *nn*
to attend for interview sich vorstellen *vr* **to
hold an interview** ein Vorstellungsgespräch
führen **to invite sb to interview** zum Vorstellungsgespräch einladen 2. *vb* ein Vorstellungsgespräch mit jemandem führen *vb*
introduce *vb* (product) ein Produkt auf dem
Markt bringen *vb*
inventory *n* Inventar (-e) *nn* **inventory control** Bestandskontrolle *nf*
invest *vb* (money) investieren *vb*
investment *n* Investition (-en) *nf* **investment
adviser** Anlageberater (-) *nm* **investment
portfolio** Effektenportefeuille (-s) *nn* **investment programme, investment program** (US)
Investitionsprogramm (-e) *nn* **investment
strategy** Investitionsstrategie (-n) *nf*
investor *n* Investor (-en) *nm*
invisible *adj* **invisible exports** unsichtbare
Exporte *nmpl* **invisible imports** unsichtbare
Importe *nmpl*
invitation *n* Einladung (-en) *nf*
invite *vb* einladen *vb*
invoice *n* Rechnung (-en) *nf* **duplicate invoice**
Rechnungsduplikat (-e) *nn* **to issue an
invoice** eine Rechnung ausstellen **to settle
an invoice** eine Rechnung begleichen
irrecoverable *adj* (loss) uneinbringlicher

Verlust (-e) *nm*

irrevocable *adj* unwiderruflich *adj* **irrevocable letter of credit** unwiderrufliches Akkreditiv (-e) *nn*

issue 1. *n* **bank of issue** Notenbank (-en) *nf* **share issue, stock issue** (US) Aktienemission (-en) *nf* **2.** *vb* (cheques,shares, tickets, notes) ausgeben *vb* (policy) ausstellen *vb* **to issue sb with sth** etwas an jemanden ausgeben *vb*

issuing *adj* **issuing bank** Notenbank (-en) *nf*

item *n* Artikel (-) *nm*

itemize *vb* aufgliedern *vb*

itemized *adj* **itemized account** spezifizierte Rechnung (-en) *nf*

itinerary *n* (Reise)Route (-n) *nf*

jackpot *n* Hauptgewinn (-) *nm*

jingle *n* **advertising jingle** Werbespruch (-üche) *nm*

job *n* **job analysis** Arbeitsanalyse (-n) *nf* **job creation** Arbeitsbeschaffung *nf* **job description** Stellenbeschreibung (-en) *nf* **job offer** Stellenangebot (-e) *nn* **job rotation** Stellenrotation *nf* **job satisfaction** Arbeitsfreude *nf* **job shop** Arbeitsamt (-ämter) *nn*

jobber *n* Jobber (-) *nm*

Jobcentre (GB) *n* Arbeitsamt (-ämter) *nn*

jobless *adj* arbeitslos *adj* **the jobless** die Arbeitslosen *npl*

joint *adj* gemeinsam *adj* **joint account** Gemeinschaftskonto (-konten) *nn* **joint obligation** gemeinsame Verpflichtung *nf* **joint ownership** Mitbesitz *nm* **joint responsibility** gemeinsame Verantwortung *nf* **joint-stock company** Aktiengesellschaft (-en) *nf* **joint venture** Gemeinschaftsunternehmen (-) *nn*

jointly *adv* gemeinsam *adv*

journal *n* Tagebuch (-bücher) *nn*

journalism *n* Journalismus *nm*

judicial *adj* gerichtlich *adj*

junior *adj* untergeordnet *adj*

junk *n* **junk bond** Junk Bond (-s) *nm*

jurisdiction *n* Zuständigkeitsbereich *nm*

juror *n* Geschworene/r *nmf*

jury *n* die Geschworenen *npl*

K *abbr* (1000) K *abbr*

keen *adj* (competition) scharf *adj* (price) extrem niedrig *adj*

keep *vb* (goods) führen *vb* **to keep an appointment** einen Termin einhalten **to keep the books** die Bücher halten/führen **to keep the business running** das Geschäft führen

keep back *vb* (money) Geld zurückhalten

keep down *vb* (prices) Preise niedrig halten

keep up with *vb* (events) sich auf dem laufenden halten *vr*

key *adj* **key currency** Schlüsselwährung (-en) *nf* **key industry** Schlüsselindustrie (-n) *nf* **key person** Schlüsselkraft (-kräfte) *nf*, Hauptperson (-en) *nf* **key question**

Schlüsselfrage (-n) *nf*

key in *vb* eingeben *vb*

keyboard *n* Tastatur (-en) *nf*

keynote *adj* **keynote speech** programmatische Rede (-n) *nf*

keyword *n* (computer) Stichwort (-wörter) *nn*

kill *vb* **to kill a project** ein Projekt streichen

kilowatt *n* Kilowatt (-) *nn*

kind 1. *adj* nett *adj* **would you be so kind as to...** würden Sie bitte so nett sein... **2.** *n* Sorte (-n) *nf*

king-size(d) *adj* riesengroß *adj*

kiosk *n* (phone) Kabine (-n) *nf*

kit *n* (equipment) Ausrüstung *nf*

kite *n* **kite mark (GB)** Gütezeichen (-) *nn*

knock *vb* (disparage) schlagen *vb*

knock down *vb* (price) herabsetzen *vb*

knock off* *vb* (finish work) Arbeit einstellen *vb*

knock-for-knock *adj* gegenseitige Aufrechnung *nf* **knock-for-knock agreement** Regreßverzichtsvereinbarung (-en) *nf*

knock-on *adj* **knock-on effect** Folgewirkung (-en) *nf*

knockdown *adj* **knockdown price** niedrigster Preis (-e) *nm*

know-how *n* Know-how *nn*

knowledge *n* Wissen *nn* **knowledge base** Wissensbasis (-basen) *nf* **it is common knowledge** es ist allgemein bekannt, daß... **to have a thorough knowledge of sth** etwas gut kennen **to have a working knowledge of sth** vertraut sein mit **to my knowledge** soviel ich weiß

knowledgeable *adj* kenntnisreich *adj*

known *adj* **known facts** die anerkannten Tatsachen *nfpl*

krona *n* (Swedish) Krone (-n) *nf*

krone *n* (Danish, Norwegian) Krone (-n) *nf*

kudos *n* Ansehen *nn*

kWh *abbr* KwS (Kilowattstunde) *abbr*

label 1. *n* Etikett (-e) *nn* **2.** *vb* etikettieren *vb*

labour, labor (US) *n* Arbeit *nf* **labour costs** Arbeitskosten *npl* **labour dispute** Arbeitskampf (-kämpfe) *nm* **labour-intensive** arbeitsintensiv *adj* **labour law** Arbeitsrecht (-e) *nn* **labour market** Arbeitsmarkt *nm* **labour relations** Arbeitsbeziehungen *nfpl*

labourer *n* ungelernter Arbeiter (-) *nm*

lack *n* Mangel (Mängel) *nm* **lack of investment** Investitionsmangel *nm*

land *n* **land purchase** Grundstückskauf *nm* **land reform** Bodenrechtsreform (-en) *nf* **land register** Grundbuch *nn* **land tax** Grundsteuer (-n) *nf* **land tribunal** Enteignungsausschuß (-üsse) *nm*

landlord *n* Wirt (-e) *nm*

landowner *n* Grundbesitzer (-) *nm*

language *n* Sprache (-n) *nf* **language specialist** Sprachexperte (-n) *nm*

large *adj* **large-scale** groß angelegt

launch 1. *n* **product launch**
Produkteinführung (-en) *nf* **2.** *vb* (product)
einführen *vb*
law *n* Gesetz (-e) *nn* **business law**
Handelsrecht *nn* **civil law** Zivilrecht *nn*
criminal law Strafrecht *nn* **international law**
internationales Recht *nn* **law of diminishing
returns** Gesetz des abnehmenden Ertrags *nn*
public law öffentliches Recht *nn*
lawsuit *n* Prozeß (-sse) *nm*
lay off *vb* (workers) entlassen *vb*
LBO (leveraged buy-out) *abbr* Leveraged
Buyout (-s) *nm*
leader *n* **market leader** Marktführer (-) *nm*
leadership *n* Führung *nf*
leading *adj* führend *adj*, Haupt- *cpd* **leading
product** Hauptprodukt (-e) *nn*
lease *vb* (ver)mieten *vb*
leasehold *n* Pachtbesitz *nm*
leaseholder *n* Pächter (-) *nm*
leave 1. *n* Urlaub *nm* **leave of absence**
Beurlaubung *nf* **sick leave** Genesungsurlaub
nm **to take leave** sich beurlauben lassen *vr*
to take leave of sb von jemandem Abschied
nehmen **2.** *vb* abfahren *vb* (resign from)
zurücktreten von *vb*
ledger *n* Hauptbuch (-bücher) *nn* **bought
ledger** Wareneinkaufsbuch (-bücher) *nn*
ledger entry Hauptbucheintragung *nf*
left *adj* **left luggage** Gepäckaufbewahrung *nf*
left-luggage locker Schließfach (-fächer) *nn*
left-luggage office Gepäckaufbewahrung *nf*
legacy *n* Erbschaft (-en) *nf*
legal *adj* gesetzlich *adj* **legal tender** gesetzliches Zahlungsmittel (-) *nn* **to take legal
action** Klage erheben (gegen jemanden)
legislate *vb* Gesetze erlassen
legislation *n* Gesetzgebung *nf* **to introduce
legislation** ein Gesetz einführen
lend *vb* leihen *vb*
lender *n* Kreditgeber (-) *nm*
lessee *n* Leasingnehmer (-) *nm*
lessor *n* Leasinggeber (-) *nm*
let *vb* (property) (ver)mieten *vb*
letter *n* **letter of application**
Bewerbungsschreiben (-) *nn* **letter of credit**
Akkreditiv (-e) *nn* **letter of introduction**
Empfehlungsschreiben (-) *nn*
letterhead *n* Briefkopf (-köpfe) *nm*
level *n* **level of employment**
Beschäftigtenstand *nm* **level of inflation**
Inflationsrate (-n) *nf* **level of prices**
Preisniveau (-s) *nn*
levy *vb* (tax) erheben *vb*
liability *n* Haftung *nf* **current liabilities**
Verbindlichkeiten *nfpl* **fixed liability** langfristige Verbindlichkeiten *nfpl* **limited liability** beschränkte Haftung *nf*
liable *adj* haftbar *adj* **liable for damages**
schadenersatzpflichtig *adj* **liable for tax**
steuerpflichtig *adj*
libel *n* (schriftliche) Verleumdung *nf*

licence *n* Lizenz (-en) *nf* **licence fee**
Lizenzgebühr (-en) *nf*
license *vb* genehmigen *vb*
licensee *n* Konzessionsinhaber (-) *nm*
licensor *n* Lizenzgeber (-) *nm*
life *n* **life assurance/insurance**
Lebensversicherung *nf* **life member** Mitglied auf Lebenszeit (-er) *nn*
LIFO (last in first out) *abbr* Lifo-Methode (-n)
nf
limit *n* Grenze (-n) *nf* **credit limit** Kreditlinie
(-n) *nf*
limited *adj* begrenzt *adj* **limited capital**
begrenztes Kapital *nn* **limited company**
Gesellschaft mit Haftungsbeschränkung
(-en) *nf* **limited liability** beschränkte Haftung
nf **limited partnership**
Kommanditgesellschaft (-en) *nf*
line *n* **above the line** zum ordentlichen
Haushalt gehörig **assembly line**
Montageband (-bänder) *nn* **below the line**
nicht zum ordentlichen Haushalt gehörig
line management Fachgebietsleitung *nf* **line
manager** Fachgebietsleiter (-) *nm* **line of
business** Sparte (-n) *nf* **product line**
Sortiment (-e) *nn*
liquid *adj* liquide *adj* **liquid assets** liquide
Mittel *nnpl* **liquid capital** liquides Kapital *nn*
liquidate *vb* liquidieren *vb*
liquidation *n* Liquidation (-en) *nf* **liquidation
value** Liquidationswert *nm*
liquidity *n* Liquidität *nf*
list 1. *n* Liste (-n) *nf* **list price** Listenpreis (-e)
nm **2.** *vb* verzeichnen *vb*, registrieren *vb*
listed *adj* **listed share, listed stock** (US)
börsennotierte Aktie (-n) *nf*
litigant *n* streitende Partei (-en) *nf*
litigate *vb* einen Prozeß führen
litigation *n* Rechtsstreit (-e) *nm*
load 1. *n* Ladung (-en) *nf*, Belastung (-en) *nf*
2. *vb* laden *vb*
loan *n* Kredit (-e) *nm* **loan agreement**
Kreditvertrag (-äge) *nm* **bank loan**
Bankkredit (-e) *nm* **bridging loan, bridge
loan** (US) Überbrückungskredit (-e) *nm*
personal loan Personalkredit (-e) *nm* **to
grant a loan** einen Kredit gewähren **to
request a loan** einen Kredit beantragen
local *adj* örtlich *adj* **local taxes** örtliche
Steuern *nfpl*
location *n* Standort (-e) *nm*
lockout *n* (of strikers) Aussperrung (-en) *nf*
logistics *npl* Logistik *nf*
Lombard Rate *n* Lombardsatz *nm*
long *n* **long capital** langfristiges Kapital *nn*
long credit langfristiger Kredit *nm* **long
deposit** langfristige Einlage *nf* **long-
distance** Langstrecken- **long-range**
Langstrecken- *cpd* **long-term** langfristig *adj*
long-term planning langfristige Planung *nf*
lose *vb* (custom) verlieren *vb*
loss *n* Verlust (-e) *nm* **financial loss** finan-

zieller Verlust (-e) *nm* **gross loss**
Bruttoverlust (-e) *nm* **loss leader** Lockartikel
(-) *nm* **net loss** Nettoverlust (-e) *nm* **loss of
earnings** Verdienstausfall (-fälle) *nm* **loss of
job** Arbeitsplatzverlust (-e) *nm* **to minimise
losses** Verluste minimieren
lost-property *adj* **lost-property office**
Fundbüro (-s) *nn*
lot *n* (at auction) Partie (-n) *nf*
low *adj* (price) niedrig *adj*
lower *vb* (price, interest rate) herabsetzen *vb*
lucrative *adj* lukrativ *adj*
luggage *n* Gepäck *nn* **excess luggage**
Übergewicht *nn* **luggage insurance**
Reisegepäckversicherung *nf*
lump *n* **lump sum settlement**
Pauschalentschädigung *nf*
luxury *adj* **luxury goods** Luxusartikel *nmpl*
luxury tax Luxussteuer (-n) *nf*
machine 1. *n* Maschine (-n) *nf* 2. *vb*
bearbeiten *vb*
machinery *n* Maschinerie *nf* **machinery of
government** Regierungsapparat *nm*
macroeconomics *npl*
Makrowirtschaft(slehre) *nf*
made *adj* hergestellt *adj* **made in France** in
Frankreich hergestellt
magazine *n* (journal) Zeitschrift (-en) *nf*
magnate *n* Magnat (-en) *nm*
magnetic *adj* magnetisch *adj* **magnetic tape**
(DP) Magnetband (-bänder) *nn*
mail order *n* Versandhandel *nm*
mailing *n* **mailing list** Adressenkartei (-en) *nf*
main *adj* Haupt- *cpd* **main office**
Hauptverwaltung (-en) *nf* **main supplier**
Hauptlieferant (-en) *nm*
mainframe *n* (DP) Großrechner (-) *nm*
maintenance *n* Unterhaltung *nf*, Wartung *nf*
maintenance costs Unterhaltungskosten *npl*
major *adj* führend *adj*
majority *n* Mehrheit (-en) *nf* **majority holding**
Mehrheitsbeteiligung *nf* **in the majority**
meistens
make *vb* **to make a fortune** ein Riesengeschäft machen **to make a living** sich seinen
Lebensunterhalt verdienen **to make money**
Geld verdienen
malingerer *n* Simulant (-en) *nm*
mall *n* **shopping mall** Einkaufszentrum (-en)
nn
malpractice *n* Berufsvergehen (-) *nn*
man-made *adj* künstlich *adj*
manage *vb* führen *vb*, leiten *vb*
management *n* Management *nn* **business
management** Geschäftsleitung *nf* **management buy-out** Management Buyout (-s) *nn*
management by objectives zielgesteuerte
Unternehmensführung *nf* **management
consultant** Unternehmensberater (-) *nm*
financial management Finanzmanagement
nn **middle management** mittleres
Management *nn* **personnel management**

Personal-Management *nn* **top management**
Unternehmensspitze *nf* **management training** Management-Ausbildung *nf*
manager *n* Manager (-) *nm*
manpower *n* Personalbestand *nm*
manual *adj* **manual worker** (manueller)
Arbeiter (-) *nm*
manufacture 1. *n* Herstellung *nf* 2. *vb*
herstellen *vb*
manufacturer *n* Hersteller (-) *nm*
margin *n* (Handels-)Spanne (-n) *nf* **profit
margin** Gewinnspanne (-n) *nf*
marginal *adj* Grenz- *cpd* **marginal cost**
Grenzkosten *npl* **marginal revenue**
Grenzertrag *nm*
marine 1. *adj* See- *cpd* **marine engineering**
Schiffsmaschinenbau *nm* **marine insurance**
Seeversicherung *nf* 2. *n* **merchant marine**
Handelsmarine *nf*
mark *n* **Deutschmark** deutsche Mark (DM) *nf*
mark down *vb* (price) herabsetzen *vb*
mark up *vb* erhöhen *vb*
markdown *n* Herabsetzung *nf*
market 1. *n* Markt (Märkte) *nm* **market
analysis** Marktanalyse (-n) *nf* **bear market**
Baissemarkt *nm* **black market** schwarzer
Markt *nm* **bond market** Bondmarkt *nm* **bull
market** Haussemarkt *nm* **buyer's market**
Käufermarkt *nm* **capital market**
Kapitalmarkt *nm* **Common Market** Gemeinsamer Markt *nm* **domestic market**
Binnenmarkt *nm* **down-market** (product)
von niedriger Qualität **market economy**
Marktwirtschaft (-en) *nf* **falling market** fallender Markt *nm* **firm market** fester Markt
nm **market forces** Marktkräfte *nfpl* **foreign
market** Außenmarkt *nm* **futures market**
Terminkontraktmarkt *nm* **labour market**
Arbeitsmarkt *nm* **market leader** Marktführer
(-) *nm* **money market** Geldmarkt *nm* **mar-
ket opportunity** Marktgelegenheit (-en) *nf*
market price Marktwert (-e) *nm* **property
market (GB)/real estate market (US)**
Immobilienmarkt *nm* **market research**
Marktforschung *nf* **retail market**
Einzelhandelsmarkt *nm* **market segmentation** Marktsegmentierung *nf* **seller's market**
Verkäufermarkt *nm* **market share**
Marktanteil (-e) *nm* **stock market**
(Aktien)Börse (-n) *nf* **the bottom has fallen
out of the market** der Markt erreichte seinen
Tiefststand *nm* **to play the market** an der
Börse spekulieren **up-market** (product) von
guter Qualität **market value** Marktwert (-e)
nm **wholesale market** Großhandelsmarkt
nm 2. *vb* verkaufen *vb*, vermarkten *vb*
marketable *adj* absetzbar *adj*
marketing *n* Marketing *nn* **marketing consultant** Vertriebsberater (-) *nm*,
Marketingberater (-) *nm* **marketing department** Marketingabteilung (-en) *nf* **marketing
director** Vertriebsleiter (-) *nm*

markup n Erhöhung nf
mart n (Finanz)Markt (Märkte) nm
mass adj **mass marketing** Massenabsatz nm
mass media Massenmedien npl **mass production** Massenfertigung nf **mass unemployment** Massenarbeitslosigkeit nf
material adj 1. **material needs** materielle(n) Bedürfnisse 2. npl Material nn **building materials** Baumaterial nn **raw materials** Rohstoffe nmpl
maternity n **maternity leave** Schwangerschaftsurlaub nm
matrix n Matrix (-izen) nf
mature vb (business, economy) fällig werden vb
maximise vb maximieren vb
maximum adj **maximum price** Höchstpreis (-e) nm
MBA (Master of Business Administration) abbr MBA abbr
mean 1. adj (average) durchschnittlich adj 2. n (average) Durchschnitt (-e) nm
means npl Mittel nnpl **financial means** Finanzmittel npl **to live beyond one's means** über seine Verhältnisse leben vb **we do not have the means to...** wir sind nicht in der Lage...
measure 1. n Maßnahme (-n) nf **financial measure** finanzielle Maßnahme (-n) nf **safety measure** Sicherheitsmaßnahme (-n) nf 2. vb messen vb
mechanical adj mechanisch adj **mechanical engineering** Maschinenbau nm
media npl Medien npl
median adj mittler adj, Mittel- cpd
mediate vb vermitteln vb
mediation n Vermittlung nf
mediator n Vermittler (-) nm
medical adj ärztlich adj **medical insurance** Krankenversicherung nf
medium 1. adj mittler adj, Mittel- cpd **medium-sized firm** mittelgroßes Unternehmen (-) nn **medium term** mittelfristig adj 2. n **advertising medium** Werbemittel (-) nn
meet vb treffen vb
meeting n Sitzung (-en) nf **board meeting** Vorstandssitzung (-en) nf **business meeting** Geschäftssitzung (-en) nf **to hold a meeting** eine Sitzung abhalten
megabyte n Megabyte nn
member n Mitglied (-er) nn **Member of Parliament (MP) (GB)** Bundestagsabgeordnete/r nmf **Member of the European Parliament (MEP)** Abgeordnete/r des Europaparlaments nmf
memo n Mitteilung (-en) nf
memorandum n Mitteilung (-en) nf
memory n (DP) Speicher (-) nm **memory capacity** Speicherkapazität nf
mercantile adj Handels- cpd
merchandise vb vertreiben vb

merchandizer n Händler (-) nm
merchandizing n Vertrieb nm
merchant n Handelsvertreter (-) nm **merchant bank** Handelsbank (-en) nf **merchant navy, merchant marine (US)** Handelsmarine nf **merchant ship** Handelsschiff (-e) nn
merge vb fusionieren vb
merger n Fusion (-en) nf
merit n **merit payment** Leistungszulage (-n) nf
message n Mitteilung (-en) nf
messenger n Bote (-n) nm
metal n Metall (-e) nn
meter n Meter (-) nmn
method n **method of payment** Zahlungsmethode (-n) nf **production method** Produktionsmethode (-n) nf
metre, meter (US) n Meter (-) nmn **cubic metre** Kubikmeter nmn **square metre** Quadratmeter (-) nmn
metric adj metrisch adj
metrication n Umstellung auf das metrische Maßsystem nf
metropolis n Metropole (-n) nf
microchip n Mikrochip (-s) nn
microcomputer n Mikrocomputer (-) nm
microeconomics n Mikroökonomik nf, Betriebswirtschaft nf
microfiche n Mikrofiche (-s) nm
microprocessor n Mikroprozessor (-en) nm
middle adj **middle management** mittleres Management nn **middle manager** mittlerer Manager (-) nm
middleman n Zwischenhändler (-) nm
migrant n **migrant worker** Gastarbeiter (-) nm
mile n Meile (-n) nf **nautical mile** Seemeile (-n) nf
mileage n Meilenzahl nf
million n Million (-en) nf
millionaire n Millionär (-e) nm
mine n Mine (-n) nf **coal mine** Kohlengrube (-n) nf
mineral n Mineral (-ien) nn
minimal adj minimal adj
minimum adj **index-linked minimum wage** indexgekoppelter Mindestlohn (-löhne) nm **minimum lending rate** Mindestzins (-en) nm
mining n Bergbau nm **mining industry** Bergbau nm
minister n Minister (-) nm
ministry n Ministerium (-ien) nn **Ministry of Transport** Verkehrsministerium (-ien) nn
minor adj unbedeutend adj
minority n Minderheit (-) nf **minority holding** Minderheitsbeteiligung nf **in the minority** in der Minderheit
mint 1. n Münzanstalt (-en) nf 2. vb prägen vb **he/she mints money** er/sie macht einen Haufen Geld
minutes npl **the minutes of the meeting** Protokoll nn

misappropriation *n* Veruntreuung *nf*
miscalculation *n* Rechenfehler (-) *nm*, Fehlkalkulation (-en) *nf*
misconduct *n* (bad management) Berufsvergehen *nn*
mishandling *n* falsche Behandlung *nf*
mismanagement *n* Mißmanagement *nn*
mistake *n* Fehler (-) *nm* **to make a mistake** einen Fehler machen
mix *n* **marketing mix** Marketing-Mix *n* **product mix** Produktmix *nm*
mixed *adj* **mixed economy** Mischwirtschaft (-en) *nf*
mode *n* (method) Art *nf*
model *n* (person) Modell (-e) *nn*
modem *n* Modem (-s) *nm*
moderate 1. *adj* gemäßigt *adj* 2. *vb* mäßigen *vb*
moderation *n* Mäßigung *nf*
modern *adj* modern *adj*
modernization *n* Modernisierung *nf*
modernize *vb* modernisieren *vb*
module *n* Modul (-e) *nn*
monetarism *n* Monetarismus *nm*
monetary *adj* monetär *adj* **European Monetary System (EMS)** Europäisches Währungssystem *nn* **International Monetary Fund (IMF)** Internationaler Währungsfonds *nm* **monetary policy** Finanzpolitik *nf*
money *n* **dear money** teures Geld *nn* **money market** Geldmarkt (-märkte) *nm* **money order** Zahlungsanweisung (-en) *nf* **public money** öffentliches Geld *nn* **money supply** Geldangebot *nn* **to raise money** Mittel aufbringen **money trader** Geldhändler (-) *nm*
moneymaking *adj* (profitable) gewinnbringend *adj*
monopoly *n* Monopol (-e) *nn* **Monopolies and Mergers Commission** Monopolkommission *nf*, (Germany) Bundeskartellamt (-ämter) *nn*
monthly *adj* monatlich *adj*
moonlight* *vb* schwarz arbeiten *vb*
moor *vb* festmachen *vb*
mooring *n* Anlegeplatz (-plätze) *nm* **mooring rights** Anlegerecht *nn*
mortgage *n* Hypothek (-en) *nf* **mortgage deed** Hypothekenvertrag (-äge) *nm* **mortgage loan** Hypothekendarlehen (-) *nn*
mortgagee *n* Hypothekengläubiger (-) *nm*
mortgagor *n* Hypothekenschuldner (-) *nm*
motor *n* **motor industry** Autoindustrie *nf*
multilateral *adj* multilateral *adj*
multinational *adj* multinational *adj* **multinational corporation** multinationales Unternehmen (-) *nn*
multiple *adj* mehrfach *adj* **multiple store** Filialgeschäft (-e) *nn*
multiply *vb* vermehren *vb*
multipurpose *adj* Vielzweck- *cpd*

municipal *adj* **municipal bonds** Kommunalanleihen *nfpl*
mutual *adj* gegenseitig *adj* **mutual fund (US)** offener Investmentfonds *nm*
mutually *adv* gegenseitig *adv*
N/A (not applicable) *abbr* nicht zutreffend
name 1. *n* **brand name** Markenname (-n) *nm* **by name** mit Namen **full name** voller Name *nm* **in the name of** im Namen... **registered trade name** eingetragener Firmenname (-n) *nm* 2. *vb* nennen *vb*, ernennen *vb*
named *adj* **named person** der/die genannte...
narrow *adj* **narrow margin** kleine Spanne (-n) *nf* **narrow market** begrenzter Markt (-märkte) *nm*
nation *n* Nation (-en) *nf* **the United Nations** die Vereinten Nationen *nfpl*
national *adj* **national debt** Staatsschuld *nf* **national income** Volkseinkommen *nn* **national insurance (GB)** Sozialversicherung *nf* **national interest** nationales Interesse *nn* **National Bureau of Economic Research (US)** Institut für Wirtschaftsforschung *nn*
nationality *n* Staatsangehörigkeit *nf*
nationalization *n* Verstaatlichung *nf*
nationalize *vb* verstaatlichen *vb*
nationalized *adj* **nationalized industry** verstaatlichte Industrie (-n) *nf*
nationwide *adj* landesweit *adj*
natural *adj* **natural rate of increase** natürliche Zuwachsrate (-n) *nf* **natural resources** Bodenschätze *nmpl*
necessary *adj* erforderlich *adj* **necessary qualifications** erforderliche Qualifikationen *nfpl*
necessity *n* (goods) Notwendigkeit *nf*
need *n* **needs assessment** Bedarfserfassung *nf* **needs of industry** industrielle Bedürfnisse *nnpl* **to be in need** brauchen (dringend) *vb*
negative *adj* **negative cash flow** Einnahmeunterdeckung *nf* **negative feedback** negative Rückmeldung *nf*
neglect *n* Vernachlässigung *nf* **neglect clause** Freizeichnungsklausel für Fahrlässigkeit (-n) *nf*
negligence *n* Fahrlässigkeit *nf* **negligence clause** Fahrlässigkeitsklausel (-n) *nf* **contributory negligence** mitwirkendes Verschulden *nn* **gross negligence** grobe Fahrlässigkeit *nf*
negligent *adj* fahrlässig *adj*
negotiable *adj* begebbar *adj* **negotiable bill** durch Indossament übertragbarer Wechsel (-) *nm* **negotiable cheque** begebbarer Scheck (-s) *nm*
negotiate *vb* verhandeln (über) *vb*
negotiated *adj* **negotiated price** vereinbarter Preis (-e) *nm*
negotiating *adj* **negotiating session** Sitzungsperiode (-n) *nf* **negotiating skills** Verhandlungsgeschick *nn*
negotiation *n* Verhandlung (-en) *nf* **by**

negotiation durch Verhandlung **to begin negotiations** Verhandlungen beginnen **under negotiation** unter Verhandlung **wage negotiations** Lohnverhandlungen *nfpl*
negotiator *n* Verhandlungsführer (-) *nm*
net, nett 1. *adj* netto **net amount** Nettobetrag (-äge) *nm* **net assets** Nettovermögen *nn* **net cost** Nettokosten *npl* **net earnings** Nettoverdienst *nm* **net interest** Nettozinsen *nmpl* **net investment** Nettoinvestition *nf* **net loss** Reinverlust (-e) *nm* **net price** Nettopreis (-e) *nm* **net proceeds** Auszahlung *nf* **net profit** Reingewinn *nm* **net result** Endergebnis (-sse) *nn* **net sales** Nettoauftragseingang (-änge) *nm* **net saving** Nettoersparnisse *nfpl* **terms strictly net** zahlbar sofort ohne Abzug **net wage** Nettolohn (-öhne) *nm* **net weight** Nettogewicht *nn* 2. *vb* einbringen *vb*
network 1. *n* **banking network** Banknetz (-e) *nn* **computer network** Computernetz (-e) *nn* **distribution network** Verteilernetz (-e) *nn* 2. *vb* ausstrahlen (im Netzbereich) *vb*
neutral *adj* neutral *adj*
new *adj* **new account** neues Konto (-ten) *nn* **new business** Neugeschäft *nn* **new product** neues Produkt (-e) *nn* **new technology** neue Technologie (-n) *nf*
newly *adv* **newly-appointed** neu angestellt **newly-industrialised** neu industrialisiert
news *n* Nachrichten *nfpl* **news agency** Nachrichtenagentur (-en) *nf* **bad news** schlechte Nachrichten *nfpl* **news bulletin** Bulletin (-s) *nn* **news coverage** aktuelle Berichterstattung *nf* **financial news** finanzielle Nachrichten *nfpl* **good news** gute Nachrichten *nfpl*
newsdealer (US) *n* Nachrichtenagentur (-en) *nf*
newsletter *n* Mitteilungsblatt (-blätter) *nn*
newspaper *n* Zeitung (-en) *nf* **newspaper advertisement** Zeitungsanzeige (-n) *nf* **daily newspaper** Tageszeitung (-en) *nf* **newspaper report** Zeitungsbericht (-e) *nm*
nil *n* Null *nn* **nil profit** Nullgewinn (-e) *nm*
no *det* **no agents wanted** wir brauchen keine Agenten **no-claims bonus** Schadensfreiheitsrabatt *nm* **of no commercial value** ohne Marktwert
nominal *adj* nominell *adj* **nominal amount** Nominalbetrag (-äge) *nm* **nominal assets** Nominalvermögen *nn* **nominal damages** nomineller Schadenersatz *nm* **nominal inflation** Nominalinflation *nf* **nominal price** Nennwert (-e) *nm* **nominal value** Nennwert (-e) *nm*
nominate *vb* vorschlagen *vb* **nominate sb to a board/committee** ernennen (als Mitglied des/der...)
nomination *n* Nominierung (-en) *nf*, Ernennung (-en) *nf*
nominee *n* Kandidat (-en) *nm* **nominee**

shareholder vorgeschobener Aktionär (-en) *nm*
non-acceptance *n* Annahmeverweigerung *nf*
non-attendance *n* Abwesenheit *nf*
non-completion *n* Nichtabschluß (-üsse) *nm*
non-contributory *adj* beitragsfreies Programm (-e) *nn*
non-convertible *adj* nicht konvertierbar *adj*
non-delivery *n* Nichtlieferung *nf*
non-discriminatory *adj* nichtdiskriminierend *adj*
non-essential *adj* unnötig *adj*, verzichtbar *adj*
non-interest-bearing *adj* zinsfrei *adj*
non-intervention *n* Nichteingreifen *nn*
non-negotiable *adj* nichtbegebbar *adj*
non-payment *n* Nichtzahlung *nf*
non-profitmaking *adj* nicht erwerbswirtschaftlich *adj*
non-returnable *adj* Einweg- *cpd*
non-stop *adj* nonstop *adj*
non-transferable *adj* nicht übertragbar *adj*
norm *n* Norm (-en) *nf*
normal *adj* **normal trading hours** allgemeine Geschäftsstunden *nfpl*
not *adv* **not applicable** nicht zutreffend *adj* **not available** nicht verfügbar *adj* **not dated** undatiert *adj*
notary *n* Notar (-en) *nm*
note *n* **advice note** Gutschriftsanzeige (-n) *nf* **cover note** Deckungsbestätigung (-en) *nf* **credit note** Gutschriftsanzeige (-n) *nf* **debit note** Belastungsanzeige (-n) *nf* **delivery note** Lieferschein (-e) *nm* **dispatch note** Versandanzeige (-n) *nf* **open note (US)** offener Kredit *nm* **to compare notes** Notizen vergleichen **to make a note of sth** sich etwas notieren
noteworthy *adj* beachtenswert *adj*
notice *n* **advance notice** (An)Kündigung (-en) *nf* **at short notice** kurzfristig **final notice** letzte Mahnung *nf* **notice period** Kündigungsfrist (-en) *nf* **term of notice** Kündigungsfrist (-en) *nf* **to come to the notice of sb** erfahren **to give notice of sth** etwas bekanntgeben **to take notice** merken *vb* **until further notice** bis auf weiteres
notification *n* Benachrichtigung *nf*
notify *vb* benachrichtigen *vb*
null *adj* **null and void** null und nichtig
number *n* **account number** Kontonummer *nf* **opposite number** Pendant *nn* **order number** Bestellnummer (-n) *nf* **serial number** Seriennummer (-n) *nf* **telephone number** Telefonnummer (-n) *nf* **wrong number** (phone) falsche Nummer (-n) *nf*
numeracy *n* Rechnen *nn*
numerate *adj* rechenkundig *adj*
numeric *adj* **alpha-numeric** numerisches Alphabet *nn* **numeric character** Ziffer (-n) *nf*
numerical *adj* **numerical analysis** Zahlenanalyse *nf*
NYSE (New York Stock Exchange) *abbr*

New Yorker Börse
object *vb* protestieren *vb*
objection *n* Einwand (-wände) *nm* **to make/
raise an objection** Einwände erheben gegen
objective *n* Ziel (-e) *nn* **to reach an objective**
das Ziel erreichen
obligation *n* Verpflichtung (-en) *nf* **to meet
one's obligations** seinen Verpflichtungen
nachkommen
obligatory *adj* obligatorisch *adj*
oblige *vb* **to be obliged to do sth** verpflichtet
sein, etwas zu tun
observation *n* **under observation** unter Beobachtung
observe *vb* **observe the rules** die Regeln
einhalten
obsolescence *n* Veralten *nn* **built-in obsolescence** geplanter Verschleiß *nm*
obsolete *adj* veraltet *adj*
obtain *vb* bekommen *vb* **to obtain credit**
Kredit aufnehmen
occupant *n* Bewohner (-) *nm*
occupation *n* Beruf (-e) *nm*
occupational *adj* **occupational disease**
Berufskrankheit (-en) *nf* **occupational
hazard** Berufsrisiko (-iken) *nn*
occupier *n* Inhaber (-) *nm*
occupy *vb* (premises) bewohnen *vb*
off-the-job *adj* **off-the-job training** außerbe-
triebliche Weiterbildung *nf*
offence, offense (US) *n* Vergehen (-) *nn*
offer *n* **firm offer** festes Angebot *nn* **offer in
writing** schriftliches Angebot *nn* **offer subject to confirmation** Angebot vorbehaltlich
der Bestätigung (-e) *nn* **offer valid until...**
Angebot gilt bis... *nn*
offeree *n* Empfänger eines Angebots *nm*
offeror *n* Anbieter (-) *nm*
office *n* Büro (-s) *nn* **office equipment**
Büroeinrichtung (-en) *nf* **office hours**
Geschäftsstunden *nfpl* **office management**
Büroverwaltung *nf* **office staff** Büropersonal
nn **to hold office** im Amt sein **to resign from
office** zurücktreten *vb*
official *n* Beamte/r *nmf* **official strike** offizieller Streik (-s) *nm*
offshore *adj* **offshore company** Offshore-
Gesellschaft (-en) *nf*
oil *n* **oil industry** Erdölindustrie *nf* **oil state**
ölproduzierender Staat (-en) *nm*
oilfield *n* Ölfeld (-er) *nn*
oligopoly *n* Oligopolie (-n) *nf*
ombudsman *n* Ombudsmann (-männer) *nm*
on-line *adj* on-line *adj*
on-the-job *adj* **on-the-job training** betriebliche Weiterbildung *nf*
onus *n* **the onus is on us to...** es liegt an
uns...zu...
open 1. *adj* offen *adj* **open cheque**
Barscheck (-s) *nm* **open credit** Blankokredit
nm **open market** freier Markt (Märkte) *nm*
open shop Firma, die nicht gewerkschafts-

gebunden ist **2.** *vb* **to open an account** ein
Konto eröffnen
open up *vb* (market) den Markt erschließen
opening *adj* **opening price** Eröffnungskurs
(-e) *nm* **opening times** Öffnungszeiten *nfpl*
operate *vb* **to operate a business** ein Geschäft führen
operating *adj* **operating expenditure**
Betriebsausgaben *nfpl* **operating expenses**
Betriebskosten *npl* **operating income**
Betriebseinkommen *nn* **operating profit**
Betriebsergebnis *nn* **operating statement**
Betriebsbilanz (-en) *nf*
operation *n* (of business) Betrieb *nm*,
Verwaltung *nf* (of machine) Unterhaltung *nf*
operator *n* Betreiber (-) *nm*
opportunity *n* Gelegenheit (-en) *nf* **market
opportunities** Marktgelegenheiten *nfpl* **to
seize an opportunity** die Gelegenheit ergreifen
option *n* Option (-en) *nf* **share option, stock
option** (US) Aktienbezugsrecht (-e) *nn* **options market** Optionsmarkt (-märkte) *nm*
option to buy Kaufoption *nf* **option to
cancel** Stornierungsoption *nf*
optional *adj* freiwillig *adj*
order *n* **order book** Auftragsbuch (-bücher)
nn **order form** Bestellformular (-e) *nn* **order
number** Bestellnummer (-n) *nf* **pay to the
order of...** zahlbar an **to cancel an order** eine
Bestellung widerrufen **to place an order**
einen Auftrag erteilen
ordinary *adj* gewöhnlich *adj* **ordinary general
meeting** gewöhnliche Sitzung *nf* **ordinary
share, ordinary stock** (US) Stammaktie (-n)
nf
organization *n* Organisation (-en) *nf*,
Unternehmen (-) *nn*
organize *vb* organisieren *vb*
organized *adj* **organized labour** (trade
unions) Gewerkschaftsmitglieder *nnpl*
origin *n* (of a product) Ursprung (-ünge) *nm*
country of origin Herkunftsland (-länder) *nn*
statement of origin Ursprungsangabe (-n) *nf*
original *adj* **original cost** Selbstkosten *npl*
outbid *vb* überbieten *vb*
outcome *n* Ergebnis (-sse) *nn*
outgoings *npl* Ausgänge *nmpl*
outlay *n* **capital outlay** Kapitalkosten *npl*
outlet *n* **market outlet** Absetzgebiet (-e) *nn*
sales outlet Verkaufsstelle (-n) *nf*
outlook *n* **business outlook**
Geschäftsaussichten *nfpl*
output *n* Output *nm*, Produktion *nf* **to
increase output** die Produktion steigern
outstanding *adj* ausstehend *adj* **outstanding
amount** ausstehender Betrag (-äge) *nm*
outstanding debt Außenstände *npl* **outstanding stock** Aktien im Publikumsbesitz
npl
overcharge *vb* jemandem zu viel berechnen
overdraft *n* Überziehung *nf* **to request an**

overdraft einen Überziehungskredit beantragen
overdraw *vb* überziehen *vb*
overdrawn *adj* **overdrawn account** überzogenes Konto (Konten) *nn*
overdue *adj* überfällig *adj*
overhead *adj* **overhead costs** Gemeinkosten
npl
overheads *npl* allgemeine Geschäftskosten
npl
overheating *n* (of economy) Überheizen *nn*
overload *vb* überladen *vb*
overlook *vb* übersehen *vb*
overman *vb* eine zu große Belegschaft haben
overmanned *adj* (mit einer zu großen Belegschaft)
overmanning *n* (excess staff) zu große Belegschaft
overnight *adj* **overnight delivery** Lieferung
bis Morgen *nf*
overpay *vb* überzahlen *vb*
overpayment *n* Überzahlung *nf*
overpopulation *n* Überbevölkerung *nf*
overproduce *vb* überproduzieren *vb*
overproduction *n* Überproduktion *nf*
overseas *adj* Übersee- *cpd* **overseas market**
Überseemarkt (-märkte) *nm* **overseas terri-**
tory Überseegebiet (-e) *nn* **overseas trade**
Überseehandel *nm*
oversell *vb* überverkaufen *vb*
oversight *n* Versehen (-) *nn* **due to an**
oversight aus Versehen
oversold *adj* überverkauft *adj*
oversubscribed *adj* überzeichnet *adj*
oversupply *vb* Überangebot *nn*
overtime *n* Überstunden *nfpl*
overvalue *vb* überbewerten *vb*
overworked *adj* überarbeitet *adj*
owe *vb* schulden *vb*
own *vb* besitzen *vb*
owner *n* Besitzer (-) *nm*
owner-occupier *n* Besitzer im eigenen Haus
(-) *nm*
ownership *n* Eigentum *nn*
pack *vb* packen *vb*
package *n* Paket (-e) *nn* **package deal**
Verhandlungspaket (-e) *nn* **package tour**
Pauschalreise (-n) *nf*
packaging *n* Verpackung *nf*
packet *n* Paket (-e) *nn*
paid *adj* bezahlt *adj* **paid holiday** bezahlter
Urlaub *nm*
paid-up *adj* **paid-up capital** voll eingezahltes
Kapital *nn*
pallet *n* Palette (-n) *nf*
palletized *adj* palettisiert *adj* **palletized**
freight palettisierte Fracht *nf*
paper *n* **commercial paper** Wertpapiere *nnpl*
paper loss nicht realisierter Kursverlust (-e)
nm **paper profit** nicht realisierter
Kursgewinn (-e) *nm*
paperwork *n* Schreibarbeit (-en) *nf*

par *n* **above par** über pari **below par** unter
pari
parent *n* **parent company** Muttergesellschaft
(-en) *nf*
parity *n* Parität *nf*
part *n* (of a machine) Teil (-e) *nn* **part**
payment Teilzahlung (-en) *nf* **part shipment**
Teillieferung (-en) *nf* **spare part** (for
machine) Ersatzteil (-e) *nn*
part-time *adj* Teilzeit- *cpd*
participation *n* **worker participation**
Mitbestimmung *nf*
partner *n* Partner (-) *nm* **sleeping partner**
stiller Gesellschafter (-) *nm*
partnership *n* Personengesellschaft (-en) *nf*
trading partnership Handelsgesellschaft
(-en) *nf*
passenger *n* Passagier (-e) *nm*
patent *n* Patent (-e) *nn*
patented *adj* patentrechtlich geschützt *adj*
patronage *n* Kundschaft *nf*
pattern *n* **spending patterns**
Ausgabenstruktur *nf*
pay 1. *n* (salary, wages) Lohn (-öhne) *nm*
equal pay gleicher Lohn *nm* **pay rise**
Gehaltserhöhung (-en) *nf* **severance pay**
Abfindungszahlung (-en) *nf* **unemployment**
pay Arbeitslosengeld *nn* 2. *vb* **to pay an**
invoice eine Rechnung begleichen **to pay by**
credit card mit Kreditkarte zahlen **to pay for**
a service für einen Dienst zahlen **to pay in**
advance im voraus zahlen **to pay in cash** bar
zahlen
payable *adj* **accounts payable**
Verbindlichkeiten *nfpl*
payee *n* Zahlungsempfänger (-) *nm*
payer *n* **prompt payer** prompter Zahler (-) *nm*
slow payer säumiger Zahler (-) *nm*
payload *n* (of vehicle) Ladung *nf*
payment *n* Zahlung (-en) *nf* **down payment**
Anzahlung *nf*
payola (US) *n* Auszahlung (-en) *nf*
payroll *n* Lohnliste (-n) *nf*, Gehaltsliste (-n) *nf*
to be on the payroll auf der Lohnliste sein
peak *n* Spitze (-n) *nf* **peak demand**
Spitzennachfrage *nf* **peak period** Spitzenzeit
(-en) *nf*
pecuniary *adj* **for pecuniary gain** um Geld zu
verdienen
peddle *vb* feilbieten *vb*
peg *vb* (prices) festsetzen *vb* **the HK dollar is**
pegged to the US dollar der HK-Dollar hängt
an dem US-Dollar
penetration *n* **market penetration**
Markteindringen *nn*
pension *n* Rente (-n) *nf* **pension fund**
Rentenfonds *nm* **retirement pension**
Altersrente (-n) *nf* **pension scheme**
Pensionsplan (-äne) *nm*
per *prep* pro *prep* **per annum** pro Jahr **per**
capita pro Kopf **per cent** Prozent *nn*
percentage *n* Prozentsatz (-ätze) *nm* **percen-**

tage of profit Prozentsatz des Gewinns *nm*
performance *n* (behaviour) Leistung *nf* **performance appraisal** Leistungsbewertung *nf* **performance-related bonus** Leistungsprämie (-n) *nf*
period *n* **cooling-off period** Karenzzeit *nf* **period of grace** Karenzzeit *nf*
peripheral *adj* Rand- *cpd*
perishable *adj* leicht verderblich *adj* **perishable goods** leicht verderbliche Güter *nnpl*
perk *n* Nebenleistung (-en) *nf*
permanent *adj* **permanent employment** Dauerbeschäftigung *nf*
permit *n* Lizenz *nf* **building permit** Baugenehmigung (-en) *nf*
perquisite *n* (formal) Nebenleistung (-en) *nf*
person *n* **third person** Dritte/r *nmf*
personal *adj* persönlich *adj*
personnel *n* Personal *nn* **personnel department** Personalabteilung (-en) *nf* **personnel management** Personal-Management *nn*
peseta *n* Peseta (-s) *nf*
petrodollar *n* Öldollar *nm*
petroleum *n* **petroleum industry** Ölindustrie *nf*
pharmaceutical *adj* **pharmaceutical industry** Pharmazieindustrie *nf*
phoney* *adj* gefälscht *adj* **phoney* company** Schwindelunternehmen (-) *nn*
photocopier *n* Kopiergerät (-e) *nn*
photocopy 1. *n* Fotokopie (-n) *nf* 2. *vb* fotokopieren *vb*
pick up *vb* (improve) sich erholen *vb*
picket *n* (strike) Streikposten (-) *nm*
piecework *n* Akkordarbeit *nf*
pig iron *n* Roheisen *nn*
pilferage *n* Diebstahl *nm*
pilot *n* **pilot plant** Pilotanlage (-n) *nf* **pilot scheme** Pilotprojekt *nn*
pipeline *n* Pipeline (-s) *nf*
piracy *n* (at sea) Piraterie *nf* **software piracy** Softwarepiraterie *nf*
place *vb* **to place an order** eine Bestellung erteilen
plan 1. *n* Plan (-äne) *nm* **economic plan** Wirtschaftsplan (-äne) *nm* **plan of campaign** Werbeplan (-pläne) *nm* **to make plans** Pläne machen 2. *vb* planen *vb*
planned *adj* **planned economy** Planwirtschaft (-en) *nf* **planned obsolescence** geplanter Verschleiß *nm*
planning *n* Planung *nf* **regional planning** Gebietsplanung *nf*
plant *n* (machinery) Anlage (-n) *nf* **plant hire** Anlagenvermietung *nf* **plant manager** Betriebsleiter (-) *nm*
plastics *npl* **plastics industry** Plastikindustrie *nf*
pledge *n* Versprechen (-) *nn*
plenary *adj* (assembly, session) Plenar- *cpd*
plough back, plow back, to (US) *vb* (profits) Gewinne reinvestieren

point *n* Punkt (-e) *nm* **point of sale** Verkaufspunkt (-e) *nm*
policy *n* **insurance policy** Versicherungspolice (-n) *nf* **pricing policy** Preispolitik *nf*
political *adj* politisch *adj*
politics *npl* Politik *nf*
port *n* Hafen (Häfen) *nm*
portable *adj* tragbar *adj*
portfolio *n* Portefeuille (-n) *nn* **investment portfolio** Effektenportefeuille (-s) *nn*
post 1. *n* (job) Stelle (-n) *nf* **post office** Postamt (-ämter) *nn* 2. *vb* einwerfen *vb*
postal *adj* **postal services** Postdienste *nmpl*
postdate *vb* vordatieren *vb*
poste restante *n* postlagernd *adj*
poster *n* (advertising) Plakat (-e) *nn*
postpone *vb* aufschieben *vb*
potential *n* **sales potential** Verkaufspotential *nn*
pound *n* (weight) Pfund *nn* **pound sterling** Pfund Sterling *nn*
power *n* Macht *nf* **power of attorney** Vollmacht *nf*
preference *n* Vorzug *nm* **community preference** Vorzugszollsystem in EU *nn*
preferential *adj* Vorzugs- *cpd*
premises *npl* Räumlichkeiten *nfpl* **office premises** Bürogebäude *nn*
premium *n* Prämie (-n) *nf* **at a premium** hoch im Kurs
prepayment *n* Vorauszahlung (-en) *nf*
president *n* (of company) Aufsichtsratsvorsitzende/r *nmf*
press *n* **press baron** Pressezar (-en) *nm* **press conference** Pressekonferenz (-en) *nf*
price *n* Preis (-e) *nm* **market price** letzter Kurs *nm* **stock exchange prices** Kurse *nmpl* **threshold price** Höchstpreis (-e) *nm*
pricing *adj* **pricing policy** Preisbildungspolitik *nf*
primary *adj* **primary industry** Grundstoffindustrie (-n) *nf*
prime *adj* **prime lending rate** Prime Rate *nf*
priority *n* Priorität *nf*
private *adj* **private sector** Privatbereich (-e) *nm*
privatization *n* Privatisierung *nf*
privatize *vb* privatisieren *vb*
pro 1. *n* **pros and cons** Für und Wider *nn* 2. *prep* **pro rata** anteilig
probate *n* gerichtliche Testamentsbestätigung *nf*
proceeds *npl* Erlös *nm*
process 1. *n* Verfahren (-) *nn* 2. *vb* bearbeiten *vb*
produce 1. *n* Agrarerzeugnisse *nfpl* 2. *vb* produzieren *vb*
producer *n* Produzent (-en) *nm*
product *n* Produkt (-e) *nn* **primary product** Rohstoff (-e) *nm*
production *n* Produktion *nf* **production line**

Fertigungsstraße (-n) *nf*
productive *adj* produktiv *adj*
productivity *n* Produktivität *nf* **productivity gains** Produktivitätssteigerung *nf*
profession *n* Beruf (-e) *nm* **the professions** die gehobenen Berufe *nmpl*
profit *n* Gewinn *nm* **profit and loss** Gewinn und Verlust *nm/nm* **profit margin** Gewinnspanne (-n) *nf* **net profit** Reingewinn *nm* **operating profit** Betriebsergebnis *nn* **profit-sharing scheme** Gewinnbeteiligung *nf* **to make a profit** einen Gewinn machen
profitability *n* Rentabilität *nf*
profiteer *vb* Preise treiben
program *n* (DP) Programm (-e) *nn*
programmer *n* (DP) Programmierer (-) *nm*
programming *n* (DP) Programmieren *nn*
progress 1. *n* Fortschritt (-e) *nm* 2. *vb* (research, project) Fortschritte machen
project *n* Projekt (-e) *nn*
promissory *adj* **promissory note** Solawechsel (-) *nm*
promote *vb* (person) befördern *vb* (product) werben für
promotion *n* (of product) Werbung *nf* (of person) Beförderung *nf*
promotional *adj* Werbe- *cpd* **promotional budget** Werbeetat (-s) *nm*
prompt *adj* unverzüglich *adj*
property *n* Besitz *nm* **property company** Immobiliengesellschaft (-en) *nf* **property developer** Bauträger (-) *nm* **private property** Privateigentum *nn*
proprietary *adj* Marken- *cpd* **proprietary brand** Markenartikel *nm*
proprietor *n* Inhaber (-) *nm*
prospect *n* **future prospects** die Aussichten *nfpl*
prospectus *n* Prospekt (-e) *nm*
prosperous *adj* florierend *adj*
protectionism *n* Protektionismus *nm*
protectionist *adj* protektionistisch *adj*
provide *vb* (supply) versorgen *vb*
provision *n* (stipulation) Versorgung *nf*
proxy *n* (power) Vollmacht *nf*
public *adj* öffentlich *adj* **public company** Publikumsgesellschaft (-en) *nf* **public funds** Staatsanleihen *npl* **public relations** Öffentlichkeitsarbeit *nf* **public sector** öffentlich *adj* **public service** Staatsdienst *nm*
publicity *n* Publizität *nf*
publishing *n* Verlagswesen *nn* **desk-top publishing** DTP *nn*, Desk-Top-Publishing *nn*
purchase 1. *n* Kauf (-äufe) *nm* **purchase price** Kaufpreis (-e) *nm* 2. *vb* kaufen *vb*
purchasing *n* **purchasing power** Kaufkraft *nf*
pyramid *n* **pyramid scheme** mehrmaliger Erwerb der gleichen Aktie **pyramid selling** Vertrieb nach dem Schneeballprinzip *nm*
qualification *n* Qualifikation *nf* **academic qualification** Qualifikation *nf* **educational qualification** Qualifikation (-en) *nf* **profes-**

sional qualification berufliche Qualifikation *nf*
qualified *adj* **qualified acceptance** eingeschränktes Akzept **qualified personnel** qualifizierte Arbeitskräfte
qualitative *adj* qualitativ *adj*
quality *n* Qualität *nf* **quality control** Qualitätskontrolle (-n) *nf* **quality report** Qualitätsbericht (-e) *nm* **quality standard** Qualitätsnorm (-en) *nf*
quantitative *adj* quantitativ *adj*
quantity *n* Quantität *nf* **quantity discount** Mengenrabatt *nm* **quantity theory of money** Quantitätstheorie des Geldes
quarter *n* (of year) Viertel (-) *nn*
quarterly *adj* vierteljährlich *adj* **quarterly interest** Vierteljahreszinsen *nmpl* **quarterly trade accounts** vierteljährliche Kundenkonten *npl*
quasi-contract *n* Quasi-Vertrag (-äge) *nm*
quasi-income *n* Quasi-Einkommen *nn*
quay *n* Kai (-s) *nm*
quayage *n* Kaigebühren *nfpl*
questionnaire *n* Fragebogendesign *nn* **market research questionnaire** Marktforschungsfragebogen (-) *nm*
queue *n* Schlange (-n) *nf*
quick *adj* **quick assets** flüssige Mittel *nnpl*
quiet *adj* **quiet market** ruhiger Markt (Märkte) *nm*
quit *vb* (resign) zurücktreten *vb*
quittance *n* Schuldenerlaß *nm*
quorate *adj* (meeting) beschlußfähig *adj*
quorum *n* Quorum (-a) *nn* **quorum of creditors** Gläubigerquorum (-a) *nn*
quota *n* Quote (-n) *nf* **quota agreement** Produktionskartell (-e) *nn* **quota buying** Quotenkauf *nm* **import quota** Einfuhrquote (-n) *nf* **sales quota** Absatzquote (-n) *nf* **quota sampling** Quotenauswahlverfahren *nn* **quota system** Quotensystem (-e) *nn*
quotation *n* (price) Preisangabe (-n) *nf*
quoted *adj* **quoted company** börsennotiertes Unternehmen (-) *nn* **quoted investment** börsennotierte Wertpapiere *nnpl* **quoted shares, quoted stocks** (US) börsennotierte Aktien *nfpl*
racket *n* Schwindelgeschäft (-e) *nn*
racketeer *n* Gauner (-) *nm*
racketeering *n* Gaunereien *nfpl*
rag *n* **the rag trade** (informal) Kleiderbranche *nf*
rail *n* **by rail** per Bahn
railway, railroad (US) *n* Eisenbahn (-en) *nf*
raise *vb* (price, interest rate) erhöhen *vb* (capital, loan) aufbringen *vb*
RAM (random access memory) *abbr* (DP) RAM *abbr*
random *adj* **at random** willkürlich *adj* **random selection** Stichprobe *nf*
range *n* (of products) Reihe (-n) *nf*
rate *n* **base rate** Basiszins (-en) *nm* **rate of**

exchange Wechselkurs (-e) *nm* **rate of expansion** Wachstumsrate *nf* **rate of growth** Wachtumsrate (-n) *nf* **rate of inflation** Inflationsrate (-n) *nf* **rate of interest** Zinskurs (-e) *nm*, Zinssatz (-sätze) *nm* **rate of investment** Investitionsrate (-n) *nf* **rate of return** Rendite *nf* **rates** (tax) Kommunalsteuern *nfpl*

ratification *n* Ratifizierung *nf*

ratify *vb* ratifizieren *vb*

ratio *n* Verhältnis (-sse) *nn*

rationale *n* Gründe *nmpl*

rationalization *n* Rationalisierung *nf* **rationalization measures** Rationalisierungsmaßnahmen *nfpl*

rationalize *vb* rationalisieren *vb*

raw *adj* (unprocessed) roh *adj*

re *prep* Betreff *nm*

re-elect *vb* wieder wählen *vb*

re-election *n* Wiederwahl (-en) *nf*

ready *adj* **ready for despatch** versandbereit *adj*

real *adj* **real estate** Immobilien *npl* **real price** effektiver Preis (-e) *nm* **real time** Echtzeit *nf* **real value** Realwert (-e) *nm* **real wages** Effektivlohn (-löhne) *nm*

realization *n* **realization of assets** Flüssigmachung von Vermögenswerten *nf*

realize *vb* (profit) erkennen *vb*

reallocate *vb* (funds) erneut zuteilen *vb*

reallocation *n* (of funds) Umschichten *nn*

realtor (US) *n* Immobilienmakler (-) *nm*

reappoint *vb* wiederernennen *vb*

reappointment *n* Wiederernennung (-en) *nf*

reasonable *adj* (price) vernünftig *adj*

rebate *n* Rabatt (-e) *nm* **to grant a rebate** einen Rabatt gewähren

receipt *n* **to acknowledge receipt** den Empfang bestätigen **to issue a receipt** eine Quittung geben

receive *vb* erhalten *vb*

receiver, administrator (US) *n* (bankruptcy) Konkursverwalter (-) *nm*

recession *n* Rezession (-en) *nf*

recipient *n* Empfänger (-) *nm*

reciprocal *adj* gegenseitig *adj*

reclaimable *adj* (materials) nutzbar *adj*

recommend *vb* empfehlen *vb*

recommendation *n* Empfehlung (-en) *nf*

recompense *n* Entschädigung (-en) *nf*

record *n* Urkunde (-n) *nf* **according to our records** gemäß unseren Aufzeichnungen

recover *vb* **to recover money from sb** Geld einziehen von

recovery *n* (of debt) Einziehung (-en) *nf* (economic) Erholung *nf*

recruit *vb* einstellen *vb*

recruitment *n* Einstellung (-en) *nf* **recruitment campaign** Einstellungskampagne (-n) *nf*

recyclable *adj* recycelbar *adj*

recycle *vb* wiederverwerten *vb*

red *adj* rot *adj* **red tape** Amtsschimmel *nm* **to be in the red** Verluste haben

redeem *vb* einlösen *vb*, amortisieren *vb*

redeemable *adj* amortisierbar *adj* **redeemable bond** Amortisationsschuld (-en) *nf*

redemption *n* Amortisierung *nf* **redemption fund** Amortisationsfonds (-) *nm*

redirect *vb* (mail) nachschicken *vb*

reduce *vb* (prices) reduzieren *vb* (taxes) ermäßigen *vb*

reduced *adj* vermindert *adj* **at a greatly reduced price** zu einem stark herabgesetzten Preis

reduction *n* Ermäßigung (-en) *nf*

redundancy *n* Arbeitslosigkeit *nf*

redundant *adj* arbeitslos *adj* **to make sb redundant** entlassen *vb*

refer *vb* **we refer to our letter of...** wir beziehen uns auf unser Schreiben vom... **we refer you to our head office** wir verweisen Sie an unser Hauptbüro

referee *n* Referenz (-en) *nf* **to act as referee** (Herr X ist bereit,) als Referenz zu dienen

reference *n* Empfehlung (-en) *nf* **credit reference** Kreditauskunft (-ünfte) *nf* **reference number** Geschäftszeichen (-) *nn* **to take up a reference** den Auskunftgeber anschreiben **with reference to** mit Bezug auf

referendum *n* Plebiszit (-e) *nn*

reflation *n* expansive Konjunkturpolitik *nf*

reflationary *adj* expansiv *adj*

reform *n* Reform (-en) *nf* **currency reform** Währungsreform (-en) *nf*

refund 1. *n* Rückerstattung (-en) *nf* 2. *vb* zurückzahlen *vb*

refundable *adj* rückvergütbar *adj*

refurbish *vb* renovieren *vb*

refurbishment *n* Renovierung (-en) *nf*

refusal *n* Ablehnung (-en) *nf*

refuse *vb* **to refuse a claim** einen Anspruch ablehnen **to refuse goods** die Warenannahme verweigern **to refuse payment** die Zahlung verweigern

regard *n* **with regard to...** in bezug auf

regarding *prep* bezüglich *prep*

regional *adj* regional *adj* **regional office** Regionalbüro (-s) *nn*

register *n* Verzeichnis (-sse) *nn*

registered *adj* eingetragen *adj* **registered bond** Namensschuldverschreibung (-en) *nf* **registered capital** Grundkapital *nn* **registered company** handelsgerichtlich eingetragene Gesellschaft (-en) *nf* **registered letter** eingeschriebener Brief (-e) *nm* **registered mail** Einschreibpost *nf* **registered office** Hauptniederlassung (-en) *nf* **registered share** Namensaktie (-n) *nf* **registered trademark** eingetragenes Warenzeichen (-) *nn*

regret *vb* **we regret to inform you that...** wir bedauern, Ihnen mitzuteilen, daß...

regular *adj* regulär *adj* **regular customer** Stammkunde (-n) *nm*

regulation n Vorschrift (-en) nf **according to the regulations** vorschriftsgemäß adj
reimburse vb rückvergüten vb
reimbursement n Rückvergütung (-en) nf
reimport vb wieder einführen vb
reimportation n Wiedereinfuhr nf
reinsurance n Rückversicherung nf
reinsure vb rückversichern vb
reject vb (goods) ablehnen vb
relation n **business relations** Geschäftsbeziehungen nfpl **industrial relations** Beziehungen zwischen Arbeitgebern und Gewerkschaften npl
relationship n **working relationship** Arbeitsverhältnis (-sse) nn
relax vb (restrictions) lockern vb
relevant adj entsprechend adj
reliability n Zuverlässigkeit nf
reliable adj verläßlich adj
relocate vb den Sitz verlegen vb
relocation n Umsiedlung (-en) nf
remaining adj (sum) verbleibend adj
reminder n Mahnung (-en) nf
remittance n Überweisung (-en) nf **remittance advice** Überweisungsanzeige (-n) nf
remunerate vb vergüten vb
remuneration n Vergütung (-en) nf
renew vb (policy, contract) erneuern vb
renewable adj erneuerbar adj
rent 1. n Miete (-n) nf 2. vb (house, office) mieten vb
rental n Miete (-n) nf
repair 1. n **costs of repair** Reparaturkosten npl 2. vb reparieren vb
reparation n Wiederherstellung (-en) nf
repatriation n Repatriierung (-en) nf
repay vb zurückzahlen vb
repayment n (of loan) Rückzahlung (-en) nf
repeat adj **repeat order** Nachbestellung (-en) nf
replace vb ersetzen vb
replacement n (person) Ersatzperson (-en) nf
reply n **in reply to your letter of...** in Antwort auf Ihr Schreiben vom...
report n Bericht (-e) nm **annual report** Jahresbericht (-e) nm **to draw up a report** einen Bericht verfassen **to submit/present a report** einen Bericht vorlegen
repossess vb wieder in Besitz nehmen
repossession n Wiederbesitznahme (-n) nf
representative n Vertreter (-) nm **area representative** Gebietsvertreter (-) nm **sales representative** Handelsvertreter (-) nm
repudiate vb (contract) zurückweisen vb
reputation n Ruf nm **to enjoy a good reputation** einen guten Ruf haben
request n Bitte (-n) nf **request for payment** Zahlungsaufforderung (-en) nf
requirement n Bedarf nm **in accordance with your requirements** Ihren Anforderungen entsprechend **it is a requirement of the contract that...** vertragsgemäß wird ver-

langt, daß...
resale n Weiterverkauf nm
rescind vb widerrufen vb
research n Forschung nf **research and development (R&D)** Forschung und Entwicklung nf/nf **market research** Marktforschung nf
reservation n Reservierung (-en) nf **to make a reservation** eine Reservierung vornehmen
reserve 1. adj **reserve currency** Reservewährung (-en) nf **reserve stock** Vorratslager (-) nn 2. n **currency reserve** Währungsreserve (-n) nf **to hold sth in reserve** auf Lager haben 3. vb reservieren vb
residual adj restlich adj
resign vb zurücktreten vb
resignation n Rücktritt (-e) nm **to hand in one's resignation** seinen Rücktritt erklären
resolution n (decision) Beschluß (-üsse) nm **to make a resolution** einen Beschluß fassen
resolve vb (sort out) lösen **to resolve to do sth** beschließen vb
resort to vb (have recourse) sich auf etwas verlegen
resources npl Mittel nnpl
respect n **in respect of...** hinsichtlich (gen)
response n **in response to...** als Antwort auf
responsibility n **to take responsibility for sth** die Verantwortung übernehmen
responsible adj verantwortlich adj
restrict vb beschränken vb
restriction n Beschränkung (-en) nf **to impose restrictions on** Beschränkungen auferlegen
restrictive adj beschränkend adj **restrictive practices** Wettbewerbsbeschränkung nf
restructure vb umstrukturieren vb
retail adj **retail outlet** Einzelhandelsgeschäft (-e) nn **retail price** Ladenpreis (-e) nm **retail sales tax** Einzelverkaufssteuer nf **retail trade** Einzelhandel nm
retain vb behalten vb
retention n Beibehaltung nf **retention of title** Eigentumsvorbehalt nm
retire vb in den Ruhestand treten vb
retirement n Ruhestand nm **to take early retirement** in Frührente gehen
retrain vb umschulen vb
retraining n Umschulung nf **retraining programme, retraining program** (US) Umschulungsprogramm (-e) nn
return n Rückgabe nf **in return** dafür adv **return on capital** Kapitalverzinsung nf **return on equity** Eigenkapitalrendite nf **return on investment** Ertrag des investierten Kapitals **return on sales** Gewinnspanne (-n) nf **returns** Ertrag nm
returnable adj (deposit) rückgabepflichtig adj
revaluation n (currency) Aufwertung (-en) nf
revalue vb (currency) aufwerten vb
revenue n Einnahmen nfpl
reverse vb umkehren vb
revert vb zurückkehren vb

revert to *vb* zurückkommen auf *vb*
revise *vb* revidieren *vb*
revocable *adj* **revocable letter of credit** widerrufliches Akkreditiv (-e) *nn*
revoke *vb* (offer) rückgängig machen *vb* (licence) zurücknehmen *vb*
right *n* Recht (-e) *nn* **right of recourse** Rückgriffsrecht *nn* **right of way** Vorfahrtsrecht *nn* **the right to do sth** das Recht haben, etwas zu tun **the right to sth** das Recht auf etwas *nn*
rights *npl* **rights issue** Bezugsrechtsangebot (-e) *nn* **sole rights** alleiniges Recht *nn*
rise, raise (US) **1.** *n* (in earnings, unemployment) Anstieg (-e) *nm* (in bank rate) Steigerung *nf* (in inflation) Zunahme (-n) *nf* **2.** *vb* steigen *vb*
risk *n* Risiko (-iken) *nn* **all-risks insurance** globale Risikoversicherung *nf* **risk analysis** Risikoanalyse (-n) *nf* **risk assessment** Risikoeinschätzung (-en) *nf* **at the buyer's risk** vom Käufer übernommenes Risiko *nn* **risk capital** Risikokapital *nn* **risk management** Absicherung von Risiken *nf* **the policy covers the following risks...** die Police bietet folgenden Versicherungsschutz
road *n* Straße (-nn) *nf* **by road** per Spedition **road haulage** Spedition *nf* **road haulage company** Spedition (-en) *nf* **road traffic** Straßenverkehr *nm* **road transport** Straßengüterverkehr *nm*
ROM (read only memory) *abbr* ROM (nur lesbare CD) *abbr*
Rome *n* Rom *nn* **the Treaty of Rome** Vertrag von Rom *nm*
room *n* Raum (-äume) *nm* **room for manoeuvre** Spielraum *nm*
royal *adj* **the Royal Mint (GB)** Britische Münzanstalt *nf*
RSVP (répondez s'il vous plaît) *abbr* U.A.w.g. (Um Antwort wird gebeten) *abbr*
run *vb* (manage) betreiben *vb*
run down *vb* (stocks) Vorräte abbauen
run low *vb* (stocks) einen geringen Vorrat haben
running *n* Betrieb *nm* **running costs** laufende Kosten *npl*
rush *adj* **rush hour** Stoßzeit (-en) *nf* **rush job** eiliger Auftrag (-äge) *nm* **rush order** Eilauftrag (-äge) *nm*
sack, fire* (US) *vb* entlassen *vb*
safe *adj* sicher *adj*
safety *n* Sicherheit *nf* **safety officer** Sicherheitsbeauftragte/r *nmf*
salary *n* Gehalt (-älter) *nn* **salary scale** Gehaltsskala (-en) *nf*
sale *n* Verkauf (-äufe) *nm* **closing-down sale, closing-out sale** (US) Räumungsverkauf (-äufe) *nm* **sales campaign** Verkaufskampagne (-n) *nf* **sales conference** Verkaufskonferenz (-en) *nf* **sales department** Verkaufsabteilung (-en) *nf* **export sales**

Auslandsabsatz *nm* **sales figures** Verkaufsziffern *nfpl* **sales forecast** Absatzprognose (-n) *nf* **home sales** Inlandsabsatz *nm* **sales ledger** Warenausgangsbuch (-bücher) *nn* **sales management** Verkaufsleitung *nf*
salesperson *n* Verkäufer (-) *nm*
salvage *vb* retten *vb*
sample 1. *n* Muster (-) *nn* **2.** *vb* probieren *vb*
sampling *n* Probe *nf*
sanction *n* **trade sanctions** Handelssanktionen *nfpl*
savings *npl* Einsparungen *nfpl*, Ersparnisse *nfpl* **savings bank** Sparkasse *nf*
scab* *n* Streikbrecher (-) *nm*
scale *n* Skala (-en) *nf*
scarcity *n* Knappheit (-en) *nf*
schedule 1. *n* Zeitplan (-pläne) *nm* **2.** *vb* planen *vb*
scheme *n* **pension scheme** Pensionsplan (-pläne) *nm* **recovery scheme** Bergungsplan (-pläne) *nm*
scrap *n* (metal) Altmetall *nn*
scrip *n* Interimsschein (-e) *nm*
SDRs (special drawing rights) *abbr* Sonderziehungsrechte *nnpl*
sea *n* **by sea** auf dem Seeweg, per Schiff **sea freight** Seefracht *nf*
seal 1. *n* Siegel (-) *nn* **2.** *vb* versiegeln *vb*
sealed *adj* **sealed bid** Submissionsgeld im versiegelten Umschlag *nn*
season *n* Jahreszeit (-en) *nf* **high season** Hochsaison (-s) *nf* **low season** Nebensaison (-s) *nf*
seasonal *adj* jahreszeitlich bedingt *adj*
SEC (Securities and Exchange Commission) (GB) *abbr* Börsenaufsichtsrat *nm*
secondary *adj* sekundär *adj* **secondary industry** verarbeitende Industrie (-n) *nf* **secondary market** Nebenmarkt (-märkte)
secondment *n* Abordnung (-en) *nf*
secretary *n* Sekretär/in (-en/innen) *nm/nf* **executive secretary** Geschäftsführer (-) *nm*
sector *n* Sektor (-en) *nm* **primary sector** Grundstoffindustrie *nf* **secondary sector** Fertigungsindustrie *nf* **tertiary sector** Dienstleistungsindustrie *nf*
secure *adj* sicher *adj*
secured *adj* gesichert *adj* **secured loan** gesicherter Kredit (-e) *nm*
securities *npl* Wertpapiere *nnpl* **gilt-edged securities** mündelssichere Wertpapiere *nnpl* **listed securities** amtlich notierte Werte *nmpl* **unlisted securities** nicht notierte Werte *nmpl*
security *n* Sicherheit *nf* **Social Security (GB)** Sozialversicherung *nf*
self-assessment *n* Selbsteinschätzung *nf*
self-employed *adj* freiberuflich *adj*
self-financing *adj* Eigenfinanzierung *nf*
self-management *n* Selbstverwaltung *nf*
self-sufficient *adj* autark *adj*
sell 1. *n* **hard sell** aggressive Verkaufstaktik

nf **soft sell** weiche Verkaufstaktik *nf* **2.** *vb* verkaufen *vb* **to sell sth at auction** versteigern *vb* **to sell sth in bulk** im Großhandel verkaufen *vb* **to sell sth on credit** auf Kredit verkaufen *vb* **to sell sth retail** im Einzelhandel verkaufen *vb* **this article sells well** diese Ware verkauft sich gut **to sell sth wholesale** im Großhandel verkaufen *vb*
sell off *vb* abverkaufen *vb*
sell up *vb* (Besitz) verkaufen *vb*
seller *n* Verkäufer (-) *nm*
semi-skilled *adj* angelernt *adj*
send *vb* senden *vb*
send back *vb* zurücksenden *vb*
sendee *n* Empfänger (-) *nm*
sender *n* Absender (-) *nm*
senior *adj* höher *adj* **senior management** Geschäftsleitung *nf*
seniority *n* höhere Position *nf*
service *n* Dienstleistung *nf* **after-sales service** Kundendienst *nm* **civil service** öffentlicher Dienst *nm* **service included** inklusive Bedienung **service industry** Dienstleistungsindustrie *nf* **National Health Service (GB)** britischer staatlicher Gesundheitsdienst *nm*
set up *vb* (company) einrichten *vb*, gründen *vb*
settle *vb* (dispute) beilegen *vb* (account) erledigen *vb*
severance *n* Lösen *nn* **severance pay** Abfindung (-en) *nf*
shady* *adj* (dealings) dunkel *adj*
share 1. *n* Aktie (-n) *nf* **a share in the profits** Gewinnbeteiligung *nf* **market share** Aktienmarkt (-märkte) *nm* **ordinary share** Stammaktie (-n) *nf* **2.** *vb* teilen *vb* **to share the responsibilities** gemeinsam die Verantwortung tragen
shareholder *n* Aktionär (-en) *nm*
shark* *n* Geschäftshai (-e) *nm*
sharp *adj* scharf *adj* **sharp practice** unsaubere Geschäfte *nnpl*
shift *n* Schicht (-en) *nf* **the three-shift system** dreischichtiger Betriebsplan (-pläne) *nm* **shift work** Schichtarbeit *nf*
shipbuilding *n* Schiffbau *nm*
shipment *n* (consignment) Versand *nm*
shipper *n* Spediteur (-e) *nm*
shipping *n* Verladung *nf* **shipping agent** Spediteur (-e) *nm* **shipping broker** Schiffsmakler (-) *nm* **shipping line** Schiffahrtslinie (-n) *nf*
shipyard *n* Schiffswerft (-en) *nf*
shirker* *n* Drückeberger (-) *nm*
shoddy* *adj* minderwertig *adj*
shop *n* Laden (-äden) *nm* **shop assistant** Verkäufer (-) *nm* **closed shop** gewerkschaftspflichtiger Betrieb (-e) *nm* **shop steward** Gewerkschaftsvertreter (-) *nm* **to shut up shop** (informal) den Laden schließen, das Geschäft aufgeben **to talk shop** (informal)

fachsimpeln *vb*
shopping *n* Einkauf *nm* **shopping centre** Einkaufszentrum (-en) *nn*
short *adj* kurz *adj* **short delivery** Teillieferung (-en) *nf* **to be on short time** kurz arbeiten *vb*
shortage *n* Mangel (Mängel) *nm*
show *n* (exhibition) Ausstellung (-en) *nf*
showroom *n* Schauraum (-räume) *nm*
shredder *n* Reißwolf (-wölfe) *nm*
shrink *vb* schrumpfen *vb*
shrinkage *n* Rückgang (-gänge) *nm* **stock shrinkage** Lagerverlust (-e) *nm*
shutdown *n* Stillegung (-en) *nf*
shuttle *n* Pendelverkehr *nm*
SIB (Securities and Investment Board) (GB) *abbr* Amt für Anlagen und Wertpapiere *nn*
sick *adj* krank *adj* **sick leave** Krankenurlaub *nm*
sickness *n* Krankheit (-en) *nf* **sickness benefit** Krankengeld (-er) *nn*
sight *n* Sicht *nf* **sight draft** Sichtwechsel (-) *nm*
sign *vb* unterschreiben *vb*
signatory *n* Unterzeichner (-) *nm*
signature *n* Unterschrift (-en) *nf*
silent *adj* still *adj* **silent partner** stiller Teilhaber (-) *nm*
sinking *adj* **sinking fund** Ablösungsfonds (-) *nm*
sit-in *n* (strike) Sitzstreik *nm*
size *n* Größe (-n) *nf*
skill *n* Fertigkeit *nf*
skilled *adj* (worker) gelernter Arbeiter *nm*
slackness *n* (laxity) Nachlässigkeit *nf*
sliding *adj* gleitend *adj* **sliding scale** gleitender (Lohn)Tarif (-e) *nm*
slogan *n* Slogan (-s) *nm*
slow down *vb* verlangsamen *vb*
slowdown *n* Verlangsamung *nf*
slump 1. *n* Preissturz (-ürze) *nm* **2.** *vb* fallen *vb*
slush *adj* **slush fund** Schmiergeldfonds (-) *nm*
small *adj* klein *adj* **small ads** Kleinanzeigen *nfpl* **small scale** begrenzt *adj*
smuggle *vb* schmuggeln *vb*
society *n* **building society** Bausparkasse (-n) *nf* **consumer society** Verbrauchergesellschaft (-en) *nf*
socio-economic *adj* sozioökonomisch *adj* **socio-economic categories** sozialwirtschaftliche Begriffe *nmpl*
software *n* Software *nf* **software package** Softwarepaket (-e) *nn*
sole *adj* **sole agent** Alleinvertreter (-) *nm*
solicitor, lawyer *n* (US) *n* Anwalt (-älte) *nm*
solvency *n* Zahlungsfähigkeit *nf*
solvent *adj* zahlungsfähig *adj*
source *n* Quelle (-n) *nf*
sourcing *n* Beschaffung *nf*
specialist *n* Fachmann (Fachleute) *nm*

speciality n Spezialität (-en) nf
specialize vb spezialisieren vb
specification n Angabe (-en) nf
specify vb angeben vb
speculate vb spekulieren vb
speculator n Spekulant (-en) nm
spend vb ausgeben vb
spending n Ausgaben nfpl
spendthrift adj verschwenderisch adj
sphere n **sphere of activity** Wirkungskreis (-e) nm, Tätigkeitsfeld (-er) nn
spin-off n Nebenprodukt nn
split 1. adj **split division** nicht einstimmige Abstimmung nf **2.** vb teilen vb, spalten vb
spoilage n Schadenhaftigkeit nf
spoils npl Ausbeute nf
spokesperson n Sprecher (-) nm
sponsor n Förderer (-) nm
sponsorship n Förderung (-en) nf
spot adj **spot cash** sofortige Bezahlung nf **spot market** Spotmarkt (-märkte) nm **spot price** Kassapreis (-e) nm **spot rate** Kassakurs (-e) nm
spread vb (payments) ausbreiten vb
spreadsheet n Tabellenkalkulation nf
squander vb verschwenden vb
squeeze 1. n **credit squeeze** Kreditbeschränkung (-en) nf **2.** vb (spending) drücken vb
stable adj (economy) stabil adj
staff n Belegschaft nf
staffing n Stellenbesetzung nf
stage n **in stages** stufenweise adv
staged adj **staged payments** Ratenzahlungen nfpl
stagger vb (holidays) staffeln vb
stagnation n Stagnierung nf
stake n Anteil (-e) nm
stakeholder n Anteilseigner (-) nm
stalemate n Patt nn
standard 1. adj Standard- cpd **standard agreement** Modellvertrag (-äge) nm **2.** n **gold standard** Goldstandard nm **standard of living** Lebensstandard (-s) nm
standardization n Vereinheitlichung nf
standardize vb vereinheitlichen vb
standing adj **standing charges** laufende Unkosten npl **standing order** Dauerauftrag (-äge) nm
staple adj **staple commodities** Hauptprodukte nnpl
start-up n Beginn nm **start-up capital** Startkapital nn
state n **state-owned enterprise** verstaatlichter Betrieb (-e)
statement n **bank statement** Kontoauszug (-üge) nm
statistics npl Statistik nf
status n **financial status** Finanzlage (-n) nf **status quo** Status quo nm
statute n Statut (-e) nn
steel n Stahl (-e) nm **steel industry**

Stahlindustrie (-n) nf
sterling n englisches Pfund nn **sterling area** Sterlinggebiet nn **sterling balance** Pfundguthaben (-) nn **pound sterling** Pfund Sterling (-) nn
stock, inventory (US) n (goods) Lager (-) nn **stock control** Lagerkontrolle nf **stock exchange** Börse (-n) nf **in stock** auf Lager **stock market** Wertpapiermarkt (-märkte) nm **out of stock** ausverkauft **stocks and shares** Aktien und Obligationen npl
stockbroker n Börsenmakler (-) nm
stockholder n Anteilseigner (-) nm
stocktaking n Inventur nf
stoppage n (strike) Stillegung (-en) nf
storage n **storage capacity** Lagervermögen nn **cold storage plant** Kühlhaus (-häuser) nn
store n (shop) Geschäft (-e) nn **chain store** Kettenladen (-läden) nm **department store** Warenhaus (-häuser) nn
stowage n Laderaum nm
strategic adj strategisch adj
strategy n Strategie (-n) nf
stress n **executive stress** Führungsstress nm
strike 1. n Streik (-s) nm **strike action** Streikmaßnahmen nfpl **strike ballot** Streikabstimmung (-en) nf **wildcat strike** wilder Streik (-s) nm **2.** vb streiken vb
strikebreaker n Streikbrecher (-) nm
striker n Streikende/r nmf
subcontract vb weitervergeben an vb
subcontractor n Subunternehmer nm
subordinate n Untergeordnete/r nmf
subscribe vb abonnieren vb
subsidiary n Tochtergesellschaft (-en) nf
subsidize vb subventionieren vb
subsidy n Subvention (-en) nf **state subsidy** öffentlicher Zuschuß (-üsse) nm
suburbs npl Vororte nmpl **outer suburbs** Außenbezirke nmpl
supermarket n Supermarkt (-märkte) nm
supertanker n Riesentanker (-) nm
supertax n Zusatzsteuer (-n) nf
supervisor n Aufseher (-) nm
supervisory n aufsichtsführend adj **supervisory board** Aufsichtsrat (-räte) nm
supplementary adj ergänzend adj
supplier n Lieferant (-en) nm
supply 1. n Lieferung (-en) nf, Bestand (-ände) nm **supply and demand** Angebot und Nachfrage nn/nf **2.** vb liefern vb
surface n **surface mail** Post auf dem Landweg/Seeweg nf
surplus n Überschuß (-üsse) nm **budget surplus** Haushaltsüberschuß (-üsse) nm **trade surplus** Handelsüberschuß (-üsse) nm
surtax n Steuerzuschlag (-äge) nm
survey n **market research survey** Marktforschungsstudie (-n) nf
swap 1. n Tausch (-e) nm **2.** vb tauschen vb
sweetener* n (bribe) Schmiergeld (-er) nn
swindle* n Schwindel (-) nm

swindler* n Schwindler (-) nm
switchboard n Telefonzentrale (-n) nf
  switchboard operator Telefonist (-en) nm
syndicate n Syndikat (-e) nn
synergy n Synergie (-n) nf
synthesis n Synthese (-n) nf
synthetic adj synthetisch adj
system n System (-e) nn expert system
  Expertensystem (-e) nn systems analyst
  Systemanalytiker (-) nm
table vb (motion, paper) einbringen vb
tabulate vb (data) tabellarisieren vb
tabulated adj tabellarisch adj tabulated data
  tabellarische Datenaufstellung nf
tacit adj stillschweigend adj by tacit agreement aufgrund einer stillschweigenden Vereinbarung
tactic n Taktik nf delaying tactics
  Verzögerungstaktik nf selling tactics
  Verkaufsmethoden nfpl
tailor vb (adapt) anpassen vb
take vb to take legal action gerichtlich
  vorgehen vb to take notes Notizen machen
  vb to take part in teilnehmen an (+dat) vb
  to take the chair den Vorsitz übernehmen vb
  to take the lead die Führung übernehmen to
  take one's time Zeit nehmen
take over vb (company) übernehmen vb
takeover n Übernahme (-n) nf
takeup n Inanspruchnahme nf
takings npl Einkünfte nfpl
talk 1. n Gespräch (-e) nn sales talk
  Verkaufsgespräch nn 2. vb to talk business
  etwas Geschäftliches besprechen
tally 1. n Rechnung (-en) nf 2. vb
  übereinstimmen vb
tally up vb zusammenrechnen vb
tally with vb übereinstimmen mit
tangible adj tangible asset Sachanlage (-n)
  nf
tap vb anzapfen vb to tap a market einen
  Markt erschließen to tap resources Geldmittel flüssig machen
target n Ziel (-e) nn target date Stichtag (-e)
  nm target market Zielmarkt (-märkte) nm
  production target Produktionsziel (-e) nn
  sales target Verkaufsziel (-e) nn to set a
  target ein Ziel setzen
targeted adj targeted campaign gezielte
  Aktion nf
tariff n Tarif (-e) nm tariff barrier Zollschranke
  (-n) nf tariff negotiations Zollverhandlungen
  nfpl tariff quota Zollkontingent (-e) nn tariff
  reform Zollreform (-en) nf to raise tariffs
  Zölle erhöhen vb
task n Aufgabe (-n) nf task management
  Aufgabenverteilung nf
tax n Steuer (-n) nf after tax nach Abzug der
  Steuern tax allowance Steuervergünstigung
  (-en) nf before tax vor Abzug der Steuern
  capital gains tax Kapitalzuwachssteuer (-n)
  nf tax claim Steuerforderung nf tax-deduc-

tible steuerlich absetzbar adj direct tax
  direkte Steuer (-n) nf tax-free steuerfrei adj
  income tax Einkommensteuer (-n) nf indirect tax indirekte Steuer (-n) nf tax liability
  Steuerpflicht (-en) nf tax rate Steuersatz
  (-sätze) nm to levy taxes Steuern einheben
  vb value-added tax, sales tax (US)
  Mehrwertsteuer (-n) nf tax year Finanzjahr
  (-e) nn
taxable adj taxable income
  Steuereinkommen nn
taxation n Besteuerung nf corporate taxation Firmenbesteuerung nf
taxpayer n Steuerzahler nm
team n Team (-s) nn research team
  Forschungsteam (-s) nn
technical adj technical director technischer
  Direktor (-) nm
technician n Techniker (-) nm
technique n sales technique
  Verkaufsmethode (-n) nf
technology n Technologie (-n) nf information
  technology Informationstechnik nf technology transfer Technologietransfer nm
telebanking n Telefonbankdienst (-e) nm
telecommunications npl Fernmeldewesen
  nn
telecopier n Fernkopierer (-) nm
telefax n Fax nn
telephone n Telefon (-e) nn telephone box,
  telephone booth (US) Telefonzelle (-n) nf
  telephone call Anruf (-e) nm telephone
  directory Telefonbuch (-bücher) nn telephone number Telefonnummer (-n) nf
teleprocessing n Datenfernübertragung nf
telesales npl Telefonverkauf nm
televise vb im Fernsehen bringen vb
teleworking n Heimarbeit am Computer
telex 1. n Fernschreiber (-) nm 2. vb
  (message) eine Mitteilung per Telex schicken
teller n Schalterbeamte (-n) nm
temporary adj provisorisch adj temporary
  employment befristete Stellung (-en) nf
tenant n Mieter (-) nm
tend vb tendieren vb to tend toward
  anstreben vb
tendency n Tendenz (-en) nf market tendencies Markttrend (-s) nm
tender n Angebot (-e) nn tender offer
  Übernahmeangebot (-e) nn tender price
  Angebotspreis (-e) nm sale by tender Verkauf aufgrund einer Ausschreibung (-äufe)
  nm to lodge a tender ein Angebot
  einreichen to put sth out for tender
  ausschreiben vb
tenderer n Angebotsteller (-) nm
tendering n Ausschreibung nf
tentative adj tentative offer unverbindliches
  Angebot (-e) nn tentative plan vorläufiger
  Plan (-äne) nm
tenure n Amtszeit nf
term n at term zum festgesetzten Termin

long term langfristig *adj* **medium term** mittelfristig *adj* **term of office** Amtszeit (-en) *nf* **terms and conditions** Bedingungen *nfpl* **short term** kurzfristig *adj* **terms of reference** Aufgabenbereich *nm* **terms of trade** Austauschrelationen *nfpl*

terminal 1. *adj* Abschluß- *cpd*, End- *cpd* **terminal bonus** Endprämie *nf* **terminal market** Terminalmarkt (-märkte) *nm* **2.** *n* **air terminal** Flughafenterminal (-e) *nm* **computer terminal** Computerterminal (-e) *nn*

termination *n* Beendigung (-en) *nf* **termination date** Verfalltag (-e) *nm* **termination of employment** Beendigung des Dienstverhältnisses (-en) *nf*

tertiary *adj* **tertiary industry** Dienstleistungsbereich (-e) *nm*

test *n* **test case** Musterfall (-fälle) *nm* **test data** Testdaten *nnpl* **to put sth to the test** auf die Probe stellen *vb* **to stand the test** die Probe bestehen

test-market *vb* Testmarkt (-märkte) *nm*

testimonial *n* Referenz (-en) *nf*

textile *n* Textil (-ien) *nn* **textile industry** Textilidustrie (-n) *nf*

theory *n* **in theory** theoretisch *adj*

third *adj* dritte/r *adj* **third party** dritte Person (-en) *nf* **third-party insurance** Haftpflichtversicherung *nf* **the Third World** Dritte Welt *nf*

thirty *adj* dreißig *adj* **Thirty-Share Index (GB)** Dreißig-Aktien-Index *nm*

thrash out *vb* (agreement, policy) ausdiskutieren *vb*

three *adj* drei *adj* **three-way split** Dreiteilung (-en) *nf*

threshold *n* **tax threshold** Steuerschwelle (-n) *nf*

thrive *vb* florieren *vb*

through *prep* durch *prep* **to get through to sb** (phone) durchkommen zu jemandem *vb* **to put sb through (to sb)** (phone) verbinden mit *vb*

tick over *vb* (ganz) normal laufen *vb*

ticket *n* Fahrkarte (-n) *nf*, Flugkarte (-n) *nf* **ticket agency** Verkaufsstelle (-n) *nf* **ticket office** Fahrkartenschalter (-) *nm*, Kasse (-n) *nf* **price ticket** Preisetikett (-e) *nn* **return ticket, round-trip ticket** (US) Rückfahrkarte (-n) *nf* **season ticket** Zeitkarte (-n) *nf*, Jahreskarte (-n) *nf* **single/one-way ticket** (rail/flight) einfache Fahrkarte (-n) *nf*

tide over *vb* ausreichen *vb*

tie up *vb* (capital) festmachen *vb*

tied *adj* **tied loan** zweckgebundene Anleihe (-n) *nf*

tier *n* Rang (-änge) *nm* **two-tier system** zweistufiges Verwaltungssystem (-e) *nn*

tight *adj* eng *adj* **to be on a tight budget** ein knapp bemessenes Budget haben

time *n* Zeit (-en) *nf* **time and a half** 50% Lohnzuschlag *nm* **double time**

Lohnzuschlag (-äge) *nm* **time frame** Zeitraum (-räume) *nm* **lead time** Einführungszeit (-en) *nf* **time limit** Zeitbeschränkung (-en) *nf* **time management** Zeiteinteilung *nf*

time-consuming *adj* zeitraubend *adj*

time-saving *adj* zeitsparend *adj*

timescale *n* Zeitmaßstab (-stäbe) *nm*

timeshare *n* Wohnung auf Timesharing-Basis (-en) *nf*

timetable *n* Fahrplan (-äne) *nm*, Stundenplan (-äne) *nm*

timing *n* Terminierung *nf*

tip *n* (suggestion) Hinweis (-e) *nm* **market tip** Börsentip (-s) *nm*

title *n* (to goods) Titel (-) *nm* **title deed** Eigentumsurkunde (-n) *nf*

token *n* **token payment** Teilzahlung (-en) *nf* **token strike** Warnstreik (-s) *nm*

toll *n* Abgabe (-n) *nf*

ton *n* Tonne (-n) *nf* **metric ton** metrische Tonne (-n) *nf*

tone *n* **dialling tone, dial tone** (US) (phone) Amtszeichen (-) *nn*

tonnage *n* Tonnage *nf* **bill of tonnage** Meßbrief (-e) *nm* **gross tonnage** Bruttotonnage *nf* **net tonnage** Nettotonnage *nf*

top *adj* **top management** Führungsspitze (-n) *nf* **top prices** Höchstpreise *nmpl* **top priority** höchste Dringlichkeit *nf*

top-level *adj* Spitzen- *cpd*

top-of-the-range *adj* Spitzenqualität *nf*

total 1. *adj* total *adj* **total sales** Gesamtumsatz *nm* **2.** *n* Gesamtsumme (-n) *nf* **the grand total** Gesamtsumme (-n) *nf*

tough *adj* **tough competition** harte Konkurrenz *nf*

tour *n* **tour of duty** Amtsperiode (-n) *nf*

tourism *n* Tourismus *nm*

tourist *n* Tourist (-en) *nm* **the tourist trade** Fremdenverkehrsbranche *nf*

town *n* Stadt (-ädte) *nf* **town centre** Stadtmitte (-n) *nf* **town council** Gemeinderat (-räte) *nm* **town hall** Rathaus (-häuser) *nn* **town planning** Stadtplanung *nf*

TQM (Total Quality Management) *abbr* Total Quality Management *nn*

track *n* Spur (-en) *nf*, Schiene (-n) *nf* **track record** bisherige Erfolge *nmpl* **to be on the right track** auf dem richtigen Weg sein

trade 1. *adj* **trade agreement** Handelsabkommen (-) *nn* **trade balance** Handelsbilanz (-en) *nf* **trade barrier** Handelsschranke (-n) *nf* **trade cycle** Konjunkturzyklus (-klen) *nm* **trade directory** Firmenverzeichnis (-sse) *nn* **trade fair** Messe (-n) *nf* **trade figures** Handelsziffern *nfpl* **trade name** Handelsbezeichnung (-en) *nf* **trade price** Großhandelspreis (-e) *nm* **trade restrictions** Handelsbeschränkungen *nfpl* **trade secret** Branchengeheimnis (-sse) *nn*

trade talks Handelsgespräche *nnpl* **Trade Descriptions Act** Warenkennzeichnungsgesetz (-e) *nn* **Trades Union Congress** Dachorganisation der britischen Gewerkschaften *nf* **trade union** Gewerkschaft (-en) *nf* **2.** *n* Handel *nm*, Gewerbe *nn* **balance of trade** Handelsbilanz (-en) *nf* **by trade** von Beruf **fair trade** Preisbindung *nf* **foreign trade** Außenhandel *nm* **retail trade** Einzelhandel *nm* **to be in the trade** (informal) in der Branche sein *vb* **3** *vb* handeln *vb* **to trade as** (name) geschäftlich tätig sein als... *vb* **to trade with sb** handeln mit *vb*

trademark *n* Warenzeichen (-) *nn* **registered trademark** eingetragenes Warenzeichen (-) *nn*

trader *n* Händler (-) *nm*

trading *adj* **trading area** Verkaufsgebiet (-e) *nn* **trading capital** Betriebskapital *nn* **trading company** Handelsgesellschaft (-en) *nf* **trading estate** Industriesiedlung (-en) *nf*, Industriegelände (-) *nn* **trading loss** Betriebsverlust (-e) *nm* **trading margin** Handelsspanne (-n) *nf* **trading nation** Handelsnation (-en) *nf* **trading partner** Handelspartner (-) *nm* **trading standards** Handelsnormen *nfpl* **Trading Standards Office (US)** Handelsnormenausschuß *nm* **trading year** Geschäftsjahr (-e) *nn*

traffic *n* **air traffic** Luftverkehr *nm* **rail traffic** Schienenverkehr *nm* **road traffic** Straßenverkehr *nm* **sea traffic** Schiffsverkehr *nm*

train 1. *n* **goods train, freight train** (US) Güterzug (-üge) *nm* **passenger train** Personenzug (-üge) *nm* **2.** *vb* (staff) ausbilden *vb*

trainee *n* Auszubildende/r *nmf* **trainee manager** Nachwuchsführungskraft (-äfte) *nf*

training *n* Ausbildung *nf* **advanced training** Fortbildung *nf* **training centre** Ausbildungszentrum (-en) *nn* **training course** Ausbildungslehrgang (-gänge) *nm*

transaction *n* Transaktion (-en) *nf* **cash transaction** Kassegeschäft (-e) *nn* **transaction management** Transaktionsverwaltung *nf*

transcribe *vb* übertragen *vb*

transfer 1. *adj* **transfer desk** (transport) Transitschalter (-) *nm* **transfer duty** Umschreibungsgebühr (-en) *nf* **transfer lounge** (transport) Transitraum (-räume) *nm* **transfer payments** Übernahmezahlung (-en) *nf* **transfer price** Tageskurs (-e) *nm* **transfer tax** Kapitalverkehrssteuer (-n) *nf* **transfer technology** Transfertechnik *nf* **2.** *n* Transfer (-s) *nm* **bank transfer** Banküberweisung (-en) *nf* **capital transfer** Kapitaltransferierung *nf* **credit transfer** bargeldlose Überweisung (-en) *nf* **3** *vb* (call) ein R-Gespräch vornehmen *vb* (ownership)

überschreiben *vb* (transport) umsteigen *vb*

transferable *adj* übertragbar *adj*

transit *n* Durchreise *nf* **transit goods** Transitgüter *npl* **in transit** unterwegs **lost in transit** auf dem Transport verlorengegangen **transit lounge** (transport) Warteraum für Transitpassagiere (-räume) *nm* **transit passenger** (transport) Durchreisende/r *nmf*

transmit *vb* senden *vb*

transnational *adj* überstaatlich *adj*

transport *n* Transport *nm* **transport agent** Spediteur (-e) *nm* **air transport** Lufttransport *nm* **transport company** Verkehrsbetrieb (-e) *nm* **public transport** öffentlicher Verkehr *nm* **rail transport** Bahntransport *nm* **road transport** Straßentransport *nm*

transportation *n* Versand *nm*

transship *vb* umladen *vb*

travel *n* **travel agency** Reisebüro (-s) *nn* **air travel** Flugreisen *nfpl* **business travel** Geschäftsreisen *nfpl* **travel insurance** Reiseversicherung *nf*

traveller, traveler (US) *n* Reisende/r *nmf* **traveller's cheque, traveler's check** (US) Reisescheck (-s) *nm*

travelling, traveling (US) *n* Reisen *nn* **travelling expenses, travel expenses** (US) Reisespesen *npl*

treasurer *n* **treasurer check** (US) Schatzanweisung *nf* **company treasurer** Finanzdirektor (-en) *nm*

treasury *n* **Treasury bill** Schatzanweisung (-en) *nf* **the Treasury** britisches Finanzministerium (-ien) *nn* **the Treasury Department (US)** US-Finanzministerium *nn*

treaty *n* Vertrag (-äge) *nm* **commercial treaty** Handelsabkommen (-) *nn* **to make a treaty** einen Vertrag abschließen

trend *n* Trend (-s) *nm* **trend analysis** Trendanalyse (-n) *nf* **current trend** aktueller Trend (-s) *nm* **economic trend** Konjunkturverlauf *nm* **market trend** Markttrend (-s) *nm* **price trend** Preisentwicklung (-en) *nf* **to buck a trend** der Konjunkturentwicklung entgegenhandeln **to set a trend** richtungsweisend sein *vb*

trial *n* **trial and error** Ausprobieren *nn* **trial offer** Probeangebot (-e) *nn* **trial period** Probezeit *nf* **to carry out trials** Tests durchführen

tribunal *n* **industrial tribunal** Arbeitsgericht (-e) *nn*

trim *vb* (investment) kürzen *vb* (workforce) abbauen *vb*

trimming *n* Kürzung *nf* **cost trimming** Kosteneinsparung *nf*

trip *n* **business trip** Geschäftsreise (-n) *nf* **round trip** Rundfahrt (-en) *nf*

triplicate *n* dreifache Ausführung *nf* **in triplicate** in dreifacher Ausführung

trust *n* Vertrauen *nn* **trust agreement**

Treuhandvertrag (-äge) *nm* **trust company**
Trust (-s) *nm* **trust estate**
Treuhandvermögen (-) *nn* **trust fund**
Treuhandmittel *nnpl* **investment trust**
Kapitalanlagegesellschaft *nf* **to hold sth in
trust** treuhänderisch verwalten **to set up a
trust** eine Stiftung errichten **to supply sth
on trust** auf Kredit liefern *vb* **unit trust**
Kapitalanlagegesellschaft (-en) *nf*
trustee *n* Treuhänder (-) *nm* **trustee department** (bank) Sparkasse (-n) *nf*
trusteeship *n* Treuhandschaft *nf*
try out *vb* probieren *vb*
turn *vb* (market) ändern *vb*
turn down *vb* (offer) ablehnen *vb*
turn on *vb* (machine) einschalten *vb*
turn out *vb* (end) sich herausstellen *vb*
turn over *vb* wenden *vb*
turnabout *n* Umkehr *nf*
turning *adj* **turning point** Wendepunkt (-e)
nm
turnover *n* Umsatz (-ätze) *nm* **capital turnover** Kapitalumschlag *nm* **turnover rate**
Umsatzrate (-n) *nf* **turnover ratio**
Umsatzquote (-n) *nf* **turnover tax**
Umsatzsteuer (-n) *nf*
twenty-four *adj* **twenty-four-hour service**
Dienst rund um die Uhr *nm*
two *adj* zwei *adj* **two-speed** Zweigang- *cpd*
two-tier zweistufig *adj* **two-way** zweibahnig
adj
tycoon *n* Großindustrielle/r *nmf*
type 1. *n* **bold type** Fettschrift *nf*, fett
gedruckt *adj* **italic type** Kursivdruck *nm*
large type Großgedrucktes *nn* **small type**
Kleingedrucktes *nn* **2.** *vb* tippen *vb*
typewriter *n* Schreibmaschine (-n) *nf*
typing *n* Tippen *nn* **typing error** Tippfehler (-)
nm
typist *n* Typist/in (-en/-innen) *nm/nf*
ultimo *adj* letzte/r *adj*
unanimous *adj* einstimmig *adj*
uncleared *adj* (customs) unabgefertigt *adj*
(cheque) noch nicht verrechnet *adj*
unconditional *adj* bedingungslos *adj*
unconfirmed *adj* unbestätigt *adj*
undeclared *adj* (goods) nicht deklariert *adj*
undercapitalized *adj* unterkapitalisiert *adj*
undercharge *vb* zu wenig berechnen *vb*
undercut *vb* unterbieten *vb*
underdeveloped *adj* **underdeveloped country** Entwicklungsland (-länder) *nn*
underemployed *adj* unterbeschäftigt *adj*
underinsured *adj* zu niedrig versichert
underpay *vb* unterbezahlen *vb*
underpayment *n* Unterbezahlung (-en) *nf*
undersell *vb* verschleudern *vb*
understanding *n* Vereinbarung *nf*
undersubscribed *adj* unpopulär *adj*
undertake *vb* unternehmen *vb*
undertaking *n* Unternehmen (-) *nn*
undervalue *vb* unterbewerten *vb*

underwrite *vb* (risk) Versicherung unter Risi-
koverteilung übernehmen
underwriter *n* Unterzeichner (-),
Versicherungsagent (-en)
undischarged *adj* (bankrupt) nicht
rehabilitiert *adj*
unearned *adj* **unearned income** Einkünfte
aus Kapitalvermögen *npl*
unemployed *adj* arbeitslos *adj*
unemployment *n* Arbeitslosigkeit *nf* **unemployment benefit** Arbeitslosenunterstützung
nf **unemployment insurance**
Arbeitslosenversicherung *nf* **level of unemployment** Arbeitslosenziffer (-n) *nf* **rate of
unemployment** Arbeitslosenrate (-n) *nf*
unexpected *adj* unerwartet *adj*
unfair *adj* **unfair dismissal** ungerechtfertigte
Kündigung (-en) *nf*
unforeseen *adj* **unforeseen circumstances**
unvorhergesehene Umstände *nmpl*
unification *n* Vereinigung *nf*
unilateral *adj* (contract) einseitig bindend *adj*
uninsurable *adj* nicht versicherungsfähig *adj*
union *n* Verband (-bände) *nm*, Gewerkschaft
(-en) *nf* **union membership**
Gewerkschaftsmitgliedschaft *nf* **union
representative** Gewerkschaftsvertreter (-)
nm **trade union, labor union** (US)
Gewerkschaft (-en) *nf*
unit *n* Einheit (-en) *nf* **unit cost** Stückkosten
npl **unit of production** Produktionseinheit
(-en) *nf* **unit price** Stückpreis (-e) *nm* **unit
trust** Kapitalanlagegesellschaft (-en) *nf*
united *adj* vereint *adj* **the United Nations** die
Vereinten Nationen *nfpl*
unlimited *adj* unbeschränkt *adj* **unlimited
company** Gesellschaft mit unbeschränkter
Haftung (-en) *nf* **unlimited credit**
Blankokredit (-e) *nm* **unlimited liability** unbeschränkte Haftung *nf*
unload *vb* entladen *vb*
unmarketable *adj* unverkäuflich *adj*
unofficial *adj* inoffiziell *adj* **unofficial strike**
wilder Streik (-s) *nm*
unpack *vb* auspacken *vb*
unpaid *adj* unbezahlt *adj* **unpaid balance**
Restschuld (-en) *nf* **unpaid bill** unbezahlter
Wechsel (-) *nm* **unpaid cheque** unbezahlter
Scheck (-s) *nm*
unprofessional *adj* unfachkaufmännisch *adj*
unprofitable *adj* unprofitabel *adj*
unsaleable *adj* unverkäuflich *adj*
unsatisfactory *adj* unzureichend *adj*
unsecured *adj* ungesichert *adj* **unsecured
bond** ungesicherter Schuldschein (-e) *nm*
unsecured credit offener Kredit *nm*
unskilled *adj* ungelernt *adj* **unskilled worker**
Hilfsarbeiter (-) *nm*
unsold *adj* unverkauft *adj*
unsolicited *adj* freiwillig *adj* **unsolicited offer**
unverbindliches Angebot (-e) *nn*
up-to-date *adj* aktuell *adj* **to bring sth up-to-**

date etwas auf den neuesten Stand bringen
update *vb* (records) auf den neuesten Stand bringen *vb*
upgrade *vb* befördern *vb*
upswing *n* Aufschwung (-ünge) *nm*
upturn *n* Aufschwung (-ünge) *nm*
upward *adj* Aufwärts- *cpd* aufwärts *adv*
  upward trend Aufwärtsentwicklung (-en) *nf*
urban *adj* städtisch *adj* **urban renewal** Stadterneuerung *nf* **urban sprawl** Stadtausbreitung *nf*
urgency *n* Dringlichkeit *nf* **a matter of urgency** dringende Angelegenheit (-en) *nf*
urgent *adj* dringend *adj*
urgently *adv* dringlich *adv*
usage *n* Brauch *nm*, Praxis *nf* **intensive usage** intensive Anwendung *nf*
use *n* verwenden *vb*, benützen *vb* **to make use of sth** Gebrauch machen von
user-friendly *adj* benutzerfreundlich *adj*
usury *n* Wucher *nm*
utility *n* Nutzen *nm* **marginal utility** Grenznutzen *nm* **public utility** Versorgungsbetrieb (-e) *nm*
utilization *n* Verwendung *nf*
utilize *vb* verwenden *vb*
vacancy *n* freie Stelle (-n) *nf*
vacant *adj* leer *adj*
valid *adj* gültig *adj*
validate *vb* anerkennen *vb*
validity *n* Gültigkeit *nf*
valuable *adj* wertvoll *adj*
valuation *n* Wertung (-en) *nf*
value *n* Wert (-e) *nm* **face value** Nennwert (-e) *nm* **market value** Marktwert (-e) *nm* **to gain value** an Wert zunehmen **to get value for one's money** preiswert kaufen **to lose value** an Wert verlieren
variable *adj* veränderlich *adj* **variable costs** veränderliche Kosten *npl* **variable rate** veränderlicher Kurs (-e) *nm*
variance *n* **budget variance** Budgetabweichung (-en) *nm*
VAT (value added tax) *abbr* Mehrwertsteuer (-n) *nf*, MwSt *abbr*
vendee *n* Käufer (-) *nm*
vending machine *n* Automat (-en) *nm*
vendor *n* Verkäufer (-) *nm* **vendor capital** Verkaufskapital *nn* **joint vendor** Mitverkäufer *nm*
verbatim *adv* wörtlich *adj*
vertical *n* vertikal *adj*, senkrecht *adj* **vertical integration** Vertikalintegration *nf*
vested *adj* übertragen *vb* **vested interests** finanzielle Beteiligung *nf* **vested rights** erworbene Rechte *nnpl*
veto 1. *n* Einspruch (-sprüche) *nm* 2. *vb* Einspruch einlegen gegen
viability *n* Leistungsfähigkeit *nf*
video *n* Video (-s) *nn*, Videofilm (-s) *nm*, Videorekorder (-) *nm* **video facilities** Videogeräte *nnpl*

viewer *n* Zuschauer (-) *nm*
VIP (very important person) *n* VIP (-s) *nm*, prominente Persönlichkeit (-en) *nf*
visa *n* Visum (-en) *nn*
visible *adj* sichtbar *adj* **visible exports** Warenausfuhr *nf*
visit 1. *n* Besuch (-e) *nm* 2. *vb* besuchen *vb*
visitor *n* Besucher (-) *nm*
visual *adj* visuell *adj* **visual display unit (VDU)** Sichtgerät (-e) *nn* **visual telephone** Sichtfernsprecher (-) *nm*
vocational *adj* Berufs- *cpd*
volatile *adj* (prices) unbeständig *adj*
volume *n* Volumen *nn* **volume discount** Mengenrabatt (-e) *nm* **trading volume** Handelsvolumen *nn*
voluntary *adj* freiwillig *adj* **to go into voluntary liquidation** in freiwillige Liquidation treten **voluntary wage restraint** freiwillige Lohnbegrenzung *nf*
vote 1. *n* Stimme (-n) *nf* **vote of no confidence** Mißtrauensantrag (-äge) *nm* **vote of thanks** Dankadresse (-n) *nf* 2. *vb* abstimmen *vb*
voting *adj* Abstimmung *nf* **voting right** Stimmrecht *nn*
voucher *n* Gutschein (-e) *nm*
wage 1. *adj* **wage demand** Lohnforderung (-en) *nf* **wage earner** Verdiener (-) *nm* **wage increase** Lohnerhöhung (-en) *nf* **wage negotiations** Lohnverhandlungen *nfpl* **wage packet, salary package** (US) Lohntüte (-n) *nf* **wage policy** Lohnpolitik *nf* **wage restraint** Verhinderung von Lohnsteigerungen *nf* **wage rise** Lohnerhöhung (-en) *nf* **wage(s) agreement** Tarifabkommen (-) *nn* **wage(s) bill** Lohnetat *nm* **wage scale** Lohntarif (-e) *nm* **wage(s) claim** Lohnanspruch (-sprüche) *nm* **wage(s) freeze** Lohnstopp (-s) *nm* **wage(s) settlement** Tarifabkommen (-) *nn* 2. *n* Lohn (-öhne) *nm* **average wage** Durchschnittslohn (-löhne) *nm* **minimum wage** Mindestlohn (-löhne) *nm* **net(t) wage** Nettolohn (-löhne) *nm* **real wage** Reallohn (-löhne) *nm* **starting wage** Anfangslohn (-löhne) *nm* 3 *vb* führen *vb* **to wage a campaign** eine Kampagne führen
waiting *n* Warten *nn* **waiting list** Warteliste (-n) *nf*
waive *vb* verzichten (auf) *vb*
waiver *n* Verzicht *nm* **waiver clause** Verzichtsleistungsklausel (-n) *nf*
wall *n* Mauer (-n) *nf* **tariff wall** Zollmauer (-n) *nf* **to go to the wall** in Konkurs gehen *vb* **Wall Street (US)** Wallstreet *nf*
war *n* Krieg (-e) *nm* **price war** Preiskampf (-kämpfe) *nm* **trade war** Wirtschaftskrieg (-e) *nm*
warehouse *n* Lagerhaus (-häuser) *nn* **bonded warehouse** Transitlager (-) *nn*
warehousing *n* Lagerhaltung *nf*
wares *npl* Waren *nfpl*

warn *vb* warnen *vb* **to warn sb against doing sth** jemandem von einer Sache abraten

warning *n* Warnung (-en) *nf* **due warning** rechtzeitiger Bescheid *nm* **warning sign** Alarmzeichen (-) *nn* **without warning** unerwartet *adj*

warrant **1.** *n* Vollmacht *nf* **warrant for payment** Zahlungsanweisung (-en) *nf* **2.** *vb* bestätigen *vb*, garantieren *vb*

warranty *n* Garantie (-n) *nf*, Berechtigung (-en) *nf* **under warranty** unter Garantie

wastage *n* Verschleiß *nm* **wastage rate** Verlustquote (-n) *nf*

waste **1.** *adj* **waste products** Abfallprodukte *nnpl* **2.** *n* Verschwendung *nf* **industrial waste** Industriemüll *nm* **waste of time** Zeitvergeudung *nf* **to go to waste** verkümmern *vb*, ungenutzt sein **3** *vb* verschwenden *vb*

wasting *adj* **wasting asset** kurzlebiges Wirtschaftsgut (-güter) *nn*

watch *vb* beobachten *vb* **to watch developments** Entwicklungen verfolgen

watchdog *n* (fig.) Wachthund (-e) *nm* **watchdog committee** Überwachungsausschuß (-üsse) *nm*

water down *vb* verdünnen *vb*, verwüssern *vb*

watered *adj* verwässert *adj* **watered capital** verwässertes Aktienkapital *nn* **watered stock** verwässertes Aktienkapital *nn*

watertight *adj* (fig.) stichhaltig *adj*

wave *n* (of mergers, takeovers) Welle (-n) *nf*

wavelength *n* Wellenlänge (-n) *nf* **to be on the same wavelength** auf derselben Wellenlänge sein

weaken *vb* (market) schwächer werden *vb*

wealth *n* Reichtum *nm*, Vermögen *nn* **national wealth** Volksvermögen *nn* **wealth tax** Vermögenssteuer (-n) *nf*

week *n* Woche (-n) *nf* **twice a week** zweimal wöchentlich *adj* **working week** Arbeitswoche (-n) *nf*

weekly *adj* wöchentlich *adj* **weekly wages** Wochenlöhne *npl*

weigh *vb* abwägen *vb*, abwiegen *vb* **to weigh the pros and cons** das Für und Wider abwägen

weight *n* Gewicht *nn* **dead weight** Eigengewicht *nn* **excess weight** Mehrgewicht *nn*, Übergewicht *nn* **gross weight** Bruttogewicht *nn* **net(t) weight** Nettogewicht *nn* **weights and measures** Maße und Gewichte *npl*

weighted *adj* beeinflußt *adj*, verfälscht *adj* **weighted average** Bewertungsdurchschnitt (-e) *nm* **weighted index** Bewertungsindex (-e) *nm*

weighting *n* Zulage *nf*

weighty *adj* gewichtig *adj*

welfare **1.** *adj* **welfare benefits** Sozialhilfeleistung *nf* **welfare state** Wohlfahrtsstaat (-en) *nm* **2.** *n* Wohl *nn*

well-advised *adj* gut beraten *adj*

well-informed *adj* wohl informiert *adj*

well-known *adj* bekannt *adj*

well-made *adj* solide *adj*, von guter Qualität *adj*

well-paid *adj* gutbezahlt *adj*

well-tried *adj* wohlerprobt *adj*, bewährt *adj*

WEU (Western European Union) *abbr* Westeuropäische Union *nf*

white *adj* **white-collar worker** Angestellte/r *nmf*

wholesale *n* Großhandel *nm* **at/by wholesale** im Großhandel, en gros **wholesale price** Großhandelspreis (-e) *nm* **wholesale trade** Großhandel *nm*

wholesaler *n* Großhändler (-) *nm*

wholly *adv* vollständig *adj* **wholly-owned subsidiary** hundertprozentige Tochtergesellschaft (-en) *nf*

wide-ranging *adj* weit *adj*, breit *adj*

will *n* Testament (-e) *nn*

win *vb* gewinnen *vb* **win customers** Kunden gewinnen **to win support** Unterstützung finden

wind up *vb* beendigen *vb*

windfall *n* unerwarteter Glücksfall (-fälle) *nm* **windfall profit** unerwarteter Gewinn (-e) *nm*

winding-up *n* Liquidation *nf* **winding-up arrangements** Liquidationsmaßnahmen *nfpl* **winding-up order** Konkursbeschluß (-üsse) *nm*

window *n* Fenster (-) *nn* **window of opportunity** Chance (-n) *nf*, Gelegenheit (-en) *nf*

withdraw *vb* zurückziehen *vb* **to withdraw an offer** ein Angebot zurückziehen

withdrawal *n* Zurückziehen *nn* **withdrawal of funds** Abhebungen *nfpl*

withhold *vb* vorenthalten *vb* **to withhold a document** eine Urkunde nicht herausgeben

withstand *vb* standhalten *vb*

witness **1.** *n* Zeuge (-n) *nm* **2.** *vb* bezeugen *vb* **to witness a signature** beglaubigen *vb*

word *n* Wort *nn* **word processing** Textverarbeitung *nf* **word processor** Textverarbeitungsgerät (-e) *nn* **to give one's word** versprechen *vb* **to keep one's word** sein Wort halten

wording *n* Wortlaut *nm*

work **1.** *adj* **work experience** Berufserfahrung *nf* **work permit** Arbeitsgenehmigung (-en) *nf* **work schedule** Arbeitsplan (-pläne) *nm* **work sharing** Arbeitsteilung *nf* **work study** Zeitstudie (-n) *nf* **2.** *n* Arbeit *nf* **casual work** Gelegenheitsarbeit *nf* **day off work** freier Tag (-e) *nm* **day's work** Tagewerk *nn* **factory work** Fabrikarbeit *nf* **office work** Bürotätigkeit *nf* **to be in work** berufstätig sein *vb* **to be out of work** arbeitslos sein *vb* **to look for work** Arbeit suchen **3** *vb* arbeiten *vb* **to work to rule** Dienst nach Vorschrift machen **to work unsocial hours** außerhalb

der normalen Arbeitszeit arbeiten *vb*
workable *adj* durchführbar *adj*
workaholic *n* Arbeitswütige/r *nmf*
workday (US) *n* Arbeitstag (-e) *nm*
worker *n* Arbeiter (-) *nm* **casual worker**
Gelegenheitsarbeiter (-) *nm* **clerical worker**
Bürokraft (-kräfte) *nf* **worker-director**
Arbeiterdirektor (-en) *nm* **manual worker**
manueller Arbeiter (-) *nm* **worker participation** Mitbestimmung *nf* **skilled worker**
Facharbeiter (-) *nm* **unskilled worker**
Hilfsarbeiter (-) *nm*
workforce *n* Belegschaft *nf*
working *adj* berufstätig *adj*, funktionierend
adj **working agreement** Absprache (-n) *nf*
working area Arbeitsbereich (-e) *nm* **working capital** Betriebskapital *nn* **working conditions** Arbeitsbedingungen *nfpl* **working
environment** Arbeitsumwelt *nf* **working
hours** Arbeitszeit *nf* **working knowledge**
Grundkenntnisse *nfpl* **working language** offizielle Sprache (-n) *nf* **working life**
Berufsleben *nn* **working majority** arbeitsfähige Mehrheit *nf* **working model** Modell
(-e) *nn* **working paper** Arbeitspapier (-e) *nn*
working party Arbeitsgemeinschaft (-en) *nf*,
Arbeitsgruppe (-n) *nf* **working population**
arbeitende Bevölkerung *nf* **working week
(GB)** Arbeitswoche (-n) *nf*
workload *n* Arbeit *nf*
workmate *n* Mitarbeiter (-) *nm*,
Arbeitskollege (-n) *nm*
workplace *n* Arbeitsplatz *nm*
works *n* Betrieb *nm* **public works programme (GB)** öffentliches Bauprogramm (-e)
nn **works committee** Betriebsauschuß
(-üsse) *nm* **works council** Betriebsrat (-räte)
nm **works manager** Werksleiter (-) *nm*
workshop *n* Werkstatt *nf*
workweek (US) *n* Arbeitswoche (-n) *nf*
world *n* Welt *nf* **the commercial world**
Handelskreise *nmpl* **world consumption**
Weltverbrauch *nm* **world exports**
Weltexporte *npl* **world fair** Weltausstellung
(-en) *nf* **World Bank** Weltbank *nf* **World
Court** Weltgerichtshof (-höfe) *nm*
worldwide *adj* weltweit *adj*
worth *adj* wert *adj* **to be worth** wert sein *vb*
wpm (words per minute) *abbr* Anschläge

pro Minute *npl*
wreck *vb* zerstören *vb*
writ *n* gerichtliche Verfügung (-en) *nf* **to issue
a writ** eine Verfügung herausgeben *vb*
write down *vb* (depreciation) Wert
herabsetzen *vb*
write off *vb* (debts) abschreiben *vb* (vehicle)
zu Schrott fahren *vb*
write-off *n* Abschreibung *nf*, Totalschaden
nm
wrongful *adj* unrechtmäßig *adj* **wrongful
dismissal** unberechtigte Entlassung (-en) *nf*
xerox *vb* fotokopieren *vb*
Xerox (R) *n* (machine) Fotokopiermaschine
(-n) *nf*
year *n* Jahr (-e) *nn* **year-end dividend** Sonderdividende am Schluß des Jahres (-n) *nf*
year-end inventory Jahresschlußinventar
(-e) *nn* **financial year** Geschäftsjahr (-e) *nn*
fiscal year Steuerjahr (-e) *nn* **tax year**
Steuerjahr (-e) *nn*
yearly *adj* jährlich *adj* **yearly income**
Jahreseinkommen *nn*
yellow *adj* gelb *adj* **the Yellow pages (R) (GB)**
Branchenverzeichnis (-isse) *nn*
yen *n* (currency) Yen *nm* **yen bond** Yen-
Auslandsanleihe (-n) *nf*
yield 1. *adj* **yield curve** Renditekurve (-n) *nf*
2. *n* Ertrag *nm* **yield on shares** Aktienrendite
nf **3** *vb* bringen *vb*
young *adj* jung *adj* **young economy** junge
Wirtschaft (-en) *nf*
zenith *n* Höhepunkt (-e) *nm*
zero *n* Null *nf* **zero address** Adresse
unbekannt **below zero** unter Null **zero
defect** fehlerfrei *adj* **zero growth**
Nullwachstum *nn* **zero hour** Stunde Null *nf*
zero rate/rating abgabenfrei *adj* **zero-rate
taxation** steuerfrei *adj* **to be zero-rated for
VAT** mehrwertsteuerfrei *adj*
zip code (US) *n* Postleitzahl (-en) *nf*
zone 1. *n* Zone (-n) *nf* **currency zone**
Währungsgebiet (-e) *nn* **enterprise zone**
wirtschaftliches Fördergebiet (-e) *nn* **postal
zone** Postbezirk (-e) *nm* **time zone** Zeitzone
(-n) *nf* **wage zone** Tarifzone (-n) *nf* **2.** *vb* in
Zonen einteilen *vb*
zoning *n* Einteilung in Zonen *nf*

Index

Index

Business Situations
how to use 3

On the Telephone

Face to Face

Business Correspondence

Business Practice

Grammar

Glossary